FINANCING
THE 1992
ELECTION

AMERICAN POLITICAL INSTITUTIONS AND PUBLIC POLICY

Stephen J. Wayne
Series Editor

VICTORY
How a Progressive Democratic Party Can Win and Govern
Arthur Sanders

THE POLITICS OF JUSTICE
The Attorney General and the Making of Legal Policy
Cornell W. Clayton

A KINDER, GENTLER RACISM?
The Reagan–Bush Civil Rights Legacy
Steven A. Shull

CONGRESS, THE PRESIDENT, AND POLICYMAKING
A Historical Analysis
Jean Reith Schroedel

RISKY BUSINESS
PAC Decisionmaking in Congressional Elections
Robert Biersack, Paul S. Herrnson, and Clyde Wilcox, Editors

PUBLIC ATTITUDES TOWARD CHURCH AND STATE
Ted G. Jelen and Clyde Wilcox

FINANCING THE 1992 ELECTION
Herbert E. Alexander and Anthony Corrado

AMERICAN POLITICAL INSTITUTIONS AND PUBLIC POLICY

FINANCING THE 1992 ELECTION

HERBERT E. ALEXANDER
ANTHONY CORRADO

M.E. Sharpe
Armonk, New York
London, England

Library of Congress Cataloging-in-Publication Data

Alexander, Herbert E.
Financing the 1992 election / Herbert E. Alexander and Anthony Corrado.
p.   cm.—(American political institutions and public policy)
Includes bibliographical references and index.
ISBN 1-56324-437-3.—ISBN 1-56324-428-1 (pbk.)
1. Campaign funds—United States.
2. Presidents—United States—Election—1992.
3. United States. Congress—Elections, 1992.
I. Corrado, Anthony, 1957–   .
II. Title.
III. Series.
JK1991.A687   1995
324.7'8'097309049—dc20
95-3540
CIP

Printed in the United States of America

The paper used in this publication meets the minimum requirements of
American National Standard for Information Sciences—
Permanence of Paper for Printed Library Materials,
ANSI Z 39.48-1984.

BM (c)   10   9   8   7   6   5   4   3   2   1
BM (p)   10   9   8   7   6   5   4   3   2   1

Contents

Tables and Figure

Tables

Figure

Foreword

I cannot enter/continue/win [pick one] the current campaign
because of the lack of adequate funds.

The lament is always the same. We heard this refrain in 1992 from Pat
Buchanan, Tom Harkin, Bob Kerrey, Paul Tsongas, even Jerry Brown, and
again in 1995 from Dick Cheney, Jack Kemp, and Dan Quayle. It is never
the candidate's fault. The problem is money, pure and simple.

Is money that critical to electoral success? How much does it take to
mount an effective campaign, to communicate with the American electorate, to organize potential supporters and turn them out on election day?

Herbert E. Alexander and Anthony Corrado seek to answer these questions in their comprehensive description and analysis of campaign finance
in the 1992 election. They provide an everything-you-want-to-know guide
about revenue and expenditures for federal office during that election cycle.
In doing so, they also discuss generic issues of strategy and tactics, issues
that pertain to the timing, targeting, and techniques of resource acquisition
and allocation. At what point is fund raising deemed to be most important
for political campaigns? When and for what types of campaign-related activities should the bulk of expenditures be made to have maximum impact?
To whom should financial appeals be directed, and what methods have
proved to be most successful in generating needed revenues? How have
new communications technologies affected the ways in which candidates go
about soliciting and spending their funds? Which of these newer technologies packs the biggest bang for the buck?

Students of electoral politics in general and the 1992 and forthcoming
1996 campaigns in particular will find the data and analyses that are presented in this book fascinating and, if they are involved in campaigns, an

extremely valuable guide. Much of the information is presented in easy-to-read tables and charts, supplemented by data from previous election campaigns. Thus readers are able to make a comparative judgment based on a wealth of cumulative data.

But that is not all this book is about. The authors tackle larger issues that bear on the relationship between finance and democracy, issues of equity, of representation, and of participation by the people. Do the costs of elections and the need to solicit private contributions reinforce or undermine the goals of a democratic electoral process? Do the wealthy still have an advantage in running and/or in influencing who wins? Do PACs exercise a disproportionate influence, and if so, on whom? How adequately are different segments of the society represented by the resources that individuals and nonparty groups expend during an election campaign? And what about the party's fund-raising and spending activities? Is there near equity between the Democrats and the Republicans on national, state, and local levels? How disadvantaged are third parties and independent candidates? Are the communications media financially accessible to them? How costly are the various methods candidates use to make appeals and mobilize their supporters? And how do these costs affect the information the electorate receives and the judgment it is able to make on election day?

Alexander and Corrado's discussion, which responds to these and related issues, enriches the academic and public dialogue on campaign finance and the reforms of the system that have occurred since the 1970s. Moreover, the authors take their discussion beyond the election to the transition and start-up costs of the new presidential administration, looking, for example, at the relationship between campaign contributions and ambassadorial appointments. In this way, they demonstrate how money affects and afflicts our electoral process and governing institutions. Readers can then decide for themselves whether or to what extent money is the root of all, some, or no evil in American electoral politics and what follows from it—democratic government.

Stephen J. Wayne
Georgetown University

Preface and
Acknowledgments

In this ninth quadrennial book on the financing of presidential-year election campaigns, the research and analytical techniques used previously were reexamined, and considerable modifications were made to accommodate the new data. The 1992 elections constituted the fifth experience with public funding, leading to new ways of dealing with, and thinking about, the subject. Each study is an educational experience, and the 1992 campaign was notable in the diversity of ways found to raise, handle, and spend the large amounts of money used.

The authors added an important chapter of materials worthy of the fullest treatment: chapter 6, "Soft Money: The Last Hurrah?" This was written by Anthony Corrado and expanded upon data analyzed in Corrado, *Paying for Presidents: Public Financing in National Elections* (New York, 1993).

The Federal Election Commission (FEC) came into being in 1975, producing immense amounts of data and information and affecting greatly the contours and analyses of the 1992 study. Some amounts reported in this book as spent by a given candidate may differ from other figures because audit totals of the FEC do not agree with totals in its published compilations or with information that the Citizens' Research Foundation (CRF) received. Closing dates for some CRF analyses differed from those in FEC or other compilations. A number of definitions of categories differ, affecting which groups are included or excluded in certain totals. And for some purposes, soft money, independent expenditures, compliance costs, and communication costs were included. Moreover, the FEC compilations often give totals only for general election candidates, dating to January 1 of the election year or previous year, without separating primary election from general election spending and not accounting for the totals of dollars raised and spent by primary election losers. Of course, the FEC disclosure forms are not designed to differentiate accurately between primary election and general election spending.

So many events and facts required description independently by topic that it was difficult to organize the book efficiently. There would have been so many notes cross-referencing topics such as fund raising or public financing that, for the most part, we dispensed with these. Accordingly, readers should use the table of contents and the index for cross-referencing.

This study attempts to update analyses and categories of data developed over the years by Professors James Pollock, Louise Overacker, and Alexander Heard; the Senate Subcommittee on Privileges and Elections (under the chairmanship of Senator Albert Gore Sr. of Tennessee) in 1956; and the eight previous volumes authored or coauthored by Herbert E. Alexander in his series on finance and elections.

Acknowledgments

The data in this study were collected by the CRF. Special appreciation is due to many individuals for providing information in personal interviews, through correspondence, and by telephone. Many finance managers and others preferred to remain anonymous. Because it would be unfair to name some and not others, we regretfully do not list the many persons in such capacities who graciously cooperated.

The authors acknowledge with special thanks the help of Professor Warren E. Miller of Arizona State University for his assistance with data from the University of Michigan National Election Study, as set forth in chapter 1. We also are grateful to David Beiler for his comprehensive research on election reform and his editing of chapter 9. Kent Cooper and Michael Dickerson of the FEC's Public Records Division helped ensure that the most recent financial reports were made available to us and expertly responded to our queries. A special note of acknowledgment is due to Robert Biersack, statistician at the FEC, who gave unstintingly of his time and willingly provided data and guidance.

Students at the University of Southern California made substantial contributions: Martin Dupuis, who served as Herbert Alexander's research assistant, exhibited unparalleled research and drafting capabilities, apparent in chapters 3 and 5; a graduate student, Melissa Wye, provided great help with the media portions of chapter 8; Oliver Klug, a visiting German student intern from the University of Konstanz, made sense of the varied data on "Independent Expenditures" and "Communication Costs," also in chapter 8;

and Alexander Wathen, an undergraduate, did work on portions of chapter 5 that was on a par with the high quality expected of graduate students.

The authors also appreciate the efforts of two Colby College students, Erik Belenky and John Daly, who served as Anthony Corrado's research assistants and helped compile the data for chapter 6. Much of the research for chapter 6 was made possible with the support of the Colby College Social Sciences Grants Committee, which the authors gratefully acknowledge. Patricia Kick contributed to the preparation of sections of the draft manuscript and helped construct a number of the tables.

Throughout, CRF's assistant director, Gloria Cornette, was a constant source of strength, managing superbly the preparation of the manuscript at all stages, editing the manuscript under deadline, and preparing the index.

None of those who were so helpful are responsible for errors of omission or commission; for those, as for interpretations, we bear sole responsibility. We appreciate the cooperation and encouragement received from officers and members of the board of trustees of the CRF, but this presentation is ours and does not necessarily reflect their views.

Without the contributions of numerous supporters of the CRF, this study would not have been possible.

Herbert E. Alexander
Anthony Corrado

Introduction

In 1992, Bill Clinton was elected president with 370 electoral votes from thirty-two states and the District of Columbia. Incumbent George Bush lost, receiving 168 electoral votes from eighteen states. The presidential elections were marked by a strong independent candidate, Ross Perot, who, though winning no states, received 18.9 percent of the total vote, compared with 43.0 percent for Clinton and 37.4 percent for Bush. Voter turnout was 55.2 percent, and the Democrats retained their majority in the U.S. Senate and the House.

Developments in financing the campaigns were notable in many ways, although they generally have received far less systematic attention than other aspects of the elections. Accordingly, these developments are the subject of this book. Campaign money may be conceived of as a tracer element in politics; much valuable information about the patterns of political events and results and the distribution of political power may be obtained by following the path of money through the course of election campaigns.

During the 1991–92 election cycle, total political campaign spending at all levels—national, state, and local—exceeded $3.2 billion, a 19 percent increase over the estimated amount spent in the previous presidential election cycle. Although the $3.2 billion figure indicates that campaign spending continues to grow at a rate slightly greater than inflation, the increase over the corresponding 1987–88 figure also is due in part to the availability of more complete information regarding campaign costs.

The 1992 national elections were the ninth to be conducted under the Federal Election Campaign Act (FECA) and its 1974 amendments, and the presidential election was the fifth conducted under the system of public funding initiated by the act and its companion legislation. While the FECA was enacted in part to control campaign spending, which had reached unprecedented levels in the 1972 presidential campaigns, more than one-half of the $3.2 billion campaign expenditure total of 1992 was used to influence federal election results. The costs of the items and services many federal campaigns must purchase, including media broadcast time, air travel, telephones, and the specialized expertise of campaign consultants, rose dramatically. Candidates and their supporters responded by adopting some previously used methods of raising and spending funds and devising various new means, some of which provoked controversy and triggered demands for further regulation.

This study's focus on finances is not intended to slight the numerous nonfinancial factors that influenced the 1992 election results. Indeed, political party rules, national and local issues, the prestige of office and advantages of incumbency, leadership and communication skills, the composition of election districts, and the mood of the electorate played important roles in determining election outcomes. But it is campaign money, as the late journalist Theodore H. White pointed out, that enables candidates to purchase items and services needed to influence party rules, to make their views on issues known, to gain office and demonstrate their communication skills, and to sway the electorate. "Money buys attention," he wrote. "It buys . . . television and radio time; it buys expertise, computers, organization, travel, visuals for the evening news."[1] By shedding light on these and other uses of campaign money and clarifying its relationships with other factors that help determine election results, we hope to illuminate the political process and contribute to the understanding of political influence and power in the United States.

Note

1. Theodore H. White, *America in Search of Itself* (New York: Harper and Row, 1982), p. 426.

1

Spending in the 1992 Elections

During the 1991–92 election cycle, political candidates, committees, and other organizations and individuals spent $3.2 billion on political campaigns. This spending covered not only campaigns for nomination and election to federal offices—the presidency and seats in Congress—but also nomination and election campaigns for state and local offices; campaigns for and against ballot propositions; efforts by political parties and numerous independent organizations to register and turn out voters; and the costs of administering national, state, and local political party organizations and numerous political committees sponsored by interest and ideological groups.

The $3.2 billion represents an increase of only 19 percent over the Citizens' Research Foundation (CRF) estimate for the 1987–88 election cycle. Notably, this increase was close to the 18.6 percent rise in the Consumer Price Index (CPI) during the period from 1988 to 1992, but it was enough to continue stoking the fires of criticism of political campaign costs. Critics maintain that high campaign costs force candidates to devote an inordinate amount of time to raising money. They also hold that special interest groups seeking to exercise influence by satisfying candidates' needs for campaign funds threaten the integrity of the election and governmental processes. Compared with some other categories of spending, however, the amounts expended for political campaigns are low. The amount spent in 1991–92 is less than the sum that the nation's two leading commercial advertisers—Procter and Gamble and Philip Morris—spent in 1992 to proclaim the quality of their products.[1] It represents a mere fraction of 1 percent of the $2.1 trillion spent in 1992 by federal, state, and local governments.[2] And it is just a fraction of what is spent on cosmetics or gambling.

As with many types of spending, there is no universally accepted criterion by which to determine when political spending becomes excessive. Many factors have contributed to what sometimes appear to be high political campaign costs. No candidate wants to lose for having spent too little. During the last two decades, political campaigning at most levels has become a highly professionalized undertaking, involving pollsters, media specialists, computer specialists, fund-raising consultants, and a host of other experts whose services are expensive and, in the estimation of many candidates and committees, essential. The costs of items and services many campaigns must purchase, including travel, telephones, and broadcast time, have risen dramatically. In addition, federal, state, and local laws enacted to compel disclosure of campaign finances and, in some cases, to impose limits on political contributions and expenditures, have required candidates to hire election attorneys and political accountants to ensure compliance. Candidates and political committees must compete for attention not only with each other but also with commercial advertisers that have access to large budgets and are able to advertise regularly—in the electronic and print media—and not just during a concentrated season. Finally, the Supreme Court has encouraged greater spending by determining that limits on campaign expenditures are unconstitutional except when imposed on candidates as a condition of accepting public funding. It has ruled further that even when campaigns are publicly funded, no limits may be placed on independent expenditures by individuals and committees that seek to advocate candidates' election or defeat.

Categories of Political Spending, 1992

The campaign bill of $3.2 billion in the 1991–92 election cycle may be classified in eight major categories (see Table 1.1):

1. Spending on presidential campaigns ($550 million), including spending on prenomination campaigns that began in 1991; spending by nominating convention committees; spending by major party, minor party, and independent presidential general election campaigns; and spending by national party committees on behalf of their presidential nominees.[3] (There were 273 presidential candidates filed with the Federal Election Commission (FEC), though most did not spend any money. Some twenty-three were on the general election ballot somewhere; Republican Bush, Democrat Clinton, Perot, and Libertarian candidate Andre Marrou qualified on the November ballot in all fifty states. Lenora Fulani of the New Alliance Party

Table 1.1

Campaign Spending in 1992 (in $ millions)

Presidential[a]	$ 550
Congressional[b]	678
National Party[c]	320
Nonparty[d]	389
State and local party (nonpresidential, federal)[e]	251
State (nonfederal)[f]	515
Local (nonfederal)[g]	350
Ballot issues[h]	175
Total	$3,228

Source: Citizens' Research Foundation.

[a]Includes all presidential election-related spending in prenomination, convention, and general election periods.
[b]Includes all spending by congressional candidates.
[c]Includes all spending by national political party committees except money contributed to presidential and congressional candidates, coordinated expenditures on behalf of presidential candidates, and that portion of money spent on media advertising in presidential campaigns. Includes hard and soft money.
[d]Includes all spending reported by federally registered, nonparty political committees and their sponsors, except money contributed to federal candidates and political party committees and money spent independently on behalf of presidential and congressional candidates. Includes an estimated $200 million in political action committee administration and fund-raising costs paid by PAC sponsors but not reported to the FEC.
[e]Includes all spending reported by federally registered state and local party committees, minus money contributed to, or spent on behalf of, presidential candidates; money contributed directly to congressional candidates; and estimated expenditures on grass-roots activities to support presidential tickets.
[f]Includes all spending by, or on behalf of, candidates for state offices.
[g]Includes all spending by, or on behalf of, candidates for local offices.
[h]Includes all spending in campaigns to support or oppose state and local ballot issues.

was on the ballot in forty states; she received matching funds only for her prenomination campaign. John Hagelin of the Natural Law Party, who was on the ballot in twenty-nine states, also qualified for matching funds in the prenomination campaign.)[4]

2. Spending on congressional prenomination and general election campaigns ($678 million), including money contributed directly to candidates by party and nonparty political committees.[5] This represents a remarkable 52 percent increase over the 1990 elections.

3. Spending by national political party committees on administration, fund raising, and other costs ($320 million), excluding coordinated expenditures on behalf of presidential candidates and direct contributions to congres-

sional candidates that are already counted in the first two categories.[6]

4. Spending by nonparty political committees and their sponsors ($389 million), including an estimated $200 million in political action committee (PAC) administration and fund-raising costs paid by PAC sponsors but not reported to the FEC, excluding funds contributed directly to federal candidates or spent independently to influence presidential or congressional elections.[7]

5. Spending by federally registered state and local party committees ($251 million), including administrative expenses shared with state-oriented party committees but excluding money contributed to, or spent on behalf of, presidential candidates and money contributed directly to congressional candidates.[8]

6. Spending on state election campaigns ($515 million), including the costs in twelve states to nominate and elect governors and other statewide officials; the money spent on legislative elections; and the maintenance of political party organizations.[9]

7. Spending on local campaigns to nominate and elect county, regional, and municipal officials ($350 million).

8. Spending on campaigns supporting or opposing state and local ballot propositions ($175 million); there were some 232 statewide proposals in thirty-nine states and the District of Columbia in 1992. This amount is based on a study of twenty-one states in which some $117.3 million was spent on statewide ballot issues, plus other state and local measures.[10]

Adding together the first five categories, approximately $2.2 billion was spent at the federal or national level.

From 1952, the first year for which total political costs in the United States were calculated, to 1992, spending in presidential election cycles has steadily increased, as follows:[11]

U.S. Political Costs, 1952–92

1952	$140,000,000
1956	155,000,000
1960	175,000,000
1964	200,000,000
1968	300,000,000
1972	425,000,000
1976	540,000,000
1980	1,200,000,000
1984	1,800,000,000
1988	2,700,000,000
1992	3,220,000,000

The increases reflect not only inflation, higher levels of competition, the professionalization of politics, and more applications of high technology to politics, but also the greater availability of data due to laws requiring better public disclosure of political receipts and expenditures.

Patterns of Political Giving

Although the costs of television, the total costs of campaigning, and the general availability of funding have risen dramatically over recent decades, the percentage of those who donate to candidates and parties has not changed much since 1952. An overview of responses to public opinion surveys on political contributions from 1952 to 1992 is given in Table 1.2. Although these figures are subject to a polling error of up to 4 percent, their replication at various levels over the years gives confidence that the upper and lower parameters of giving are accurate.

The surveys show a rather steady increase in the number of contributors in the 1950s through 1964, when the numbers began to drop. The number rose again in 1972, only to drop in the post-Watergate period.

The post-Watergate era has become known for great disillusionment with candidates and politics. At the same time, electoral reform has re-strained the large giver, prompting alternative techniques of fund raising—sophisticated direct mail appeals and other means—which seek relatively small sums of money from a large number of people. Even with the wide-spread use of these techniques by candidates and political organizations in 1992, the proportion of the population giving to political causes does not appear to have increased. Furthermore, there are no indicators that a reser-voir of untapped potential for campaign funds continues to exist, despite the inroads made by PACs. This notion has been reinforced by survey findings spanning more than four decades.

The percentage of contributors, steady in the late 1970s, dropped consid-erably in 1980, 1984, and 1992, with only a blip upward in 1988. Interest-ingly, increased spending in the 1980s and 1990s is not reflected in the results of surveys on giving. Of course, the national adult civilian popula-tion, on which these surveys are based, has grown, so 4 or 5 percent in later years represents a larger aggregate because the universe is larger than in the earlier years.

A broader series of surveys of differentiated contributors has been car-ried out by the Center for Political Studies at the University of Michigan since 1980. This series, results of which are summarized in Table 1.3, has been conducted every two years, in congressional as well as presidential years.

It is worth noting that the congressional years include many more guber-

Table 1.2

Percentage of National Adult Population Making Political Contributions, 1952–92

Year	Polling Organization	Contributed to		Total[a]
		Republican	Democrat	
1952	SRC	3	1	4
1956	Gallup	3	6	9
1956	SRC	5	5	10
1960	Gallup	4	4	9
1960	Gallup			12
1960	SRC	7	4	12
1964	Gallup	6	4	12
1964	SRC	5	4	10
1968	SRC	3	3	8[b]
1972	SRC	4	5	10[c]
1974	SRC	3	3	8[d]
1976	Gallup	3	3	8[e]
1976	SRC	4	4	9[f]
1980	CPS	3	1	4
1984	CPS	2	2	4
1988	CPS	4	2	6
1992	CPS	2	2	4

Sources: Survey Research Center (SRC), and later the Center for Political Studies (CPS), both at the University of Michigan: data direct from the center or from Angus Campbell, Philip E. Converse, and Donald E. Stokes, *The American Voter* (New York: John Wiley and Sons, 1960), p. 91; 1980 data from Ruth S. Jones and Warren E. Miller, "Financing Campaigns: Macro Level Innovation and Micro Level Response," *Western Political Quarterly* 38, no. 2 (1987); 1984 data from Ruth S. Jones, "Campaign Contributions and Campaign Solicitations: 1984" (paper presented at the meeting of the Southern Political Science Association, Nashville, TN, November 6–9, 1985); Gallup data direct or from Roper Opinion Research Center, Williams College, and from the American Institute of Political Opinion (Gallup Poll).

[a]The total percentage may add to a total different from the total of Democratic and Republican contributors because of individuals contributing to both major parties, or to candidates of both major parties, nonparty groups, or combinations of these.
[b]Includes 0.7 percent who contributed to the American Independent Party (AIP).
[c]Includes contributors to the American Independent Party.
[d]Includes 0.7 percent who contributed to both parties and 0.8 percent who contributed to minor parties.
[e]Includes 1 percent to another party and 1 percent to "do not know" or "no answer."
[f]Republican and Democratic figures are rounded. The total includes 0.6 percent who gave to both parties, 0.4 percent to other, and 0.3 percent "do not know."

Table 1.3

Mode of Political Contributions, 1980–92 (in percent)

	1980 (N = 1395)	1982 (N = 1418)	1984 (N = 1944)	1986 (N = 2176)	1988 (N = 1775)	1990 (N = 2000)	1992 (N = 2252)
Federal tax checkoff[a]	26.0	30.0	31.0	32.0	26.0	25.0	26.0
State tax checkoff[b]	6.0	7.0	N.A.	N.A.	N.A.	N.A.	N.A.
Candidate organization[c]	6.0	7.0	5.0	5.0	6.0	5.0	6.0
Republican	3.8	2.8	2.1	2.1	2.7	2.2	2.2
Democrat	2.0	4.0	2.4	2.4	2.6	2.5	3.0
Both	N.A.	N.A.	0.3	0.2	0.4	0.2	0.4
Other[d]	0.5	0.4	0.2	0.2	0.2	0.2	0.4
Party Organization[e]	4.0	4.0	5.0	5.0	6.0	4.0	4.0
Republican	3.0	2.7	2.6	2.7	4.0	1.9	1.9
Democrat	1.0	1.3	2.0	1.9	1.9	1.8	1.8
Both	N.A.	N.A.	0.2	0.3	0.1	0.1	0.1
Other[f]	0.0	0.0	0.2	0.1	0.0	0.1	0.1
PAC[g]	7.0	8.0	N.A.	N.A.	N.A.	N.A.	N.A.
Ballot issue[h]	N.A.	N.A.	2.0	N.A.	N.A.	N.A.	N.A.
Other group[i]	N.A.	N.A.	2.0	3.0	4.0	5.0	5.0
Summary							
Noncontributor[j]	68.0	63.0	65.0	64.0	68.0	69.0	69.0
Checkoff only[k]	20.0	21.0	26.0	27.0	20.0	20.0	20.0
Organizational giver[l]	11.0	15.0	10.0	9.0	12.0	10.0	11.0

Source: Based on data of the Center for Political Studies, University of Michigan, and compiled by Warren E. Miller.

Note: Entries do not always total 100 percent because of rounding.

[a]"Did you use the $1 checkoff option on your federal income tax return to make a political contribution?" The entries are those who said "yes."

[b]"Did you make a political contribution by checking off that item on your state income tax return?" The entries are those who said "yes."

[c]"Did you give money to an individual candidate?" The entries are those who said "yes."

[d]"Which party did that candidate belong to?" Missing values are not included.

[e]"Did you give money to a political party?" The entries are those who said "yes."

[f]"To which party did you give money?" Missing values are not included.

[g]"Did you give money to political action groups?" The entries are those who said "yes."

[h]"Did you give any money to help support or oppose any ballot proposition this election year?" The entries are those who said "yes."

[i]"Did you give any money to any other group that supported/opposed candidates?" The entries are those who said "yes."

[j]The entries are an index that counts those who did not make political contributions at all.

[k]The entries count those who have made only checkoff contributions.

[l]The entries count those who made other kinds of contributions and may have used the checkoff.

natorial elections—some thirty-three—compared with only twelve in presidential years, so the percentages of organizational contributors (which includes party givers shown in Table 1.3) was relatively steady in congressional as well as in presidential election years. The data also suggest that the opportunity to give to a growing number of PACs has not stimulated an increase in the percentage of the population willing to contribute to an organized group. While PAC contributors were at as high a level as party contributors in 1980 and 1982, the proportion of such donors, which is included in the category "other group" in recent years and presumably includes PAC donors, has remained steady at 4 to 5 percent.

Other survey data offer somewhat different findings. Throughout the 1940s and 1950s, the Gallup Poll asked individuals if they would be willing to make political contributions; approximately one-third of those surveyed said they would be willing to contribute. In the 1960s, this figure rose to 40 percent. A June 1981 Gallup Poll found that 39 percent of respondents expressed a desire to join one or more special interest groups.[12] These data, which suggest that a significant share of the population is willing to participate financially, should raise an alarm about overreporting in surveys that inadvertently may solicit prestigious answers to questions on voting or contributing.

From 1952 to 1992, between 4 and 12 percent of the total adult population said they contributed to politics at some level. Clearly, some persons contribute in more than one category. The conclusion of one study of patterns of giving is insightful:

> While it is true that more and more people are now asked, by phone and mail, to make political contributions, the response rate is generally very low. Modern technology notwithstanding, face-to-face appeals continue to be the most effective way of soliciting political contributions. There does not seem to be a large, undifferentiated electorate just waiting for an invitation to contribute to campaigns.[13]

The data seem to bear out this conclusion. It should be noted, however, that one factor in the years 1972 to 1984 was missing in 1988: a federal income tax credit for portions of political contributions. The Tax Reform Act of 1986 repealed the credit.[14] Whatever incentive the tax benefit may once have given contributors has not been available in later years.

The Federal Tax Checkoff

The Revenue Act of 1971 established a voluntary tax checkoff provision on federal income tax forms that allows taxpayers to designate a contribution to the Presidential Election Campaign Fund (PECF), a separate account maintained by the Treasury Department to finance the public funding program for presidential elections. From 1972 to 1992, the law allowed individuals with a federal tax liability to check off a specific amount—$1 for individuals and $2 for married persons filing jointly—without increasing their tax obligation or reducing the amount of any anticipated refund. In 1993, the amount of the checkoff was increased to $3 for individuals and $6 for married persons filing jointly.[15]

Although survey data reveal that the percentages of those who claim to use the checkoff have remained relatively stable since 1988 (see Table 1.3), the reported checkoff participation rates have steadily declined since 1981. As noted in Table 1.4, the early years of the checkoff were characterized by rising participation and substantial growth in the annual revenues deposited into the PECF. These trends peaked in 1981, when 28.7 percent of all tax returns designated a contribution to the public financing program. Since then, participation has fallen to a low of 17.7 percent in 1992. Annual receipts also have declined sharply, dropping from a high of more than $41 million in 1981 to less than $30 million in 1992.

The discrepancy between these figures on checkoff activity, which are compiled by the Internal Revenue Service (IRS) and Treasury Department and reported by the FEC, and the findings of survey research may be explained in part by the conclusions of a recent Twentieth Century Fund study of the tax checkoff system. This analysis revealed that the decline in participation may not be as steady or steep as is often assumed. It further noted that although the rate of checkoff participation has steadily declined since 1981, the actual number of participants has not.[16] Between 1983 and 1991, when the rate of participation fell from 24.2 percent to 19.5 percent, the actual number of returns that earmarked a contribution remained relatively stable, ranging from 23.2 million to 22.3 million. In three of those years, 1986, 1988, and 1990, the number of participants was higher than in the previous years. This suggests that the sharpness of the decline is not due simply to the number of participants; it also is a function of the increase in the number of tax returns filed each year. For example, in 1985, 22.8 million tax returns designated a contribution, yielding a participation rate of 23 percent. In 1988, the same number of tax returns designated a contribution, but the participation rate fell to 21 percent.[17]

It is also important to note that despite the overall decline in participation over the past decade, the checkoff has served to expand the number of individuals who participate financially in the political system. About 80 percent of those who use the checkoff are not organizational contributors, which suggests that these individuals would not have participated finan-

Table 1.4

The Federal Income Tax Checkoff

Calendar Year	Percent of Returns with Checkoff[a]	Dollar Amount Designated	Fund Balances
1992	17.7	$29,592,735	$ 4,061,061
1991	19.5	32,322,336	127,144,469
1990	19.8	32,462,979	115,426,713
1989	20.1	32,285,646	82,927,013
1988	21.0	33,013,987	52,462,359
1987	21.7	33,651,947	177,905,677
1986	23.0	35,753,837	161,680,423
1985	23.0	34,712,761	125,870,541
1984	23.7	35,036,761	92,713,782
1983	24.2	35,631,068	177,320,982
1982	27.0	39,023,882	153,454,501
1981	28.7	41,049,052	114,373,289
1980	27.4	38,838,417	73,752,205
1979	25.4	35,941,347	135,246,807
1978	28.6	39,246,689	100,331,986
1977	27.5	36,606,008	60,927,571
1976	25.5	33,731,945	23,805,659
1975	24.2	31,656,525	59,551,245
1974[b]	.0	27,591,546	27,591,546
1973[b]	.0	2,427,000	2,427,000

Source: Federal Election Commission.

[a]The percentages refer to the tax returns of the previous year. For example, the 17.7 percent of 1991 tax returns that indicated a checkoff of $1 or $2 directed $29,592,735 into the Presidential Election Campaign Fund in calendar year 1992.
[b]The 1973 tax forms were the first to have the checkoff on the first page; in 1972 taxpayers had to file a separate form to exercise the checkoff option. To compensate for the presumed difficulty caused by the separate form, taxpayers were allowed to designate $1 for 1972 as well as 1973 on the 1973 forms. Given these circumstances, total and percentage figures for these returns would be misleading.

cially had there been no checkoff. Moreover, the 30 million or more individuals represented by the checkoff percentages constitute a large body of support, especially when compared with the numbers of those who contribute money, who give service to parties and candidates, or who vote in congressional election years.

The checkoff system admittedly has experienced a substantial decline in annual receipts. Most observers assume that this decline is a result of the decline in participation. The problem with this assumption is that the annual revenue loss does not correspond to the drop in participation. For instance, between 1983 and 1991, the number of returns that included a checkoff contribution fell from 23.2 million to 22.3 million, and annual receipts fell from $35.6 million to $32.3 million. A decline of 900,000 returns thus resulted in an annual revenue loss of about $3.3 million. But since the maximum amount that can be checked off was $2 (and this only if the return was a joint filing), the total loss should have been no more than $1.8 million, or $1.5 million less than the actual difference. Similarly, in 1986, the number of returns with a contribution rose by 1.1 million, but receipts increased by less than $1.1 million, or by less than the minimum checkoff of $1 per return. The likely explanation for these discrepancies is that some of those who earmarked a contribution had no tax liability and were ineligible to participate in the program. Even though these individuals chose to support the public financing program and marked the "yes" box on their tax forms, no money was deposited into the fund as a result of their actions, because the regulations that govern the checkoff specify that only those with a tax liability may designate a contribution to the fund. The declining PECF revenues, therefore, are not simply a result of declining participation; they also are related to the tax status of checkoff participants.

For years, FEC officials have assumed that the low level of checkoff participation was largely a result of inadequate citizen understanding of the public financing system, a view supported by a number of research surveys.[18] To address this problem and enhance participation, the FEC initiated a number of projects in advance of the 1992 election to improve public awareness of the checkoff. The agency sponsored focus group surveys of public attitudes toward the checkoff; produced television and radio public service announcements in English and Spanish; and undertook an extensive public outreach effort that included the distribution of informational brochures, numerous media appearances by commission members, and special information packages for tax preparers and accounting software companies.

The FEC estimated that its announcements and education materials reached a potential audience of more than 90 million citizens in 1991 and about 200 million in 1992.[19] While extensive, this effort was relatively modest in its resources and intensity. In most instances, the public service advertisements were broadcast infrequently, if at all. The program did not produce a level of exposure great enough to provide taxpayers with a clear understanding of the relatively complex provisions of the checkoff system. Nor was it strong enough to outweigh the public perception that the system is not working, or the growing feelings of frustration and alienation among the electorate. As a result, the FEC's efforts appear to have had little effect: checkoff participation did not change appreciably in either 1991 or 1992.

Yet even if a major improvement in the level of public awareness is achieved, there is no guarantee that participation or checkoff receipts will

increase. Recent studies sponsored by the FEC show that most noncontribu-
tors are unlikely to become contributors even with further education.[20]
There also appears to be limited potential for additional contributions from
those who are presumably passive nonparticipants, that is, whose who leave
the checkoff boxes on their tax forms blank from year to year. Surveys of
selected tax returns conducted by the IRS since 1989 show that on average
only about 16 to 18 percent of tax filers fail to check "no" or "yes" on the
checkoff question on their forms.[21] While some of these individuals may
simply be overlooking this question, others surely leave the boxes blank
because they have no tax liability and are ineligible to participate. But even
if all of these individuals were potentially eligible and participated at rates
comparable to the rest of the taxpaying population, their contributions
would increase participation by only 3 or 4 percent. There does not appear
to be a large bloc of checkoff nonparticipants within the electorate who can
easily be identified and encouraged to contribute.

Notes

1. "100 Leading National Advertisers," *Advertising Age,* September 23, 1992, p. 1.
2. U.S. Department of Commerce, Bureau of Economic Analysis, *Survey of Current Business,* August 1993, p. 71.
3. Amount is based on Table 2.1 in this volume, derived from Federal Election
Commission (hereafter referred to as FEC), *The Presidential Public Funding Program*
(Washington, DC: FEC, 1993); FEC, *Annual Report 1992* (Washington, DC: FEC,
1993), pp. 3–18; and direct assistance by Robert Biersack, supervisory statistician, FEC.
4. FEC, *Annual Report 1992,* p. 5.
5. FEC, "1992 Congressional Election Spending Jumps 50% to $678 Million,"
press release, March 4, 1993, pp. 1–70.
6. Based on FEC, "Democrats Narrow Financial Gap in 1991–92," press release,
March 11, 1993, pp. 1–8; and Robert Biersack, "Hard Facts and Soft Money: Party
Finance in the 1991–92 Election Cycle" (paper presented at State of the Parties Conference, Ray C. Bliss Institute of Applied Politics, Akron, OH, September 23–24, 1993).
7. FEC, "PAC Activity Rebounds in 1991–92 Election Cycle—Unusual Nature of
Contests Seen as Reason," press release, April 29, 1993, pp. 1–38.
8. Based in part on Biersack, "Hard Facts and Soft Money."
9. Based in part on spending by some ninety-seven candidates in the twelve gubernatorial contests in 1992, amounting to $60.2 million. See Thad L. Beyle, "The 1992
Gubernatorial Elections," *Comparative State Politics* 15, no. 1 (February 1994), pp.
28–31.
10. Based in part on David Magleby, "Campaign Spending and Referendum Voting" (paper delivered at the annual meeting of the Western Political Science Association,
Albuquerque, NM, March 10–12, 1994), p. 4.
11. See Herbert E. Alexander and Brian A. Haggerty, *Financing the 1984 Election*
(Lexington, MA: Lexington Books, 1987), p. 127, fn. 1.
12. Gallup Poll, "Participation in Interest Groups High," *Gallup Report* (August
1981), p. 45.
13. Ruth S. Jones, "Contributing as Participation," in Margaret Latus Nugent and

John R. Johannes, eds., *Money, Elections, and Democracy: Reforming Congressional Campaign Finance* (Boulder, CO: Westview Press, 1990), p. 40.

14. *Tax Reform Act of 1986* (Public Law 99–514), *U.S. Statutes at Large* 100 (1986): 2085.

15. This change was made under the Omnibus Budget Reconciliation Act signed into law by President Clinton on August 10, 1993. See FEC, *Annual Report 1993* (Washington, DC: FEC, 1994), p. 5.

16. Anthony Corrado, *Paying for Presidents* (New York: Twentieth Century Fund Press, 1993). The discussion of the tax checkoff on pages 19–25 of this study served as the basis for the discussion that follows.

17. Ibid., p. 19.

18. See, among others, Frank Sorauf, *Money in American Elections* (Glenview, IL: Scott, Foresman, 1988), p. 219; and Market Decisions Corporation, *Presidential Election Campaign Fund Focus Group Research* (Portland, OR: Market Decisions Corporation, 1990).

19. Based on the usage reported in *Final Report: Federal Election Commission Broadcast Media Public Education Program on the Tax Checkoff* (Washington, DC: Washington Independent Productions, 1991).

20. Market Decisions Corporation, *Presidential Election Campaign Fund.*

21. Internal Revenue Service (hereafter referred to as IRS), "1992 Taxpayer Usage Study," report no. 13 (Washington, DC: IRS, 1994).

2

Seeking the Nominations:
An Overview

In the 1970s, the laws regulating federal election campaign financing in the United States underwent dramatic changes. In regard to presidential campaigns, enactments were intended to minimize opportunities for undue financial influence on officeholders and to make the election process more open and competitive. The laws have accomplished some of their aims, but they have had some unintended, and not always salutary, consequences. The degree to which the laws have failed to achieve their intended effects testifies at least as much to the inventiveness of political actors in circumventing the laws and to the intractability of election campaign finance in a pluralistic society as to the deficiencies of the laws.

The Federal Election Campaign Act of 1971 (FECA),[1] the Revenue Act of 1971,[2] and the FECA Amendments of 1974,[3] 1976,[4] and 1979[5] thoroughly revised the rules of the game for candidates, parties, and contributors. In regard to presidential campaigns, the laws provided for public matching funds for qualified candidates in the prenomination period (including minor party candidates who qualify), public grants to pay the costs of the two major parties' national nominating conventions, and public grants for the major party general election candidates. They also established criteria whereby minor parties and new parties can qualify for public funds to pay nominating convention and general election campaign costs.

The public funds, earmarked through a federal income tax checkoff, were intended to help provide or to supply in entirety the money serious candidates need to present themselves and their ideas to the electorate. In the prenomination period, public funding was intended to make the nomination process more competitive and to encourage candidates to broaden their

16

bases of support by seeking out large numbers of relatively small contributions matchable with public funds. In the general election period, flat grants to major party candidates were intended to provide the basic money needed soon after the nominating conventions, to be supplemented by national party–coordinated expenditures on behalf of the presidential ticket.

Contribution limits and expenditure limits also were enacted, although the Supreme Court subsequently ruled that spending limits are permissible only in publicly financed campaigns.[6] These laws were intended to control large donations that have the potential for corruption, to minimize financial disparities among candidates, and to reduce opportunities for abuse. Laws requiring full and timely disclosure of campaign receipts and expenditures were put in place to help the electorate make informed choices among candidates and to make it possible to monitor compliance with the campaign finance laws. Finally, Congress also established the FEC as the regulatory body responsible for administering and enforcing the law.

The Regulatory Framework

Candidates who seek presidential nomination do not enjoy unrestricted access to the electorate. Interposed between the candidates and potential voters is the government, acting through campaign finance and political broadcast regulations intended to ensure that candidates compete, as much as possible, on a fair and equitable basis. Political parties at national and state levels also intervene in the communication process between candidates and voters through party rules for delegate selection. Laws and procedures, then, circumscribe the candidates' activities. At the same time, they are the object of much probing and testing by candidates seeking advantage over their opponents while remaining within the bounds established by government and party.

The basic laws that governed fund raising, spending, and reporting the use of campaign money in the 1992 prenomination campaigns were the same as those that had been in effect four years earlier and had changed little since they were first applied in the 1976 campaigns. Candidates for the presidential nomination in 1992 were permitted to accept no more than $1,000 from any individual contributor and no more than $5,000 from any political action committee (PAC). The candidates were allowed to contribute an unlimited amount to their own campaigns—as Ross Perot did—unless they accepted public funding. In that case they were permitted to contribute a maximum of $50,000 in personal or family funds. No candidate was permitted to accept a contribution from certain sources, including corporate and labor union treasury funds, or cash contributions in excess of $100.

Public matching funds were available for candidates who raised $5,000 in each of twenty states in contributions from individuals of $250 or less. Contributions from PACs were not eligible for matching funds. The federal government matched each contribution to qualified candidates from individuals up to $250 per contributor, but the total federal subsidy to any candidate could not exceed $13.8 million, one-half of the prenomination campaign spending limit. The matching funds were drawn from the PECF. Taxpayers were permitted to use a checkoff procedure on their federal income tax forms to earmark a small portion of their liabilities—$1 for individuals and $2 for married persons filing jointly—for public funding of presidential election campaigns. Although the FEC could not begin releasing matching funds to candidates until January 1, 1992, the candidates were permitted to begin collecting matchable contributions as early as January 1, 1991.

Each candidate for presidential nomination in 1992 who accepted public matching funds was permitted to spend no more than $27.6 million, plus 20 percent—$5.5 million—for fund raising. Unlike the contribution limits, which have remained at the level fixed by the 1974 FECA Amendments, the expenditure limit is adjusted for inflation, using 1974 as the base year. As Table 2.3 indicates, the 1992 prenomination campaign spending limit (minus fund-raising costs) represents a net increase of about $16.7 million over the 1976 limit and an increase of about $4.5 million over the 1988 limit. Candidates accepting matching funds also were bound by spending limits in the individual states. They were permitted to spend no more than the greater of $200,000 or 16 cents per eligible voter, plus a cost-of-living increase using 1974 as the base year. Payments made by the candidates for legal and accounting services to comply with the campaign law were exempted from the limits, but the candidates were required to report such payments to the FEC. Candidates who do not accept public funding are not bound by the overall or the individual state spending limits. All eleven major candidates for nomination, however, accepted public funding and were required to honor the limits.

Finally, all the candidates were required to submit regular reports to the FEC, disclosing information about their campaign organizations' receipts and disbursements. The FEC, in turn, made these reports available to the public. The reports had to identify by name, address, occupation, and principal place of business contributors of more than $200 and itemize each campaign expenditure of more than $200, indicating the name and address of the recipient and the purpose of the expenditure.

Five presidential elections—1976, 1980, 1984, 1988, and 1992—have been conducted under the FECA, its amendments, and its companion laws, a sufficient experience from which to draw some conclusions about the impact of the laws and to determine whether they have had their intended effects.[7] The costs to the voters, the taxpayers, and the candidates' campaigns have been considerable. An assessment is in order of how well the public funding system for presidential campaigns, and the accompanying expenditure limits, served the candidates and the American people.

The 1992 Presidential Costs

In the 1991–92 election cycle, political candidates and committees at all levels—federal, state, and local—spent $3.2 billion on political campaigns. About 17.2 percent, or $550 million, was spent to elect a president. The spending in each phase was apportioned as indicated in Table 2.1. Some $153.2 million was spent by and on behalf of candidates seeking nomination, $59.6 million related to the two major party conventions, and $310.5 million in the general election period. Miscellaneous spending accounted for the remainder of the $550 million.

While the 1992 spending was high, when seen in perspective in Table 2.2, the long-term trends are not so alarming. When adjusted for inflation since 1960, the costs of presidential campaigns have increased only by a factor of four, whereas aggregate unadjusted costs have risen more than eighteenfold from 1960 to 1992. The $550 million, however, represents only a 10 percent increase from the 1988 presidential campaign cost.[8] In 1988, with no incumbent running, the presidency was wide open for the first time in twenty years; in 1992, with an incumbent seeking renomination, the prenomination costs were much reduced from 1988. And despite an open contest for the Democratic nomination, the costs were much less than in 1988; in 1991–92, the best-known Democrats did not contend, and those who did started later in 1991 than others had in 1987.

Table 2.2 even shows a decrease in 1992 in adjusted spending, that is, as measured by the value of 1960 dollars. The decrease from 1988 to 1992 occurred because the presidential costs increase of 10 percent was less than the inflation increase over the four-year period.

In 1992, the competition for nomination in both major parties combined cost about $117.6 million in candidate spending, much less than the 1988 amount of $199.6 million, when there were fiercely competitive contests in both parties. General election spending rose over 1988 mainly because of inflation and Perot's campaign. The amount each of the major presidential candidates could spend in the general election was adjusted according to the CPI, from $46.1 million in 1988 to $55.2 million in 1992. The amount each national party committee could spend on behalf of its nominee similarly rose from $8.3 million to $10.3 million, while the soft money amounts

Table 2.1

Costs of Electing a President, 1992 (in $ millions)

Prenomination (as of September 30, 1993)
    Spending by major party candidates $117.6
    Compliance   8.0
    Independent expenditures[a]   1.2
    Communication costs[a]   0.7
    Labor spending   20.0
    Minor parties[b]   5.7
      Subtotal $153.2

Conventions (including host cities and committees)
    Republicans $21.0
    Democrats   38.6
      Subtotal $59.6

General election
    Spending by major party candidates[c] $110.4
    Compliance   10.3
    Parties[d]   63.4
    DNC and RNC media[e]   14.5
    Independent expenditures[f]   3.0
    Communication costs   2.7
    Labor, corporate, association spending   35.0
    Perot and minor parties[g]   71.2
      Subtotal $310.5

Miscellaneous expenses[h]   26.7

Grand total $550.0

Source: Citizens' Research Foundation.

[a]Prenomination independent expenditures and communication costs are through July 15 for Democrats, August 15 for Republicans.
[b]Reported for prenomination campaigns by Lenora Fulani, Andre Marrou, and John Hagelin.
[c]Includes $55.2 million in public funds spent by each major party candidate.
[d]Includes $43 million in "soft money" expenditures related to presidential campaigns, convention activities, and coordinated expenditures by the DNC and the RNC.
[e]The RNC spent $10 million on a national media advertising campaign; the Democrats spent $14.2 million on a similar media campaign; 60 percent of the value was assigned to the presidential campaigns.
[f]Negative advertising comprised $570,650 of the total.
[g]Includes $68.3 million spent by Ross Perot; $1.1 million by Lyndon LaRouche; $608,000 by Andre Marrou, the Libertarian Party candidate; and other minor party and independent candidates.
[h]Includes a reasonable portion of funds spent by nonpartisan organizations to conduct voter registration and turnout drives that benefited specific presidential candidates; costs for advertising and communications by various organizations on issues closely related to presidential campaigns; and miscellaneous out-of-pocket expenses.

Table 2.2

Presidential Spending, 1960–92
(adjusted for inflation, 1960 = 100)

Year	Actual Spending[a]	CPI (1960 base)	Adjusted Spending[a]
1960	30.0	100.0	30.0
1964	60.0	104.7	57.3
1968	100.0	117.5	85.1
1972	138.0	141.2	97.7
1976	160.0	192.2	83.2
1980	275.0	278.1	98.9
1984	325.0	346.8	93.7
1988	500.0	385.4	126.5
1992	550.0	446.9	117.8

Source: Citizens' Research Foundation.

[a]All spending figures are in millions and include prenomination, convention, and general election costs.

raised and spent in the major party campaigns decreased only slightly from 1988. More important was the spending of Perot, who spent $68.4 million in his presidential campaign.

Congressional efforts in 1991–92 to extend public financing to Senate and House campaigns diverted attention from the fine-tuning that was desirable in the laws governing presidential campaigns. There had been no basic change in federal election law since 1979, but most of the presidential election provisions had not been changed since 1974. There was one exception, however: amounts of public financing and expenditure limits were adjusted to changes in the CPI—but not enough to keep pace with the escalation of campaign costs at a much higher rate than inflation over the sixteen-year period. Table 2.3 demonstrates the amounts of public funding and expenditure limits as officially adjusted and set by the FEC from 1976 to 1992.

One significant change in the law occurred in mid-1993, well after the 1992 elections, when the federal income tax checkoff was increased to $3 on a single return and $6 on a joint return. This was enacted by the Congress as part of the Omnibus Budget Reconciliation Act of 1993, and was designed to raise sufficient tax dollars for public funding of the 1995–96 presidential election cycle.[9] The change began with 1993 tax returns, and was revised according to inflation and entitlement increases set by the CPI, assisting eligible parties to hold their 1992 conventions, and assisting candidates in the prenomination and general election phases. The entitlement

Table 2.3

Major Party Presidential Expenditure Limits and Public Funding, 1976–92
(in $ millions)

	Prenomination Campaign				General Election Campaign		
	National Spending Limit[a]	Exempt Fund Raising[b]	Overall Spending Limit[c]	Nominating Convention	Public Treasury Grant[d]	National Party Spending[e]	Overall Spending Limit[c]
1976	$10.9 +	$2.2 =	$13.1	$2.2[f]	$21.8 +	$3.2 =	$25.0
1980	14.7 +	2.9 =	17.7	4.4	29.4 +	4.6 =	34.0
1984	20.2 +	4.0 =	24.2	8.1	40.4 +	6.9 =	47.3
1988	23.1 +	4.6 =	27.7	9.2	46.1 +	8.3 =	54.4
1992	27.6 +	5.5 =	33.1	11.0	55.2 +	10.3 =	65.5

Source: Citizens' Research Foundation.

[a]Based on $10 million plus cost-of-living increases (COLA) using 1974 as the base year. Eligible candidates may receive no more than one-half the national spending limit in public matching funds. To become eligible, candidates must raise $5,000 in private contributions of $250 or less in each of twenty states. The federal government matches each contribution to qualified candidates up to $250. Publicly funded candidates also must observe spending limits in the individual states equal to the greater of $200,000 + COLA (base year 1974), or 16 cents × the voting-age population (VAP) of the state + COLA.
[b]Candidates may spend up to 20 percent of the national spending limit for fund raising.
[c]Legal and accounting expenses to ensure compliance with the law are exempt from the spending limit.
[d]Based on $20 million + COLA (base year 1974).
[e]Based on 2 cents × VAP of the United States + COLA.
[f]Based on $2 million + COLA (base year 1974). Under the 1979 FECA Amendments, the basic grant was raised to $3 million. In 1984, Congress raised the basic grant to $4 million.

increases were urgent because payments had begun to eat up the balances of the PECF, which were dwindling due to the decline in revenues from the income tax checkoff.

Precandidacy PACs

Once a person declares his or her intention to run for the presidency and registers a principal campaign committee with the FEC, the meter begins to run on contribution and expenditure limits. One way of circumventing these limits is to remain an undeclared candidate for as long as possible and to establish a PAC for use as a vehicle for supporting precandidacy political activity. A PAC is an organization usually formed by a business, labor, professional, or other interest group to provide funds to candidates and other political committees. Groups form PACs so that they may raise funds on a voluntary basis from members, stockholders, employees, or, in some cases, the general public, to generate meaningful amounts that can be contributed to candidates or otherwise spent on activities designed to influence election results. Like any other individual, a prospective presidential contender can establish a PAC. Such a PAC is considered to be completely independent of a presidential aspirant's future campaign, even if that individual is the head of the PAC, so long as the PAC and its members avoid a handful of specific activities that are used by the FEC to determine whether an individual should be regarded as a candidate subject to the presidential campaign finance regulations. These activities, which include the financing of a media campaign to announce an individual's intention to seek a party's presidential nomination, the use of PAC money to qualify an individual for state ballots, and describing an individual as a future candidate in PAC publications, are so narrowly defined that they can easily be avoided. As a result, an increasing number of candidates throughout the 1980s relied on PACs to launch their campaigns for the Oval Office.[10]

The first candidate to use this tactic was Ronald Reagan, who formed Citizens for the Republic after his unsuccessful bid for the Republican presidential nomination in 1976. Reagan's PAC, which was partly funded by the $1.6 million remaining from his 1976 campaign, eventually spent close to $6.3 million. Only about 10 percent of this amount, however, was disbursed in the form of contributions to candidates for federal office. Most of the money went to activities designed to keep Reagan in the political spotlight and allow him to expand his political organization in preparation for a possible presidential run in 1980. PAC funds were used to hire staff and consultants, develop fund-raising programs, recruit volunteers, subsidize Reagan's travel and expenses, and host receptions on his behalf. This spending benefited Reagan's 1980 bid for office, but because no funds were spent on purposes considered to be directly related to the presidential campaign as defined by the FEC, none of the money raised or spent by the PAC was subject to the limits imposed on presidential campaign committees.

Following Reagan's lead, an increasing number of prospective presidential candidates established PACs throughout the 1980s. Prior to the 1984 contest, four Democratic challengers mimicked Reagan's approach. The five committees (including Reagan's PAC, which continued to operate until he left office) spent a total of $7 million. An even larger number of presidential hopefuls took advantage of this tactic in anticipation of the 1988 election—the first presidential nomination race since the adoption of the FECA in which a president was not seeking reelection. As a result, the level of early political activity among those considering a presidential bid was particularly high. To gain some relative advantage over potential opponents, five of the eventual Republican candidates and four of the Democrats established personal PACs. (Interestingly, Michael Dukakis, the eventual Democratic nominee, was one of the few candidates who did not have such an organization.) These committees spent a total of more than $25 million, almost twice the amount spent by similar committees in the previous two election cycles. About 85 percent of this sum was spent by the PACs associated with then-Vice President George Bush, Robert Dole, and Jack Kemp. Despite their relatively extravagant level of spending, almost none of these expenditures was counted against the candidates' respective campaign spending limits.[11]

The initial stage of the 1992 election cycle suggested that those contemplating a presidential bid would follow the basic pattern established in previous elections. After his victory in 1988, Bush maintained his PAC, Fund for America's Future, and it appeared that he would follow the model set by Reagan and use this committee to conduct political activities that would prepare the way for his reelection effort. A number of potential Democratic aspirants organized PAC operations early in the cycle and began to engage in the tasks associated with the beginnings of presidential candidacy. But the unique political circumstances that developed prior to the election year led many of these hopefuls to decide not to enter the race. As a result, personal PACs did not play a significant role in the financing of the 1992 prenomination campaigns.

The most prominent Democrat to form a PAC in anticipation of the 1992 election was the Reverend Jesse Jackson, who had unsuccessfully competed for the party's nomination in 1984 and 1988. In June 1988, while still technically a candidate for the nomination (Dukakis had received the support of enough delegates to secure the nomination, but the national convention was still a month away), Jackson announced that he would form a PAC to serve as the "basis for his activities beyond the 1988 election."[12] It was further reported that the PAC "would not only serve as an operational base but, for the first time, would also provide money to candidates aligned with [Jackson] and set the stage for him to increase his political influence around the country among . . . 'progressive candidates.'"[13] The committee was filed with the FEC on June 30, 1988, as Keep Hope Alive PAC, and Steven Cobble, a member of Jackson's presidential campaign staff, became the group's executive director.

After the 1988 election, Jackson's PAC quickly began to raise money, organize a staff, and undertake various political activities. According to FEC reports, by mid-1989 the PAC had raised approximately $280,000. A substantial portion of this sum was used as seed money to develop a national direct mail effort and lists of supporters.[14] By the end of 1989, the committee had raised approximately $561,000 and spent $513,000. It raised an additional $211,000 in 1990, while spending about $244,000. The PAC, however, donated relatively little money to candidates. By mid-1989, the committee contributed approximately $8,000 to candidates for public office, most of whom were involved in mayoral and local judgeship races in Mississippi, Texas, and New Jersey. In 1990, it donated a total of about $7,000 to Democratic candidates seeking federal office. Most of the funds raised by the committee were used to develop a political organization and finance some of Jackson's travel and political activities.

Richard Gephardt, another unsuccessful 1988 contender, also sought to keep his options open for 1992 by maintaining the PAC he founded in advance of his 1988 candidacy. His Effective Government Committee, which had spent about $1.2 million before Gephardt entered the 1988 race, raised about $280,000 in 1989 and $571,000 in 1990, according to FEC reports. The committee spent $240,000 in 1989 and $616,000 in advance of the 1990 midterm election. Unlike most personal PACs, however, Gephardt's organization disbursed a significant amount of money in the form of contributions to federal candidates. During the 1990 congressional election cycle, the PAC contributed $252,000 to seventy-four federal candidates, representing about 30 percent of the total raised by the committee in this period. This relatively high level of giving reflected Gephardt's position as House majority leader, an office he won after the 1988 election. He thus relied on his PAC to assist fellow party members and try to increase the Democratic majority in Congress. The political support developed through these gifts not only would help Gephardt in his relations in the Congress, but also would help to develop political support if he were to seek the presidency in the future.

Mario Cuomo also had a federal PAC, the Empire Leadership Fund, at the start of the 1992 election cycle. This committee, however, was relatively inactive, spending only about $13,000 before the 1990 election. Cuomo's supporters chose to concentrate their efforts on his 1990 New York gubernatorial reelection campaign, which raised close to $8.4 million. After the election, his campaign had a surplus of approximately $3.8 million.[15] Cuomo was thus positioned to jump-start a presidential campaign in the same way Dukakis had in 1987, by transferring his extensive donor list and any monies from his gubernatorial campaign that met federal regulations to a presidential committee.[16]

Another Democrat who considered the PAC option was L. Douglas Wilder, governor of Virginia. On November 13, 1990, Wilder filed papers with the FEC to establish a PAC named the Committee on Fiscal Responsibility. He was reportedly planning to finance the PAC in part by transferring nearly $1 million from his gubernatorial inaugural fund to the committee, but this transaction never took place.[17] In fact, the PAC did not raise any money, according to FEC reports. Instead, Wilder decided to launch his presidential campaign by forming an exploratory committee on March 27, 1991. On the same date, he terminated his PAC.

There are a number of reasons why potential 1992 challengers to Bush did not take advantage of the opportunities for precandidacy politicking offered by a personal PAC. In general, the level of early political activity would not have equaled that of 1988 under any normal circumstances because the Democratic nominee would be facing an incumbent. This prospect usually leads potential challengers to approach a race more cautiously, unless the incumbent is unpopular, which was the case with Jimmy Carter in the last two years of his administration, and Reagan in 1982 and early 1983. Bush, however, enjoyed notably high approval ratings throughout his first two years in office. During most of this period, Bush's public approval rating was higher than 60 percent, and after the invasion of Panama in late 1989 his approval rating reached 80 percent, a mark exceeded in the Gallup Poll only once since World War II, by John F. Kennedy after the 1961 Bay of Pigs invasion.[18]

The president's popularity discouraged widespread Democratic politicking, and the dramatic events surrounding the August 1990 invasion of Kuwait by Iraq and the subsequent Gulf War produced an abrupt chilling effect on presidential campaigning. No Democrat was willing to pursue open campaigning while the nation was engulfed in this crisis. After the war, Bush's popularity soared again, rising above the 80 percent mark from mid-February to mid-April 1991.[19] Consequently, none of the prominently mentioned potential Democratic candidates was willing to risk a race against such a popular likely opponent. Mario Cuomo, Richard Gephardt, and Senator Bill Bradley, among others, decided to focus on their reelection campaigns rather than pursue a possible presidential candidacy. Jackson also shifted his attention to nonpresidential politics, campaigning in support of statehood for the District of Columbia and winning election as one of D.C.'s "shadow senators" to promote the cause of statehood.

More interesting perhaps than the actions of the Democrats was Bush's course. At the outset of the 1992 election cycle, many observers believed that Bush would rely on his PAC to continue some of his political activities, just as Reagan had done when he was in office and as Bush had done prior to his 1980 quest for the Republican nomination and again in advance of his successful 1988 effort. The PAC remained active after the 1988 election, but it ceased its fund-raising operations. The PAC spent only $43,000 in 1989 and 1990, and then closed down on June 4, 1990, transferring the $137,000 remaining in its account to the Republican National State Election Committee for use in state and local elections.[20]

No explanation was given as to why the PAC chose to cease its operations. One reason may be that the president no longer needed the committee to build a political and financial organization. Including his 1980 experience, Bush had spent twelve consecutive years running for president or serving as vice president and thus had already developed an extensive nationwide political and financial network. As president, he also would have access to the Republican National Committee (RNC) as a vehicle for promoting his political interests. Yet he still could have used the PAC to maintain his political organization, as Reagan did during his first term in office. This approach, however, may have made it more difficult for Bush to assist his party in Congress, which was engaged at the time in a heated debate on campaign finance reform legislation. A cornerstone of the Republican position on this issue was the need for legislation that severely restricted or, preferably, eliminated the role of PACs in the financing of congressional campaigns. Bush supported this reform and, in his 1991 State of the Union address, urged Congress to "totally eliminate political action committees."[21] It would have been difficult for the president to defend this proposal if he had continued his PAC operation.

Whatever the specific reasons, the unusual political circumstances that characterized the early portion of the 1992 election cycle created a political climate that was not conducive to early campaigning and caused many potential Democratic challengers to wait until 1996. As a result, precandidacy PACs were not a prominent feature of the precampaign period. But the factors that encourage the formation of such committees, such as strategists' concerns about the restrictive effects of federal contribution and spending limits, and the financial demands of the front-loaded presidential delegate selection system, remain. Consequently, it is likely that many of those considering presidential bids in the future will consider the PAC alternative when planning their financial strategies, and that future election cycles will be more similar to those of the 1980s than to the precampaign period of 1992.

Prenomination Campaigns

The 1991–92 presidential campaigns for nomination stood in stark contrast to those of 1987–88. As indicated, Bush dominated the thinking because his early popularity ratings were high and accordingly a number of prominent Democrats—among them Albert Gore Jr., Mario Cuomo, Jay Rockefeller, Richard Gephardt, and Jesse Jackson—decided not to run. Bush's popularity in this period was as high as 89 percent, and Democratic chances did not seem promising. By January 1992, Bush's popularity had fallen to 69 percent, and it plummeted further as the year progressed. Only Paul Tsongas announced early, on April 30, 1991. By the time Bush's decline became certain, it was late for prominent Democrats to gear up a campaign. Accordingly, the Democratic field in fall 1991 consisted of relatively little-known and, with the exception of Tsongas, late-starting candidates.[22]

In 1988, Super Tuesday had been a major event, including primaries or caucuses in twenty states for the Democrats and seventeen for the Republicans.[23] On March 10, 1992, the numbers were down to a dozen for each party, but the key ones, Texas and Florida, remained, as did the stretch from Massachusetts to Hawaii. There was an emphasis on the South, but without Alabama, Arkansas, Kentucky, and North Carolina, there was no drama of a southern primary, as had occurred four years earlier.

Nevertheless, by March 17—a week after Super Tuesday—more than half the states holding primaries or caucuses had voted, and about half the delegates to the Democratic convention were chosen. By April 1, it was clear that Clinton would be nominated at his convention, and that is the date chosen in this study to start the general election period in the work of the national party committees and in the collection of soft money for the November election.

Meanwhile, in the Republican contest, Pat Buchanan voiced stronger and stronger criticism of Bush for betraying the conservative tradition established by Reagan. As Bush's popularity declined, Buchanan's criticisms became harsher, and in December 1991, Buchanan announced his candidacy. A futile campaign by David Duke fizzled, and the Republican field was narrowed to two. Buchanan did well in New Hampshire, and overall scored 30 percent or more in four primaries but failed to win any, and by April 1 it was clear that the general election would be a contest between Bush and Clinton.

As usual, the candidates had to be selective in marshaling and allocating their resources so they would have enough for the long presidential primary and caucus season. With the $33.3 million total limitations, as shown in Table 2.3, are sublimits in each state based on population size.[24] These limitations on how much a candidate could spend in each state became wholly unrealistic in these days of media-dominated, regional campaigning. The ultimate absurdity of the state limits can be demonstrated by adding the total of allowable state spending. The 1992 total of all fifty states produced a total of $86.7 million, a little less than three times the $33.1 million national limit (including fund-raising costs). The FEC came to the rescue by rationalizing the system.

In 1991, the FEC promulgated regulations to loosen the restrictions on how much a presidential campaign could spend in each state. By exempting certain advertising, travel, and consulting costs, which were considered part of a campaign's spending in a state, the rules, which took effect in November 1991, were designed to end the practices of subterfuge to which some candidates resorted to circumvent the state limits in important early primaries or caucuses.[25] The practices included arranging overnight accommodations for staffs in a state bordering on a nearby state so the costs could be counted against the bordering state's spending limit, and the purchase of television time in cities outside a primary or caucus state (when the cities' media markets included portions of the state) so television costs could be applied in part to another state's limit.

In 1988, the FEC decided that if requests for contributions were tagged onto television ads, one-half of the costs of airing the ad could be allocated to fund-raising costs, and that portion of costs would not be credited against the New Hampshire or Massachusetts limits.[26] To justify dodging the limits and/or to point out the need for raising the limits, many candidates complained that the FEC rules and formulas for allocating expenditures to individual states were illogical and arbitrary.

Under the 1991 FEC regulations, fees for placing television, radio, or print advertisements did not apply to the state expenditure limits at all. In addition, candidates' staff salaries while in the state and their travel expenses no longer applied to the state limits. Moreover, neither fees paid in a state for consultants who were advising on national campaign strategy nor a candidate's travel expenses applied to the limits. In spite of the new regulations, some observers maintain that the state spending limits, particularly in states with early prenomination contests, encourage independent expenditures on behalf of candidates who are approaching the limits.

The FEC was justified in seeking to reduce severe pressures on the candidates. Consider the psychological stake of winning in the first two contests: in Iowa, where the 1992 spending limit was $914,332; and in New Hampshire, where the 1992 limit was $552,400. In earlier years, candidates found ways to assign spending to their national headquarters; to surrounding states; or to fund-raising costs, a separate accounting procedure. For example, autos were rented in Massachusetts for use in New Hampshire and credited against the larger Massachusetts limit with a later primary. Earlier, the commission also allowed for 80 percent of the television time purchased on Boston stations, reaching 80 percent of the New Hampshire population, to be allocated to the Massachusetts limit, where the primary was not held until Super Tuesday. And in 1988, Gephardt put tag-end requests for contributions on his television ads and allocated half the costs to fund raising; thus the expenditures were not credited against the New Hampshire limits. By sanctioning such allocations, the FEC allowed the candidates to avoid exceeding the state limits. And in any case, documented excessive spending brought only a FEC fine in the amount of the overspending represented by public funds, which is usually about one-third of the amount of total spending. Moreover, this fine is assessed months after the event and is considered by pragmatic candidates as a cost of "doing business." As L. Sandy Maisel has written, "Certainly the intent of the law was not to create incentives for candidates to cheat on the state-by-state limits, because the consequences of being caught cheating were less serious for a campaign than the consequences of losing a caucus or primary."[27]

Consider also the resource allocation choices candidates faced on Super Tuesday. On that day campaigns had to choose where to campaign from among twelve states; candidates could not afford to spend the $5 million minimum that most experts said was necessary to campaign effectively in that many states, or to purchase spot announcements in the forty or so media markets involved. The $33.1 million limit had to cover all the fifty states plus national headquarters spending over the entire period of the prenomination campaigns.

Candidate Receipts and Expenditures

According to FEC records, prenomination candidate spending among those who received matching funds totaled about $120.8 million, as shown in Table 2.4. Excluding minor party candidate spending by John Hagelin, Andre Marrou, and Lenora Fulani, the total spent was $115.1 million, with $65.3 million expended by Democrats and $49.8 million by Republicans. Slightly more was raised by these Democratic and Republican candidates, but the approximately $42.7 million derived from matching funds accounted for 37 percent of the total spent, making the United States government the largest single contributor. As shown in Table 2.4, total individual contributions amounted to about $82.6 million, almost a 2-to-1 ratio over the $42.7 million in matching funds.

As Table 2.4 also shows, only $920,976 was derived from PAC or other political committee receipts, less than 1 percent of receipts or expenditures. Clinton, Tsongas, and fellow Democrat Jerry Brown refused PAC contributions, hoping to gain some political mileage from their refusals. Bush also

Table 2.4

1992 Prenomination Campaign Receipts and Expenditures, by Candidate

Candidate	Adjusted Total Receipts[a]	Individual Contri- butions	PAC Contri- butions	Matching Funds	Adjusted Total Disburse- ments[a]
Agran	$610,831	$331,631	0	$269,691	$607,218
Brown	9,420,374	5,176,336	0	4,239,345	8,994,722
Clinton	37,641,819	25,105,044	$5,204	12,518,130	33,900,254
Harkin	5,681,056	3,069,474	492,069	2,103,351	5,227,520
Kerrey	6,466,079	3,913,332	349,757	2,198,284	6,461,751
LaRouche	1,599,861	1,599,840	0	100,000	1,605,386
Tsongas	8,099,564	5,056,620	3,566	3,003,973	7,682,978
Wilder	799,334	508,519	750	289,026	805,972
Buchanan	12,205,269	7,157,808	24,750	4,999,983	11,551,379
Bush	38,013,375	27,088,825	44,250	10,658,513	37,945,656
Duke	271,815	220,715	0	0	354,838
Hagelin	926,304	561,820	449	353,160	875,143
Marrou	578,067	562,770	181	0	575,795
Fulani	4,137,368	2,201,577	0	1,935,524	4,206,857
Total	$126,451,136	$82,554,311	$920,976	$42,668,980	$120,795,469

Source: Federal Election Commission, data as of September 30, 1993.

[a]Adjusted to take into account transfers from or to affiliated committees, loan repayments, contribution refunds, and refunds or rebates to the campaigns.

refused PAC contributions, and he really did not need them. Political committee transfers of funds showed up on the Tsongas and Bush records, but they were not PAC gifts; these were proceeds from joint fund-raising committees, or gifts from committees of candidates for Congress. The two United States senators running, Tom Harkin and Bob Kerrey, were alone in seeking out PAC contributions, with Harkin raising $492,069 and Kerrey $349,757. Labor PAC contributions accounted for the bulk of Harkin's money in this category.

Prenomination spending in 1992 was augmented by an accounting provided by the FEC of twenty-two "minor" Democratic and Republican candidates who raised or spent $5,000 or more, indicating an additional $2.4 million.[28] None of these candidates qualified for matching funds and none received much publicity. In all, sixteen Democrats spent $1,530,516, and six Republicans spent $875,104. For example, Democrat Charles Woods spent $960,338, campaigning mainly in a number of southern states and winning 15,247 votes in the Alabama primary;[29] Republican James Lennane spent $793,255, mostly on anti-Bush commercials in New Hampshire,

Table 2.5

Payouts from the Presidential Election Campaign Fund, 1992 (in $ millions)

Prenomination		
Republicans	$15,858,507	
Democrats[a]	24,630,921	
National Alliance	2,013,323	
Natural Law	353,159	
Subtotal		$42,855,910
Conventions		
Democrats	$11,048,000	
Republicans	11,048,000	
Subtotal		$22,096,000
General Election		
Bush–Quayle	$55,240,000	
Clinton–Gore	55,240,000	
Subtotal		$110,480,000
Total		$175,431,910

Source: Federal Election Commission, *The Presidential Public Funding Program,* (Washington, DC: FEC, 1993), p. 71.

[a]Includes $100,000 to Lyndon LaRouche per court order.

where he received 1,684 votes;[30] some $255,789 was spent by Tom Laughlin, an actor who received 3,251 votes in New Hampshire; better-known candidates included former U.S. Senator and 1968 presidential contender Eugene McCarthy, who spent $77,680, and Endicott Peabody, a former governor of Massachusetts, who ran for vice president and spent $35,575.

Matching Funds

Table 2.5 shows the U.S. Treasury payouts from the PECF for all three phases of the presidential selection process: the prenomination period, the conventions, and the general election period. The payouts aggregated $175.4 million, a minimal reduction from 1988 payouts.

Table 2.6 presents additional information about matching funds, showing $43.4 million that included amounts received by Lenora Fulani, John Hagelin, and Lyndon LaRouche. Interestingly, Clinton received almost $2

Table 2.6

Summary of Matching Fund Activity for 1992 Presidential Prenomination Candidates

Candidate	Number of Submissions	Average Contribution on Submissions	Number of Contributions	Amounts Certified by FEC
Agran	2	$63	4,335	$269,692
Brown	8	52	84,567	4,239,405
Clinton	10	75	169,230	12,536,135
Harkin	15	51	44,421	2,103,362
Kerrey	14	53	41,767	2,195,530
LaRouche	1	179	3,217	568,435
Tsongas	15	80	38,710	3,003,981
Wilder	2	128	2,324	289,027
Buchanan	11	33	165,744	5,199,987
Bush	13	76	141,752	10,658,521
Fulani	14	20	101,932	2,013,323
Hagelin	4	97	3,658	353,160
Total	107	$76	801,657	$43,430,558

Source: Federal Election Commission, data as of July 31, 1994.

million more in matching funds than Bush, although their average contributions were similar. Buchanan received almost $5.2 million, a testimony to his smaller average contribution derived from a successful direct mail campaign. Brown benefited from the fourth largest amount of matching funds, more than $4.2 million. This is a tribute to his aggressive financial campaign in which he accepted only individual contributions of up to $100, not up to the $250 that was matchable under the law. Fulani received almost as much as Kerrey and Harkin, and more than twice the amount she received in her 1988 campaign.[31]

Table 2.6 also shows a few more than 800,000 contributions to the various candidates, down from the 1,245,501 to the candidates in 1988.[32] Of the major party candidates, Buchanan had the lowest average contribution, only $33, one-half the amount of the average of all the candidates, $66. Buchanan received more contributions than Bush. Clinton, at 169,230 contributions, and Brown, at 84,567 contributions, led the Democratic list.

Major Candidate Contributions/Loans to Their Own Campaigns

As of September 30, 1993, contributions and loans from the candidates themselves accounted for relatively little money, as follows:

Contributions to Own Campaigns

Agran	$500
Harkin	4,533
Marrou	116

Loans to Own Campaigns

Agran	$5,000
Tsongas	45,000
Buchanan	50,000
Duke	1,000
Marrou	15,000

Under federal law, a presidential candidate who accepts public financing is limited in the amount—$50,000—he and his immediate family can contribute or lend to his own campaign. Only Buchanan lent that much to his campaign for early direct mail, but he repaid the loan from campaign funds in August 1992.[33] Tsongas lent his campaign $45,000, raising the money by selling stocks;[34] because of additional campaign debts, he has not been able to repay the loan.

A Center Study

In late October 1992, the Center for Responsive Politics (CRP) issued a report that compared the size of contributions in the Clinton and Bush prenomination campaigns through August. It showed Clinton having received 38 percent of his individual contributions in amounts of $200 or less, compared with Bush's 14 percent in this category; inversely, it showed Bush receiving 86 percent of his contributions in amounts in excess of $200, compared with Clinton's 62 percent in this category. This analysis confirms that Bush was more reliant on larger contributions, and Clinton was more dependent on smaller contributions.[35]

The same report provided a profile of those who gave more than $200 to Bush or Clinton by industry. It found that lawyers and lobbyists were the leading identifiable source of funds for the Clinton campaign, providing $3.4 million. The leading identifiable source of funds for the Bush campaign was a combined category of finance, insurance, and real estate, providing a total of almost $4 million. This combined category was the second largest source for Clinton, at almost $2 million, while lawyers and lobbyists were third largest for Bush, at $2.1 million.[36]

Questions can be raised about the reliability of the profile, however, because donors of some $9.2 million to Bush were unidentified, and donors of some $5.1 million to Clinton were unidentified. Also, the percentage of

Table 2.7

Funding Sources for Major Party Nominees, 1991–92 Prenomination Campaigns (in $ millions)

Contributions from Individuals	Bush	Clinton
Less than $500	$5.3	$14.0
$500-$749	2.6	3.8
$750-$1,000	19.8	7.6
Matching funds	10.1	12.5

Source: Federal Election Commission, *The Presidential Public Funding Program* (Washington, DC: FEC, 1993), p. 31.

unidentified donations was at odds with the percentage the CRP used in a June 1992 study.[37]

Overview

In the contests for nomination, the eleven candidates receiving matching funds (plus LaRouche, belatedly), with the exception of Bush, all needed exposure. Only Bush, Brown, and Fulani (not counting LaRouche, who was in prison) had run previously.

Clinton demonstrated an ability to overcome adversity in the form of allegations about his infidelity and draft evasion. He received tremendous attention and name recognition, even if much of it was negative, but in the main, he had sufficient funds to carry on, abetted by a large bank line of credit, as will be noted. Buchanan demonstrated that he could do relatively well in challenging a president, with modest financing but support activated by strong feelings. As Clyde Wilcox has suggested, "campaign spending matters most when little-known candidates contest the nomination, and matters considerably less when the candidates are well known and when free media provide voters with sufficient information to make up their minds."[38]

Comparing the Nominees

George Bush and Bill Clinton, the prenomination winners, had two common characteristics: they had the most money early, and they had enough money to sustain their campaigns throughout, though not without rough spots for both candidates. A breakdown of funding sources is shown in Table 2.7.

Bush's successes, though less impressive than in 1987–88, were more related to his incumbency and to the political obligations people owed to him than to his actual spending. As his popularity fell, it became more difficult to raise funds. He got off to a later start in 1991 than in 1987 and had more difficulty, even once his nomination was assured, and he was still raising money just a few weeks prior to the Republican convention.

Clinton raised more than other Democrats by far, but more and more as his nomination became more likely. He, too, was raising money right up to the time of his convention.

As Table 2.7 shows, Bush had a clear advantage in raising large numbers of the legally maximum $1,000 contributions. Clinton relied more on smaller contributions and received more in matching funds than Bush.

A measure of the nature of the 1991–92 prenomination campaigns is indicated by the amounts of money the major party candidates had raised as of December 31, 1991. The listing among Democrats, in rounded numbers, was as follows:[39]

Clinton	$3.3 million
Harkin	2.2 million
Kerrey	1.9 million
Tsongas	1.3 million
Brown	0.5 million
Wilder	0.5 million
LaRouche	0.3 million
Agran	0.2 million

The Republican listing, in rounded numbers, was:

Bush	$10.0 million
Buchanan	0.7 million
Duke	0.1 million

Other party candidates, in rounded numbers, raised these amounts:

Hagelin	0
Marrou	$0.3 million
Fulani	0.9 million

The major party total of $21.3 million compares with $88.8 million as of December 31, 1987, four years before.[40] Bush, who had raised $18.7 million four years earlier, raised only $10 million by December 31, 1991. Clinton had raised only $3.3 million, less than one-third of the amount raised by Dukakis by that date—$10.6 million—four years earlier. Obviously, campaigns can be won for relatively less, but the amounts depend upon the extent of competition and whether an escalating arms race is under way. In 1988, the competition for open nominations in both major parties was intense and costly, while in 1992, there was no arms race and the level of competition financially was much less.

Including minor party candidates, the 1991 receipts came to $21.3 million. Adjusted total disbursements by all candidates were only $11.5 million.

Considering the amounts raised and spent, candidates began 1992 with about $10.5 million cash on hand. The FEC certified and the Treasury Department paid out $6.4 million in matching funds in the first week of January 1992 for 1991 candidate collections.

In addition, independent expenditures in the prenomination period were $1.1 million for all presidential candidates, $1 million of that on behalf of Bush; and an additional $166,059 was spent in negative campaigning in opposition to various candidates. Independent expenditures on behalf of Democratic candidates were only $55,834, but the negative spending in opposition to Democratic candidates was $54,572, including $45,603 against Clinton, the front-runner. A more extensive discussion of presidential independent expenditures is found in chapter 9, and in Table 9.1. Other related expenditures, such as those by labor unions in parallel campaigning, were shown earlier in Table 2.1.

Notes

1. *Federal Election Campaign Act of 1971* (Public Law 92-225), *U.S. Statutes at Large* 86 (1973): 3 (codified as amended in *U.S. Code,* vol. 2, secs. 431 et seq., and in scattered sections of *U.S. Code,* vols. 18 and 47).

2. *Revenue Act of 1971* (Public Law 92-178), secs. 701–3, 801–2, *U.S. Statutes at Large* 85 (1972): 497, 560–74 (codified as amended in scattered sections of U.S. Code, vol. 26).

3. *Federal Election Campaign Act Amendments of 1974* (Public Law 93-443), *U.S. Statutes at Large* 88 (1974): 1263 (codified in scattered sections of *U.S. Code*).

4. *Federal Election Campaign Act Amendments of 1976* (Public Law 94-283), *U.S. Statutes at Large* 90 (1976): 1263 (codified in scattered sections of *U.S. Code*).

5. *Federal Election Campaign Act Amendments of 1979* (Public Law 96-187), *U.S. Statutes at Large* 93 (1979): 1339 (codified in scattered sections of *U.S. Code*).

6. *Buckley v. Valeo,* 424 U.S. 1 (1976).

7. For a thorough analysis of the impact of federal campaign finance law on the conduct of the 1988 presidential campaigns, see Herbert E. Alexander and Monica Bauer, *Financing the 1988 Election* (Boulder, CO: Westview Press, 1991).

8. Ibid., pp. 11–13.

9. *Omnibus Budget Reconciliation Act of 1993* (Public Law 103-66), *U.S. Statutes at Large* 107 (1993): 567. Also see FEC, "Congress Increases Tax Check-off—FEC Says '96 Presidential Elections Will be Fully Funded," press release, August 20, 1993.

10. For a more detailed discussion of precandidacy PACs, see Anthony Corrado, *Creative Campaigning: PACs and the Presidential Selection Process* (Boulder, CO: Westview Press, 1992); and Alexander and Bauer, *Financing the 1988 Election.*

11. Audits of these campaigns conducted by the FEC after the election found that less than 1 percent of these expenditures could be considered campaign spending subject to federal caps.

12. Bernard Weintraub, "Jackson Says His PAC Will Have a Wide Impact," *New York Times,* June 21, 1988.

13. Ibid.
14. Tom Sherwood, "PUSHing and Rainbowing and Keeping Hope Alive," *Washington Post National Weekly Edition,* November 6–12, 1989, p. 14.
15. See Frank Lynn, "In a Party Split, Kemp Endorses Conservative's Bid for Governor," *New York Times,* October 6, 1990; "Mr. Cuomo's Fund-Raising Overkill," *New York Times,* November 3, 1990; and Adam Pertman, "Democrats in '92 Field Already Feel a Cuomo Chill," *Boston Globe,* October 24, 1991.
16. Corrado, *Creative Campaigning,* pp. 83–84.
17. "Wilder Still Keeps Inaugural Fund Secret," *Campaign Practices Reports,* June 24, 1991, p. 8.
18. George C. Edwards III, "George Bush and the Public Presidency: The Politics of Inclusion," in Colin Campbell and Bert A. Rockman, eds., *The Bush Presidency: First Appraisals* (Chatham, NJ: Chatham House, 1991), pp. 131–32.
19. Ibid., p. 132.
20. See Fund for America's Future, Termination Report, Schedule B. A copy of this report is on file with the FEC.
21. See the text of Bush's State of the Union Address in *New York Times,* January 30, 1991.
22. Karen DeWitt, "Tsongas Pitches Economic Austerity, Mixed With Patriotism," *New York Times,* January 1, 1992.
23. Alexander and Bauer, *Financing the 1988 Election,* p. 17.
24. FEC, "FEC Announces 1992 Presidential Spending Limits," press release, February 12, 1992.
25. 11 C.F.R. 106.2.
26. Richard L. Berke, "Election Unit Eases TV Ad Limits, Rejecting Advice of Own Counsel," *New York Times,* February 26, 1988.
27. L. Sandy Maisel, "Spending Patterns in Presidential Nominating Campaigns, 1976–1988" (paper prepared for the American Political Science Association annual meeting, Washington, DC, September 1–4, 1988), p. 21.
28. FEC, "List of Republican and Democratic Candidates," as of June 1, 1994.
29. FEC, *Federal Election 92* (Washington, DC: FEC, 1993), p. 101.
30. R.W. Apple Jr., "Bush, Slipping in New Hampshire, Aiming for 'Home Run' on Visit," *New York Times,* February 15, 1992.
31. Alexander and Bauer, *Financing the 1988 Election,* Table 2.7, p. 19.
32. Ibid.
33. Robert Shogan, "Buchanan Starts 'America First' Bid for President," *Los Angeles Times,* December 11, 1992.
34. Martin Tolchin, "Tsongas's Life, and Finances, Changed Course When Illness Struck," *New York Times,* February 1, 1992.
35. Center for Responsive Politics, "Lawyers, Wall Street, Insurance Industry, Oil and Gas Lead All Contributors in 1992 Election," press release, October 22, 1992, unnumbered pages.
36. Ibid.
37. See chapter 5, pp. 34–35.
38. Clyde Wilcox, "Financing the 1988 Prenomination Campaigns," in Emmett H. Buell Jr. and Lee Sigelman, eds., *Nominating the President* (Knoxville, TN: University of Tennessee Press, 1991), p. 92.
39. FEC, "Adjusted Disbursements," as of December 31, 1991, p. 2.
40. Alexander and Bauer, *Financing the 1988 Election,* p. 20.

3

The Prenomination Campaigns: The Candidates

The FECA provisions that require candidates and committees to make full and timely disclosure of campaign receipts and expenditures were put in place to help the electorate make informed choices among candidates. If voters know the sources of a candidate's financial support, advocates of disclosure reason, they will be better able to determine whether the candidate deserves their support. The disclosure requirements also were intended to make it possible to monitor compliance with the campaign finance laws. Thus candidates who accept matching funds are required to supply the FEC with substantial documentation to demonstrate that their campaigns have remained within the spending limits specified by the law. All candidates are required to file regular reports with the FEC to demonstrate that their campaigns have complied with the contribution limits.

No doubt more information is available about details and trends in campaign financing than ever before, but there is no empirical method by which to establish whether this increased availability has increased the political sophistication of voters. Few "average citizens" go directly to the FEC for campaign finance information about candidates and committees in which they are interested. They depend instead on journalists who write about the financing of campaigns and, in some cases, on candidates or their opponents. Coverage of campaign financing in some newspapers and journals is consistently superior; in many others it is highly selective or nonexistent. Moreover, contending parties in election contests should hardly be considered unimpeachable sources of campaign finance data.

While available official data are abundantly used throughout this volume, the candidate-by-candidate section that follows includes internal information from the campaigns, as will be evident. This section also relies on newspaper accounts because they give some sense of the ongoing character of the various campaigns for nomination. Newspaper and newsmagazine stories depict the tone and flavor of the campaigns, and the activities they describe all had budgetary consequences in terms of the costs of the campaigns, along with indications of where the money was coming from.

Clinton: Prenomination

Governor Bill Clinton declared his candidacy for the Democratic presidential nomination on October 3, 1991, outside the Old State House in Little Rock, Arkansas. He pledged to expand economic opportunity and restore the American Dream for the "forgotten middle class."[1] In addition, he urged the American public to "take some personal responsibility for the future of this country."[2] In an effort to separate himself from Washington, at least symbolically, Clinton established his campaign headquarters in Little Rock, where it remained throughout the campaign.

Clinton, who was associated with the Democratic Leadership Council, is a centrist who embraces traditional Democratic social concerns with more conservative economic policies. Clinton established himself as a viable contender for the nomination with a clear message, organizational and fundraising strength, and the ability to gather endorsements. The political calendar also worked in his favor, since many southern states participated in the Super Tuesday round of primaries, which allowed Clinton to capitalize on his early popularity and support in these states.

Clinton had vowed to forsake national office when he won the governorship in 1990 and decided to enter the race only about two weeks before his announcement. This uncertainty may have prevented his campaign from getting off to a vigorous start. The campaign did not have a manager when it was announced, although longtime Clinton friend and political associate Bruce Lindsey agreed to serve temporarily as coordinator. But the campaign quickly went about the task of recruiting staff members. James Carville and Paul Begala were hired as consultants to the campaign; these men had masterminded Harris Wofford's upset victory over former U.S. Attorney General Dick Thornburgh for a U.S. Senate seat from Pennsylvania.[3] David Wilhelm, a political consultant from Illinois, was selected to serve as chairman. After the November 1992 general election, he became chairman of the Democratic National Committee (DNC).[4]

Clinton began campaigning at once and visited Los Angeles in mid-October. He had three fund raisers in his one-and-one-half-day trip. One was given by environmentalists, another by television producers Harry Thomason and Linda Bloodworth-Thomason, and a third by Peter Guber, Sony Pictures Entertainment chairman. Clinton's visit marked an escalation in the competition for Southern California money. Senator Harkin had already raised money from Hollywood liberals, and Senator Kerrey had fund raisers in Los Angeles in late October.[5]

Until his Chicago address to the Association of State Democratic Chairs in November, Clinton's fund raising had not been robust. But after this important gathering of party leaders, his financial prospects improved significantly. Clinton's speech was given a very favorable review, and the campaign's fund-raising staff took advantage of the opportunity it presented. Comments from the press and participants were distributed to potential contributors. In the twenty days following the speech, finance director Rahm Emanuel put together twenty-seven events. By late November, Clinton's popularity was becoming evident and commentators were beginning to identify Clinton as one of the front-runners. Veteran political columnists Jack W. Germond and Jules Witcover, for example, noted, "[T]here is a rough consensus developing in the political community these days that Gov. Bill Clinton has become the leading man in the drama of the campaign for the Democratic presidential nomination."[6]

In early December, two prominent 1988 Bush supporters hosted a breakfast for Clinton to hear his views on the economy. The hosts were Roger W. Johnson, chairman of Western Digital Corporation, and Kathryn G. Thompson, a real estate developer and member of Bush's Team 100, a group of contributors who gave at least $100,000 each to the 1988 Republican campaign. The campaign said the breakfast was evidence that Clinton's economic message had appeal across party lines. Johnson and Thompson said the event did not represent an endorsement of Clinton.[7]

Clinton was back in Hollywood in early December for fund raisers hosted by Dawn Steel, former president of Columbia Pictures, and her husband, Charles Roven. Many celebrities and the heads of four motion picture studios attended.[8] This event and another in Hollywood jointly raised $225,000.

Clinton spent $25,000 to $30,000 on Florida's Democratic Party straw vote in mid-December. Clinton's campaign supplied placards illuminated by built-in flashlights, bussed in college students from Arkansas to cheer, and mailed videotapes to all the delegates. Clinton received 54 percent of the vote, which was a nonbinding preference poll. Clinton aides said this was a continued sign of their candidate's momentum.[9]

At the end of December 1993, Clinton raised $75,000 in Atlanta and was endorsed by U.S. Senator Sam Nunn and Governor Zell Miller, both of Georgia. He then went on to Memphis and Nashville for fund raising. One ploy the Clinton campaign used was to release the reports of its 1991 fund raising early in January 1992, weeks before the law's deadline, forcing other candidates to do the same. Clinton's financial lead over the other candidates then was used to contribute to the impression of a Clinton popularity surge.[10] In all, he raised $3.3 million in 1991, most of it from mid-November to year's end. But nearly one-third of that money came from one event in Little Rock, and despite the Hollywood input, most of it came from the South.[11]

The advantage of being the front-runner was that it made it easier for Clinton to attract donations. The disadvantage was that others were targeting Clinton as the person to beat. His rivals accused Clinton of being the darling of the media, but these charges had little effect. Clinton commanded the most attention in early 1992 because he had been more effective than the others in maximizing his strengths and neutralizing his weaknesses during 1991. The campaign operated effectively, paid attention to details, and consisted of a cohesive inner circle of advisors.[12]

Clinton attracted New Hampshire voters with TV ads and the assiduous advance work of his staff, which blanketed targeted voters with mailings and leaflets. Clinton's television advertisements gave the phone number of his Manchester, New Hampshire, headquarters so people could call for a copy of his economic plan. Some 1,300 phone calls were received during the first two days the commercial aired. The issue of electability also worked in Clinton's favor.[13] Organized labor, which was more aligned with Harkin's message, held off making an endorsement out of concern that Harkin could not win the White House.[14] While the Democratic contenders increased their criticism of Clinton's record and proposals, no negative television advertisements were run as of early February.[15] But just before the election, the sparring had increased and the advertisements were becoming more pointed.

Clinton took advantage of his connections to Arkansas money. Early on, the campaign had raised $200,000, and employees of Worthen National Bank of Arkansas were among the most frequent contributors. As will be seen, this bank established various credit lines for the Clinton campaign. In addition, people such as Warren A. Stephens, president and chief executive officer of Stephens, Inc., which has vast holdings in natural gas, finance, and real estate, helped raise more than $100,000 for the campaign. The Stephens family had previously been supportive of the Republican Party and started supporting Clinton when one of his Republican gubernatorial challengers expressed criticism of the family's influence.[16] Obviously, his incumbency as governor helped Clinton raise money. A number of Arkansas contributors commented that they gave to the presidential campaign because they wanted to appear supportive of the person who controlled the state's lucrative bond market, pension fund, and other regulated businesses.[17] Contributors from Arkansas, with a population of only 2.3 million, accounted for $2.5 million by the time of the nomination.[18]

Clinton returned to the heart of Republican fund-raising territory in California in mid-January and raised $40,000 to $50,000 at a standing-room-only luncheon in Santa Ana. Organizers estimate that at least one-fourth of the 100 people in attendance were Republicans.[19] Clinton raised $1,607,000 in January, $650,000 of which would qualify for federal matching funds.[20]

As well as courting the independent and Republican vote, Clinton was active in the South, shoring up support from the Democratic establishment and reaching out to blacks and more liberal elements of the party. The other candidates had not campaigned in the South and so by early 1992, Clinton had out-hustled his competitors. Clinton also campaigned actively in Texas. An aide to Kerrey said, "Clinton has spent so much time in Texas, it's like he's running for Governor of the state."[21]

The front-runner mantle caused Clinton's personal life and policy proposals to be scrutinized extensively. Ironically, the issue of electability, which first propelled Clinton's campaign, began to undermine his popularity after issues of infidelity and charges of his avoiding the draft received much publicity.[22] Allegations of extramarital affairs surrounded Clinton from the beginning but peaked in early 1992.

The accusations of Gennifer Flowers hounded Clinton in late January. The matter escalated when Flowers played a tape of a telephone conversation between her and Clinton in which Clinton stated that New York Governor Mario Cuomo behaved like a "mafioso." Clinton apologized to Cuomo, but Cuomo reacted by suggesting the comment was a racial slur.[23]

Polls at the end of January showed that most New Hampshire voters cared little about the extramarital affair accusations. But the issue was on the minds of even his staunchest supporters. The issue surfaced again when Flowers made allegations of an affair that she claimed had ended in 1989. Clinton appeared on the CBS television show "60 Minutes" with his wife, Hillary, to refute the charges. Airing just after the Super Bowl, the show potentially reached 24 million households, an audience no other politician except the president could attract. Clinton hoped to end the questions surrounding his personal life by dealing directly with them.[24] Next, Clinton turned his focus on the president and the State of the Union address.[25]

Despite this negative publicity, many political leaders continued to support Clinton. Extensive committees of supporters were established in Texas, Mississippi, and Louisiana. George Stephanopoulos, deputy campaign manager, said, "The fact is, at the height of the scandal, Clinton raised almost half a million dollars in three days and received public endorsements from a host of public officials, while the polls either held steady or rose in New Hampshire."[26]

While Clinton's popularity in some polls did not seem to suffer, other polls indicated that 26 percent of those surveyed would not vote for someone who had had an affair, and 40 percent viewed adultery as something that should be considered in evaluating a candidate's character. A number of Democratic leaders felt that Clinton had been "mortally wounded" as a general election candidate and called on other party leaders to enter the race.[27] Representative Richard Gephardt came close to deciding to enter the contest.

In early February, another controversial issue hit the campaign when Clinton's draft status during the Vietnam years was called into question. Clinton claimed no wrongdoing and countered that he had no influence to pull strings. But five days before the New Hampshire primary, a letter was leaked that Clinton had written in 1969 to the army officer overseeing the ROTC program at the University of Arkansas. The letter indicated that Clinton misled army officials about his plans. This revelation caused further concern about his character and his electability.[28]

Clinton campaigned vigorously in the week before the New Hampshire primary. He purchased a half-hour television slot to field questions from callers. Paul Tsongas, who had moved ahead of Clinton in the polls, scheduled only a few public appearances in the days before the election and even turned down an offer for a live interview on the most-watched news program in the state.[29] Clinton's extensive campaigning enabled him to make up the support he had lost over the alleged affairs and draft-avoidance issues. Clinton placed second in New Hampshire with 25 percent of the vote, nine points behind Tsongas, who lived in nearby Massachusetts and was better known. Clinton was pleased that he significantly outpaced Kerrey and Harkin, who received 11 percent and 10 percent of the vote, respectively. Clinton felt confident that eventually he could beat Tsongas, who was thought to have only regional appeal.[30]

Clinton's finances were so low at this point that some staff members paid bills on their own credit cards. Earlier, Clinton had established a $3.5 million line of credit with the Worthen National Bank of Arkansas, which some claim rescued the campaign after the New Hampshire primary.[31] The loan, with interest, was repaid with matching funds that were claimed to have been wired directly to the bank by the Treasury Department, according to one report.[32]

Despite his funding problems, Clinton led his rivals in fund raising, collecting $2.3 million in February, almost twice as much as Tsongas.

President Bush, however, raised $3.9 million in that month. Nonetheless, Clinton qualified for $1.1 million in matching funds to Bush's $672,000 and Tsongas's $370,000.[33] By maintaining his fund-raising advantage over Tsongas, Clinton was in a better position to contest the early March primaries.

The next campaign stop was Georgia, and Clinton needed to win to show his strength in the South and to demonstrate that the past accusations had not tarnished his popular support. None of the other Democratic contenders were broadly organized in Georgia, and only Kerrey had attracted any visible support.[34] Clinton wanted to shift the public debate from questions of his character to the differences between himself and the other candidates. To distinguish himself on the issues, Clinton began to focus his advertising on the weaknesses of the other candidates and their positions, while stressing his own message. This prompted Tsongas to accuse Clinton of "negative campaigning."

By early March, the contest had become a two-way race between Clinton and Tsongas, with Clinton clearly in the lead. With the field narrowed, Clinton resorted to a campaign theme that differentiated himself from Tsongas and his economic policies.

Clinton and Tsongas entered the March series of southern and midwestern primaries with about the same amount of debt and available cash. According to FEC reports filed on March 20, 1992, Clinton ended February with $102,068 in cash and $711,406 in debts. Clinton, however, was able to borrow large amounts of money from his Worthen Bank line of credit, using future matching funds as collateral. Tsongas had already borrowed against his future matching funds. Clinton took out $1.4 million in loans in the month of March to outspend Tsongas in the primaries. Clinton used the loans in addition to $900,000 in private donations and another $650,000 in federal matching funds received since March 1 to campaign and advertise heavily in the South and Midwest.[35]

Controversy continued to follow the Clinton campaign. At the end of February, Clinton unknowingly made a comment into an open microphone about the Reverend Jesse Jackson's supposed back-stabbing tendencies. In early March, questions arose about the Clintons' involvement in a real estate deal with a former Clinton assistant and a failed Arkansas savings and loan.

Clinton and Tsongas took their now unfriendly battle to the airwaves of Florida. Clinton spent about $500,000 on television commercials, while Tsongas spent roughly $300,000. These expenditures were not excessive by presidential campaign standards for a state with six major media markets. The other Democratic candidates could not afford to sponsor TV advertising.[36] Clinton won in Florida with 51 percent of the vote.

After a string of impressive victories in the Super Tuesday primaries, and with Kerrey and Harkin out of the race, Clinton sought support and financial contributions from organized labor. Labor had rallied behind Harkin before his withdrawal. Tsongas was not embraced by labor unions and Jerry Brown was not considered a serious contender. Some unions decided not to endorse anyone, but Clinton gained the most support, adding to the perception that he had the nomination secured. This made it even more difficult for Tsongas to raise funds.

Tsongas, for the first time, spent more than Clinton on television advertising in Michigan. Clinton's fund raisers, Rahm Emanuel and Amy Zisook, were trying to raise $500,000 to fund the campaign's efforts in Michigan and Illinois. Almost $8 million had been raised in less than six months. Emanuel summed up the fund-raising effort: "In December, 27 events raised $2.4 million; in January, 27 events raised $1.6 million; in February, 11 events, $2.3 million."[37] As of April, Clinton was raising twice as much money as Tsongas. Clinton was an aggressive fund raiser, attending five events in one night in Chicago, for example.

Tsongas suspended his campaign in mid-March after the Michigan and Illinois primaries, citing his inability to raise sufficient funds. At this point, Clinton had raised twice as much as Tsongas. With Tsongas out of the race, Clinton became the clear choice to win the nomination and subsequently was able to raise the funds to retire most of his debt. Clinton came under attack in late March for golfing at an exclusive Arkansas country club that has no nonwhite members. He also was confronted with allegations of steering a lucrative state bond issue to a wealthy backer, who was later indicted for selling cocaine. He admitted to experimenting with marijuana in the 1960s, raising questions about how straightforward his previous responses to this question were.

Brown spent more than Clinton on television advertising in Connecticut, and Clinton lost to Brown in the primary on March 24. This surprising loss spurred Clinton to focus on Brown rather than running against Bush. Brown also won the Vermont caucuses, but Clinton did not campaign actively there.

Clinton and Brown waged a heavy advertising campaign against each other in New York. Clinton was concerned about the race but ended up winning the primary. Brown placed third, behind Tsongas, who had dropped out of the race. The Clinton campaign spent almost $1 million on the New York primary. By mid-April, Clinton had raised $11 million and qualified for $4 million in federal matching funds.

By the end of April, the Clinton campaign took a new direction and began looking to the general election. Brown was being dismissed as a contender for the nomination. Clinton picked up a number of labor endorsements. He also reduced his campaign appearances, in part to devote more time to fund-raising efforts.[38]

In early May, Clinton had to suspend temporarily the paychecks of twenty staff members in Washington, DC. The shortfall was made up but the pay cut hurt morale at the office.[39] Clinton's debt soared to almost $4 million, with $1.2 million of debt accumulating in May alone. The cash balance in May was $161,853. Clinton spent almost $1 million in California for the June 2 primary. In both April and May, Clinton raised nearly $2.3 million.[40] By the end of May, Clinton had reached almost $20 million in total contributions, $5 million less than the amount Dukakis had raised by the end of May 1988.

Then Ross Perot's candidacy made it harder for Clinton to raise money. In June, Clinton was running in third place in the polls behind Perot and Bush, which also hurt his fund-raising appeal. The recession and the lack of any hotly contested primaries in the late spring were factors cited to explain the slower fund-raising pace. In June, his cash on hand was only $258,000, less than a quarter of what Dukakis had at that time.[41] But Clinton's debt was reduced in June and practically wiped out by the time of the convention.

Talk shows and "infomercials" played a large role in the contest, with all three candidates—Bush, Clinton, and Perot—appearing on the major networks and Cable News Network (CNN).[42] The Clinton campaign arranged for the DNC to pay $373,000 for a one-half-hour question-and-answer "national town meeting" on NBC-TV. Clinton used the format to reintroduce himself to the people and to articulate his views. Perot's independent candidacy had been getting significant publicity and this show helped Clinton recapture the media's attention. Taking to the airwaves "is the best way to engage real issues and let voters speak their minds," said George Stephanopolous, who was now serving as Clinton's communication director.[43] Clinton said, "What we're finding is, the more I can directly communicate with the people, the better I do."[44] His mail tripled after several national television appearances and his own talk show.

The RNC filed a complaint with the FEC, alleging that it was improper for the DNC to pay for Clinton's television program because it was used to solicit primary election campaign funds by displaying an 800 fund-raising telephone number. The FEC stated in a 1984 advisory opinion that political parties are allowed to spend general election funds before the end of the official primary season if the money is used for "influencing the outcome of the general election."[45] The Clinton campaign acknowledged that it made a technical error and returned contributions made in response to the program's toll-free number.[46]

Creative Fund Raising

Unlike most other candidates, Clinton actively sought funds from the gay community. This constituency, having been ignored by most candidates in the past, proved very valuable in fund raising. Gay voters are important due to their visibility in states such as New York, Illinois, and California, which had a large number of convention delegates and thus were crucial to the Clinton strategy.[47]

Clinton held a fund raiser in Los Angeles in early May, with more than 600 leaders of the gay and lesbian community, raising close to $100,000. This fund raiser was the largest one ever held by gays for a presidential candidate. It was also unique in that it was open and covered by the media, making Clinton vulnerable to voters offended by the gay rights agenda. Clinton promised to establish a "Manhattan Project" in search of a cure for AIDS and, by executive order, to make it possible for homosexuals to serve in the military. "I have a vision," Clinton declared, "and you are part of it."[48]

The Human Rights Campaign Fund, with a membership of 38,000, is a bipartisan gay and lesbian organization headquartered in Washington, DC. The mission of the fund is to support candidates who are for gay rights. The fund is one of the fastest growing PACs in the nation, giving $528,000 to candidates for the Senate and House in the 1989–90 election cycle and $712,684 in the 1991–92 election cycle. In this cycle, the fund ranked forty-second among all PACs measured by direct contributions to candidates. In addition, there was the Gay and Lesbian Victory Fund, which supports gay and lesbian candidates. This fund spent $331,163 during the first season in which it was active, but contributed only $1,283 to federal candidates.

Because gays have not previously been very active as a group in national politics, other than in issues of special concern to them, coordinated campaign contributions from this group on a large scale is very new. The gay community had been previously upset with candidates of both parties, such as in 1988, when Dukakis got only one-half the gay vote, perhaps over his unwillingness to favor adoption of children by gay couples. Clinton clearly was successful in obtaining gay support. David Mixner, one of Clinton's more successful fund raisers, stated that gays contributed more than $3.5 million to the Clinton campaigns—pre- and post-nomination. Mixner collected contribution check records to back up his claim. In addition to his historic fund-raising success with gays, Clinton attracted 72 percent of their votes.[49]

Another of Clinton's more creative fund-raising ventures was the effort by Bob Raymar, a New Jersey lawyer, who raised at least $1.6 million through the Yale Law School Graduate Committee, a group of Clinton supporters and fellow law school alumni of the Clintons. Nearly one-half of this amount came from graduates of Clinton's class, 1972 and 1973.[50]

Douglas Eakeley, a Yale roommate of Clinton's, raised $100,000 in New Jersey by using only the Rhodes scholar and Yale Law School directories as his guides.[51]

Overview

Clinton used the end of the primary season to organize for the general election, especially in key states such as California and Ohio. As Clinton locked up the nomination, his fund-raising staff merged with the DNC's organization. Clinton's treasurer, Robert A. Farmer, concentrated on raising big-dollar "soft" contributions for the party, as he had for Dukakis in 1988. In all, Clinton had raised $25.1 million from individuals, and received $12.5 million in federal matching funds, more than any other candidate. The campaign reported 169,230 contributors who qualified for matching funds, with an average contribution of $75.

Independent expenditures in favor of Clinton's campaign before the nominating convention totaled $32,234. Opponents of Clinton's nomination spent $45,603 in independent expenditures. More significantly, communication costs of nearly $646,500 were spent on behalf of Clinton, mainly by labor unions.[52] (See Table 8.9).

Tsongas

Paul Tsongas became the first Democrat to enter the race when he announced his campaign on April 30, 1991. On May 3, 1991, just five days after announcing his campaign, Tsongas had raised $350,000 and had fourteen paid staff members.[53] Yet two months into his campaign, Tsongas had raised only a little money; as of June 30, 1991, Tsongas had a campaign fund of only about $500,000. In comparison, by the summer of 1987, Michael Dukakis, another Greek-American Democrat from Massachusetts, had raised $4.6 million. Whereas Tsongas was invisible in the South at the end of summer in 1991, Dukakis had opened an office in Atlanta and established at least some presence there.[54]

Tsongas had previously served two terms in the House and one term as a senator from Massachusetts. He left the Senate in 1984 due to cancer of the lymphatic system, which had gone into remission. He had been out of the public eye since 1985.[55] Upon declaring his candidacy for the presidency,

Tsongas described himself as pro-business and liberal on social issues. He emphasized the need to redirect the thinking of the Democratic Party and the nation regarding economic policy. In particular, he advocated proposals to restore the country's manufacturing base and supported such measures as cuts in the capital gains tax and increased gasoline taxes. He summarized his economic plan in a lengthy campaign manifesto entitled "A Call to Economic Arms," which he distributed widely to voters in New Hampshire. The plan criticized many traditional Democratic economic policies and made Tsongas unpopular with the party establishment.

Although he had accepted PAC contributions in his congressional and senatorial campaigns, Tsongas took a strong stand against the influence of PAC money on the political process. His chief fund raiser said that this decision could cost the campaign $500,000, although none of this money would qualify for federal matching funds.[56] On June 15, before an Americans for Democratic Action audience, Tsongas said that PAC money had become a destructive "stench." Evidently no one told his longtime fund raiser, Nick Rizzo, who had already raised $70,000 from PACs. Rizzo commented to a reporter, "I don't get it. He never had a problem with it before."[57] The PAC money was returned to the donors.

Through September 1991, Tsongas had raised $800,000, compared with the $8.1 million Dukakis had collected by September 1987. Tsongas relied heavily on the Greek-American network that Dukakis built in 1988, but Tsongas said the Greek community was "traumatized" by Dukakis' defeat and "for every dollar that Michael got, I get 10 cents."[58] Tsongas, whose total net worth was estimated at between $1.2 million and $1.4 million, sold $45,000 worth of stock and loaned the money to the campaign.[59]

But Tsongas was competitive with other Democratic contenders early in the race: Harkin had raised $712,857, and none of the other declared candidates had raised more than $500,000 by the end of September.[60] A good portion of Tsongas's campaign budget during this early period was spent on travel. He visited thirty states in the first nine months of the campaign.[61] By the end of 1991, he had increased his staff to forty-two full-time paid campaign workers and begun to focus on New Hampshire, Maryland, Florida, Washington, and other states holding early primaries or caucuses.[62]

Tsongas's position quickly changed when Clinton and Kerrey entered the race in October. By the end of 1991, Clinton had raised $3.3 million to Tsongas's $1.3 million.[63] Tsongas was declared eligible for federal matching funds on November 20, 1991. He was the second candidate to become eligible, behind Lenora B. Fulani of the New Alliance Party.[64] Despite this early start, Tsongas qualified for only $556,444 in matching funds as of February 1, 1992, far behind Clinton, Harkin, Kerrey, and even Fulani.[65]

Tsongas's fund raising was slow in part because he had been out of office for seven years and had low name recognition outside of New England. His fund raising was conducted mainly through events, direct mail, and one-on-one phone calls by the candidate.[66] The fund-raising events, however, were relatively inexpensive, with the expensive ones running from $250 to $500 a ticket. There were numerous low-ticket events in the $10 and $25 range. He had a fund raiser on Wall Street, which demonstrated that his economic theme had some appeal there.[67]

The Tsongas campaign used direct mail successfully. Goldman Associates, a Boston-based firm, ran the operation. It began with an 8,000-person house list, which was pared to 6,000, then grew to 27,000 by the end of the campaign. The response rate was 7 percent. Three repeat mailings to this base were sent in 1991. Prospect mailings were highly targeted. In May 1991, the first letter went out to 10,000 Greek-Americans who had given to Dukakis's 1988 campaign. The response rate was 5.5 percent with an average contribution of $49.59, which was considered a notable return. The second nationwide mailing went to 44,000 former Peace Corps volunteers, highlighting Tsongas's participation in the Corps in early 1960s, and yielded a 2.5 percent response with an average contribution of $44.77. These two letters and a general prospecting piece were worked into a mail rotation. Tsongas swapped his lists for other Massachusetts donor lists and picked up 77,000 more names. Just as the campaign was terminated, the most ambitious mailing project to date was being prepared: a 150,000-person nationwide appeal. A total of $10,000 had been spent on the list and $20,000 in printing costs.[68]

Although Tsongas was running first in the polls for the New Hampshire primary, many commentators felt he was dull and unelectable. He was compared with Dukakis, who lost overwhelmingly to Bush in 1988. Tsongas believed he was the best candidate but also felt it was important that his message be spread. He felt that the electorate was tired of slick, professional candidates who spoke in sound bites. He sought to rely on people to make an informed, well-thought-out decision.

To save money, Tsongas had only one office in Manchester, New Hampshire, and staff assistants operated from the homes of campaign supporters around the state.[69] Tsongas wanted to save his money for TV ads so he could compete with the better-financed candidates. Nearly $100,000 was spent on television spots in New Hampshire, which ran for two weeks. One thirty-second television advertisement showed Tsongas swimming the butterfly stroke the length of a pool while the commentators discussed Tsongas's beating the odds in other political campaigns and in his bout with cancer.[70] He was the first candidate to air commercials and spent the most time in the state, approximately forty-three days as of January 10. This enabled him to build a good grass-roots organization.

Tsongas won the New Hampshire primary with 33 percent of the vote. This upset over Clinton, who received 25 percent, resulted in part over questions of Clinton's personal life and allegations of extramarital affairs. The victory significantly boosted his fund-raising effort and gave credibility to his candidacy. On the Friday following Tsongas's victory in New Hampshire, a full back-page ad ran in the *Boston Globe* with a cut-out response card asking for contributions. The advertisement cost $18,000 and raised $108,000.[71]

Tsongas, however, quickly ran into problems that undermined his efforts to capitalize on his victory. Because he had focused most of his campaign's limited financial resources on New Hampshire, he did not develop extensive organizations in other states or begin early television advertising as he had in New Hampshire. As a result, his campaign was not well positioned for the quick succession of primary contests that took place at the beginning of March. Only a week after New Hampshire, he finished a distant fourth in the South Dakota primary, well behind Kerrey, Harkin, and Clinton. On March 3, he focused on Maryland, where he campaigned actively, especially in the white-collar suburbs around Washington, and won with 40 percent of the vote. But on the same day, he lost badly to Clinton in Georgia and finished third in Colorado behind Clinton and Brown. Tsongas next focused on Florida, hoping to show that he could defeat Clinton in an important southern state on Super Tuesday.

Tsongas asked Democratic chairman Ronald Brown to offer a "nonaggression pact" for all the Democratic candidates that would put a moratorium on negative campaigning. He "very reluctantly" authorized his staff to put out "counter-punch" commercials refuting claims made by other candidates, especially Clinton.[72] Tsongas and Clinton competed heavily in Florida's television market. In response to Clinton's attack on Tsongas, Tsongas reluctantly agreed to issue negative ads.

Tsongas conserved his funds and effectively conceded many of the southern states to favorite son Clinton. He competed in Florida, which has many northern transplants, but placed a distant second with 35 percent of the vote to Clinton, who received 51 percent.[73] Tsongas spent $1 million on advertising in Michigan and Illinois.[74] Tsongas hoped that his economic message would be well-received in Michigan with its manufacturing-based economy, but Jerry Brown scored more points with the voters, and Tsongas finished third with only 17 percent of the vote.

Tsongas suspended his campaign on March 19, citing a lack of financial support. Without adequate money to win, Tsongas felt the alternative was to play the spoiler, and that he would not do. Tsongas did not have the funds to fight the media war in New York. Without the ability to campaign aggressively, he was worried his message would be damaged. Tsongas said that money was presently coming in, but there were no reserves to respond to Clinton and Brown attacks. Tsongas felt his message of "economic growth with our traditional social compassion" was catching on.[75] By suspending the campaign, Tsongas kept his delegates and they were able to go to the convention and articulate his message.

The Tsongas campaign was nearly $500,000 in debt when it was suspended.[76] Tsongas was raising $93,000 a day just before suspending the campaign.[77] He stayed on the ballot across the country. Even though he was not actively campaigning, he did well in New York. Tsongas considered reentering the race but finally declined.[78] He thought his campaign was successful in that it moved the Democratic Party closer to the economic center, where he thought it belonged. Tsongas had won five primaries (New Hampshire, Maryland, Utah, Massachusetts, and Rhode Island) and three caucuses (Maine, Arizona, and Delaware). The termination of his campaign in effect yielded the nomination to Clinton.

Direct mail continued to be used to retire the $500,000 campaign debt. The first house appeal to 20,000 donors raised $62,000 and it was expected to raise a total of $100,000. The committee held on to the list for the future.[79] The campaign provided source data as follows:

Tsongas Campaign Receipts

Mail/direct mail	$1,867,835
Telemarketing	106,739
Newspaper advertising	138,541
Fund raising (direct solicitation)	2,834,569
Matching funds	2,922,814

The *Wall Street Journal* stated in an editorial that the public financing laws made it difficult for Tsongas to raise the money necessary to mount a national presidential campaign. Because he challenged the party's traditional wisdom, he was not well-liked by the Democratic leadership across the country. If Tsongas could have accepted larger donations from individuals, rather than the $1,000 personal limit, he might have found a few supporters to keep the campaign going. Former Senator Eugene McCarthy, who waged his own campaign for the presidency in 1968, said an insurgent such as Tsongas "can't fairly compete" under a $1,000 contribution limit, especially when that limit has not been indexed for inflation, and was worth approximately $350 in 1992.[80]

In a serious reversal after the campaign, Tsongas's fund-raising chairman was indicted for embezzlement, bank fraud, mail fraud, and soliciting more than $1 million worth of illegal campaign contributions while serving the campaign.[81] Allegedly, Rizzo fraudulently obtained loans from Tsongas supporters and submitted false bills and expenses for reimbursement and diverted funds from the campaign into a secret personal bank account. The money was allegedly used to pay Rizzo's gambling debts and to repay personal loans.[82] Prosecutors called the case the largest campaign fraud case in U.S. history.[83] Rizzo pleaded guilty in September 1993 to a twenty-five count indictment charging him with defrauding Tsongas's campaign in excess of $1 million. He was sentenced to fifty-two months in prison, ordered to pay $899,000 in restitution to the campaign, and was required to forfeit $600,000 to the federal government. The embezzlement may have denied Tsongas access to badly needed federal matching funds.[84]

Also after the campaign, the U.S. Justice Department filed criminal charges against a businessman contributor, James T. Lichoulas Jr., for allegedly providing the Tsongas campaign with thirty-eight blank money orders, each for $250 and totaling $9,500. Tsongas aides filled out the checks with the names of other people, illegally making matchable contributions and filing false campaign reports.[85]

Tsongas raised a bit more than $5 million. He received in excess of $3 million in federal matching funds, and had 38,710 qualifying contributions with an average contribution of $80. The campaign had $754,000 in fund-raising exemptions and $179,000 in legal and accounting costs. Independent expenditures on his behalf totaled $23,000, and $4,250 in independent expenditures was spent against his campaign.

Kerrey

On September 30, 1991, Senator Robert Kerrey announced his decision to run for the Democratic presidential nomination against the backdrop of the Nebraska state capitol, which he portrayed as "a monument to prairie optimism in the depths of the Depression."[86] His speech sought to echo John F. Kennedy's 1960 appeal to "get the country moving again." Like Kennedy, Kerrey hoped to run for the presidency as a self-proclaimed generational candidate.[87] "I want to lead America's fearless, restless voyage of generational progress," said the senator. "We have been led off course by a federal government whose engine has become inertia, whose direction is drift, and whose compass is cynicism."[88]

Kerrey's decision represented another unexpected choice in his unconventional political career. After successfully building a chain of restaurants and health fitness centers that made him a millionaire, Kerrey made his first bid for public office in 1982, when he challenged a Republican incumbent, Charles Thone, for the office of governor. Kerrey won, even though a majority of the voters in the state are Republican, and went on to a successful term in office. Though he was a well-respected governor who drew attention for his management of state government, as well as his relationship with actress Debra Winger, he decided not to run again after one four-year term, despite a record 74 percent public approval rating in statewide polls.[89] Then, in 1988, he entered the race for the U.S. Senate, defeating Republican David Karnes, who had been appointed to fill the vacancy created by the death of Senator Edward Zorinsky. Less than halfway through his first term in the Senate, he decided to launch a bid for the Oval Office.

Kerrey was the fourth major candidate to enter the Democratic race. But unlike Tsongas, Harkin, and Wilder, he began his quest amid high expectations. Kerrey had a number of potential strengths that attracted the interest of many party activists and political professionals: he had a compelling personal background, varied experience in business and government, and a distinctly nonideological approach to politics. A former member of the Navy's elite Sea/Air/Land (SEAL) special operations unit, Kerrey served in Vietnam and earned the Congressional Medal of Honor for his valor. He was, therefore, immediately cast as the type of Democrat who could compete with Bush's record of military service and might help his party overcome its "weak-on-defense" image.[90] Kerrey also was viewed as an atypical politician, running at a time when most of the electorate was tired of "politics as usual." He sought to appeal to a wide range of voters, given that he was a Democrat with a business background who had a liberal record on social issues and advocated universal federal health care programs, but also had a reputation as a fiscal conservative who was tough-minded on trade issues.

Kerrey's campaign had a seasoned look. A number of campaign veterans joined his staff, including some of the top strategists from former candidate Gary Hart's 1984 and 1988 presidential campaigns. The campaign got off to a quick start, raising $200,000 in Lincoln, Nebraska, on the day of his announcement—a feat never before accomplished in a Democratic prenomination contest.[91] Two days later, Kerrey embarked on an eight-day campaign swing through New Hampshire.[92] Soon thereafter, an early October poll showed him to be the front-runner in the race, with 21 percent support nationwide.[93]

Kerrey continued to ride his fast start and positive press coverage through November, and enjoyed substantial success in raising money. Although he lacked Clinton's contacts and Harkin's direct mail base, his campaign raised about $1.6 million by the first week of December. According to campaign records, most of this amount, about $1.3 million, was raised through individual contributions and fund-raising events. The campaign also raised $58,350 from PACs, $66,644 through direct mail, and $179,100 through a telemarketing program that began in the first week of November. In addition, these donations generated more than $500,000 in matching funds that the campaign was due to receive on January 1, 1992, for a total yield of about $2 million.

Almost one-half of the money raised during the first two months of the campaign came from supporters in Nebraska, which was the focal point of the campaign's early fund-raising efforts. Upon entering the race, Kerrey set a goal of raising between $750,000 and $1 million in Nebraska by January 1. This goal was met by late December. Kerrey's Nebraska finance chair, Denny Jorgensen, reported that the campaign had received $630,000 and had outstanding pledges for another $155,000 as of December 26. About 60 percent of these donations, or approximately $385,000, was received in individual contributions of $250 or less and thus was eligible for matching funds.[94] Kerrey also aggressively sought financial support from California, where he relied on the contacts he had made in Hollywood through his friendship with Winger and the efforts of one of his chief fund raisers, Robert Burkett, a well-known California Democratic money man.[95] On November 12, the campaign raised $200,000 at a Los Angeles fund raiser hosted by Fox Broadcasting Company chairman Barry Diller.[96] Florida was another important source of early money, due to the efforts of Kerrey's campaign treasurer, Hugh Westbrook, who headed a successful Miami-based health care hospice organization.

By late November, however, the initial enthusiasm for Kerrey's candidacy began to wane. Many observers noted that the senator lacked a focused message beyond his personal story and was vague with respect to the policy initiatives he would pursue as president.[97] "In the early period, 1991," one campaign official observed in retrospect, "Senator Kerrey hadn't developed the comprehensive yet concise answers on a broad range of issues that you must have in presidential politics if you're going to be accepted as credible by the press and political community."[98] As a result, Kerrey failed to define his candidacy clearly, which left many Democratic activists wondering what he stood for and how he differed from his opponents.

More important, the campaign entered a period of major missteps and negative press coverage. This began in late November at a New Hampshire political event, when Kerrey, unaware of an open microphone being used by C-SPAN to broadcast the event, told Clinton a joke involving lesbians. The comment provoked strong criticism from gay, lesbian, and women's groups, and the campaign was forced to apologize.[99] Then, on December

17, the Labor Department reported that the restaurant chain partly owned by Kerrey had been assessed a $64,650 fine for 116 violations of child labor laws, most of which involved teenagers working late-night shifts or longer hours than allowed by law.[100] The fine undermined one of Kerrey's potential strengths vis-à-vis his opponents—that he was the only candidate with hands-on business experience.[101] Finally, in late December, a news report revealed that Kerrey's businesses failed to provide health insurance to most of their employees. Although the business offered health insurance to full-time employees, part-time workers were not covered. As a result, only about seventy-five to 100 of the 700 to 800 restaurant employees and twenty-five to thirty of the 300 health club employees received health insurance.[102] This report generated extensive press coverage because Kerrey had introduced a bill in the Senate calling for comprehensive federal health insurance and was attempting to make national health insurance a cornerstone of his campaign. Kerrey explained that the situation his businesses faced demonstrated the need for national legislation, since under the current system small businesses like his would go bankrupt if they tried to provide coverage to all workers.[103] Whatever the reality, the press accounts generated a perception that led some voters to question whether Kerrey could be trusted to create a national health insurance program.

The one bright spot during this period was the nationally televised Democratic candidate forum on December 15, moderated by Tom Brokaw of NBC News. Most observers judged Kerrey as having performed well in this "debate," noting in particular his stern retort to Jerry Brown, when he disagreed with Brown's implied charge that he was "bought and paid for" as a result of his campaign fund raising.[104] Otherwise, the Kerrey campaign was stalled. Kerrey's state coordinator in Florida advised him not to make any effort in a mid-December Democratic state convention straw poll to avoid the embarrassment of a defeat.[105] His fund raisers were increasingly frustrated with the campaign's lack of progress, and the campaign lacked an organization outside the state campaigns in New Hampshire, South Dakota, and Nebraska.[106] As a result, fund raising suffered. From mid-December to mid-January, the campaign raised less than $350,000, or less than one-half the average amount raised in each of the first two months of the campaign. By the end of December, the campaign was beginning to struggle with its cash flow. Although the FEC report filed by the campaign at the end of the year showed about $589,000 cash on hand, an internal campaign analysis revealed that when outstanding payables were taken into account, the campaign would have a balance of only about $252,000.[107]

Thus, at a time when Clinton was beginning to emerge as the clear Democratic front-runner and enjoying noteworthy fund-raising success,

Kerrey faced a growing perception among political insiders that his campaign was in disarray. Instead of being regarded as the man to beat, many observers began to cast the Nebraskan as "the underachiever in the field."[108] In an effort to revive the campaign, a decision was made to change management, and on December 23, campaign manager Susan Casey, a well-known Democratic Party operative and a veteran of Hart's 1988 campaign, resigned. She was soon replaced with Tad Devine, the manager of Lloyd Bentsen's 1988 vice presidential campaign and one of the Democratic Party's leading experts on the presidential selection process.

Devine acted quickly to strengthen the campaign organization and shore up the fund-raising effort. He then turned his attention to the media campaign. Kerrey had originally hired Rothstein and Company, a Washington-based firm that had handled advertising for his successful 1988 Senate race, to develop the advertising for his presidential campaign. The firm was authorized to spend $225,000 on advertising production in 1991, and spent about $200,000 producing a number of television spots in a cinema verité style for use in the early stages of the selection process. None of these ads were used, however, since Devine decided on a different direction and hired Doak and Shrum, the high-profile Washington media firm that had worked with presidential candidate Gephardt in 1988.

The new campaign team decided on a strategy that would concentrate on the issues of health care and trade, as well as Kerrey's biography.[109] Initially, they considered contesting the Iowa caucuses through a relatively low-key effort conducted primarily from Nebraska. They felt that Kerrey might be able to build some momentum by finishing a surprising second to Harkin. But the campaign lacked the resources to campaign on a number of fronts, so the decision was made to focus on New Hampshire.

New Hampshire Primary

On January 10, the Kerrey campaign began its television advertising in New Hampshire, purchasing $84,000 worth of time to air a spot on trade issues. The ad, which began airing soon after Bush's ill-fated trip to Japan, showed Kerrey in an empty hockey rink talking about the need to take a tougher stance on trade with the Japanese. In the spot, Kerrey vowed, "If I'm president, the time for begging is through. I'll tell the Japanese if we can't sell in their markets, they can't sell in ours." The ad had its intended effect; it highlighted the trade issue and increased Kerrey's profile in the race, forcing Clinton and Tsongas to respond to this message. But it also generated a substantial amount of criticism for its protectionist overtones from journalists, other Democratic challengers, and ultimately from within the campaign itself.[110] While some of Kerrey's supporters claimed a "fantastic reaction" to the ad, Kerrey's New Hampshire coordinator, Paul Johnson, argued that it failed to help the candidate and may have turned off voters, a view that Kerrey later expressed, noting that the ad was a mistake.[111] After the campaign, Devine argued the contrary: "I have to disagree with that assessment. I believe that the hockey ad brought us back from the dead. We were really on the verge of collapse. When the ad came out, for the first time in the campaign our opponents began to respond to us."[112]

Devine's view seemed to be supported by Kerrey's standing in New Hampshire public opinion polls. At the end of December, Kerrey stood at 6 or 7 percent in most statewide polls, but by mid-January, after the hockey ad had been broadcast, his support rose to 16 to 18 percent.[113] With this rise in support came a surge in fund raising. According to campaign records, from mid-January through the first week of February, Kerrey received about $618,000 in individual and PAC contributions, and slightly more than $97,000 in direct mail and telemarketing receipts. In addition, the campaign took out a $225,000 loan in the third week of January against a portion of the anticipated February 1 matching fund payment.

Armed with this war chest, Kerrey launched an aggressive media campaign in New Hampshire. After the hockey ad, the campaign aired a thirty-second spot about the senator's health care plan and a sixty-second biographical ad. After Clinton and Tsongas had responded with health care ads, Kerrey aired a number of other health-related spots in an effort to define his position on this issue. In addition, on February 10, a full week before any other candidate, Kerrey purchased media time in South Dakota and began airing a health care ad and a biographical ad. These were followed the next week by a thirty-second spot directed toward family farmers.

Overall, the campaign spent almost $1.2 million on New Hampshire media, including the costs of cable and radio advertisements and ad production costs.[114] About $700,000 of this amount represented the actual sum spent to purchase time to air twelve separate ads.[115] The rest represented Kerrey's production costs, which were extremely high because he changed media consultants and some ads were never used. This effort was partially financed by an additional $950,000 in loans taken against a portion of the anticipated March 1 matching fund payment and projected telemarketing receipts.

Despite this extensive media campaign, Kerrey's support in New Hampshire began to decline. Analysts offered a number of explanations. First, although Kerrey had improved his message by early February, wrapping it in a call for "fundamental change," on the stump he often veered from his standard themes, leaving his audience unclear as to his core message. While he had made a strong case on trade, he did not develop this argument and link it to jobs and economic recovery, which were crucial concerns of the New Hampshire electorate, given the state's depressed economy. Nor did he respond effectively to the counterattacks of his opponents, especially Tsongas, who claimed that protectionist approaches would not solve the nation's economic woes.[116] More important, after his initial success in making health care a cornerstone issue, the other candidates began touting their own health care proposals, which undermined Kerrey's effort to distinguish himself on this issue. Polls showed that the public was most concerned with costs, not coverage, and Kerrey never convinced voters that his program was a better alternative for controlling costs than the market-based plans of his opponents.[117] Furthermore, focus groups conducted by his campaign on February 6 showed that the press reports of the health coverage problems at Kerrey's businesses had taken a toll on the senator's credibility on this issue. Finally, with Clinton's problems and Tsongas's emergence as the leading contender dominating the press coverage in the final weeks, Kerrey found it difficult to inject himself into what was rapidly becoming a two-man race. Consequently, Kerrey finished third in New Hampshire with 11 percent of the vote, well behind Tsongas and Clinton, and barely 1 percentage point ahead of Harkin.

Other States

Given his poor showing in New Hampshire, it became essential for Kerrey to win the primary in South Dakota on February 25, where polls showed him in first place ahead of Harkin. Campaign officials considered this contest especially important because they believed that if Kerrey was to be regarded as a viable candidate, he would have to show that he could win in his "own backyard." They also felt that Kerrey could do well in South Dakota against Tsongas and that a victory over Harkin might force the Iowan from the race. The campaign thus intensified its media effort in the state, spending about $43,000 on television and $5,000 on radio. Kerrey also campaigned actively in the state, and appeared more comfortable on the stump than he did in New Hampshire, as he met with farmers, rode horses, visited an Indian reservation, and climbed Mount Rushmore. The campaign aired a thirty-second comparative spot that asked voters to decide which candidate would be best at fighting to save the family farm: Kerrey, who was described as "one of us, from the Great Plains"; Clinton, whose top economic adviser had suggested that "we should end farm subsidies"; or Tsongas, whose "economic plan doesn't even mention agriculture." Kerrey won with 40 percent of the vote, Harkin finishing a distant second.

After South Dakota, the Kerrey campaign was broke; the organization had little cash on hand and $1.1 million in debts. Campaign fund raisers hoped that a victory in South Dakota would produce a sorely needed influx of cash, but additional contributions were not forthcoming. The staff was banking on a New York fund-raising event, scheduled two days after the South Dakota primary, as a major revenue source, but the event was so poorly attended that the campaign was obliged to give away tickets to fill a small reception room.[118] Out of cash and running out of time, the campaign was forced "to fly blind" for the rapidly approaching March 3 contests, which included primaries in three states and caucuses in four others, since it lacked the funds to engage in any polling and had less than $100,000 available to spend.

The campaign's strategists decided to bypass the Maryland primary, conceding it to Tsongas, and focus on the primaries in Georgia and Colorado. The campaign had only enough money to advertise on television in one of these states and decided to concentrate on Colorado, considered to be the best chance to win. Lacking the funds to pursue the media strategy that had proved successful in South Dakota, which involved a mix of health care and biographical spots with a strong comparative ad, the campaign spent $60,000 airing one thirty-second spot that attacked Clinton and Tsongas on their environmental records. Kerrey's campaign team hoped that the ad would have a similar effect among Colorado's environmentally conscious party activists. In addition, the campaign spent $6,600 on radio ads in Idaho, hoping that this would be enough to win this low-turnout caucus state.

In Georgia, Kerrey was forced to rely on press coverage to promote his candidacy. To guarantee coverage, he went to Georgia and attacked Clinton, who was considered to be the front-runner in the state, on his draft record. At a news conference in Atlanta, Kerrey predicted that if Clinton was nominated, his avoidance of the draft would be an issue in the general election. He further declared: "I think he's going to get opened up like a soft peanut in November of 1992."[119] This statement generated substantial nationwide press attention. While it kept the draft issue alive and highlighted Kerrey's record of military service, it gained him little support in Georgia, where he finished with only about 5 percent of the vote, compared with Clinton's 57 percent.

In the other states with March 3 events, the results were much the same. In Colorado, Kerrey's environmental ad did not have the effect that his strategists intended. Kerrey and Clinton attacked Tsongas on the airwaves for his support of nuclear power. Kerrey's team hoped that this would benefit the Nebraskan, who had a strong record of support for clean air legislation and was a long-time opponent of further expansion of the nuclear industry. But in a surprising outcome, the candidate who seemed to gain the greatest benefit from these tactics was Brown, who ended up winning the state with almost 29 percent of the vote. Kerrey finished a poor fourth, with only 12 percent of the vote.

Withdrawal

On March 5, Kerrey dropped out of the race. "We were ready to go full throttle," he said, "but unfortunately we ran out of gas."[120] Overall, Kerrey's campaign raised approximately $6.5 million and spent about the same amount. At the time he quit the race, the campaign faced a debt of about $1.2 million. The campaign received slightly more than $3.9 million in individual contributions and about $350,000 from PACs. The committee also earned close to $2.2 million in matching funds, most of which was used to pay off $1.2 million in bank loans that had been received in anticipation of matching fund payments.[121]

By the time he announced his decision to end his candidacy, Kerrey had raised about $3.4 million in private contributions. About 75 percent of this amount, $2.6 million, was raised through 10,600 contributions generated through fund-raising events and the personal solicitations of members of the campaign's finance committee. Telemarketing solicitations produced an additional 18,800 contributions totaling about $372,000, and the campaign's limited direct mail program produced 5,600 contributions totaling $222,000. Kerrey also received $152,000 from seventy-three PAC gifts, almost all of which were from nonlabor PACs, since the labor committees that were willing to make donations in the presidential race were primarily supporting Harkin.

The campaign maintained a small fund-raising and accounting operation after Kerrey withdrew to resolve the organization's debt. This debt retirement staff raised approximately $450,000 in private contributions in the first three months after Kerrey's withdrawal. About one-third of this total, $151,900, was received from fifty-nine PACs, including many labor committee gifts, since these committees now viewed Kerrey as an incumbent senator whom they were willing to assist, rather than Harkin's opponent. In addition, Kerrey successfully solicited donations from PACs that do not contribute to active presidential candidates but do give to debt-retirement operations, especially if the former candidate is a member of Congress. The campaign also raised $187,000 through events and finance committee solicitations, as well as $64,600 from its

Table 3.1

Kerrey for President Committee: Geographical Distribution of Contributions (as of June 1992)

State	Total Amount	Number of Contributions	Percentage of Total Revenue
Nebraska	$868,252	19,428	21.4
California	561,456	6,577	13.8
New York	458,398	1,289	11.3
Washington, DC	342,450	679	8.4
Florida	254,383	977	6.3
Illinois	174,555	1,444	4.3
Texas	173,639	712	4.3
Subtotal	$2,833,133	31,106	69.8
Other states	1,222,243	10,828	30.2
Total	$4,055,376	41,934	100.0

Source: Citizens' Research Foundation.

telemarketing effort, which produced 3,660 additional contributions, and $45,600 from direct mail, which produced about 1,100 contributions.

As of June 1992, the campaign had received approximately $4 million from 41,934 separate contributions, not including matching funds. About one-third of this total, $1.4 million, was raised through 1,382 contributions of $1,000. Another $350,700 was received from 108 PAC gifts in excess of $1,000 and around $1.1 million was generated by 37,569 contributions of $250 or less. Of the $4 million raised, almost 70 percent had been solicited from six states and the District of Columbia (see Table 3.1). Nebraska led the way, accounting for more than $1 out of every $5 donated to the campaign, with more than 19,000 gifts totaling more than $868,000. Donors from California represented 13.8 percent of the campaign's total contributions, giving about $561,000, and supporters from New York represented 11.3 percent, or close to $460,000.

Although a complete accounting of Kerrey's expenditures is not available, the campaign had spent $5,218,000 through June 1992. Among the major costs included in this total were:

Media production and media time expenses	$1,530,000
Payroll and consulting fees	1,055,907
Travel and advance costs	596,370
Direct mail expenses	438,770
Telemarketing expenses	272,798
Polling costs	91,973

As of July 1, 1992, the Kerrey campaign had a remaining gross debt of about $615,742, excluding the costs of the debt retirement operation. The debt retirement staff worked throughout the election year to resolve these obligations. By early 1993, the $1.1 million in debt that existed after Kerrey dropped out had been completely paid, in part by negotiating the final $200,000 in debts and paying vendors about sixty-two cents on the dollar, which reduced the campaign's costs by about $80,000.[122]

Harkin

Senator Tom Harkin, the self-described "prairie populist," was reelected to the Senate in 1990. He is an outspoken, unabashed liberal, having never drawn a rating of less than 90 percent from Americans for Democratic Action during his seven years in the Senate. Harkin's father was a coal miner who suffered from black lung disease and his mother died when he was ten years old. Harkin was a poverty lawyer before his election to the House in 1974 and was first elected to the Senate in 1984. Harkin boasted that his campaign for reelection to the Senate raised more money from organized labor than any senatorial campaign in history, and he was proud of that support. Harkin's 1990 campaign manager, Tim Raftis, said that labor PACs contributed more than $490,000 of the almost $6 million raised by the campaign.[123]

Harkin's campaign for the Democratic nomination was announced on September 15, 1991. He was the third Democrat to enter the race, following Tsongas and Wilder. He planned an aggressive, confrontational campaign against George Herbert Walker Bush, as he called the president, emphasizing the president's patriarchal roots. As the only traditional liberal in the race, his goal was to position himself to stake out the left-labor wing of the party and to seek inroads with groups that play an oversized role in the Democratic nomination process. One news article suggested that the Iowa senator perfectly fit the profile of a Democratic loser: someone who can stir the party faithful in the primaries and provide an easy target for Bush in November.[124]

Harkin was not apologetic about collecting PAC money, saying, "I'm not going to fight with one hand behind my back. In George Bush, we are up against the mother of all money machines."[125] Harkin's decision to accept PAC money made him a target for people who were pressing for changes in campaign finance law. Harkin's credo, however, was "Never defend, always attack."[126]

Harkin's spirited, Bush-bashing campaign attracted substantial early financial support. Harkin qualified for $1.1 million in federal matching funds in early December 1991. Campaign manager Tim Raftis said, "It was the Clinton campaign that said that money was the first primary. Well, they got whipped."[127] Part of Harkin's early success is attributable to the time he devoted to it. Nathan Landow, chairman of the Democratic Party in Maryland, where Harkin's campaign was based, stated, "In the number of events, Tom has probably done twice as many as the others."[128] Harkin held fund raisers in Hollywood hosted by such celebrities as Roseanne and Tom Arnold, Ed Asner, David Crosby, and Steve Allen.

Harkin's direct mail was productive. He began a mail campaign in September, immediately upon announcing his candidacy. Direct mail requires a large initial investment and can produce uncertain returns, but more money than even campaign officials expected was generated from it. The direct mail program was handled by Mal Warwick and Associates of Berkeley, California, the company that handled Jesse Jackson's effort in 1988. Carter Eskew, a political consultant who worked on Harkin's Senate campaigns, commented, "Tom's message lends itself to mail, and it is a tremendous advantage to have a good direct mail program because it gives you a real boost in the beginning when you need matching funds."[129] By December 31, 1991, Harkin's campaign had raised $2.2 million, ranking second among the Democratic candidates.

To maximize resources for a television and radio advertising blitz in New Hampshire starting in January, Harkin kept his campaign staff comparatively small. Media consultant Ken Swope, who produced some of Dukakis's commercials, was hired. Harkin hoped to win enough support in the early primaries to be able to survive a poor showing on Super Tuesday, March 10, which is made up of many southern states that might be more inclined to vote for Clinton. Selected southern states such as Texas and Florida would be targeted, and then Harkin hoped to do well in the Northeast with its strong labor base.

Harkin's fund raising, however, was inhibited while Mario Cuomo considered entering the race, and he was seen as benefiting the most from Cuomo's decision not to run. In mid-January, fund raising was sluggish and polls showed only little support. Harkin thought he could distinguish himself from previous liberal, unsuccessful, Democratic presidential nominees by his aggressive style.

Harkin's status as a favorite son made the Iowa caucus, the first delegate selection process in the nation, insignificant for other candidates. Kerrey paid $10,000 for a list of previous caucus-goers. Jerry Brown mounted the most serious challenge and spent a few days in Iowa in January 1992. Clinton did some polling in the fall of 1991. Tsongas spent the most time campaigning in the state, even more than Harkin, but much of this was before Harkin entered the race. Harkin mainly had to run against the expectations of how successful he should be in his home state.

Harkin's aides estimated that he campaigned nine days in Iowa. Organizational efforts in Iowa were estimated at $250,000 to operate phone banks, send out mailings, and stage rallies. Harkin mailed to 60,000 frequent caucus participants. Some Iowans feared that Harkin's campaign would make the caucuses less meaningful, which would hurt the state party's organizational and fund-raising drives, as well as its ability to attract candidates for local offices.[130] Polls just before the Iowa caucus showed Harkin declining in popularity and Clinton rising, despite not campaigning in the state. Harkin, however, won the Iowa caucuses.

Harkin assembled a fairly strong organization in New Hampshire and campaigned in the state for forty-four days. He enjoyed a high standing among union leaders and the rank and file and was the front-runner for labor support, but he was not strong enough to win a preprimary endorsement from the AFL-CIO. Harkin was endorsed by fifteen national or international unions with an aggregate membership of more than 7.7 million. This did him little good in the early primary states, which do not have a strong union presence.[131]

Harkin, who has a deaf brother, courted disabled voters. In 1990, he introduced the Americans With Disability Act, which Bush had signed into law. The sole job of one campaign staff member was to organize disabled voters. All of his campaign offices were accessible to the handicapped and special phones were installed for people with speech or hearing difficulties. He had a sign language interpreter with him while campaigning.

Harkin spent many days working at different jobs—laying sewer pipe, going out on a lobster boat, waiting tables, serving as a police officer and short order cook—to emphasize his solidarity with working people. This generated considerable exposure on the evening newscasts. Also, Harkin aired two thirty-second television spots in New Hampshire starting January 16, 1992. Clinton and Kerrey were already advertising on television, and Harkin intended to make up for this slow start by purchasing more TV time. Harkin ran a third television advertisement about creating jobs. A fourth ad assailed his Democratic rivals for backing "tax giveaways to the rich." But Harkin's style and highly personal attacks did not play well on television.

At the end of January, polls showed Harkin in last place among the five Democratic contenders in New Hampshire. Some observers felt that his campaign speeches were redundant. To counter charges that his message was too general, Harkin produced a thirty-five-page booklet laying out his plan for the economy.

Harkin went on the attack in a sixty-second radio advertisement in New Hampshire in early February. In addition to criticizing Bush, Harkin attacked his Democratic rivals. He risked offending voters who would be turned off by this negative approach, and his attacks invited counterattacks from the pack of candidates. This put Harkin on the spot and he did not respond effectively. Although nuclear power production has long been a controversial issue in New Hampshire, he was unable to answer questions about his campaign's acceptance of contributions from companies that pollute and promote the presence of nuclear power plants in Iowa. He also mailed out a letter in the name of a dummy women's organization containing inaccurate charges against Clinton and Kerrey. The women's organization had the same mailing address as the Harkin campaign headquarters.

Harkin came in fourth out of five Democrats in the New Hampshire primary with 10 percent of the vote. Funds dwindled as he lost in Maine and South Dakota. By early March, Harkin was nearly out of funds and was scraping by to get to the primaries in the industrial Midwest, where he could take advantage of his labor ties. Black voters were aggressively courted in South Carolina. Harkin looked toward Michigan, where he was endorsed by Detroit Mayor Coleman Young and was heavily backed by the United Auto Workers, to boost his campaign back into the race. Fund raising from union members was seen as a last source of additional money.

Harkin's campaign did not make it to the Michigan primary, however. On March 9, when Harkin withdrew from the race, his campaign coffers were empty. His withdrawal sent the three remaining candidates scrambling for labor's support. Harkin was not successful in winning any primaries but won caucuses in Iowa, Idaho, and Minnesota. Analysts suggested that Harkin's campaign succumbed due to organizational problems and the expectation, emphasized by the media, that Clinton or Tsongas would get the nomination. Harkin was seen by many as abrasive and many of his proposals seemed dated. His Midwest, farm-state style and attitudes were not well received in other parts of the country. His campaign was politically nostalgic, citing Franklin Roosevelt and Hubert Humphrey often, which did not attract younger voters, and he was reluctant to offer specific policy proposals. Some journalists suggested that Harkin did not appear presidential, and his often-humorous remarks were not consistent with many voters' sense of respect for the presidency. He ran as the "Real Democrat" when much of the electorate did not care about party identification.

These factors combined to prevent him from attracting sufficient financial support to continue the campaign. Harkin would have lost his eligibility for federal matching funds because he failed to win at least 10 percent of the vote in two consecutive primaries, and he would not have regained eligibility unless he won at least 20 percent of the vote in a primary within thirty days. Raftis claimed, "We are stopping because we just ran out of money, not because people didn't support the policies of our campaign. It's difficult to get your message through when you don't have any money."[132] The campaign had debts of $300,000 and was having trouble raising additional funds.

Harkin's campaign ended up raising more than $3 million from individuals and $492,069 from PACs. He received $2.1 million in federal matching funds. There were no independent expenditures for or against him. Some $4,615 was spent on his behalf as communication costs, which was a labor union endorsement to its members.

Brown

Former California Governor Edmund G. "Jerry" Brown, Jr., announced on September 3, 1991, that he was launching an exploratory campaign for the Democratic presidential nomination. Brown, who had run for president twice, in 1976 and 1980, had been considering a run for the U.S. Senate. In a ten-page letter to supporters, he said that American politics had been taken over by "corruption, careerism and campaign consulting,"[133] and that only contributions of $100 or less would be accepted. He said that he knew firsthand the power fund raisers hold over politicians. Jabbing at his chest, Brown said, "When I point the finger, I point it right here." The importance of campaign finance reform was stressed. If Brown decided to seek the presidency, he would run "not a campaign but a cause."[134]

Critics suggested that Brown would enter the presidential race as a symbolic gesture because he could not win a real, down-to-earth race for the Senate and that he was only accepting contributions of $100 or less because he was not able to raise big money, especially "after a career of unashamedly courting millions of dollars in special-interest funds."[135] He had previously raised an estimated $20 million in his various political campaigns. In 1990, Brown raised thousands of dollars from "special interest" lobbyists to wage a successful legal challenge to overturn Proposition 73, the ballot initiative that imposed a $1,000 contribution limit on California campaigns. At the time, he called the proposition "one of the most pernicious campaign laws ever enacted."[136] Brown solicited even more money as chairman of the California Democratic Party.

Brown formally announced his campaign on October 21, 1991, now claiming that government today is "an unholy alliance of private greed and corrupt politics." He suggested that there were no longer two political parties but only one, "a Washington's Incumbent Party," that needed to be replaced.[137] Brown had recast himself as the populist defender against special interests.

Unlike any other presidential candidate in history, Brown made campaign reform the main issue of his campaign. "Money is the problem, not the answer," Brown remarked. The $100 limit for campaign contributions dramatized his message that campaign spending by the wealthy and powerful has corrupted the American system. This theme registered with many people, but the economic problems of Americans were deemed a more serious issue by most voters. Furthermore, many of those who embraced Brown's message felt that he was the wrong messenger.

The campaign was chaired by Jodie Evans, an aide to Brown when he was governor. The mostly volunteer staff consisted of about a dozen casually dressed men and women in their twenties who worked out of an austere office building in Santa Monica, California.[138] Brown used the radio as his most significant means of communicating with the voters. In part, this was due to the low cost of being on the radio. Brown's campaign had raised nearly $250,000 at the end of 1991, all of which qualified for matching funds.

At the first televised presidential forum among Democratic candidates, Brown spoke about the powerful connection between campaign contributions, elected officials' actions, and the influence of PACs. Brown ignored NBC's request not to solicit money during the debate, and gave out his 800 phone number for making pledges.[139] The announcement of his number brought in thousands of calls. Brown, however, showed no movement in the polls and his fund raising overall continued to lag.

In January 1992, Brown raised $159,713, all of which qualified for federal matching funds. At the end of January, Brown's campaign reported that $700,000 had been raised, the least amount for the five Democratic contenders.[140] Brown had received $390,000 in matching funds, almost 40 percent of his total receipts.[141] Through the first week in February, approximately 13,000 people had made contributions, a response level that compared favorably to that of his Democratic rivals, and Evans said that overall 103,000 calls were received on the 800 number.[142] While Brown's fund raising was modest, so were his expenses. He had only seven paid staff members and stayed at the homes of supporters on the road.

In early February, Brown held a fund raiser in Los Angeles with 1,500 supporters. A multi-racial church choir opened the program. Actresses Talia Shire and Bonnie Bedelia were in attendance, and actor Martin Sheen led the group in prayer before Brown spoke. The event raised $40,000. This event was Brown's largest fund raiser.

Brown explored new ways of reaching voters. He appeared on many talk radio and cable television interview programs that other national candidates usually ignored. He relentlessly promoted the 800 number. An interview was held with New York–based shock-radio disc jockey Howard Stern, whose nationally syndicated FM morning show commands large audiences in several markets. Brown tried to fend off Stern's sexist comments and one-liners and deliver his political pitch. The appearance generated a large number of calls on the 800 number. Evans commented, "It is very hard to get attention from the media, so we are creating our own media."[143]

Brown proposed a 13 percent flat tax with exemptions for only charitable contributions, rent, and home mortgage payments as a replacement for the current tax system. He also stressed greater energy conservation and the need for new fuel-efficient automobiles.

Brown lacked the funds necessary to buy the television time needed to reach large numbers of voters efficiently. A thirty-minute "infomercial" was produced entitled "Take Back America," which portrayed Brown as a political outsider who bucked insiders to benefit ordinary people. It suggested that policies for which he was once criticized or ridiculed had turned out to be sound. The rates for infomercials are less than those for standard advertising, and the program appeared on cable channels in New Hampshire.[144]

Campaigning in the States

Brown was drawing big crowds of supporters from among students, white liberals, gay rights activists, and consumer activists. He commented, "I certainly would like that Rainbow Coalition."[145] These crowds did not translate into voter approval at the polls, though. In March, Brown faced the loss of his eligibility for matching funds after failing to win at least 10 percent of the vote in the first two consecutive primaries, New Hampshire and South Dakota. Brown had thirty days to regain his eligibility by winning 20 percent of the vote in an upcoming primary. Colorado was targeted as the state on which to focus.

Brown tied with Tsongas for first place in Maine's caucus in late February. In early March, Brown attracted 29 percent of the vote in Colorado, allowing him to remain eligible for matching funds and giving his campaign more concentrated media attention. Brown had spent a considerable amount of time in the state. This victory and his strong second-place finish in Utah gave him credibility as the anti-establishment candidate and caused his campaign to be taken more seriously. Brown said, "The fuel of my campaign is based on very solid ground, more solid than in any campaign I have ever run. It's based on the truth of what is happening in this country. And it's not compromised by the contradictions of the rhetoric and the money paying for the rhetoric. . . ."[146]

Brown began getting the national coverage he had been denied in the past. The campaign focused on the corrosive impact of big campaign contributions, lobbyists, and entrenched incumbents. The former governor dismissed attacks on him for his past connection to big money by stating, "That's a cynical opposition to reforming the system." He said he tried for years to reform the system from the inside. Brown vowed to make Jesse Jackson his running mate if he won the nomination.

Brown spent $65,000 on media in New Hampshire and $38,000 in Colorado, compared with hundreds of thousands of dollars by the Clinton and Tsongas campaigns.[147] As of March 3, $1,078,108 had been raised from 19,406 small contributors, less than one-fifth of what Clinton had raised. By mid-March, the campaign had ten paid staff members, each earning $500 a week. No paid political consultants were used and no polling was conducted since the Iowa caucus early in the year. The 800 number had generated 120,000 calls. Brown rejected Secret Service assistance as an unnecessary perk. The campaign's shoestring budget allowed Brown to stay in the race until the end.

Brown still did not have enough money to run television advertising, the lifeblood of most presidential campaigns, but he did three thirty-minute infomercials for cable stations and some radio spots. He relied mostly on local press coverage, satellite television interviews, radio talk shows and personal appearances. Brown knew the South would not be supportive of his candidacy and focused his efforts on high stake states like Texas and Florida.[148] Commentators were suggesting that Brown could play a pivotal role at the convention if Clinton and Tsongas did not have enough delegates to secure the nomination.

Brown's strategy was to do well in Michigan, which he hoped would knock Tsongas out of the race. Having established himself as the alternative candidate, he could then win the "rust belt" state primaries in April and May, then win California in June. If Brown did poorly, he risked looking foolish, given all the attention he was drawing.

Clinton responded to the Brown campaign in Michigan, and for the first time, Clinton ran an ad attacking Brown's tax proposal. When Harkin dropped out of the race, some labor leaders in Michigan rallied around

Brown. In a heated moment of a debate between the three contenders, Brown accused Clinton of funneling money to his wife's law firm. But the campaign lacked organization, which in part affected Brown's ability to get news coverage. Brown missed an interview with the *New York Times* to go jogging. Brown's media expenditures included $10,000 in Texas for Spanish language radio and $150,000 in Michigan.[149]

On the night of the debate with Clinton in mid-March, Brown raised $100,000 through the 800 number. That week he brought in $500,000.[150] As of March 31, $5,342,917 had been pledged from 216,000 callers, 122,000 of them California residents. Of this amount, $2,245,895 had been collected.[151] Federal matching funds added $580,000, with another $320,000 forthcoming. By contrast, Clinton had raised $8 million by mid-March with more due from matching funds. Brown finished second in Michigan with 26 percent of the vote; Clinton won with 51 percent. In Illinois, a state Brown did not focus on, he ran third with 15 percent of the vote, finishing 36 percentage points behind Clinton. After his second-place finish in Michigan, $100,000 was pledged on his 800 number.

Brown, with nothing to lose, bombarded Clinton with criticisms ranging from his policy positions to his character. Brown aired a television commercial in Connecticut suggesting voters reject the notion that Clinton had secured the nomination. The ad was a major financial commitment for the campaign. Brown scored an upset in Connecticut, winning with 37 percent of the vote. In response to this victory, Brown said, "It's a miracle. It's not about me. It's about the grassroots rising up against the bounced checks, the congressional pay raises, the corrupt status quo."[152]

After the showing in Connecticut, Cuomo proclaimed New York's primary was wide open. As the anti-establishment candidate, Brown was receiving the full attention of the media. Brown said his goal of grassroots participatory democracy would be difficult to achieve, but his $100 limit on contributions was a good start because people who gave at that level "feel part of it for the first time."[153] Brown was accused of negative campaigning by Democratic Party chairman Ronald Brown and Jimmy Carter.

Brown asked Clinton to join him in not running any paid broadcast commercials in New York and in accepting a $100 limit on contributions. Brown said, "You join me in that, and we will have a reformed Democratic Party that goes to the grass roots."[154] Clinton would not agree to these conditions. Brown finished in third place in the New York primary.

Brown said his primary opponents were corrupt for taking $1,000 campaign contributions. Despite Brown's inconsistent stances on many positions over the past twenty years, he was certainly a messenger for reform. Ralph

Nader said of Brown, "When you've burned your bridges like that, you're entitled to a little credibility."[155]

The 800 number was open twenty-four hours a day. A confirmation letter was sent to each person making a pledge, and only one reminder was sent if pledges were not received. All contributors were entered into the computer, creating a potentially significant grass-roots political reform network for future elections. Campaign officials estimated the costs of the 800 line accounted for approximately one-third of all money collected through it and consisted of labor, extensive telephone charges, mailings, computer equipment, check-sorting, and administration. The director of the phone bank, Jan Krajewski, said the bill for keeping the staff fed with pizzas at odd hours was nearly $2,000 a month.[156]

But Sidney Galanty, a Brown advisor, estimated that the campaign lost approximately half of the potential contributors because the toll-free line was busy.[157] At its peak, Brown had only about eighty people staffing the phone lines, whereas the average product being advertised by way of infomercials had 3,000 operators answering phones. Sidney Blumenthal, in *The New Republic,* reported that the campaign representative answering the 800 line stated he could not comment on Brown's positions on issues and could not answer questions on the telemarketing firm that set up the operation. Compucall, which is owned by Evans's brother and ex-husband, was the firm that created the telephone network.[158]

Brown used the media to take presidential politics to places it had never been before: public-access cable channels, infomercials, 800 numbers, and radio talk shows. Local, public-access television, however, can be bought for as little as $100 a half-hour in some markets.

In March, Brown raised $1.2 million, which qualified for federal matching funds, and claimed more money than Clinton raised during the month. More significantly, Brown reported 21,458 contributors, compared with Clinton's 8,265.[159] The average contribution was $57 per caller. This spectacular fund-raising success nearly doubled the total amount of contributions raised previously. Brown had raised $2.3 million through the end of March.[160]

After defeats in New York, Pennsylvania, North Carolina, Nebraska, and West Virginia, Brown gave up any notion of denying Clinton the nomination on the first round of balloting and focused on winning enough delegates to go to the convention as a force for change. Brown vowed to stay in the race to save the Democratic Party and the country. He said, "The cause is bigger than any individual candidate. I'm running because I want to carve out an insurgent movement that will keep the tradition and the conscience of the [Democratic] Party before the electorate."[161] In April, 33,000 people contributed money to Brown, who received more federal matching funds than any other candidate, $1.7 million.[162] Independent committees did not spend any significant money in support of, or in opposition to, Brown. The Sheet Metal Workers' Union spent nearly $45,000 to publicize Brown's candidacy within its membership.

Brown said he would endorse the party's nominee if campaign contribution limits were decreased to $100, and other reforms were supported. The nominee also had to favor term limits and same-day voter registration, and declare election day a holiday.[163] Clinton declined.

Brown lost the California primary by 8 percentage points and stated that he planned on organizing nationwide platform hearings for ideas to take to the convention. To promote party unity, Brown was allowed to offer two convention resolutions seeking to establish a commission to study ways to revitalize the party, including possible changes in fund raising, grass-roots organization, and nominating rules. Delegates rejected both resolutions.

Brown's campaign introduced two significant alternative approaches to presidential campaign financing: contribution limits of $100 and 800-number telephone fund raising. The 800 number accounted for nearly 85 percent of the individual contributions the campaign received, totaling nearly $5.2 million. Federal matching funds contributed $4.2 million, with 84,567 qualified contributions averaging $52. The campaign budget of $9 million was approximately one-fourth that of Clinton's campaign. Media buys constituted half of the campaign's expenditures. Fund-raising costs totaled $2.3 million and legal and accounting exemptions totaled just $220,000.

New York–based television and political consultant Jack Hilton said, "In making it possible for someone to run for president without a massive treasury, Jerry Brown may be a trailblazer."[164] Patrick Caddell, former campaign adviser to Carter and George McGovern, praised Brown's toll-free number and $100 contribution limit as a way of political empowerment for the masses. The other significance of Brown's campaign was the rhetoric on campaign reform, never before heard in a presidential campaign so loudly or so stridently.

Wilder

L. Douglas Wilder, of Virginia, was the first elected African American governor in American history. He described himself as "a fiscal conservative with a social conscience and a deep concern for the country's middle class."[165] He formed an exploratory committee in March 1991 and had raised $118,915 by June 30, 1991.[166] Wilder announced his candidacy on September 13, 1991, and by the end of September he had collected only about $220,000.[167]

Wilder's campaign manager thought Wilder would need $3 million to get through Super Tuesday,[168] but the campaign had raised only $501,000 through December 31, 1991. Wilder had a $1 million surplus from his Virginia gubernatorial inaugural fund, but he was not permitted under federal law to transfer the funds to his presidential campaign.[169] Wilder withdrew from the contest on January 8. In all, his campaign spent $805,972, including $289,026 in matching funds. He left the Democrats without a major black contender for the first time since 1980. After unsuccessfully trying to distinguish himself from the other candidates, he shifted his focus to a campaign of racial pride, but Jackson urged African Americans to wait until their support was solicited by the presidential candidates, rather than falling in line behind Wilder.[170]

Bush: Prenomination

President George Bush entered the race with perhaps the most well-established financial base in recent electoral history. He had spent essentially twelve years developing financial support, first as a presidential candidate in 1980, then as vice president, and finally as president. In his 1988 bid for the Republican nomination, he adopted a fund-raising approach designed to exploit his ability to attract large donations.[171] In 1992, he pursued a similar strategy.

Active in campaigning throughout his term in office, Bush made more political appearances and raised more money for Republicans in 1990 than any president in history. From mid-1988 through 1990, Bush was credited with having raised $90 million at 115 fund-raising events.[172] In the months before the 1990 election, the president made twenty-three trips involving sixty-five personal appearances at campaign events. Bush often tied political stops to "official" business so the fund-raising events would not have to pick up the costs of Air Force One and his other travel expenses.[173]

White House chief of staff John Sununu stated in February 1991 that Bush intended to follow "roughly" the campaign schedule used by Ronald Reagan in 1984, with major decisions on staffing and structure made in the spring, the establishment of a full-blown campaign organization in the fall, and the president announcing his bid for reelection late in the year or in January 1992.[174] By May 1991, however, not much had been done on the campaign and RNC chairman Clayton Yeutter announced that Bush intended to establish an exploratory committee to consider his reelection and to begin collecting campaign contributions by early September.[175]

The financial side of the campaign established its base in Alexandria, Virginia, at the office of the campaign treasurer, Stanley Huckaby. Margaret Alexander, the finance director at the RNC, and a few members of her staff, left the RNC payroll and formed the nucleus of the fund-raising team.[176] A finance plan for the campaign was prepared in July 1991. It called for the president to appear at fourteen fund-raising events during 1991. Strategists planned a $25 million fund-raising blitz, even though at the time it appeared that the president would face no primary opposition. They hoped, however, that such an aggressive fund-raising effort would deny Democrats matching funds for early 1992 primaries, because a Treasury Department ruling gave campaigns that raised the earliest contributions first access to the dwindling pool of matching funds.[177] These goals, however, were not achieved. By year's end, the White House had cooperated in only four of the planned events.

Bush held his first two fund-raising events in Texas during the last week of October 1991, raising close to $2 million. The first two fund-raising letters of the campaign were mailed out during this time, both urging support for Bush in the final campaign of his career. One letter was sent to the list of major donors to prior Bush campaigns, and the other to general Republican contributors. In these letters, Bush asked for support but did not express any sharp ideology.[178] A fund raiser was held in New York City on November 12, 1991, which was most successful and brought in $2.1 million. Another event in Washington, DC, on November 20, 1991, grossed more than $1 million.[179]

Bush had thirty-eight national finance vice chairmen. Among those who raised money for Bush were Peter Terpeluk, a Washington lobbyist with the Philadelphia-based consulting firm S.R. Wojdak and Associates; Donald Bren, a prominent Southern California developer; Lodwrick Cook, chairman of ARCO, an oil company; Henry Kravis, of the New York City–based investment house Kohlberg Kravis Roberts & Co.; Alec Courtelis, a Miami developer and horse breeder; and Wally Ganzi, owner of Washington, DC–based Palm Restaurants.[180]

With his popularity dropping and the White House in disarray with the unwise use of perquisites causing problems for his chief of staff, John Sununu, Bush announced his campaign team in early December and appointed Samuel Skinner as White House chief of staff.[181] He made his candidacy official on February 12, 1992.

The Power and Privilege of Incumbency

As a sitting president, Bush had the power and prestige of the office at his disposal. Part of the campaign strategy was to remain "presidential" for as long as possible, thus appearing above the fray. At times, Bush was criticized by the Democrats for staging political or campaign-related activities under the guise of official business. A few examples illustrate this point.

Bush spent $26,750 from funds at the Department of Education to make a speech to schoolchildren, which was carried live by CNN and PBS. Secretary of Education Lamar Alexander had sent letters to all the elementary and secondary schools beforehand, urging them to let students watch. Democrats assailed the spending, but the president's spokesman, Marlin Fitzwater, denied the event was political and said that it cost less than mailing a letter to 86,000 students.[182]

On his high-profile trip to Asia in 1991, Bush was accompanied by twenty-one heavyweight corporate executives. Some of these executives and their wives also were major contributors to the Republican Party, raising questions about the political motivation for the trip. Four executives gave $15,000 each to the RNC in the first ten months of 1991. Another gave $5,000 to the RNC, while his company gave $75,000 in soft money in 1989–90.[183]

The White House condemned attempts by business executives to coerce their employees to donate to political campaigns but said there was nothing improper in luring donors with elbow-rubbing and photo opportunities. The statement was made in response to a civil suit filed in court by a corporate employee, alleging dismissal for failure to contribute to a Republican fund raiser.[184]

Drug czar Bob Martinez directed $63,644 of money refunded from his collapsed Florida gubernatorial campaign to the Florida GOP for Bush's reelection. The transmittal letter was written on his White House office stationery. This action violated federal law, and only $1,000 could be used directly for campaign-related activity.[185]

When a president runs for reelection, there will always be a thin line between political and official activities. Ethics regulations and campaign laws attempt to control this problem. It appears Bush was sensitive to these issues and at times supported broad interpretations of these regulations to avoid the appearance of impropriety. For example, a White House interpretation of the statute making it a federal crime for a government employee to make a political contribution to a supervisor prohibited millions of federal employees from contributing to Bush's campaign. Also, Bush had vetoed a measure in 1990 that would have loosened restrictions on political activities by government employees. In the past, the statute was construed more narrowly, covering only White House employees and presidential appointees requiring Senate confirmation. The White House noted that employees' spouses and families could still make such a contribution.[186] In 1993, with Clinton's approval, the law was changed.[187]

New Hampshire and Georgia

With Pat Buchanan's challenge from the right, the economic recession, and the lack of a clear campaign theme, Bush had to revise his strategy. Initially, Bush was going to stay out of a controversial campaign mode and rely on the power and prestige of the presidency for as long as possible. Bush planned to spend only three days in New Hampshire, leaving the traditional pavement-pounding to surrogates such as Dan Quayle, Jack Kemp, and Barbara Bush.[188] But polls showed his popularity increased after visiting the state and additional trips were then scheduled.

Three waves of commercials were run in New Hampshire.[189] Bush aired a thirty-second television commercial on January 24, 1992, apologizing for voters' economic pain. The campaign prepared but did not air a commercial attacking Buchanan.[190] For a limited period during the height of the campaign, the Bush and Buchanan campaigns each bought twenty-five to thirty commercial spots a day on the state's leading station as well as substantial commercial time on Boston outlets.[191] Bush's campaign is estimated to have spent slightly less than Buchanan's $1.7 million on television, but Bush started campaigning later.[192] Bush ran radio ads extolling his conservative credentials, and both New Hampshire senators supplied radio endorsements.[193] Jim Lennane, a wealthy businessman who ran for the Republican nomination as an unknown, spent some $500,000 on anti-Bush television ads; he received 1,684 votes.[194]

Bush received 53 percent of the New Hampshire vote, which was a modest showing. Buchanan's 37 percent was considered a significant victory, which gave his campaign a sense of legitimacy. Buchanan, who admitted his campaign was a long shot, now spoke of the possibility of winning. From a historical perspective, incumbent presidents who did poorly in the primary dropped out of the race or were defeated in the fall. The returns motivated the campaign to take Buchanan seriously and address his attacks directly.

Bush ran television and radio ads in Georgia highlighting Buchanan's opposition to the use of force in the Persian Gulf and some of Buchanan's controversial statements, including the suggestion that women were psychologically unsuited for certain jobs.[195] Bush spent $216,000 on advertising in Georgia, almost one-half of what Buchanan spent. Bush countered Buchanan's negative advertisements with negative rebuttals and accusations. The president received 64 percent of the vote in Georgia.[196]

Bush hoped to do extremely well in the early primaries to make it hard for Buchanan to compete effectively, by making it difficult to raise money.[197] Bush held a fund-raising dinner in Manchester, New Hampshire, in early February; in attendance were Senator Phil Gramm, Defense Secretary Richard Cheney, John Sununu, and HUD Secretary Jack Kemp.[198] California fund raisers were held on February 25, 1992, and organizers raised $1 million at a $1,000-per-plate dinner in Los Angeles, and more than $600,000 at a $1,000-per-plate luncheon in San Francisco.[199] These February fund raisers added more than $2 million to the $14.3 million in the campaign coffers at the time.[200]

Super Tuesday

Buchanan received more than 30 percent of the vote in only two of eight states holding contests on Super Tuesday. While Buchanan captured the attention of many unsatisfied Americans, his threat to Bush's nomination had dwindled. With David Duke's entry into the campaign, the conservative vote was splintered. But it also is interesting to note that in South Dakota, where Buchanan was not on the ballot, 30 percent of the Republican vote went to "uncommitted." This may indicate that Buchanan's support may have been more of a protest vote than a vote in favor of Buchanan. Bush spent less money than Buchanan in these contests.[201]

As of April 30, the Bush campaign reported raising $24 million, about $5 million more than Clinton, who was $2.7 million in debt at this time. Bush focused fund raising on individual donors. Two-thirds of the campaign's receipts came in the form of $1,000 checks, the maximum an individual can give.[202] In all, the campaign had 139,480 contributions from some 108,891 contributors listed on matching fund submissions to the FEC. By the end of May, the campaign had more than $7 million cash on hand. The economic recession slowed Bush's fund-raising effort, however. He had hoped to raise the $27.6 million the campaign could spend before the convention by March, but this limit was not reached until May. Direct mail returns were less than expected. An average of about $1 per letter was collected instead of the $2 or $3 average officials had expected. Earnings on the collected money were low because interest rates were down.[203]

The president received $10.7 million in matching funds and reported 141,752 qualifying contributions with an average contribution of $76. PAC contributions were not accepted although the FEC listed $44,250 in income from other committees. Some $5.5 million was grossed by direct mail, with an average contribution of $52. There were no loans. Fund-raising costs exempt from the spending limits, including those for direct mail, were $5.5 million. Legal and accounting exemptions totaled $4.6 million. In the end, Bush spent as much as legally permitted, even though his renomination was assured by Super Tuesday, and later spending was pro forma in some states and then allocated in ways to abet the general election spending. During the prenomination period, $4.9 million was spent on media and $850,000 was spent on polling.

The president benefited from an active independent campaign on his behalf. Independent expenditures for Bush totaled a bit more than $1 million, whereas only $32,000 was spent on behalf of Clinton during the prenomination period. The Presidential Victory Committee and right-to-life organizations were the major sources of this spending. There were no communication costs reported to the FEC in support of Bush and only $5,700 of independent communication costs were spent against him.[204]

Buchanan

Patrick J. Buchanan, conservative television commentator, columnist, and influential Nixon and Reagan administration staff member, claimed that Bush had betrayed the conservative movement. Throughout the fall of 1991, he used his talk show appearances and newspaper columns to criticize the administration. On December 10, he announced his decision to challenge an incumbent president of his own party for the nomination. Buchanan accused Bush of abandoning conservative principles, losing touch with the nation, focusing too much on world affairs, and ignoring domestic problems and the economy. In contrast, Buchanan articulated an "America First" perspective, which was rather isolationist.[205]

Buchanan Philosophy

Buchanan is well known for his acrimonious, scathing remarks on the CNN shows "Crossfire" and "The Capital Gang," and NBC's "The McLaughlin Group." He is deeply committed to his extreme views, which were influenced by his father, his traditional Catholic religious beliefs, and his fervently anti-Communist upbringing. In articulating these views, he championed isolationist foreign policies, trashed pluralism, derided secularism and immigration, and insulted African Americans, women, Jews, homosexuals, and non-Europeans. Buchanan denied being prejudiced, but his comments resonated with those who embraced intolerance. Buchanan rejected the bigotry of Duke, a former Ku Klux Klan leader, who ran briefly for the Republican nomination, and said, "I don't welcome the support of anyone who is voting out of hatred of any group or out of bigotry."[206]

Buchanan wanted to take up the mantle of conservatism, but many on the right opposed his isolationist, protectionist views. The Republican Party under Reagan favored interventionist foreign policies, especially to fight communism, opposed isolationist trade policies, and supported Israel.[207] Many conservatives did not embrace Buchanan's extreme positions but felt Bush was drifting too far to the left.

Buchanan spoke of leading the middle class but his annual income actually placed him in the top 1 percent of American workers. Buchanan balked at disclosing his personal finances to the FEC, as required by law. The candidate's disclosure was due in January 1992, but Buchanan did not comply until April. The Justice Department considered prosecuting.[208] Buchanan reported income of $809,975 for 1991 from his talk show appearances, columns, and speeches, with $1 million in an account of a major Wall Street brokerage firm, five rental properties worth at least $800,000, stock valued at a sum of at least $24,000, and a home valued at $1 million.[209]

Organization

Buchanan's initial resources were slim, and he lent $50,000 of his own money, the legal maximum, to start the campaign; as noted, he repaid himself from campaign receipts. His sister, Angela M. "Bay" Buchanan, former U.S. treasurer and unsuccessful candidate for California state treasurer, chaired the campaign. Buchanan thought that he would not have the funding to pay for high-powered television ads and planned to rely on free media such as interviews.[210] As it turned out, Buchanan was successful at raising money.

Buchanan was not well organized in any state other than New Hampshire, where he had sufficient time to prepare. Tony Fabrizio, pollster and strategist, quit after having disagreements with Buchanan and his sister.[211] Buchanan's campaign had two people as research staffers and few advance people. The volunteers and staff were young and inexperienced. There were many examples of poor or last-minute planning.[212] Buchanan hired a media consulting company, River Bank, with the account for the primary race valued at $490,000.[213]

Buchanan failed to get on the primary ballot in New York. He needed to collect 1,250 signatures of registered Republicans per congressional district to get on the ballot in that district. He failed to get on the ballot in any district. Buchanan attributed this failure to tough election laws.[214]

Buchanan's fund-raising events were not designed to raise large sums of money. Buchanan recognized that, unlike Bush, he could not go to Texas and raise $2 million in a weekend. Buchanan's fund-raising events consisted of activities such as a $50-a-plate lunch in Orlando, Florida, and a riverboat cruise in South Carolina. Parties in Los Angeles and San Diego netted about $70,000. A fund-raising dinner in Dallas generated $75,000. Since Buchanan entered the race late and had laid little groundwork, he did not think he could afford to leave the campaign trail to attend a large number of fund raisers. Conservative business groups hosted him at meetings, which was valuable in that it allowed him to meet executives who later contributed. L. Brent Bozel III, Buchanan's finance chairman, took credit for raising more than $1.7 million.[215]

Direct Mail

Buchanan's main source of fund raising was direct mail solicitation. David Tyson, a direct mail expert, commented, "This is the most successful direct mail effort in the history of conservative politics."[216] Buchanan or his sister wrote the letters, and the direct mail consulting firm of Bruce W. Eberle & Associates handled the logistics. Eberle & Associates did fund raising for Senator Jesse Helms in the 1984 and 1990 elections, among others. Buchanan rejected traditional direct mail techniques and refused professional advice. The emphasis was on the message.

Buchanan sent out the first direct mail appeal at the end of December. His goal was to have $1 million to $2 million for the New Hampshire primary. He thought it was a tough time to raise money, considering the Christmas holiday and the recession, and said, "We started early enough to make the case, but we didn't start early enough to raise money."[217]

The first mailing of 74,700 letters to people on Buchanan's newsletter subscriber list plus similar bases brought in $693,767, an incredible return for a net of nearly $600,000. Many of these donations would also qualify for matching funds. The response rate was 13.8 percent with an average contribution of nearly $62, compared with typical response rates of less than 3 percent with contributions averaging $20. Scott B. Mackenzie, Buchanan's campaign manager, reported in early January in filings for federal matching funds that more than $500,000 had been raised by direct mail and another $150,000 in "high-dollar" amounts (from $200 to $1,000).[218] In a January 31, 1992, FEC filing, Buchanan stated that the campaign had raised $1.7 million, about $700,000 in contributions of $200 or less.

On February 17, 1992, direct mail solicitations went out to 40,000 supporters and officials, which the campaign hoped would bring in $250,000. Two more mailings to 300,000 people were sent out in late February.

Mailing lists from conservative groups were rented. As a conservative, Buchanan had access to extensive mailing lists compiled by direct mail specialists such as Richard Viguerie. Conservatives had considerable experience in direct mail solicitation. A small profit was even made on "prospecting," that is, sending letters to people who have not previously contributed, which is usually a money-loser. Buchanan had success with virtually any prospect list mailed: national defense causes, religious groups, hard money advocacy, anti-drug campaigns, Catholics, evangelicals, magazine subscribers, book buyers, former Kemp, Dole, and Bush contributors, even a 1988 Bush for President list. Tyson said that profits were made using lists from such groups as Citizens for Bush and Americans for Bush, two independent expenditure groups established to raise and spend money to support Bush in 1988. Croatian-Americans donated $100,000 to $150,000 to Buchanan, much unsolicited, because they liked his views on recognizing an independent Croatia.[219]

The costs of direct mail fund raising are high and profits often are not generated until a list of actual contributors, who can be tapped for money repeatedly, is developed. By the end of February, barely six weeks into the fund-raising drive, nearly 64,000 donations were received from a mailing of less than 2 million people, and the donations were still coming in. In requesting matching funds, Buchanan's accountants reported receiving $1.1 million in donations of $250 or less between February 1 and 27. Matching funds are available for donations of $250 or less.[220]

Buchanan's appeal consisted of two long letters explaining his reasons for seeking the presidency and several follow-up letters, including one right after the New Hampshire primary, saying that he desperately needed more money to compete with Bush's threatened negative ads. The letters criticized Bush and accused him of betraying the Reagan revolution. They mentioned Bush's reversal of his "no new taxes" pledge, his continuing support for the National Endowment for the Arts, and his commitment to foreign aid, all issues that have angered conservative Republicans. These letters not only raised money but also helped stir up anti-Bush sentiment among the millions of conservative Republicans receiving them.

Buchanan officials said that 80 percent of their money came from mail solicitation. At the end of February, 50,000 people had contributed, with an average donation of $48. Approximately $2.5 million was raised by mid-February and $145,000 was received the day of the New Hampshire primary. With his strong showing in New Hampshire, Buchanan had the momentum to continue successful fund raising. Close to another $1 million was raised by the time of the Georgia primary on March 3. Compared with Bush, who had raised $2.7 million in December and had begun 1992 with $7 million in cash on hand and an organization that ran two previous presidential campaigns, Buchanan still trailed far behind.[221] The campaign received $1.1 million in federal matching funds in early March, but the campaign had borrowed $750,000 against this income. Even after taking a beating in the southern primaries, the repeat appeals to contributors continued to bring in more than $6 for every name mailed.[222] By the end of May, Buchanan had raised more than $4 million from his direct mail effort and had qualified more than 85 percent of these donations for matching funds.[223]

New Hampshire

Buchanan spent a huge amount of time and resources on his New Hampshire campaign. He spent forty-five days campaigning in the state, and had been organizing there for ten weeks. In early February, Buchanan's campaign bought twenty-five to thirty commercial spots a day on the state's leading station as well as substantial numbers of spots on Boston outlets. Approximately $1.7 million was spent on television advertising alone, with $2 million expended overall.[224] Bush is estimated to have spent less on TV advertising in New Hampshire than Buchanan, but he started campaigning later.

Buchanan waged a vicious campaign against the president and found a supportive audience. New Hampshire had experienced severe economic hardships as a result of the recession. Many voters thought that Bush had ignored New Hampshire after the state had given him his first victory in 1988, propelling his presidential campaign. Buchanan began the campaign by blasting Bush and touting his "America First" theme. As the campaign progressed, he toned down his barrages and stressed his compassion for those hurt by the recession. His caustic anti-Bush remarks were replaced by his own ideas for improving the economy.[225]

Buchanan received 37 percent of the vote, showing significant strength against the president, who received 53 percent. This strong showing conferred legitimacy to his campaign and fueled his fund-raising effort, which was now in need of replenishment. He had less than $200,000 cash on hand.

Early Primaries and Super Tuesday

Buchanan's fund raising surged after New Hampshire, bringing in $600,000 in receipts, but the response was less than campaign officials expected.[226] Buchanan was unable to finance a major campaign in all the southern states and so focused on Georgia as the best chance to inflict a humiliating defeat on the president. Bush loyalists were scarce in Georgia, and the Republican establishment was somewhat divided.

Two new television ads were targeted at the state. One emphasized the "America First" campaign theme and another "more negative" ad attacked Bush for "flip-flopping" on the tax increase and on hiring-quota issues.[227]

Buchanan also ran an ad accusing Bush of financing pornography through the National Endowment for the Arts.[228] According to Bill Thorne, Bush's Georgia campaign head, Buchanan put more ads on TV than any presidential primary candidate.[229] Buchanan spent $206,885 on TV spots in the Atlanta area, compared with $121,727 for Bush. Buchanan outspent Bush on advertising nearly 2 to 1 in Georgia, $400,000 to Bush's $216,000.

Buchanan tried to appeal to white conservatives in both parties, as the state has an open primary. He encouraged the protest vote in his advertising.[230] Buchanan did well again, receiving 36 percent of the vote to Bush's 64 percent.[231]

The Louisiana GOP chairman endorsed Buchanan over Bush, saying that Buchanan represents "the true conservative legacy of Ronald Reagan."[232] Buchanan spent considerable time and money on radio and TV in South Carolina.[233] Buchanan won 30 percent or more in four primaries, but to remain a realistic, formidable candidate, he needed to win in one state.

North Carolina, California, and Beyond

Buchanan later scaled back his efforts and concentrated on North Carolina and California. He stopped attacking Bush on his record as president and articulated his own vision for America. Buchanan said he did not want to do anything that would permanently wound Bush in the general election and did not want to be seen as a spoiler for Bush, which would perhaps stain his own reputation for a possible 1996 campaign. He was concerned about whether his campaign funds were sufficient to stay in the race, especially since he was no longer considered a serious challenger. Buchanan had raised $400,000 in early March, but $380,000 of that was from two direct mail solicitations that had gone out four to five weeks earlier, when he seemed to have a serious shot at the nomination after the strong New Hampshire showing. He hoped that North Carolina voters who had been affected by the imports of foreign textiles might be attracted to his protectionist views. While in North Carolina, Buchanan called for the repeal of the Voting Rights Act.[234] But Senator Jesse Helms supported Bush, which eroded Buchanan's strength in the state. The North Carolina campaign ran on a low budget and consisted of many small-town newspaper visits and radio interviews. Buchanan did not buy any TV commercials.[235]

Buchanan said he would not drop out of the race even if it became clear that he could not win the nomination. He cited other objectives for continuing the campaign, such as bringing the party to its conservative base. Buchanan even rejected Richard Nixon's advice to exit the race. He said he wanted to win back the heart and soul of the Republican Party. Buchanan felt his presence in the race had forced Bush to concede some positions to the conservative movement, such as Bush admitting he made a mistake when he accepted a 1990 budget agreement that raised taxes and forced out the director of the National Endowment for the Arts.[236]

Buchanan also said he wanted to stay in the race to give California conservatives an opportunity to express their frustration with a president and governor who had walked away from conservative principles, referring to Governor Pete Wilson, a moderate Republican and chair of Bush's re-election efforts in California.[237] Buchanan also hoped to take advantage of conservative interest in the two hotly contested Senate races, which pitted conservatives against moderates.[238]

Buchanan also directed his remarks at Congress, castigating it for its privileges, the House Bank affair, and what he characterized as its hypocrisy. Buchanan visited Wisconsin and Minnesota, which held primaries on April 7. He did not qualify for New York's primary on April 7.[239]

An additional incentive for staying in the race was that Buchanan would collect the names of California's conservative donors.[240] Throughout his campaign, the direct mail fund-raising effort produced a list of approximately 250,000 contributors.[241] Buchanan could use these lists, which consisted of 165,000 individual contributors, to start a conservative organization or expand his newsletter publishing business. He also could use these lists to distribute a platform for 1996.

It is uncertain to what extent the votes he received were an endorsement of Buchanan for president or were protest votes against Bush. In the South Dakota primary on February 29, where Buchanan was unable to get on the ballot, 31 percent of the Republican vote went to an uncommitted slate. This may suggest that any alternative candidate to Bush would have received this support.[242]

Buchanan vowed to take his disagreements with Bush's policies to the Republican convention and warned that it would be a terrible mistake to deny him the podium.[243] Bush must have taken Buchanan's influence seriously, for Buchanan was invited to give a major address at the convention; he helped set the tone for a convention later thought by many to have hurt Bush's chances for reelection.

Buchanan spent nearly $12.5 million in his bid for the nomination. He received $5.2 million in federal matching funds, with 165,744 contributors and an average contribution of $33. PACs and other committees contributed only $24,750. Buchanan did not have any significant support or opposition through independent expenditures or communication costs. While Buchanan did not win a single primary, he received a total of 2.6 million votes. The campaign, therefore, spent approximately $4.75 for every vote received.

Notes

1. Robert Shogan, "Clinton Enters Race, Urges Citizens to Do More for U.S.," *Los Angeles Times,* October 4, 1991.

2. Robin Toner, "Arkansas' Clinton Enters the '92 Race for President," *New York Times,* October 4, 1991.

3. "Clinton's Campaign Signs on Strategists Who Aided Wofford," *New York Times,* December 3, 1991.

4. "People: Clinton Clan," *National Journal,* December 14, 1991, p. 3043.

5. Ronald Brownstein, "Clinton Opposes Thomas, Backs Gay Rights Bill," *Los Angeles Times,* October 15, 1991.

6. Jack W. Germond and Jules Witcover, "Clinton Is Riding a Strong Message," *National Journal,* November 11, 1991, p. 2934.

7. Dave Lesher, "Invitation to Clinton Raises Hint of Mutiny Among GOP Donors," *Los Angeles Times,* December 4, 1991.

8. Liz Smith, "Most Did Help Gloria's *Ms.,*" *Los Angeles Times,* December 17, 1991.

9. Richard L. Berke, "Florida Democrats Give Victory in Poll to Clinton," *New York Times,* December 16, 1991.

10. Dan Balz and E.J. Dionne Jr., "Gathering Momentum, Money and Media Scrutiny," *Washington Post National Weekly Edition,* January 20–26, 1992, p. 12.

11. Gwen Ifill, "Trying to Deliver a Mainstream Message with a Southern Accent," *New York Times,* December 27, 1991.

12. Balz and Dionne, "Gathering Momentum, Money and Media Scrutiny," p. 12.

13. Gwen Ifill, "Clinton Seizes on Asia Trip to Depict Bush as Beatable," *New York Times,* January 15, 1992.

14. Ronald Brownstein, "Harkin's Failure to Gain Early Labor Support Boosts Clinton Campaign," *Los Angeles Times,* January 16, 1992.

15. R.W. Apple Jr., "Clinton the Front-Runner is Also the Prey as Primary Nears," *New York Times,* February 8, 1992.

16. Jeff Gerth, "Wealthy Investment Family a Big Help to Clinton," *New York Times,* February 8, 1992.

17. Neil A. Lewis, "Being Governor Helps Clinton Raise Money at Home," *New York Times,* April 27, 1992.

18. Gwen Ifill, "Clinton Defends His Character to Supporters," *New York Times,* April 21, 1992.

19. Gebe Martinez, "Clinton Visits GOP Stronghold," *Los Angeles Times,* January 15, 1992.

20. Neil A. Lewis, "In Money Race, Clinton Leading the Democrats," *New York Times,* February 1, 1992; and Ronald Brownstein, "Fund Raising for Clinton Holds Steady," *Los Angeles Times,* February 1, 1992.

21. Gwen Ifill, "Clinton Moves on 2 Fronts to Widen Support in South," *New York Times,* January 22, 1992.

22. Elaine Ciulla Kamarck, "Front-Runner Mantle May Be Clinton's Curse," *Los Angeles Times,* February 7, 1992.

23. John J. Goldman, "Clinton Apologizes for Remarks About Cuomo," *Los Angeles Times,* January 29, 1992.

24. David Lauter, "Clinton Takes the Offensive to Battle Adultery Rumors," *Los Angeles Times,* January 25, 1992.

25. Gwen Ifill, "Clinton, Cheered by New Polls, Again Assails Bush on Economy," *New York Times,* January 29, 1992.

26. Robin Toner, "Democrats, Anxiously or Eagerly, Gauge Clinton's Political Health," *New York Times,* January 31, 1992.

27. Robert Shogan, "Clinton Keeps Bid Afloat, but Polls Show Voters Wary," *Los Angeles Times,* January 31, 1992.

28. Gwen Ifill, "Clinton Thanked Colonel in '69 for 'Saving Me From the Draft,'" *New York Times,* February 13, 1992.

29. David Lauter, "Clinton Steps Up Pace in N.H. Primary Contest," *Los Angeles Times,* February 15, 1992.

30. David Lauter, "Clinton Dodges a Bullet, Looks to South," *Los Angeles Times,* February 19, 1992.

31. L.J. Davis, "The Name of Rose," *The New Republic,* April 4, 1994, p. 23.

32. "Presidential Slush Money," *Political Finance & Lobby Reporter,* March 23, 1994, p. 8.

33. "Clinton Holds Fund-Raising Lead," *Los Angeles Times,* March 4, 1992.

34. Ronald Brownstein, "Victory in Georgia Contest Viewed as Crucial to Clinton's Campaign," *Los Angeles Times,* February 21, 1992.

35. "Clinton Campaign Running $1.8 Million in the Red," *Los Angeles Times,* March 21, 1992.

36. Elizabeth Kolbert, "Clinton-Tsongas Ads Provide a Little Drama in Florida Race," *New York Times,* March 9, 1992.

37. Geraldine Baum, "Clinton's Big-Money Machine," *Los Angeles Times,* March 17, 1992.

38. Cathleen Decker, "Clinton Campaign Ignores Brown," *Los Angeles Times,* April 25, 1992.

39. "Squeezing Stones," *Newsweek,* April 27, 1992, p. 3.

40. Carol Matlack, "Clinton's Fund Raising Falling Short," *National Journal,* May 30, 1992, p. 1298.

41. Stephen Labaton, "Clinton, Lagging in the Polls, Also Faces a Cash Shortage," *New York Times,* June 13, 1992.

42. Gwen Ifill, "Clinton Discusses Policy, Not Perot, in TV Forum," *New York Times,* June 13, 1992.

43. Quoted in Edwin Chen, "Clinton Faces Voters on Own TV Talk Show," *Los Angeles Times,* June 13, 1992.

44. Ibid.

45. Quoted in "GOP Charges Clinton Campaign Wrongly Used Funds for TV Pitch," *Los Angeles Times,* June 20, 1992.

46. "Clinton to Return Money Raised in TV Forum," *New York Times,* June 21, 1992.

47. Beth Donovan, "Gay Activists' Cash, Votes Ride on Ban Decision," *Congressional Quarterly Weekly Report,* July 10, 1993, pp. 1814–16.

48. Bill Clinton and Al Gore, *Putting People First* (New York: Times Books, 1992), p. 64.

49. Donovan, "Gay Activists' Cash," p. 1815.

50. Michael Kelly, "New President Brings Opportunity to Cash In," *New York Times,* January 18, 1993.

51. Jacob Weisberg, "Clincest," *The New Republic,* April 26, 1993, pp. 22–27.

52. CRF analysis, based on data provided by the FEC. To compare with 1988, see Herbert E. Alexander and Monica Bauer, *Financing the 1988 Election* (Boulder, CO: Westview Press, 1991), pp. 105–7.

53. Cathleen Decker, "Tsongas Makes Campaign Stop Minus Glitz," *Los Angeles Times,* May 3, 1991.

54. Jon Keller, "Tsnooze," *The New Republic,* August 12, 1991, p. 16.

55. Rhodes Cook, "First Out of the Democratic Chute, Tsongas Remains Dark Horse," *Congressional Quarterly Weekly Review,* November 2, 1991, pp. 3219–24.

56. "In Brief: Tsongas Forgoes PAC Money in Presidential Bid," *Campaign Practices Reports,* June 24, 1991, p. 8.

57. Keller, "Tsnooze."

58. Martin Tolchin, "Tsongas's Life, and Finances, Changed Course When Illness Struck," *New York Times,* February 1, 1992.

59. Ibid.

60. Cook, "First Out of the Democratic Chute."

61. Paul Richter, "Tsongas Showing Signs of Winning Over N.H. Voters," *Los Angeles Times,* February 4, 1992.

62. Karen DeWitt, "Tsongas Pitches Economic Austerity, Mixed With Patriotism," *New York Times,* January 1, 1991.

63. Richter, "Tsongas Showing Signs of Winning Over N.H. Voters."

64. FEC, "Tsongas Declared Eligible by FEC," press release, November 20, 1991.

65. Richter, "Tsongas Showing Signs of Winning Over N.H. Voters."

66. DeWitt, "Tsongas Pitches Economic Austerity."

67. Maureen Dowd, "Wall Street Has a Rally, for Tsongas," *New York Times,* March 4, 1992.

68. Maura Keefe, "Solid Direct Mail Base Nearly Resurrected Tsongas Campaign," *Campaign,* May 1992, pp. 23–25.

69. James A. Barnes, "Misreading Tsongas," *National Journal,* January 11, 1992, p. 84.

70. DeWitt, "Tsongas Pitches Economic Austerity."

71. Keefe, "Solid Direct Mail Base."

72. Maureen Dowd, "Can Morality Be a Campaign Issue? Tsongas Denies Trying to Make It One," *New York Times,* February 1, 1992.

73. Elizabeth Kolbert, "Tsongas to 'Fight Back' with TV Ads," *New York Times,* March 6, 1992.

74. Elizabeth Kolbert, "Negative Tsongas Ads Become Fatal Media Error," *New York Times,* March 20, 1992.

75. Robin Toner, "Tsongas Abandons Campaign," *New York Times,* March 20, 1992.

76. B. Drummond Ayres Jr., "Tsongas Declares He Won't Re-enter Democratic Race," *New York Times,* April 10, 1992.

77. Editorial, "Tsongas's Money Ceiling," *Wall Street Journal,* March 23, 1992.

78. Ayres, "Tsongas Declares He Won't Re-enter Democratic Race."

79. Keefe, "Solid Direct Mail Base."

80. "Tsongas's Money Ceiling."

81. "Grand Jury Adds Charges to Tsongas Fundraiser," *Political Finance & Lobby Reporter,* October 27, 1993.

82. Fox Butterfield, "Tsongas Fund-Raiser Indicted in Campaign Fraud," *New York Times,* February 23, 1993.

83. "Ex-Aide to Tsongas Indicted Again," *Washington Post,* June 5, 1993.

84. "Below the Beltway: Tsongas' Fundraiser Pleads," *Political Finance & Lobby Reporter,* October 27, 1993; also see Butterfield, "Tsongas Fund-Raiser Indicted in Campaign Fraud"; and "Grand Jury Probing Loans Linked to Tsongas Associate," *Los Angeles Times,* February 7, 1993.

85. "Tsongas Donor Charged With Concealing Gifts," *Political Finance and Lobby Reporter,* September 14, 1994, p. 4.

86. Robin Toner, "Nebraska Senator Enters the 1992 Race," *New York Times,* October 1, 1992.

87. Charles Krauthammer, "A Democrat Who Bears Watching," *Washington Post,* November 15, 1991; and David Nyhan, "A Democratic Candidate for the New Generation," *Boston Globe,* October 1, 1991.

88. Toner, "Nebraska Senator Enters the 1992 Race."

89. Peter Maas, "I Have Carried with Me a Promise," *Washington Post Magazine,* December 15, 1991, p. 5.

90. Jack W. Germond and Jules Witcover, *Mad as Hell: Revolt at the Ballot Box, 1992* (New York: Warner Books, 1993), p. 94.

91. Tad Devine, Kerrey's campaign manager, described this fund-raising effort as "something that's never happened before" in Charles T. Royer, ed., *Campaign for President: The Managers Look at '92* (Hollis, NH: Hollis Publishing, 1994), p. 9.

92. Germond and Witcover, *Mad as Hell,* p. 96.

93. Royer, *Campaign for President,* p. 9.

94. Joe Brennan, "Kerrey Hits Funds Goal," *Omaha World-Herald,* December 26, 1991. This article also notes that Kerrey's home state fund-raising effort compared favorably to similar efforts by candidates in the 1988 campaign. For example, in 1988 Gephardt raised $1.3 million in Missouri over a twenty-month period, and Gore raised $1.3 million in Tennessee over a thirteen-month period. Nebraska's population, however, is only about 1.6 million, compared with about 5 million for these other states. See also Jeff Gauger, "Nebraska Leads the Way for Kerrey," *Omaha World-Herald,* January 28, 1992.

95. Richard L. Berke, "Kerrey Retells War Story in Effort to Connect with the Voters," *New York Times,* December 31, 1991.

96. Barbara Kemick, "Fund Raising This Year Takes Extra Work," *Omaha World-Herald,* January 28, 1992.

97. Ibid.; and Germond and Witcover, *Mad as Hell,* pp. 104–5.

98. Devine in Royer, *Campaign for President,* p. 9.

99. Gwen Ifill, "A Candidate's Joke Recorded at Rally, Is Bringing Criticism," *New York Times,* November 20, 1991.

100. Peter T. Kilborn, "Kerrey Concern Violates Laws on Child Labor," *New York Times,* December 18, 1991; and "Kerrey Chain Broke Youth Labor Laws, U.S. Says," *Boston Globe,* December 18, 1991.

101. Devine in Royer, *Campaign for President,* p. 9; and Berke, "Kerrey Retells War Story."

102. Robert Pear, "Kerrey's Companies Provide Few With Medical Coverage," *New York Times,* December 28, 1991.

103. "Chipping at Kerrey Cornerstone," *Washington Post,* December 29, 1991; and Berke, "Kerrey Retells War Story."

104. Germond and Witcover, *Mad as Hell,* p. 104.

105. Ibid., p. 102.

106. Devine in Royer, *Campaign for President,* p. 10.

107. A copy of this analysis was provided by the Kerrey campaign to Anthony Corrado.

108. Berke, "Kerrey Retells War Story."

109. Devine in Royer, *Campaign for President,* p. 10.

110. See, for example, Paul A. Gigot, "In New Hampshire Protectionists Slip on the Ice," *Wall Street Journal,* February 7, 1992; and David S. Broder, "Campaign Spotlights Trade Debate," *Washington Post,* January 19, 1992.

111. "Kerrey on Ice," *Wall Street Journal,* January 17, 1992; Peter S. Canellos, "Kerrey, NH Campaign Manager Show Downbeat Side," *Boston Globe,* February 4,

1992; and Howard Fineman, "Kerrey Reflects: 'The Tunnel of Unlove,'" *Newsweek*, February 10, 1992, p. 29.

112. Devine in Royer, *Campaign for President*, p. 10.

113. Canellos, "Kerrey, N.H. Campaign Manager"; and Curtis Wilkie, "Kerrey Revamps Lineup, Message," *Boston Globe*, January 24, 1992.

114. This figure includes time purchased on stations in Boston, Massachusetts; Portland, Maine; and Burlington, Vermont. Only a portion of the funds spent in these markets was allocable to the New Hampshire spending limit under FEC guidelines. For example, of the approximately $1.2 million spent on New Hampshire media, about $668,000 was associated with ads aired on Boston stations; only about 16 percent of this amount was allocable to New Hampshire since only 16 percent of the Boston market represents New Hampshire viewers. Similarly, Kerrey spent $79,000 on television in the Portland market but only 13 percent was allocated to New Hampshire; and $48,000 spent in the Burlington market, of which only 10 percent was allocated to New Hampshire.

115. Renee Loth, "Political Advertising for Success: What Experts Say," *Boston Globe*, February 22, 1992. Also see L. Patrick Devlin, "Television Advertising in the 1992 New Hampshire Presidential Primary Election," *Political Communication* 11 (1994), pp. 81–99.

116. Devine in Royer, *Campaign for President*, p. 11.

117. Peter S. Canellos, "Medium Distorted His Message," *Boston Globe*, March 6, 1992.

118. Alessandra Stanley, "Kerrey Decides to Withdraw After Poor Showing in West," *New York Times*, March 5, 1992.

119. When Bush did raise this issue at the outset of the general election, Kerrey used the occasion to launch a sharp attack on Bush for "trying to find a winning issue" because his economic policies and cold war approach to foreign policy had failed. See Senator Bob Kerrey, "George Bush and the War in Vietnam," press release, Kerrey for President Committee, September 10, 1992.

120. Alessandra Stanley, "Short on Money, Kerrey Quits Race," *New York Times*, March 6, 1992.

121. These figures are based on disclosure reports of the Kerrey for President Committee filed with the FEC.

122. Paul Goodsell, "Kerrey Settles Campaign Debts For About 62 Cents on Dollar," *Omaha World-Herald*, February 7, 1993.

123. Dan Balz, "Tom Harkin: A Democrat and Proud of It," *Washington Post National Weekly Edition*, July 1–7, 1991, p. 14.

124. Eleanor Clift and John McCormick, "Liberal and Proud of It: Iowa's 'Prairie Populist,'" *Newsweek*, August 26, 1991, p. 22.

125. Rhodes Cook, "American Dream Personified, Harkin Hits Populist Trail," *Congressional Quarterly Weekly Report*, December 7, 1991, pp. 3607–13.

126. Elizabeth Kolbert, "Harkin Seeks to Recall Democrats' History, Though Some Fear It," *New York Times*, December 26, 1991.

127. Ibid.

128. Ibid.

129. Ibid.

130. Richard L. Berke, "Harkin, in Iowa, Urges Support in Caucus Vote," *New York Times*, February 9, 1992.

131. Beth Donovan, "Harkin Signs Out of Race," *Congressional Quarterly Weekly Report*, March 14, 1992, p. 633.

132. Sam Fulwood III, "Harkin Withdraws From Democratic Presidential Race," *Los Angeles Times*, March 10, 1992.

133. "California's Brown to Seek Presidency," *Congressional Quarterly Weekly Report*, September 7, 1991, p. 2575.

134. Ronald Brownstein, "Brown Delivers a Fiery Speech to Union," *Los Angeles Times*, September 3, 1991.

135. Larry Liebert, "Washington Perspective: Jerry Brown Redux," *California Journal*, May 1992, p. 484.

136. "Below the Beltway: The Chameleon Candidate," *PACs & Lobbies*, October 2, 1991, p. 10.

137. Rhodes Cook, "Jerry Brown Makes Third Bid, Decries Political Corruption," *Congressional Quarterly Weekly Report*, October 26, 1991, p. 3148.

138. B. Drummond Ayres Jr., "Brown Hopes One-Note Campaign Strikes a Responsive Chord," *New York Times*, December 28, 1991.

139. Christopher Matthews, "Brown Wasn't Polite—But He Was Right," *Los Angeles Times*, December 19, 1991.

140. B. Drummond Ayres Jr., "Brown Avoids Doing the Expected, Even with His Own Money," *New York Times*, January 31, 1992.

141. Ronald Brownstein, "Brown Draws Big Crowds, Little Support," *Los Angeles Times*, February 28, 1992.

142. Ronald Brownstein, "Brown Presses His 'Guerrilla' Approach," *Los Angeles Times*, February 8, 1992.

143. Ibid.

144. Karen DeWitt, "The Ad Campaign—Brown: Capitalizing on 'Outsider' Role," *New York Times*, February 12, 1992.

145. Brownstein, "Brown Draws Big Crowds."

146. Alan C. Miller, "Colorado Gives Brown Firmer Footing," *Los Angeles Times*, March 4, 1992.

147. Robert Reinhold, "No Longer Target of Jokes, Brown Becomes a Force," *New York Times*, March 9, 1992.

148. Alan C. Miller, "Brown Outsider Theme Attracts New Attention," *Los Angeles Times*, March 6, 1992.

149. Patt Morrison, "Brown an Enigmatic Insurgent," *Los Angeles Times*, March 22, 1992.

150. R. W. Apple Jr., "Brown's Big Gamble: Risking Ridicule for a Victory in Michigan," *New York Times*, March 17, 1992.

151. Kenneth Reich, "A Sure Winner: Brown 800-Line Funding Idea," *Los Angeles Times*, April 4, 1992.

152. Jordan Bonfante, "1-800-Pound Guerrillas," *Time*, April 6, 1992, pp. 17–19.

153. George Skelton, "The Brown Bid Seems More an Adventure than a Plan," *Los Angeles Times*, March 30, 1992.

154. Robert Shogan, "Brown Captures Connecticut Race in Stunning Upset," *Los Angeles Times*, March 25, 1992.

155. Richard L. Berke, "Insider, Outsider, Brown Runs on Contradictions," *New York Times*, April 3, 1992.

156. Reich, "A Sure Winner."

157. Robert Guskind, "Feeding on the Roars," *National Journal*, May 2, 1992, pp. 1053–56.

158. Sidney Blumenthal, "Brownian Motion," *The New Republic*, March 2, 1992, pp. 18–20.

159. Jonathan Alter, "Jerry's Date With History," *Newsweek*, April 13, 1992, p. 31.

160. "Donors Keep Dialing Dollars to Jerry Brown's Presidential Campaign," *PACs & Lobbies*, April 15, 1992, p. 7.

161. Michael Ross, "Brown Campaign Is Ending as It Began—in Obscurity," *Los Angeles Times*, May 11, 1992.

162. "Brown Tops Matching Funds List," *New York Times*, May 20, 1992.

163. "Brown Lists His Conditions for Backing Party Nominee," *Los Angeles Times*, April 13, 1992.

164. "Brown Campaign Trailblazes Use of New Age TV," *Los Angeles Times*, April 4, 1992.

165. Quoted in B. Drummond Ayres Jr., "Wilder's Flier," *New York Times Magazine*, January 12, 1992, p. 31.

166. James A. Barnes, "Wilder: Is It Yes or No?" *National Journal*, August 17, 1991, p. 2037.

167. Rhodes Cook, "Wilder Campaigns on Message of Fiscal Responsibility," *Congressional Quarterly Weekly Report*, November 16, 1991, p. 3405.

168. "In Brief: Wilder Still Keeps Inaugural Fund Secret," *Campaign Practices Reports*, June 24, 1991, p. 8.

169. Sam Fulwood III, "Wilder Shifts Campaign's Focus to Woo Black Voters," *Los Angeles Times*, December 26, 1991.

170. Sam Fulwood III, "Jackson Hurting Campaign Effort, Wilder Aides Say," *Los Angeles Times*, January 8, 1992.

171. See Alexander and Bauer, *Financing the 1988 Election*, pp. 75–80, 86–88.

172. Maureen Dowd, "Not on the Ballot This Election, But on the Line Nonetheless," *New York Times*, November 7, 1990.

173. David Lauter, "White House Will Not Reveal Portion of Bush's Political Travel Paid for by GOP," *Los Angeles Times*, April 27, 1991.

174. Ann Devroy and Dan Balz, "An Unofficial Announcement," *Washington Post National Weekly Edition*, February 11–17, 1991, p. 13.

175. *National Journal*, May 25, 1991, p. 1247.

176. Guy Gugliotta and Ann Devroy, "Off and Not Running, Bush Schedules 2 More Fund-Raisers," *Washington Post*, October 29, 1991.

177. For information on the tax checkoff funds, see chapter 1, pp. 10–14.

178. Ibid.

179. Ibid.

180. Carol Matlack, "Money Rolls In for Bush," *National Journal*, May 23, 1992, p. 1244.

181. Andrew Rosenthal, "Bush Names New Staff Chief and Campaign Team," *New York Times*, December 6, 1991.

182. "Financing for a Bush Speech Is Attacked," *New York Times*, October 4, 1991.

183. Michael Parrish, "Has Bush Taken the Right People to Asia?" *Los Angeles Times*, January 1, 1992.

184. Richard L. Berke, "Fitzwater on Donations: No to Arm-Twisting, Yes to Elbow-Rubbing," *New York Times*, April 24, 1992.

185. "Ex-Florida Gov. Uses White House Office to Raise Bush Campaign Funds," *PACs & Lobbies*, January 15, 1992, p. 8.

186. "No Bureaucrat Bucks for Bush," *PACs & Lobbies*, January 1, 1992, p. 8.

187. *Hatch Act Reform Amendments of 1993* (Public Law 103–94), *U.S. Statutes at Large* 107 (1993): 1001.

188. R.W. Apple Jr., "Bush Forces Plan to Unveil Big One: Don't Waste Vote," *New York Times*, January 26, 1992.

189. R.W. Apple Jr., "After Bad Start, Bush Seems to Have Steadied Support," *New York Times,* February 5, 1992.

190. R.W. Apple Jr., "Bush Supporters Try to Figure Out How Their Campaign Went Wrong," *New York Times,* February 20, 1992.

191. For an in-depth article on advertising content of all the candidates, see Thomas R. Rosenstiel and James Gerstenzang, "New Bush Ad Spotlights Foreign Policy," *Los Angeles Times,* February 8, 1992.

192. R.W. Apple Jr., "Bush, Slipping in New Hampshire, Aiming for 'Home Run' on Visit," *New York Times,* February 15, 1992.

193. Andrew Rosenthal, "Bush Readies Against Buchanan," *New York Times,* February 12, 1992.

194. Apple, "Bush, Slipping in New Hampshire."

195. Robin Toner, "Bush Urges Georgia to Reject Buchanan Appeal," *New York Times,* March 2, 1992.

196. Sonni Efron, "South Carolina Battle Puts Bush, Governor on Spot," *Los Angeles Times,* March 2, 1992.

197. Apple, "Bush Slipping in New Hampshire."

198. Apple, "After Bad Start."

199. George Skelton, "Wilson Tells Bush Campaign to Have President Visit More," *Los Angeles Times,* February 2, 1992.

200. Michael Wines, "Bush Goes West, Pursued by Doubts Over Message," *New York Times,* February 26, 1992.

201. James A. Barnes, "Seasoned to Perfection?" *National Journal,* May 23, 1992, p. 1229.

202. Carol Matlack, "Money Rolls In for Bush," *National Journal,* May 23, 1992, p. 1244.

203. "Slower Bucks for Bush," *National Journal,* January 18, 1992, p. 113.

204. FEC, Communication Cost Index by Communication Filers, as of July 10, 1993.

205. Robin Toner, "Buchanan, Urging New Nationalism, Joins '92 Race," *New York Times,* December 11, 1991.

206. Peter Applebome, "Duke's Followers Lean to Buchanan," *New York Times,* March 8, 1992.

207. Steven A. Holmes, "As Buchanan Runs, the Right Fragments," *New York Times,* February 4, 1992. See also Lally Weymouth, "Buchanan's Right Hook to Bush," *Washington Post National Weekly Edition,* December 30, 1991–January 5, 1992, p. 23.

208. "Buchanan Balks at Disclosure," *PACs & Lobbies,* April 1, 1992, p. 10.

209. Steven A. Holmes, "Buchanan Income Is Put at $809,975," *New York Times,* April 2, 1992.

210. Toner, "Buchanan, Urging New Nationalism."

211. Cathleen Decker, "Buchanan Uses Whatever It Takes in Long-shot Bid," *Los Angeles Times,* December 11, 1991.

212. Steven A. Holmes, "For Buchanan's Campaign, Improvising Is the Strategy," *New York Times,* February 17, 1992.

213. David Beiler, "Is Roger Good For What Ailes Bush?" *Campaign,* March 1992, p. 8.

214. "Buchanan Fails in Bid for New York Ballot," *New York Times,* February 8, 1992.

215. Steven A. Holmes, "For Buchanan Aide, Genetic Conservatism," *New York Times,* February 9, 1992.

216. Sara Fritz, "Buchanan's Direct Mail Drive Delivers Substantial Dividends," *Los Angeles Times,* March 7, 1992.

217. Weymouth, "Buchanan's Right Hook to Bush."

218. Jack W. Germond and Jules Witcover, "Buchanan in Race for Long Haul?" *National Journal*, January 11, 1992, p. 92.

219. See Steven A. Holmes, "The Checks Are in the Mail, and Made Out to Buchanan," *New York Times*, February 24, 1992.

220. Fritz, "Buchanan's Direct Mail Drive."

221. Rhodes Cook, "Conservative Tilt," *Congressional Quarterly Weekly Report*, February 15, 1992, p. 368.

222. Bruce Eberle, "Buck Breaks the Bank," *Campaign*, May 1992, p. 20.

223. Carol Matlack, "Buchanan's Lucrative Mailing List," *National Journal*, April 4, 1992, p. 817.

224. R.W. Apple Jr., "Bush, Slipping in New Hampshire." Buchanan's FEC filings show $456,865 spent in New Hampshire, which had a state expenditure limit of $522,400.

225. Cathleen Decker and James Gerstenzang, "Bush-Buchanan Primary Race Takes on Air of Civility," *Los Angeles Times*, February 11, 1992. See also, Steven A. Holmes, "As a Candidate, Buchanan Shows Compassionate Side," *New York Times*, February 15, 1992.

226. Notes from a conversation between Scott MacKenzie, Buchanan's campaign treasurer, and Herbert E. Alexander, May 15, 1992.

227. Michael Ross, "Bush Assailed by Buchanan over Quotes," *Los Angeles Times*, February 22, 1992.

228. Robin Toner, "Bush Urges Georgia to Reject Buchanan Appeal," *New York Times*, March 2, 1992.

229. Sonni Efron, "South Carolina Battle Puts Bush, Governor on Spot," *Los Angeles Times*, March 5, 1992.

230. Michael Ross, "Buchanan Stumps Hard in Georgia, Invests in TV Ads," *Los Angeles Times*, March 2, 1992.

231. Efron, "South Carolina Battle."

232. "Louisiana G.O.P. Chairman Picks Buchanan Over Bush," *New York Times*, February 27, 1992.

233. Efron, "South Carolina Battle."

234. William J. Eaton, "Buchanan Calls for Repeal of Voting Rights Act," *Los Angeles Times*, April 29, 1992.

235. William J. Eaton, "North Carolina Tough Going for Buchanan," *Los Angeles Times*, May 3, 1992.

236. "Buchanan Declines Nixon's Exit Advice," *Los Angeles Times*, March 22, 1992.

237. Steven A. Holmes, "Buchanan Vows to Stay in Race, Despite Votes," *New York Times*, March 8, 1992.

238. Steven A. Holmes, "Buchanan Pledges to Go On, But at Quiet Pace," *New York Times*, March 19, 1992.

239. "Buchanan Rejoins G.O.P. Battle," *New York Times*, March 31, 1992.

240. Cathleen Decker, "Buchanan's Sunset Journey to California Seen as the Dawn of '96 Presidential Bid," *Los Angeles Times*, March 29, 1992.

241. Howard Fineman and Bill Turque, "Buchanan's Shock Troops," *Newsweek*, March 2, 1992, p. 30.

242. William Schneider, "Buchanan's Constituency of Protest," *National Journal*, January 25, 1992, p. 246.

243. Jack Nelson, "Buchanan Demands Voice in GOP Convention Debate," *Los Angeles Times*, April 15, 1992.

4

Financing the
National Conventions

The second phase of the presidential selection process, the national nominating conventions, has lost much of its importance since changes in the
nominating process have essentially shifted the determination of the nominees from the convention floors to state delegate selection processes. In
recent decades, the voting at a convention has served simply to confirm a
choice that was, in effect, made well before the delegates assembled. This
change has led some observers to conclude that conventions are no longer
necessary. These analysts argue that conventions are little more than highly
orchestrated media events, designed to place the best light on the party's
standard-bearer. Others note that the convention still plays a vital role in the
selection process, especially given its role in the drafting of party platforms,
in developing party rules, in choosing a vice presidential candidate, in unifying the party faithful behind the nominees, and in launching the general
election campaign.

As questions have been raised about the role of the conventions, so have
questions about their financing. The conventions are financed in part by
public funds provided to the two major parties, $11,048,000 each in
1992. But the parties' expenses greatly exceed the amount of this subsidy.
The Democrats' convention in New York City cost more than three times as
much—$38.6 million—with the remainder provided by the city and a host
committee that was established to help solicit private funds and donations
of services and other resources. Similarly, only a portion of the costs of the
Republicans' convention in Houston were financed with public monies. The
experience of recent conventions has thus led some observers to question
whether the monies provided for conventions are adequate, while others

have questioned whether parties should be allowed to supplement public subsidies with private funds. Still others have begun to wonder whether taxpayers' dollars should be used to pay for conventions at all, given their altered role in the presidential selection process. Many of these questions are difficult to answer, however, because the financing of national nominating conventions is more difficult to document and has not been as thoroughly scrutinized as other aspects of the presidential campaign finance system.

Paying for the Conventions

Prior to 1976, the year of the first national nominating convention to be regulated by the FECA as amended, there were four principal sources of funds to pay convention costs: municipal, county, and state appropriations; contributions from local businesses and individuals; contributions from state and national businesses; and revenues from the sale of advertisements in convention programs.[1] Two of these sources—contributions from business interests and convention program revenues—at times became sources of controversy, thereby contributing to the atmosphere that made enactment of the FECA possible.

Under the FECA, the two major political parties are eligible to receive convention subsidies from the Presidential Election Campaign Fund established by the Revenue Act of 1971. None of the grant money drawn from the fund may be used to defray the expenses of any candidate or delegate participating in a convention. Moreover, parties accepting the public subsidy are not permitted to spend additional funds to pay convention-related costs. The amount of the grant originally stipulated was $2 million plus a cost-of-living adjustment. The base amount was raised to $3 million by the 1979 FECA Amendments and to $4 million by an act of Congress in mid-1984.[2] A minor party is eligible for a partial subsidy if its candidate received more than 5 percent of the vote in the previous presidential election.

The federal subsidy was intended to replace state and local government appropriations, individual and corporate contributions, and revenues from convention programs as the means of paying for nominating conventions. From the beginning of this funding system, however, avenues have been created by which private money and state and local government funds may legally reenter the financing process. As a result, the public subsidy now represents less than half of the monies spent to conduct these quadrennial political spectacles.

Public Funds

In the other two phases of the presidential selection process, the public money goes to the candidates for their pre- and post-nomination campaigns. The national nominating convention grants are the only form of federal

Table 4.1

National Nominating Convention Spending, Major Parties, 1992
(in $ millions)

Spending by	Democrats	Republicans
Party convention nominating committees	$11.0	$11.0
Host cities	21.1	5.7
Host committees	6.5	4.3
Total	$38.6	$21.0

Source: Citizens' Research Foundation.

assistance that goes to the political parties. Also, these payments are made available to the parties beginning in the year before the election year so that the funds can be used to defray such early costs as rental of the convention hall and hotel deposits.

Table 4.1 demonstrates the extent of government involvement in the conventions, some $59 million in all. In addition to the federal money, the governments of the host cities made funds available to assist the parties. The assistance is one of the benefits cities offer the parties in their bids to secure the convention. For example, in its proposal for the 1992 Democratic convention, New York City offered to provide $20 million in facilities and services to the Democratic National Convention Committee (DNCC).[3] The city ultimately made $21.1 million of taxpayers' money available. The city of Houston committed to $5.7 million for the Republican event. This funding was generated by a special hotel room tax. These financial commitments essentially constitute an investment that cities hope to recoup through the increased business and revenues generated by convention attendees and their families. New York City expected close to $200 million in direct spending, some $25 to $30 million of which would be returned to the city in the form of taxes. Houston expected a more modest $100 million in convention and conventioneer spending.[4]

The amounts spent on the conventions thus exceed the amount provided by the federal government by a substantial sum. In 1992, federal funds represented only about half of the $21 million spent on the Republican convention and less than one-third of the $38.6 million spent on the Democratic convention. An accounting of the Republican Party's allocation of the $11 million federal grant, compared with four years earlier, is shown in Table 4.2. This table evidences the wide variety of costs associated with a national nominating convention.

Table 4.2

Allocation of Public Funds, Republican National Convention, 1988 and 1992

	1988	1992
Site selection	$171,201	$161,639
Administration	1,397,034	1,688,717
Rules committee	13,317	0
Arena operations	1,331,394	1,800,534
Arena logistics	1,559,847	1,807,037
Arena management/program	3,237,805	3,856,523
Special organizations	285,551	292,885
Convention services	580,214	591,555
Platform	232,411	690,410
Media support	155,323	80,858
Other	216,376	77,842
Total	$9,180,473	$11,048,000

Source: Citizens' Research Foundation.

The Republicans spent most of their federal funds on activities directly related to the party business associated with the convention and the staging of the event. More than $3.8 million was devoted to the management of the convention and the convention program, while slightly more than $3.6 million was spent on operations and logistics at the Astrodome, the site of the convention. It also is interesting to note the site selection costs and platform costs. The Republicans incurred $161,639 in costs related to visits to various cities that offered proposals to hold the convention. They also spent $690,410 on hearings held prior to the convention, in San Diego, Kansas City, Salt Lake City, and Washington, DC, to hear testimony and gather information in an effort to develop some consensus for the national party platform.

Further examples of convention costs in Houston included the services of numerous consultants: $8,599 to a production designer for outside and interior decorations; $24,000 to arrange floor seating to look best on television; $70,406 to coordinate federal and local security agencies; $10,000 to provide lighting and acoustical assistance. Legal advice accounted for expenditures of at least $131,124 to one law firm, and $125,007 to an accounting firm to ensure compliance and keep the books.[5]

Although a similarly detailed breakdown of the costs of the Democratic convention is not available, some of the major costs related to this event included:[6]

Madison Square Garden rent	$4,000,000
Construction costs	5,000,000
Transportation	650,000
Parking	175,000
Police	6,600,000

Counting the rental and construction costs, the locale alone accounted for almost as much as the federal grant. The costs of police time were covered by the resources committed by New York City. The city also made available more than 568,000 square feet of work space outside Madison Square Garden.[7] Like the Republicans, the Democrats also used some of their convention funds to finance site selection costs and a platform hearing held in Cleveland in mid-May. Another example of Democratic convention costs, erroneously charged to public funds but caught by an FEC audit, were mementos totaling $17,805 that were given as expressions of gratitude to managers of the convention.[8]

Private Funds

Ironically, the public funding was designed to provide an alternative to private funds, but the latter still can be raised under increasingly easy guidelines. Every four years since public funding went into effect in 1976, the Federal Election Commission (FEC) has interpreted the law to permit more private money for operating the conventions, and has exempted more expenditures from the spending limits. These include resources provided by state and local governments, as well as funds raised privately by host committees that are mainly solicited from corporate sponsors that donate amounts as large as $100,000 or more.

State and local governments are permitted to provide certain facilities and services, such as convention halls, transportation, and security services, the costs of which are not counted against the parties' expenditure limits. Parties may accept such items as free hotel rooms and conference facilities so long as other groups holding conventions of similar size and duration are offered similar benefits. (No other conventions really approximate the mega-size of the national nominating conventions.) Local businesses and national corporations with local outlets may contribute funds to host committees or civic associations seeking to attract or assist the conventions, so long as they can reasonably expect a commensurate commercial return during the convention.[9]

For example, as early as 1984, when the Republican Party held its convention in Dallas, state law and long-standing local tradition prevented tax revenue and other government monies from being used to finance convention-related costs. Accordingly, the city successfully sought FEC permission to establish and administer a nonprofit, nonpartisan convention fund to finance facilities and services for the convention, provided the fund pays for such items and services at their fair market value. The FEC rule stated that payments made to the city-administered fund for convention facilities and services, and donations to the fund, would not constitute contributions to the RNC and would not count against the RNC's convention-spending ceiling.[10] As a result, the fund was able to collect donations in unlimited amounts from individuals, associations, businesses, and corporations, without having to disclose the names of contributors. The IRS also ruled that contributions to the fund would be fully tax deductible.[11]

San Francisco, site of the 1984 Democratic convention, had received a similar FEC ruling in 1983 for its Convention Promotion Services Fund.[12] The 1983 advisory opinion stated that FEC regulations placed no limits on the sources from which the city could draw contributions for its convention fund or the amounts it could accept from any source.[13] The advisory further noted that payments made by the city from its convention fund for convention services and facilities would not constitute contributions to the DNC and would not count against the convention spending limit the DNC would have to observe if it accepted public funds. In this case, too, the only restriction the FEC placed on the city convention funds was that any convention services obtained from commercial vendors be purchased at their fair market value.

An additional FEC advisory opinion sanctioned the use of corporate funds for specific convention-related spending. In 1983 the commission advised the LTV Corporation, a major defense contractor, that it might establish a reception facility near the site of the 1984 Republican convention to which it might invite delegates, federal, state, and party officials, and members of the press.[14] The commission also advised the corporation that it might sponsor cocktail party receptions in conjunction with the Republican and Democratic conventions for delegates and selected attendees and observers. The advisory opinion stated that expenditures by the corporation for these purposes would not be considered contributions or expenditures under federal election law, so long as the corporation made no attempt to influence the outcome of the conventions, did not solicit funds at the sponsored events or advocate the election or defeat of any candidate for federal office, did not use its events or facilities to defray any delegates' subsistence expenses during the convention, and maintained final control over its proposed convention-related activities.

Despite the intent of the 1974 FECA Amendments to replace traditional private and local government funding of conventions with federal funding, the effect of the FEC advisories from 1975 through 1992 has been to restore the traditional funding sources to their positions of prominence. Although the sources of private funding are not subject to federal disclosure requirements if contributions are made to permissible city convention funds, press reports and the acknowledgements of at least some contributors indicate that tax-deductible corporate contributions, earlier a source of considerable controversy, continue to play an important role in convention funding.

The 1992 conventions were similarly financed in part by corporate and other large contributions, which went with the grants of federal funds supplemented by New York City and Houston public funds. The Houston Host Committee pledged to raise $4.3 million from the private sector to help pay the costs of the convention. These funds were solicited by the Houston Convention Fund, an independent, nonprofit organization formed to support the convention and chaired by Ben Love, former chairman and chief executive officer of Texas Commerce Bancshares, a nationally known trust company. The $4.3 million goal was met by March 1992, thus making Houston "the first host city for either the Democratic or Republican conventions in 20 years to complete its fund raising before the convention began."[15] Similarly, the New York City Host Committee established an independent, nonprofit organization to raise private funds for the Democratic convention. This committee, which was chaired by Robert E. Rubin, vice chairman of investment house Goldman Sachs & Co., initially pledged to raise $2.7 million and eventually raised twice that amount.

The Houston Host Committee funds were raised to remodel the Astrodome, a sports stadium, into a convention hall. To free the Astrodome for the convention, Houston persuaded the baseball Astros to take a twenty-six-game road trip, the longest trip in the history of any major league team. Houston also recruited 11,000 volunteers to serve as drivers, ushers, and other convention functionaries. Tons of sound-absorbing materials were placed to muffle noise.[16] The New York City committee also was responsible for recruiting and organizing thousands of volunteers. In addition, the committee recruited prominent city residents to host fifty-six parties for the visiting delegations. For example, Fred Wilpon, an owner of the New York Mets, hosted a party for the Nebraska delegation, while James M. Lebenthal, a Wall Street bond dealer, entertained the Idaho delegation.[17]

The party organizations further benefited from services and merchandise offered by a host of companies and retailers. Both parties were able to arrange reduced-cost services by agreeing to designate airlines and others as "official suppliers" for the conventions. Democratic delegates received free "NY '92" welcome kits containing a mug, a T-shirt, an LCD clock, two magazines, and a Zagat restaurant guide. The retail value of each kit, according to one report, was $83.80, but some of the items were provided by merchandisers free of cost.[18] At the Houston event, some 6,000 free gift bags were distributed to delegates and Republican officials. Trucks made the rounds of fifty hotels every day of the convention carrying additional gifts, such as one tasty eye-catcher: plastic cowboy boots filled with red, white, and blue M&M's.[19]

Both parties relied on large donations from corporate and labor sponsors, in contributions to the host committee funds or in services provided at the conventions. Among the corporate and labor sponsors to the Democratic convention were AT&T, American Express, Time-Warner Inc., Coca-Cola, Delta Airlines, the American Federation of State, County and Municipal Employees, the Machinists Non-Partisan Political League, and the National Education Association.[20] Among corporate contributors to the Republican convention were American Express, ARCO, Coca-Cola, Delta Airlines, Shell Oil, Exxon, Pennzoil, and Sony.[21]

In New York City and Houston, delegates and donors did not have to spend much money on food or entertainment. There were hospitality suites and private receptions sponsored by corporations and labor unions, stocked with drinks and delicacies; full breakfasts and luncheons for state delegations; and lobbyists hosting small lunches and dinners. In New York, there were excursions to theaters, museums, and a baseball game. The Democrats also sponsored a "party train" from Washington, DC, to New York, providing several hours of informal talk with party leaders, members of Congress, and celebrities.[22]

Given these sources of funding, the Democratic convention was particularly ironic. On the one hand, the party's platform vowed to "get big money out of our politics and let the people back in."[23] On the other hand, the convention accepted money from corporations, unions, lobbyists, and large donors, or allowed these outsiders to sponsor events. Convention officials issued a thirty-nine-page list of parties sponsored by the party or special interests. One of the first events was a reception for DNC chairman Ronald Brown, sponsored by his former law office, Patton, Boggs & Blow, one of Washington's most influential lobbying firms.[24] Another was a breakfast for the California delegation, sponsored by ARCO and Southern California Edison Company, at which Jerry Brown, among others, spoke. The conflict between Brown's message, which consisted of interest-group-bashing and talk of stopping "the power of the few," and corporate sponsorship of an event at which he spoke, was apparent. The event thus served as another sign of the problem of sending one message while continuing practices that now are anathema to many, among them some of the Brown delegates, who nevertheless ate heartily at the corporations' table.[25]

Other major events in New York included two parties given in honor of Speaker of the House Thomas Foley, one of which was sponsored by the Baby Bell telephone companies and the other by AT&T, Anheuser-Busch, and PepsiCo.[26] The Enron Corporation, a Houston oil and energy company, made a major contribution to a $200,000 Street Fair in honor of Senator John Breaux of Louisiana, chair of the Democratic Leadership Council and a member of the Senate Commerce and Finance committees. (The chair and CEO of Enron, Kenneth Lay, also served as chair of the Houston Host Committee for the Republican convention.) Other sponsors of the fair included the Distilled Spirits Council, the Tobacco Institute, and the National Restaurant Association.[27]

At the Republican convention, Delta Airlines picked up the costs for a major donor hospitality suite, open day and night, serving drinks and a buffet. There were hospitality suites for Eagles—$15,000 party donors— and for Team 100 members—large soft money donors—sponsored by party and corporate sources. Large contributors also received reserved parking spaces and skybox seats at the Astrodome. Even so, the Republicans employed some modesty in their provisions for large contributors. Some limousine rentals were canceled shortly before the convention and replaced with regular sedans. A big event featured Texas-style country and western music and substituted the more common cowboy look in place of traditional black ties and ball gowns. The more fancy events were held away from the public eye; one was held at a private country club, where reporters were not invited.[28]

Related Fund Raising

In recent years national party conventions also have served an important but less often publicized function: they provide the parties and their candidates with opportunities to raise funds for a variety of purposes. Many of these are related to the presidential campaigns, while others are designed to give special recognition to important party contributors. In 1992, both conventions featured fund-raising events or activities that sought to raise money to help party organizations, candidates, and political committees retire presidential prenomination campaign debts; fund permissible national party coordinated expenditures on behalf of the presidential tickets; finance national party committee operations; fund voter registration activities by a variety of tax-exempt organizations; and pay for permissible activities on behalf of federal candidates.

To the degree that fund raising thrives where large numbers of affluent persons have come together in common cause, party conventions will continue to serve an array of fund-raising purposes. This is especially true for nominating conventions, because party officials have become adept at developing special perquisites for large contributors, including such items as special floor passes, exclusive reserved seating, and high-level briefings.

In 1992, both parties held large fund-raising events during their conventions that grossed more than $3 million for each party. Both raised hard and soft money at these events. A Democratic "victory dinner" on the last night of the convention, at a cost of $1,000 to $5,000 per plate, sold out with 2,700 attending and no extra space for those who decided to come at the last minute. Attendees were bussed to the dinner, which was held at the Intercontinental Hotel, where Clinton was staying. The Republicans held a gala luncheon on the last day of their convention, at a cost of $1,000 per plate.

The Democratic victory dinner was a new event that had not been held at earlier conventions, whereas the Republican galas have become fixtures at their conventions. Both parties applied the hard money proceeds to their funds for general election coordinated expenditures, although the Democrats shared some proceeds with affiliated state and local party committees. By the time of the convention, the Democrats had raised only about $1 million toward the $10.2 million limit for coordinated spending, while the Republicans had raised only $2 million. Both parties finally reached the maximum amount and made coordinated expenditures up to the limit, but the Republicans took longer to raise the money in 1992 than they had in 1988.[29] Adding Al Gore to the Democratic ticket certainly increased the pool of potential donors because Gore had his own base of supporters, no problems of ethics, and was an indefatigable fund raiser willing to attend events. Other fund raising at the 1992 conventions included events for party soft money prospects, for members of Congress, and for women and minority candidates.

Commentary

National nominating conventions have been widely criticized in recent years. Rather than deliberative bodies that nominate candidates for the offices of president and vice president, they confirm presidential candidates chosen through the delegate selection process in state primaries and caucuses; they readily accept as candidates for vice president the personal choices of the presidential candidates; and they write platforms dictated by incumbent presidents or chosen candidates for president.

Whatever the merits or virtues of national conventions, they serve two additional functions. They attract large television audiences, showcase the candidates, and give them opportunities to highlight the rhetoric and slogans

of the upcoming campaigns. And conventions serve to unify the party behind the ticket and activate campaign workers from among delegates and
others who attend these quadrennial events. In effect, the conventions are
launching pads for both the party and the ticket.

This joint effect of conventions makes it difficult to sort out the expenses of the party from those of a candidate at the convention. This
problem is illustrated by the FEC Final Audit Report of the Democratic
convention. Prior to Clinton's acceptance speech, a film on Clinton's life,
entitled "The Man from Hope," was shown at the convention. The FEC
audit questioned several payments to a media company for production
costs made by the Democratic National Convention Committee, the Democratic National Committee, and the Clinton for President Committee. FEC
auditors concluded that the film should be considered an expense of the
candidate and, as such, an expense for which public funds should not be
used. The commissioners reversed the staff determination, because such
films had been shown at previous conventions. The case, however,
illustrates the thin line that exists between the convention as a party event
and as an event intended to launch a candidate's campaign.[30]

"The Man from Hope" also attracted the attention of the *Los Angeles
Times* in a feature article that highlighted the work of two of the Clintons'
friends, Harry Thomason and his wife, Linda Bloodworth-Thomason. The
article intimated that certain services provided by the Hollywood producers
used studio facilities and equipment leased for their television sitcoms and
thus were corporate contributions neither reimbursed nor paid for by the
Clinton campaign. Among other services were the producers' preparation of
several spot announcements for the New Hampshire primary. The article
drew no follow-up story in the *Times* and no known FEC action.[31]

The mix of public and private financing (including tax-exempt funding)
for the nominating conventions satisfies the parties because it provides
sufficient funding and involves local participation. But the development
every four years of new means of introducing private money undermines
the premise in the 1974 law that public funding would essentially replace
private funds. The FEC has permitted more avenues for private funds. Besides questioning the rationale for the use of public funds, the infusion of
large amounts of private funds makes the expenditure limits meaningless.

Notes

1. For a discussion of convention funding prior to the FECA, see John F. Bibby and
Herbert E. Alexander, *The Politics of National Convention Finances and Arrangements*
(Princeton, NJ: Citizens' Research Foundation, 1968), pp. 48–62.
2. *Quadrennial Political Party Presidential National Nominating Conventions*
(Public Law 98–355), *U.S. Statutes at Large* 98 (1984): 394.

3. Proposal of the New York City Host Committee to the Democratic National Committee's Convention Site Selection Committee, March 22, 1990, p. 4.

4. John Solomon, "Taxpayers Bear Increasing Brunt of Political Convention Costs," Associated Press, July 8, 1992; and Steven Lee Myers, "Dog and Elephant Days: Wooing G.O.P.," *New York Times,* August 4, 1994.

5. John Solomon, "GOP Convention Bills Loaded With Consultants," Associated Press, August 12, 1992.

6. Barbara Demick, "Conventions Aren't Cheap—You May Help Pay Tab," *Miami Herald*, July 13, 1992.

7. Proposal of the New York City Host Committee, p. 16.

8. James A. Barnes, "OK, Taxpayers, Read and Weep," *National Journal,* April 2, 1994, p. 786.

9. See Herbert E. Alexander and Brian A. Haggerty, *Financing the 1984 Election* (Lexington, MA: Lexington Books, 1987), p. 291.

10. Ibid., pp. 291–92.

11. Ibid., pp. 297–98.

12. Ibid., pp. 302–5.

13. FEC, AO 1983–29: Fund Used by City to Finance Presidential Nominating Convention, *Record,* December 1983, p. 3.

14. FEC, AO 1983–23: Reception Facility and Events Sponsored by a Corporation at Presidential Nominating Conventions, *Record,* November 1983, pp. 4–5.

15. Official Press Guide, 1992 Republican National Convention, August 1, 1992, p. 19.

16. Robert Suro, "A Houston-Style Convention: Republicans in Heavy Traffic," *New York Times,* August 15, 1992.

17. James Barron, "Reporter's Notebook," *New York Times,* June 29, 1992.

18. Dean Chang, "Free-For-All: Delegates Heading Home with a Wealth of Giveaways," *New York Daily News,* July 16, 1992.

19. Soro, "A Houston-Style Convention."

20. Demick, "Conventions Aren't Cheap."

21. Solomon, "Taxpayers Bear Increasing Brunt of Political Convention Costs."

22. Barbara Demick, "It's a Nonstop Free Lunch, Invitations Only," *Philadelphia Inquirer,* July 14, 1992.

23. *The Democratic Party Platform 1992,* p. 9.

24. Stephen Labaton, "Deductible Dollars Flowed Like Wine," *New York Times,* July 19, 1992.

25. John Solomon, "Anti-Corruption Candidates' Delegates Treated to Special Interest Breakfast," Associated Press, July 14, 1992.

26. Labaton, "Deductible Dollars Flowed Like Wine."

27. Ibid.

28. Barbara Demick, "It's Networking and Fund-Raising: Conventions Are Havens of Lobbyists and Special Interests. The Backdrop Is Nominations and Platforms," *Philadelphia Inquirer,* August 23, 1992; and "Conventioneers, Wooing Middle Class, Eschew Trappings of the Rich," *Philadelphia Inquirer,* August 19, 1992.

29. John Solomon, "In Stark Contrast to 1988, GOP Fund-Raising for Bush Lags Behind," Associated Press, August 17, 1992; and Barbara Demick, "At Convention, Democrats Went After Money in a Big Way," *Philadelphia Inquirer,* July 19, 1992.

30. FEC, *Final Audit Report on the 1992 Democratic National Convention Committee, Inc.* (Washington, DC: FEC, 1994), pp. 7–11.

31. Robert W. Welkos and Melissa Wye, "Producers to the President Play a Continuing Role," *Los Angeles Times,* March 24, 1994.

5

Financing the General Election Campaigns

General Election

The November election in 1992 was quite similar to that of 1968, which featured a three-man race among Richard M. Nixon, Hubert H. Humphrey, and George Wallace. Nixon won by about the same margin as Clinton, receiving 43.2 percent of the popular vote as against 43 percent for Clinton, while Humphrey received 42.7 percent. George Wallace received 13.5 percent of the vote, compared with 18.9 percent for Perot. In 1992, though an incumbent president, Bush received only 37.7 percent of the popular vote.

Unlike Wallace, Perot achieved certain spectacular successes. As will be shown, he received more media attention in the fall campaign than in the spring, although he received considerable attention throughout. Perot was able to get on the ballot in fifty states and the District of Columbia, no simple task. Bush and Clinton sent envoys to see him in late September, perhaps to talk him out of running, or to give an endorsement. Neither happened. Both invited him to participate in the presidential debates, believing that his presence would help their own campaigns and that he was too popular to ignore. The Commission on Presidential Debates belatedly recommended including Perot in the debates, despite low poll ratings at the time, and sponsored the three debates with the three presidential candidates and one with the three vice-presidential candidates. This was the first time that both major party presidential candidates debated with a third candidate.[1]

Bush Campaign Leadership

Former Vice President Dan Quayle, a participant, has called the 1992 Bush–Quayle campaign "the most poorly planned and executed incumbent presidential campaign in this century."[2] Whether true or not, the Bush campaign sputtered over the early summer, while Clinton gathered support, until Bush sought to energize the effort in August. Shortly after the convention, Secretary of State James Baker began his twin jobs as White House chief of staff and head of the Bush–Quayle campaign. Baker was allowed to replace virtually anyone in the White House to facilitate Bush's reelection effort.[3] Baker's concurrent duties in the administration and the campaign drew considerable criticism. Although the White House denied that federal law would be violated, it was difficult to believe that Baker would not do any campaign work at all on government time. The White House said on one hand that Baker would not be very involved in the campaign, and on the other hand that it would not be illegal for him to do so. It was stated that Baker's position was not covered by the Hatch Act, which prohibits such activity.[4]

Other members of the Bush campaign leadership included Robert M. Teeter, a veteran pollster who served as campaign coordinator and chief strategist, and Frederick V. Malek, who held the title of campaign manager. Robert A. Mosbacher, who had been secretary of commerce and then general chairman of the prenomination campaign, was given the task of running the soft money operation. Mosbacher was the logical choice, having operated Team 100 efforts in the 1988 Bush campaign.[5]

Clinton Campaign Leadership

The Clinton campaign did not suffer the leadership problems the Bush campaign did. Its campaign chairman was Mickey A. Kantor, a Los Angeles lawyer, and its campaign manager and chief of staff was David Wilhelm, a Chicago political consultant. This leadership was sparked by consultants James Carville and Paul Begala. Carville was credited with coining the working principle of the campaign: "It's the economy, stupid." Financial direction of the campaign was managed by Robert A. Farmer, who had played the same role for Dukakis in 1988, and by Rahm Emanuel, whose title was finance director.[6]

Soft Money

In the general election phase of the presidential selection process, apart from Perot's self-financing, the most notable financial phenomenon was the

Table 5.1

Presidential Soft Money Expenditures, 1980–1992 (in $ millions)

| | Party | |
Year	Republican	Democrat
1980	$ 15.1	$ 4.0
1984	15.6	6.0
1988	22.0	23.0
1992	15.6	22.1

Source: Citizens' Research Foundation.

Note: Amounts represent presidential campaign-related soft money expenditures, not election-cycle expenditures.

search for soft money. Soft money is money raised and spent outside the restraints of federal law and is regulated by state laws, many of which are less stringent than federal law. Efforts by the campaigns to raise soft money became as competitive and as high profile as the search for votes on November 3.

Soft money was sanctioned by the 1979 FECA Amendments. It was raised and spent in the 1980 and 1984 presidential campaigns, but the money was raised in low-key efforts, not in the high-visibility competitive ways as in 1988 or 1992, and in smaller amounts, as shown in Table 5.1.[7]

Through parallel fund-raising efforts by the candidates' prenomination campaign operatives, both major parties sought soft money contributions to supplement the public funds each presidential and vice presidential ticket received. Some $55.2 million, plus $10.3 million the national parties could spend on behalf of the ticket—both amounts in hard money—could be supplemented by whatever soft money the parties spent—approximately $22.1 million by the Democrats and $15.6 million by the Republicans. Soft money was raised centrally at a steady pace, as if no contribution limits or expenditure limits existed. It was raised not by the parties but by the same Bush and Clinton finance officials who raised the candidates' prenomination funds. And it was raised in large individual contributions—much in excess of the federal contribution limitations—some as much as $100,000 each. The Republicans claimed 198 contributors of $100,000 or more, as contributors to Team 100—down from 267 in 1988—while the Democrats counted 375 individuals who gave or raised $100,000—up from 130 in 1988 and surpassing Republican numbers in 1992.[8] In 1992, the Democrats won over a few of the 1988 Team 100 members. For example, Edgar

Bronfman, the chairman of Joseph E. Seagram & Sons Inc., gave the Republicans $450,000 during the first year and one-half of the 1991–92 election cycle, then Bronfman and his son each gave the Democrats $100,000 in September 1992.[9] According to the Center for Responsive Politics, there were forty-four soft money donors who gave $50,000 or more to both parties throughout the election cycle, not all in the presidential phase from July 1, 1992, to the end of the election year.[10]

Clinton put a $100,000 limit on soft money amounts that would be accepted from individuals and refused to accept any from corporations, labor unions, or PACs. Before Clinton was nominated, however, the Democrats had accepted soft money from corporate and labor sources for help in funding the Democratic national convention and the DNC. Most Republican soft money contributions were from individuals but some were corporate. Some Republican soft money was raised in amounts as low as $1,000 for tickets to the Gala Luncheon at the Republican convention. The costs of the gala were part of the soft money expenditures. So both conventions used up some of the soft money expenditures for 1992, as shown in Table 5.1. Additional hard money (within the restraints of federal law), in the tens of millions of dollars, was raised and spent by Republicans and Democrats on combined hard-soft money activities related to the presidential campaigns. Additional soft money was raised and spent locally by state and local party committees in amounts not included in the national soft money totals.

Figure 5.1 is a reproduction of an instruction sheet provided to fund raisers and potential contributors by the DNC on behalf of the DNC Victory Fund '92. It illustrates the legal restrictions on hard money for federal accounts, and the availability of a soft money account (nonfederal) for unlimited contributions. As can be seen, different instructions apply to individual contributions, corporate and union contributions, and PAC contributions. For example, an individual making a $100,000 contribution may contribute $20,000 in hard money and $80,000 in soft money, or he or she may give the entire amount in soft money.

Thus, during the 1992 general election period, in which candidate spending limits were set by law at $55.2 million, more than twice as much was spent, mainly by combinations of candidate and party committees at the state and local levels. The erosion of the effectiveness of the contribution and expenditure limits represents a return to big money: public and private, hard and soft, candidate and party. It threatens the general election public funding concept, which is that full public funding would be provided, with minimal national party participation, and effective expenditure limitations. Public funds were intended to help provide

> Democratic National Committee
> ## DNC VICTORY FUND '92

-------------------------------   *INDIVIDUAL CONTRIBUTIONS*   -------------------------------

WHO CAN GIVE

Any U.S. citizen or permanent resident alien ("green card" holder) may contribute an unlimited amount to the Democratic National Committee. Federal (individual) checks are preferred. Each donor must fill out and sign a donor card including the following information:

- *Full name and address*
- *Occupation and name of employer*
- *Name of person who solicited check*

FEDERAL CONTRIBUTIONS

Individuals may contribute a total of $25,000 per year to federal candidates, federal political committees and the federal accounts of the DNC and state and local parties. Of this amount, each individual may contribute **$20,000** annually to the DNC Federal Account for use in connection with federal elections (Presidential, Senate and House campaigns).

NON-FEDERAL CONTRIBUTIONS

Individuals may contribute an **unlimited** amount to the DNC Non-Federal Account. Non-federal dollars are used in connection with state and local elections as permitted by law as well as to pay a portion of generic national party activities such as fundraising and research.

HOW TO WRITE THE CHECK(S)

(A)   **Federal Contributions** from individuals of up to $20,000 should be made by personal check payable to:

DNC VICTORY '92/FEDERAL ACCOUNT

(B)   **Non-Federal Contributions** from individuals can be made payable to:

DNC VICTORY '92/NON-FEDERAL ACCOUNT

Please note: Individual contributions in excess of $20,000 **require two checks.** Each check must be made with the appropriate Federal/Non-Federal designation as outlined above.

PLEASE REMEMBER

In the general election, which is financed with a federal grant, checks solicited or directed specifically to the Clinton/Gore Committee are generally impermissible and cannot be accepted. (However, individuals may contribute up to $1,000 to the Clinton/Gore Compliance Fund. Such checks may be sent directly to the Clinton/Gore Committee, P.O. Box 615, Little Rock, AK 72203) Federal contributions to the DNC are spent on behalf of the entire ticket including Bill Clinton and Al Gore.

Please Send Contributions to:

QUESTIONS?

Please feel free to call:
Carol C. Darr
DNC General Counsel
(202) 479-5113

DNC Victory Fund '92
Democratic National Committee Headquarters
430 South Capitol Street, S.E.   Third Floor
Washington, D.C. 20003
(202) 863-8000

. . Contributions to the Democratic National Committee are not tax deductible as charitable contributions for Federal Income Tax purposes.

Figure 5.1. Democratic National Committee Fund-Raising Guide, 1992.

-------------------------- *CORPORATE AND UNION CONTRIBUTIONS* --------------------

WHO CAN GIVE

Corporations and labor organizations may make *unlimited* contributions from corporate or union treasury funds to the **DNC Non-Federal Account.** Non-federal dollars are used in conjunction with state and local elections as permitted by law as well as to pay a significant portion of national party activity.

Corporations and labor organizations are prohibited from making contributions from corporate or union treasury funds to the DNC Federal account.

HOW TO WRITE CORPORATE/UNION CHECK(S)

Checks from corporate treasury funds or labor union treasury funds may be written for an *unlimited* amount to:

DNC VICTORY '92/NON-FEDERAL ACCOUNT

Please note: Your contribution to the DNC Non-Federal Account will be used in connection with state and local election activities and to pay for a portion of DNC administrative costs.

------------------------------------- *PAC CONTRIBUTIONS* ---------------------------------

WHO CAN GIVE

Federally registered multi-candidate committees may contribute up to *$15,000* per calendar year to the DNC Federal Account. Such PACs can contribute *unlimited* amounts to the DNC Non-Federal Account.

HOW TO WRITE PAC CHECKS

Contributions up to $15,000 per year from PACs may be written to:

DNC VICTORY '92/FEDERAL ACCOUNT

Non-federal contributions from PACs may be written to:

DNC VICTORY '92/NON-FEDERAL ACCOUNT

Your contribution to the DNC Federal Account is for use in connection with federal elections and is subject to federal contribution prohibitions and limitations. Individual contributions in excess of $20,000 and all corporate or labor organization funds are used to support DNC work in connection with state and local elections. Your contribution is not tax deductible for federal income tax purposes.

or supply in entirety the money serious candidates needed to present themselves and their ideas to the electorate. Such public money also was meant to diminish or eliminate the need for financing from wealthy donors and interest groups, thereby minimizing the influence contributors possibly could exert on officeholders. And, of course, public funding was designed to relieve candidates of the need to engage in fund raising. Instead, the candidates helped to raise soft money. If soft money expenditures do violence to the rationale for public funding, the whole election law framework is opened to doubt.

Moreover, when presidential candidates accept public financing for the general election campaign, they agree not to raise private funds nor to spend more money than permitted under the expenditure limits. Yet the presidential candidates speak at events at which soft money is raised, and their finance staffs from the prenomination campaigns help to raise soft money and direct its disbursements in key states. Some observers believe this is a violation of the law.

While there is much criticism of soft money, it plays an important role in voter outreach and party renewal. Its use is required by federal law to be restricted to spending related to voluntary activities. Its purpose is to allow state and local party committees to undertake such activities as registration and get-out-the-vote drives, phone banks, and the like—widely accepted functions that attract citizen participation, activities highly valued in a democracy. Soft money also can be used for items such as bumper strips and local canvassing materials. With more money available in 1992, the definition of voluntary activity was broadened by experience to include joint state headquarters and related expenses shared with presidential campaign operatives in key states. In contrast, the public funding provided by tax checkoffs to the candidates was used directly on advertising by the presidential tickets. To some extent, soft money expenditures freed up more of the public money for advertising, travel, and other expenditures directly associated with the presidential campaigns. (For extended discussion of soft money, see chapter 6.)

Three Parallel Campaigns

In the 1992 general election, both major party campaigns expressed a need for a level playing field. As a result, the campaigns sought to supplement spending beyond the expenditure limits through the use of soft money and other means. Despite incumbency, the Republicans got a later start in raising soft money and lagged behind the Democrats in yield. But soft money was only one component of spending outside the candidates' expenditure limits. Analysis of the presidential general election period demonstrates that at least three distinct but parallel campaigns were conducted by each ticket or on each ticket's behalf.[11] Amounts of each component are shown in Table 5.2.

In the first campaign, spending was limited by law to the flat-grant amount, $55,240,000, that public funding provided. This money was supplemented by national party–coordinated expenditures of $10.3 million in hard money funds. The total of these public and party funds, $65.5 million, was entirely within the control of the major party nominees and their campaign organizations. Identical amounts were spent by

Table 5.2

Sources of Funds, Major Party Presidential Candidates, 1992 General Election (in $ millions)

	Sources of Funds	Bush	Clinton
Limited campaign			
Candidate controlled	Federal grant	$ 55.2	$ 55.2
	National party	10.3	10.3
Unlimited campaigns			
Candidate may coordinate	Party soft money[a]	15.6	22.1
	Labor[b]	1.0	35.0
	Corporate/association	1.5	1.0
	Compliance	4.3	6.0
Independent of candidate	Independent expenditures[c]	2.0	.5
Total		$89.9	$130.1

Source: Citizens' Research Foundation, based on Federal Election Commission and other data.

[a]Includes soft money raised by the national party committees and channeled to state and local party committees from July 1, 1992, through December 31, 1992.
[b]Includes hard and soft money, and internal communication costs (both those in excess of $2,000, which are reported as required by law, and those less than $2,000, which are not reported), registration and voter turnout expenditures, overhead, and related costs. Labor amount includes $2.4 million spent in partisan communications costs.
[c]Does not include amount spent to oppose the candidates: $34,648 against Bush and $506,758 against Clinton.

the Bush–Quayle and Clinton–Gore campaigns in these categories.

Bush's unpopularity was evident in RNC fund raising for the Presidential Trust account, designed to supply hard money for coordinated expenditures. The RNC spent the full amount the law permitted in coordinated expenditures for the Bush–Quayle general election, $10.3 million, but actually raised only $6 million for this purpose. The RNC drew on other accounts to make up the $4.3 million difference. The Democrats raised and spent the full amount, as they had done in 1988 but not in 1984 or 1980, when the Republicans led in such party spending.[12] The Democrats raised most of their coordinated expenditures in six weeks starting at their national convention.

In the second campaign, spending was provided for but not limited under the law. Some of it was directly controlled by the nominees and their campaign organizations, and some was outside their orbit. Even those funds outside their direct control, however, could be coordinated with spending by the nominees. This second campaign was financed, in part, by funds raised under FECA limits from private contributions to pay the legal, accounting, and related costs the organization incurred in complying with the law: $4.3 million by Bush and $6 million by Clinton.

The second campaign also was financed, in part, by soft money funds spent by state and local party committees—with Republican spending lagging behind the Democrats. Each major party has fifty state committees, 3,100 or so county committees, plus uncounted municipal committees, which worked to register voters, distribute absentee ballots, and get out the vote on November 3. In 1992, soft money was collected nationally and allocated to some of these party committees to aid them in such activities on behalf of the presidential tickets. The soft money amounts spent by the Democratic party organizations from July 1 through December 31 were roughly $22.1 million, while the Republican amounts during the same period were about $15.6 million. These figures represent the amounts spent on election-related activities; in addition, the party committees spent soft money through building funds and on activities that were not directly related to the presidential race, from January 1, 1991, to June 30, 1992. In this study, July 1 was chosen as the date when it was clear that both Bush and Clinton would be nominated, and that the national party organizations had focused their efforts on raising money for the general election campaign. The Perot campaign, of course, had no such infrastructure at work, excepting the state and other chapters he was able to organize.

In addition, in this part of the campaigns, funds were spent on the nominees' behalf by labor unions, trade associations, and membership groups, on partisan communications with their constituencies and in parallel campaigning on nominally nonpartisan activities directed to the general public. The major amount was $36 million in union support, almost exclusively on behalf of Clinton–Gore. In 1988, the Bush–Quayle ticket had better labor support, specifically from the Teamsters; however, in 1992, Teamster support went to the Clinton–Gore ticket. This parallel spending could be coordinated with spending by the nominees' campaign organizations.

In the third campaign, spending also was provided for but not limited under the law. Under *Buckley v. Valeo,* individuals and groups are permitted to spend unlimited amounts to advocate the election or defeat of specific candidates, as long as these independent expenditures are made without consultation or collaboration with the candidates or their campaigns. An advantage to the Bush campaign in independent expenditures was evident, but amounts—only $2 million—in 1992 were less than one-third the amounts spent on his behalf in 1988. The full amounts of general election independent expenditures, as shown in Table 5.2, were $2 million on behalf of Bush–Quayle, $500,000 on behalf of Clinton–Gore, as well as $34,648 in negative spending against Bush, and $506,758 in negative spending against Clinton.

These three parallel campaigns illustrate why expenditure limits are illusory in a pluralistic system with numerous openings for disbursement sanctioned by law or court decisions. Such developments demonstrate the difficulties in attempting to regulate strictly money in the American political arena. When freedom of speech and association are guaranteed, restricting money at any point in the campaign process results in new channels being carved, through which monied individuals and groups seek to bring their influence to bear on campaigns and officeholders.

With a total of almost $90 million for or on behalf of Bush, and $130.1 million for or on behalf of Clinton, as shown in Table 5.2, it is apparent that the candidates' spending limitations, plus those of the national party, are not effective. Moreover, it is apparent that both major party campaigns felt a need for additional spending.

The total amounts spent in the major party general election campaigns were remarkable, not only for the aggregate amounts raised and spent on behalf of the candidates, but also because the Democratic candidate was the beneficiary of much more spending than the Republican. Dukakis had achieved a stark reversal from all presidential elections in the twentieth century in 1988 and Clinton maintained the Democratic lead for the same reasons: The Democrats spent the full amount of party-coordinated expenditures, $10.3 million, and outspent the Republicans in soft money. Also, the Democrats continued their advantage of strong labor spending in parallel campaigns, amounting to $35 million. Indeed, the Democrats achieved more than their desired level playing field; they had a notable advantage in actual dollars spent.

Additional sums were spent on behalf of the tickets but were impossible to calculate with any precision. According to the 1992 Chairman's Report, the RNC spent more than $10 million on a national advertising campaign promoting the Republican Party and its candidates generally. If one used the 60 percent rule of the FEC regarding hard/soft money allocations, another $6 million could be allocated as Republican Party support of the presidential ticket. Similarly, Democrats spent some $14.2 million on a national media campaign, and 60 percent would be $8.5 million allocable to DNC support of the presidential ticket.

The Post-Convention Surge

In mid-July 1992, Clinton was still paying off prenomination campaign debts. He expected to be paid up by August.[13] In early August, Clinton filed for $1.8 million in matching funds for the last part of the prenomination period, based on his July fund raising in excess of $3 million. This nearly erased his debt of $2 million, which had been cut in half since May.[14]

Clinton was able to erase his debt before September in large part because of the success of the Democratic convention in mid-July. After the convention, Clinton's popularity surged twenty points, one of the largest post-convention "bounces" for a Democrat in recent elections. As a result, public opinion polls showed Clinton with a lead of 52 percent to 32 percent over Bush, the largest lead for any Democrat during the last forty years.[15] This change in the relative standing of the candidates was in part a reaction to the favorable public attention given the convention; it also was likely due to Perot's announcement on the last day of the Democratic gathering that he had decided to drop out of the race. Whatever the reason, Clinton's lead created a sense of enthusiasm within the party that translated into fund-raising success, as well as increased popularity among voters.

Moreover, unlike the 1988 election, when Dukakis's post-convention lead dwindled after the Republican gathering, Bush did not gain significant ground after his convention in 1992. Following the Republican convention and through September, Bush's level of public support stayed virtually flat.[16] Clinton's lead thus continued to serve as an encouragement to Democratic donors and voters.

One of the factors that helped Clinton maintain his lead throughout August and into September was the campaign's decision to embark on an extensive bus tour in the wake of the convention. Clinton, Gore, and their wives toured parts of the country by bus, as a way to stay in the media's eye. The bus tour was the lead story of the network evening newscasts and was given long segments on the morning programs. The tour was like a rolling advertisement with images of small town America as a backdrop, especially when juxtaposed with images of what appeared to be a frazzled, frustrated president vying for attention. The bus trips cost journalists $100 per day, much less than plane fare. Every network had "exclusive" interviews with Clinton or Gore aboard the bus or in a small town along the 1,000-mile route. The relatively low cost of the trip also enabled many local reporters to join the entourage for segments of the tour, which helped generate extensive coverage from local media outlets.

The first trip lasted six days, beginning in New York after the convention and continuing through New Jersey, Pennsylvania, West Virginia, Kentucky, Indiana, Ohio, and Illinois, and ending in Missouri. If 500 or more people gathered along the road, the buses would stop and a rally would begin, with staffers setting up a sound system and stage.[17] This first trip was considered so successful that four additional bus trips were conducted during the course of the general election campaign. The second trip was for three days and went from St. Louis to Minneapolis along the Mississippi River. These trips evoked visions of the American heritage and were designed to express the virtues of hope and change, the major themes of the campaign.

The Black Vote

As a result of Clinton's successful turnaround during the Democratic convention, his support among blacks was reported to be increased from 45 percent to 70 percent in just one week![18] Democratic Party officials reached an agreement with Jesse Jackson to recruit black voters aggressively. Jackson led a four-day bus caravan from New Orleans to Chicago for this purpose, and the party, not the Clinton campaign, provided Jackson with about $1.2 million for a twelve-state voter registration drive. Latino leaders were given $1.5 million for a similar drive in twelve states with large Latino populations. Clinton had been criticized by Jackson and other African American leaders for not reaching out more to the black community. Clinton received a $6 million proposal from three black congressmen for voter registration, but no action was taken.[19]

Business and Industry Endorsements

Fueled by Bush statements that the economy was really better than Clinton said it was, voter discontent remained high. Clearly, this discontent, to which even the business community was not immune, created opportunities for the Democrats. Clinton hoped to take advantage of these opportunities, since he felt that endorsements by business leaders would give his campaign an added level of credibility. Ellis Mottur, director of business and high-tech constituencies for the campaign, said, "Our primary objective was to show the American public that if long-term, tough-minded, Republican business leaders would go against their norm and go with Clinton, then there's no way he's a traditional tax-and-spend Democrat."[20]

In part to recruit business support, Clinton ran a $1 million advertising campaign in early September, stating that Arkansas led the nation in job growth and that state incomes were rising at twice the national rate. Clinton also pledged to create 8 million new jobs in four years, a claim that Bush challenged.[21] Clinton also broadcast ads reminding voters of Bush's "no new taxes" pledge from the 1988 campaign and the statements Bush had made denying that the economy was in a recession.

A number of prominent Republicans and businesspersons endorsed Clinton as part of an eighteen-state announcement and the formation of the Independent Americans for New Leadership Committee. A number of defectors felt that the RNC isolated them from the party and that the religious right had taken over the party.[22] On September 21, 1992, more than 100 top business leaders endorsed Clinton, including about twenty-five longtime Republicans, bringing the total of business-related endorsements to about 400.[23]

While Clinton enjoyed more support than most Democratic presidential candidates from the business establishment, leaders of the *Fortune* 500 generally retained their traditional loyalty to the Republican Party. Support for Bush, however, was often lukewarm.[24] Many executives who had previously given only to Republicans switched from Bush to Clinton. In soft money, the Republicans were behind the Democrats by approximately $3 million for July, $10 million for August, and $4 million for September, in spite of Mosbacher's efforts.[25]

The support for Clinton from the entertainment industry was much more widespread than that for Bush. By mid-July, by one count, members of the entertainment industry had contributed $382,622 in soft money to the Democrats and only $130,490 to the Republicans.[26]

After the Democratic convention, Clinton's contributions from the entertainment industry increased. The level of support and excitement rose when it became evident that Clinton had a chance of winning.[27] Lew Wasserman, chairman of MCA, held a fund raiser resulting in more than $1 million. Tickets went for $5,000.[28]

The Hollywood Women's Political Committee hosted a celebrity fund raiser with a special performance by Barbra Streisand, raising nearly $1 million in ticket proceeds. Additional funds ranging from $500,000 to $1.5 million were expected to be raised by transmitting the event via satellite hookup to fund raisers across the country. The Clinton–Gore campaign received one-half of the proceeds with the remainder divided mainly between other candidates and the party.[29]

A group of neoconservative foreign policy experts endorsed Clinton in an ad in the *New York Times*. Among the thirty-three people signing the ad were Paul Nitze, Reagan's arms control negotiator, and former Assistant Secretary of State Richard Schifter.[30] He also was endorsed by retired Admiral William J. Crowe Jr., who was chairman of the Joint Chiefs of Staff under Presidents Reagan and Bush. As president, Clinton appointed Crowe as ambassador to Great Britain.

The Final Days

Clinton raised more money than Bush in the last months of the campaign. In fact, in the last six months of 1992, the DNC and the Clinton campaign raised about $69 million, compared with almost $49 million by the RNC and Bush campaign. These amounts broke down, according to Common Cause, as follows: Democrats raised $48.9 million in hard money and $20.1 million in soft money; whereas Republicans raised $35.8 million in hard money and $12.7 million in soft money.[31] This fund-raising effort marked the second time that a Democratic presidential candidate raised more money than the Republican—Dukakis was the first in 1988—reflecting Bush's political weakness and the effects of the recession in drying up some of Bush's sources of money.[32]

But money was very important in the last days of both campaigns. To conserve funds Bush's staff stayed in less expensive hotels, while Clinton made do with older buses and less expensive airplane food. All three major candidates spent in excess of $1 million each on advertising in the weekend before the election. Clinton and Perot purchased costly one-half-hour blocks of air time on the Monday before the elections.[33]

The Anatomy of Public Opinion Surveys

Public opinion survey data is one of the most valuable resources in a presidential campaign. Presidential campaigns rely on polling to help target their resources, shape their messages, plan their media buys, and determine candidate travel schedules. Polling expenditures are thus an essential component of presidential campaign spending, even though they do not consume a substantial portion of a campaign's budget. An understanding of polling expenses can provide valuable insights into a campaign's strategy and the states that are a focal point of the campaign's efforts.

This section provides a breakdown of the types of polls conducted by the 1992 presidential campaigns and the states in which they were conducted. Because of the nature of the public opinion expenditures by the three major campaigns—each provided from internal data compiled by the spenders—the presentation is made serially and is not combined into a single table. The data for the Clinton and Bush campaigns are presented for both the prenomination and the general election periods. Of course, the Perot information is for one campaign only, the general election campaign. Media spending data supplied by the campaigns of the three presidential campaigns will be found in chapter 8.[34]

Clinton–Gore

The Clinton and Clinton–Gore survey research expenditures for polling are shown in Table 5.3: $649,000 for the prenomination period and $1,622,000 for the general election period.

Table 5.3

Polling and Focus Group Expenditures—Clinton–Gore, 1992

	Primary Amount	General Amount
National surveys	$ 75,000	$ 654,000[a]
Focus groups	152,000	309,000
Perception analyzer/dial groups	0	65,000
Statewide surveys	422,000[b]	594,000[c]
Total	$649,000	$1,622,000[d]

Source: Citizens' Research Foundation.

[a]Includes professional fees and calling costs that were subcontracted by Clinton–Gore.
[b]Includes allocated professional fees.
[c]Includes statewide surveys and buy-ons paid for by Clinton–Gore and DNC Presidential 441a(d) authority.
[d]Totals do not include travel or communication costs.

What follows gives some notion of the extent and diversity of survey methods utilized by the Clinton–Gore campaign for the general election period only. It also focuses on the electoral votes of the states the campaign strategy dictated as a means of winning the election. Not counting nationwide surveys, the polling research expenditures were made as follows:

Focus Groups, which are small, intensive questioning sessions, were held in twelve states and cost $309,000:

Alabama	Illinois	Missouri
California	Kentucky	Ohio
Colorado	Louisiana	Pennsylvania
Georgia	Michigan	South Carolina

Perception analyzer/Dial groups, also small, were held in three states and cost $65,000:

Kentucky	Michigan	Ohio

Statewide surveys, paid for by the campaign, were conducted in eight states:

California	Kentucky	Ohio
Florida	Mississippi	Texas
Georgia	North Carolina	

Statewide buyons, in which the campaign shared costs with other campaigners, were purchased in more than one-half the states:

Alabama	Louisiana	Ohio
Arizona	Maine	Oklahoma
California	Maryland	Oregon
Colorado	Michigan	Pennsylvania
Connecticut	Minnesota	South Dakota
Delaware	Missouri	Tennessee
Georgia	Montana	Vermont
Illinois	Nevada	Washington
Iowa	New Jersey	Wisconsin
Kentucky	New Mexico	

The combined cost of the statewide and state buyons totaled $594,000.

Bush–Quayle

Table 5.4 shows the costs of the Bush–Quayle survey research: $853,928 in the prenomination period and $994,713 in the general election campaign.

To give some notion of the extent and diversity of survey methods for the Bush–Quayle pre- and post-nomination period, not counting nationwide surveys, and not broken down to separate prenomination and general election surveys, the polling research occurred as follows:

Focus groups, which are small, intensive questioning sessions, were held in ten locations:

Birmingham, Alabama	Farmington Hill, Michigan
Irvine, California	Paramus, New Jersey
Los Angeles, California	Charlotte, North Carolina
Atlanta, Georgia	Cleveland, Ohio
Towson, Maryland	Milwaukee, Wisconsin

Perception analyzer groups, also small, were held in nine locations:

Fresno, California	St. Louis, Missouri
Riverside, California	Teaneck, New Jersey
Arlington Heights, Illinois	Perrysburg, Ohio
Farmington Hills, Michigan	Milwaukee, Wisconsin
Southfield, Michigan	

Statewide surveys, paid for by the campaign, were conducted in one-half the states:

Alabama	Michigan	Oregon
California	Mississippi	South Carolina
Connecticut	Missouri	Tennessee
Florida	Montana	Texas
Georgia	New Hampshire	Virginia
Illinois	New Jersey	Washington
Iowa	New Mexico	Wisconsin
Kentucky	North Carolina	
Louisiana	Ohio	

Table 5.4

Research Expenditures—Bush—Quayle, 1992

	Primary (December 1991– July 1992)		General (July 31– November 11)		Total	
	No.	Amount	No.	Amount	No.	Amount
Projects						
National surveys	8	$467,901	7	$233,750	15	$ 691,651
National tracking				94,000		94,000
National track buy-ons				39,325		39,325
Subtotal		467,901		357,075		824,976
Focus groups	24	109,282	8	32,084	32	141,366
Perception analyzer groups	2	24,000	10	109,950	12	133,950
Subtotal		133,282		142,034		275,316
Statewide surveys	14	134,218	41	397,709	55	531,927
Statewide buy-ons			63	27,705	63	27,705
Statewide tracking			7	188,717	7	188,717
Subtotal		134,218		614,131		748,349
Total		$853,928		$994,713		$1,848,641

Source: Citizens' Research Foundation.

Statewide buyons, in which the campaign shared costs with other campaigners, were purchased in seventeen states:

Arizona	Nebraska
Colorado	Nevada
Delaware	North Dakota
Hawaii	Oklahoma
Idaho	Pennsylvania
Indiana	South Dakota
Maine	Vermont
Maryland	Wyoming
Massachusetts	

The Bush—Quayle campaigns spent a combined total of $1,848,641 on public opinion surveys.

Table 5.5

Research Expenditures—Perot, 1992

	General (July 31–November 1): Amount
Projects	
National surveys	$13,100.00[a]
National tracking	0
National track buy-on	—
Focus Groups	$65,762.36[b]
Perception analyzer groups	0
Statewide surveys	$ 30,000[b]
Statewide buy-ons	0
Statewide tracking	0
Total	$108,862.36

Source: Citizens' Research Foundation.

[a]Includes $3,500 expenditure at direction of temporary staff unbeknownst to candidate (June 1992); balance $9,600 expended in October 1992.
[b]Expenditure at direction of temporary staff unbeknownst to candidate (June 1992).

Perot–Stockdale

The Perot–Stockdale polling costs, presented from July 31, 1992, to November 1, 1992, and shown in Table 5.5, indicate expenditures of only $108,862, minimal amounts for a $68 million campaign.

Conclusions

Like the media data to be presented in chapter 8, the Clinton–Gore campaign spent more than $700,000 more on polling than the Bush–Quayle general election campaign, which barely spent $1 million. But in the prenomination period, Bush spent in excess of $200,000 more than Clinton; however, this same pattern of higher Bush spending also is shown in Table 8.1 on media expenditures. Again, it is presumed that Bush spent more on media and polling while having only one opponent, Buchanan, because he had the money available, whereas Clinton, having formidable opponents who won various primaries and caucuses, spent less because he had relatively less to spend, needing to concentrate his resources across more primary and caucus states.

Compliance Costs and Their Uses

One form of spending in the presidential campaigns is for compliance costs. FEC regulations permit publicly funded campaigns to raise private contributions, up to $1,000 per contributor, in separate accounts to pay for legal and accounting expenses incurred in complying with the law. The regulations exempt compliance fund spending from the expenditure limits on the theory that laws and regulations should not be an inordinate burden on limited campaign funds.

In the last week of the campaign, Clinton found himself running short of his $55.2 million public funding grant and, in an unprecedented move, asked the FEC for permission to borrow money in anticipation of a $1.2 million reimbursement by the Secret Service. The Bush campaign denounced the request as evidence that Clinton had mismanaged public funds and was seeking an unfair late influx of cash. Bush had $7.9 million left and Malek made a point of Clinton's "failing his first test in managing federal funds."[35] Clinton refuted Bush's accusation by stating that the campaign had not run out of money but had a temporary cash-flow problem because a challenger had required up-front Secret Service costs that an incumbent does not have.

The FEC voted 4 to 0 on November 13, 1992, to allow the Clinton campaign to take an interest-free loan from its compliance fund. The campaign estimated nondeferable, post-general-election expenses from November 4 to December 3, 1992, of $844,500 for payroll and related taxes, $550,000 for telephone lines and services, $125,000 for consulting fees, and $110,000 for printing and production fees. The FEC said the money must be used for qualified campaign expenses, must be repaid promptly, and could not be used creatively to exceed the spending limit. Commissioner Trevor Potter stated that the FEC should review the legal and accounting compliance fund exception: "In my opinion, the legal and accounting fund, a creation of the Commission, has grown far beyond its intended bounds. As a result, it presents the spectacle of high profile private fund raising by a presidential campaign which has forsworn this very activity. This can only sow confusion about the public funding system."[36]

The Center for Responsive Politics (CRP), a Washington-based watchdog group, issued a June 1992 report criticizing the use of private money in presidential campaigns and charging that presidential compliance funds were being turned into campaign "slush funds."[37] The report found that between January 1, 1991, and February 29, 1992, some 656 individuals who had contributed $1,000 to Bush's prenomination campaign made a second $1,000 contribution to the Bush–Quayle '92 Compliance Committee.[38]

On March 1, 1994, the CRP filed a petition for rulemaking with the FEC, arguing that the $11 million spent on compliance funds by the major party candidates in the general election period violated the public funding statute and undermined the objectives of the presidential public funding system. The petition stated, among other details, that Clinton–Gore disclosure records showed spending of $200,000 in compliance funds to mail "The Man from Hope" videos to prospective donors; and that Bush–Quayle committee filings covered in compliance funds more than $650,000 in personnel costs and in excess of $470,000 on computer equipment.[39] The FEC staff drafted documents to hold hearings on the issue, and the outcome is unknown at this writing.

In 1992, while the campaigns were under way, the CRP issued a study indicating that in the prenomination campaign filings with the FEC, some 53 percent of Clinton donors of more than $200, and nearly 63 percent of Bush donors of more than $200, were not identified by occupation and principal place of business, as required by law.[40] Shortly thereafter, the FEC sent candidates reminders of their legal obligation to provide full information about contributors of more than $200.[41]

The irony is that the CRP's concurrent drive to achieve higher standards of "best efforts" by candidate committees to identify fully their donors is contrary to the complaint about compliance costs, because without permitted compliance funds, surely there would be even less effort by the committees to identify donors. In any case, the FEC strengthened its "best effort" rules in 1993 and later recommended that Congress clarify whether private funds should continue to be used by presidential candidates to meet the accounting and compliance requirements.[42] Nevertheless, the CRP complaint sought even tougher enforcement.

In July 1994, a federal district court judge in Washington, DC, dismissed a suit brought by the RNC and the Republican senatorial and congressional committees, claiming the "best efforts" regulation was "arbitrary, capricious and contrary to law." The FEC requires political committees to include in fund-raising materials a specific admonition, stating the law's disclosure requirements, and to make at least one specific written or oral request to the donor to provide occupation and principal place of business information.[43]

Ross Perot

During Ross Perot's ascendancy in 1992, it was reported that he had said he would spend from his personal fortune, "whatever it takes," perhaps $100 million or more, to campaign for the presidency.[44] In reality, the total cost of Perot's on-again, off-again campaigns was $68.4 million. The Perot '92 campaign had net operating expenditures of $67.3 million, as of December 31, 1992, after deducting contributions that were refunded, bank loans that were repaid, and other offsets; additional amounts of $1.1 million were spent through March 31, 1994, some for 1992 bills.

Of these amounts, Perot contributed $63,267,115 of his own money and received $5,022,575 in individual contributions, most of which were in-kind contributions made to local grass-roots groups and dollar amounts designated to such groups. Refunds of contributions totaled $1,255,652, and net operating expenditures were $68,386,947. Perot received 19,747,267 votes, so the cost per vote was $3.46.[45]

The costs of the Perot campaigns can be best understood by dividing them into six components:

1. The preliminary period in which there was speculation about his running and early spending occurred;
2. The petition drive, in which some volunteer organizations received assistance to get Perot on the ballot as an independent candidate in fifty states;
3. The first campaign, both amateurish and professional;
4. The withdrawal period in July through September, with continuing activities by some state organizations clouding Perot intentions;
5. The October–November campaign, rejoined and fully funded;
6. The post-election period, leading to the organization of United We Stand America, an ongoing entity.

Many in the media wrote of Perot's advantage in being able to underwrite a $100 million campaign, while Bush and Clinton were disadvantaged by the $65.5 million general election spending limit (including national party coordinated expenditures) they agreed to as a consequence of accepting public funds. But not many observers noted that in the end, Perot's actual spending only equaled that of the Bush–Quayle and Clinton–Gore tickets' limited spending of $65.5 million each in the general election period, although most of his spending was concentrated in October and early November. The spending totals shown in Table 5.2 by the major party tickets and in allied and related spending on their behalf, however, actually exceeded the Perot amount substantially. As noted, major party tickets have a party and interest group infrastructure that an independent or minor party candidate does not naturally have. Independent or minor party candidates have to build one, if possible, as Perot did through his state petitions and campaign chapters.[46]

Moreover, since Perot's spending ran with interruptions from February through November, it would be fairer to include in the comparison prenomination spending by Bush ($37.9 million) and Clinton ($33.9 million), and their exposure at the national nominating conventions (see Table 2.4). Perot's state petition drive could be considered—as was that of Wallace in 1968—the equivalent of a prenomination campaign, although in effect he nominated himself (of course, he would say he was responding to the people). But he did devote considerable resources to start-up costs and to getting on and staying on the ballot in fifty states, a difficult and costly process in terms of time and money.

The Perot advantage, in money amounts unique and impressive, took several forms: (1) his ability to write personal checks when and as needed, without spending time on fund raising; (2) his ability to finance a campaign without public funding (he would have been eligible retroactively, after the election, if he had followed the FECA as an independent candidate and could have contributed only up to $50,000 of his own money), giving him an issue to use against Bush and Clinton; and (3) his concurrent avoidance of spending limits, enabling him to spend unlimited amounts when and as needed. And Perot had four savings that cut down on his need to spend: (1) no competition for nomination; (2) free publicity through media attention and extensive use of his specialty, the "talk shows" and what are called "electronic town halls"; (3) the invitation by Bush and Clinton to participate in the presidential debates (the first such third-candidate participation in history); and (4) the July-to-September hiatus from active campaigning.

In short, Perot's personal spending made him competitive, and, like Clinton, Bush, and their supporters, he did spend more than the nominal $55.2 million limit allotted with the public funding grant that applied to Bush and Clinton. But even if he had spent as much as $100 million, this would only have made him competitive with the spending by and on behalf of the major party tickets.

While Perot ran on his own money, he also ran against other people's money. He made a virtue of spending from his personal fortune, saying he was buying the election "for the American people," because they could not afford it, while chastising others dependent upon special interest money or, in presidential campaigns, taxpayer dollars.[47] He stated, "I don't want to spend a penny of taxpayers' money on me ... because I want that money, which we don't have enough of, to go out to help the people who need it, and to be spent to rebuild our country."[48] Despite occasional questioning by reporters, Perot never responded directly to questions of how others not as wealthy as he could finance campaigns while avoiding special interest money or taxpayer dollars or both. He never committed to the idea of public funding as a principle, but was vociferous on the matter of his opponents' funding: "You taxpayers are going to pay for the Democrats' and the Republicans' campaigns."[49] He often criticized the operation of political action committees and the work of lobbyists, particularly lobbyists for foreign interests, and he repeatedly indicted the money-dominated process and its *modus operandi*.

Of course, Perot's campaign drew op-ed articles, such as a typical one entitled, "Perot *Is* Buying the Election, and That's Bad."[50] And many public opinion surveys were conducted. In one survey conducted in April by NBC News and the *Wall Street Journal,* 51 percent said that Perot's spending $100 million of his own money was a good thing—compared with 33 percent saying it was bad trying to buy the presidency—because he would not have to raise money from "special interest groups."[51]

The presidency has attracted wealthy candidates before, such as the Roosevelts, Rockefellers, Kennedys, and Du Ponts. But only Perot was willing to finance a campaign almost exclusively with his own money. By donating $63.3 million, Perot qualifies for a unique place: His is the single largest self-contribution in the nation's history.

Perot's campaign was by far the costliest minor party or independent candidate effort in American history, and the only one ever led by a billionaire. The available records of national committees—certainly fragmentary and not comprehensive at the time—show only $665,420 spent for Theodore Roosevelt's Progressive Party in 1912, and $236,963 for Robert LaFollette's Progressive Party in 1924.[52] For 1948, records of receipts by national committees show $1.1 million for Henry Wallace's effort and a mere $163,000 for Strom Thurmond's campaign.[53] While these were not the totals spent at all levels, they hardly compare with the almost $9 million reported by the George Wallace campaign in 1968, even considering price differentials and inflation.[54] John Anderson's independent candidacy in 1980 cost some $16.6 million.[55]

A Unique Series of Campaigns

The first indication that Perot might run for president was given in an appearance on CNN's "Larry King Live," in which he said he would agree to run a grass-roots campaign if "everyday folks" urged him to do so and placed his name on the ballot in all fifty states. After an initial surge of support, Perot opened a dozen telephone lines and a toll-free number.[56] Further appearances on "60 Minutes" and the syndicated "Donahue" show caused Perot to expand to more than 1,300 telephone lines, including 1,200 leased from cable's Home Shopping Network. By April, as many as 30,000 calls a day were claimed; supporters characterized it as the only phone bank in political history never to make an outgoing call.[57]

The first month of disclosure under federal law was March 1992, when $394,803 was spent, including some $60,000 on telephone equipment.[58] Early expenditures also were made in an effort to comply with the FECA. As self-starting supporters set up state organizations on Perot's behalf, most not knowing the requirements of federal law, the central headquarters had to instruct these people on the law, to centralize disclosure, to get information on bank accounts, and to ensure that excessive contributions were not accepted. While Perot said publicly he would ask only for $5 contributions from ordinary people, some larger contributions were accepted, as were various goods and services that were listed as "in-kind" contributions, virtually all from volunteers to local organizations.[59]

Access to general election ballots in fifty states is a difficult standard to meet. In most states, the law required a running mate, so on March 30, Perot chose as a temporary running mate retired Vice Admiral James B. Stockdale, a former combat pilot and Vietnam War participant, and a winner of the Congressional Medal of Honor.[60] Ballot access also requires legal skills, extensive signature gathering, and money.

Perot sent money to state organizations to assist in their efforts to get his ticket on the ballots, seeking to stop the circulation of competing petitions, and to ensure their FECA compliance. In most states, Perot easily qualified for the ballot, as his supporters often filed thousands or even tens of thousands more signatures than were required by law. Perot's filing for April with the FEC brought his personal contributions to $1.3 million, and his organization reported contributions of $168,000, mostly in-kind gifts in which a fair-market price of not more than $1,000 per person is permitted.[61]

Without formally declaring his candidacy, Perot achieved a notable success, propelling himself into a serious challenge to the two major parties and their tickets. Mainly through appearances on talk shows, and with very limited travel to rallies, he attracted millions of citizens into an emotional crusade largely fueled by disillusionment with Washington and professional politics.

Perot soon found himself in need of a staff.[62] On the recommendation of Tom Luce, Perot's lawyer and associate, who was campaign chairman through mid-July, he hired two key persons: as press secretary, James Squires, a former *Chicago Tribune* editor and newspaper executive; as issues director, John White. Both had been associates of Luce at the Kennedy School at Harvard University. Then in early June, Perot entered a more traditional phase of his campaign. He assembled a "world-class" bipartisan staff led by Ed Rollins, a Republican, and Hamilton Jordan, a Democrat, veteran strategists with presidential experience. In turn, they hired famous ad men such as Hal Riney and Gerald Rafshoon. The conventional campaign consultants drew up costly plans for broadcasting and mail drives. With White, Luce, and others, they sought to identify and flesh out issues; they tried to schedule events and produced pilot television commercials.

But Perot balked. He rejected a mail campaign to thank and energize state volunteers and petition signers (at a cost of $2 million to $3 million) because he opposed junk mail; he objected to a $7 million initial advertising campaign, and an overall advertising budget of $50 million; he rejected the idea of holding a national convention. Mainly, he frustrated his professional staff members, and they frustrated him. After about forty-five days, Rollins announced he was leaving, but Jordan hung on a bit longer; neither satisfied Perot's ideas on grass-roots emphasis.[63] Finally, while the Democratic convention was in progress, Perot withdrew abruptly from a campaign he had never formally entered. He had given some $12,271,803 to his aborted campaign and had received about $2.5 million in outside contributions.[64] He quit over the costs, but also because of the media scrutiny he was receiving. At the time, he voiced initial good impressions of Clinton's program and foresaw a revival with Democrats addressing needed issues.

In some states, Perot would be on the ballot unless he withdrew. In others, there was a deadline for withdrawing, or otherwise he would be on the ballot; the deadline had already passed in some states. Perot did not give a clear sign of his intentions, yet he worked to get on remaining ballots if his volunteers wanted him to. He spent as much as $40,000 per month to keep his California operation alive and, at the highest point, some $480,000 a month to retain sixty-four offices in fifty states.[65] During the hiatus, Perot undertook a massive effort to get his ticket on the New York ballot: He paid $150,000 for full-page newspaper advertisements and $30,000 for radio commercials, and he hired 600 people from fifteen employment agencies to canvass for necessary petition signatures, paying two such agencies some $85,000. In August and September, the national Perot Petition Committee paid $250,000 for office equipment, $540,000 to MCI for telephone service, and $718,000 to Perot Systems for computer time.[66] In August, he also published a book, *United We Stand,* which became a best-seller.[67]

Two weeks after his withdrawal, United We Stand America was formed as a nonprofit, noncampaign-related organization, based on the volunteer campaign groups. Offices were opened in all fifty states. A conspiracy theorist could write a scenario for Perot's taking a chance on dropping out, scrapping an expensive conventional campaign through part of July, August, and September, and then getting back in with an "October Surprise."

This is exactly what happened, and it allowed him to regroup, to purge political consultants, to prepare for a showdown, and to save considerable personal spending. Through minimal spending during this period, at the least he kept his options open for reactivating publicly his campaign.

In late September, Bush and Clinton sent emissaries to meet with Perot, to discuss his future role. Amid hints he would reenter the contest, he expressed his disappointment that the Republican and Democratic campaigns were failing to address the issues, particularly ways to reduce the federal deficit. During this period, Perot attempted to buy television time to air issue-oriented presentations by various individuals, such as Paul Tsongas and Senator Warren Rudman, but the networks turned him down, noting that he could buy time only if he became a candidate. On October 1, Perot reentered the campaign, charging that Bush and Clinton were failing to address government spending and related economic issues.[68]

A day after announcing his reentry, Perot committed to spending about $1 million for advertising the next week. His first buy was a one-half-hour "infomercial" on CBS, at a cost of $380,000; this program shocked CBS executives by outdrawing the later baseball playoffs.[69] He paid $620,000 to ABC for a one-half-hour program leading into the "20/20" program with Barbara Walters. Later, he bought thirty minutes on ABC, opposite a World Series game, at a cost of $370,000. He spent $3.2 million for a series of fifteen- to thirty-second commercials on ABC, broadcast during prime time, sports programs, and "Good Morning, America."[70]

Perot was reported to have spent $10.8 million in the first ten days following his reentry. What was heralded in the press as a $40 million television advertising blitz for the month of October actually was less because the entire Perot media placements were only $31.9 million, according to an official Perot source.[71] He wrapped up his campaign on election eve, paying $3 million for two hours in thirty-minute blocks on ABC and CBS, and sixty minutes on NBC.[72]

The Perot campaign did not end with the election. He sought to mold United We Stand America into a citizens' lobby. It was reorganized as a nonprofit, nonelection-related organization. He undertook membership campaigns for his grass-roots watchdog group, asking $15 in annual dues. The organization took on the task of monitoring the new Clinton administration and Congress in their efforts to reduce the federal deficit and get the economy going again.[73] In a period of fluidity in American politics, in which partisan loyalties have declined, the prospects for Perot's organization looked bright. While he has refused to reveal the membership or the income for United We Stand, a carefully researched article indicated that in early April 1993, he probably had more than 1 million members and had taken in more than $15 million.[74] Some of the money was spent on recruitment activities, including three "infomercials," but money also was used to sustain the organization's ongoing activities, including the conducting and dissemination of public policy polls. The "infomercials" brought in more than $3 million, and Perot's popularity grew to 60 percent by May 1993.

Another indication of his early post-election popularity was in the publication of issue presentations derived from campaign infomercials in a book, *Not for Sale at Any Price* (New York: Hyperion, 1993), and listed for several weeks on the *New York Times* best-seller list.

The legacy of Perot's candidacy was felt in other ways. He appeared before committees of Congress, at his own instigation and on invitation; he was wooed by freshman Republicans; and he cast an influence on election reform legislation to the extent that he continued his criticisms of lobbyists, PACs, and "bloated campaign budgets"—a strange charge coming from a $60 million–plus self-contributor![75] Perot also was highly visible in the debate over the North American Free Trade Agreement (NAFTA) in 1993. He opposed NAFTA and wrote a book with Pat Choate, *Save Your Job, Save Our Country, Why NAFTA Must Be Stopped—Now* (Hyperion Books, 1993). As an example of the deference shown to him, Perot was invited to engage in a debate on NAFTA with Vice President Gore, bringing CNN its biggest audience ever; however, Perot's performance was less than sparkling, and his reputation began to decline.[76]

An Evaluation

Apart from funding aspects, reference has been made to Perot's savings in view of the media attention he received. The conclusion of a detailed analysis is best captured by a headline: "Unconventional Media Boosted Perot, Mainstream Brought Him Down." The accompanying story told of a study indicating that Perot's rapid rise in the polls to a 20 percent rating in late March was due to highly successful use of unconventional media such as talk shows, and without benefit of party, election, or the attention of the establishment press. In comparison, once it became clear that Clinton could win and Perot could not, not only did Clinton (and Bush) get much more coverage, but Perot received considerable investigative reporting and negative press by the mainstream media.[77]

Throughout, Perot declined to launch a "third" party, remaining in the American tradition of seeking to maintain a following for an individual who had run for president, but not evolving into an ideological group, as most minor parties do.[78] Perot has been said to believe he helped to give a voice to a pragmatic, centrist group in the population, while parties tend to be ideological.

Nevertheless, Perot's campaign was innovative in the use of free talk shows and one-half-hour "infomercials" that drew wide audiences. The notion of electronic town halls to thrash out policies was appealing to many. And, of course, Perot's ideas struck a very responsive chord among up to 38 percent of potential voters who said they would vote for him if they thought he could win. Many did not want to waste their votes, but one-half of those did vote for him. Finally, the Perot campaign was a phenomenon about much more than money: volunteerism by scores of thousands, ideas that met widespread popular response, and an unparalleled meteoric rise in opinion polls before significant amounts of money were spent.

Minor Parties and Independent Candidates

Perot was the most important and influential independent candidate in 1992, but there were other independent candidates and candidates of minor parties; some 273 filed with the FEC. In Table 2.1, which covers the costs of electing a president, some $71.2 million is shown as spending by Perot and the minor and independent candidates. While Perot's campaign accounts for most of the spending, Table 5.6 lists those who spent $5,000 or more in nonmajor party campaigns. The time periods are different for the candidates because they were nominated or chose to run at different times. Of these, three candidates applied for and received matching funds for their campaigns for nomination; the prenomination costs for minor parties are shown in Table 2.1 as well. None of the candidates shown in Table 5.6 received any public funding for their general election campaigns, but in the cases of Fulani, Hagelin, and LaRouche, their prenomination spending, including the matching funds they received and spent, significantly exceeded their general election spending, as follows:

	Prenomination	General Election
Fulani	$4,137,368	$204,907
Hagelin	926,304	377,055
LaRouche	1,605,386	1,213,459

These figures show the impact of public funding for Fulani, Hagelin, and LaRouche, although the latter only received public funds belatedly and under court order.

As noted in chapter 1, in addition to the major party candidates for president, only Ross Perot and Andre Marrou of the Libertarian Party were

Table 5.6

Minor Parties and Independent Candidates: General Election Campaigns, 1992

Candidate	Identification	Amount
Ross Perot	Independent	$68,314,358
Lyndon LaRouche	Independents for Economic Recovery	1,213,459
Andre V. Marrou	Libertarian Party	656,910
John Hagelin	Natural Law Party	377,055
Lenora Fulani	New Alliance	204,907
Bob Congdon		9,998
James "Bo" Gritz	Populist/America First	176,056
Howard Phillips	U.S. Taxpayers	228,215
Robert Allen Mark Selwa		5,008
James MacWarren	Socialist Workers	29,811
John Andrew Yiamouyiannis	Independent	8,509
Total		$71,224,286

Source: Federal Election Commission, data as of December 31, 1993.

Note: Time periods differ for each candidate, since the candidates were nominated or chose to run at different times.

on the ballot in all fifty states. Lenora Fulani of the New Alliance Party was on the ballot in forty states, and John Hagelin of the Natural Law Party was on the ballot in twenty-nine states. Lyndon LaRouche was on the ballot in eighteen states and received write-in votes in thirteen states as well.

Fulani

Lenora B. Fulani, presidential candidate of the New Alliance Party, qualified for matching funds in 1992 and 1988. Funds were raised mostly through some 200 volunteers who collected 40,000 contributions, mainly on street corners and by knocking on doors, particularly in California and New York City. About 10 percent of contributions were raised over the phone from people who had contributed in the past. The party had raised close to $1 million from 60,000 contributors as of mid-February 1992. Fulani said her fund-raising success was "a loud statement by the people of this country for a broader range of candidates and viewpoints."[79]

The New Alliance Party was founded twenty-five years ago by Fred Newman and has been accused of operating like a cult and of being anti-Semitic. The party and groups affiliated with it support local political campaigns, psychotherapy groups, a lobbying operation in Washington, DC, and a publishing arm that supports Louis Farrakhan, a controversial Muslim leader. The party describes itself as a black-led, woman-led, pro-gay, pro-socialist, multiracial progressive movement. Fulani was the party's presidential candidate in 1988 also, when she received $922,000 of public money.

In addition to her independent race for president, Fulani appeared on the New Hampshire ballot as a Democrat in 1992. She received only 402 votes in the primary. In late February, Fulani dropped out of the Democratic primary race but continued her independent campaign. She would have lost her matching funds as a Democratic candidate if she did not receive 20 percent of the vote in an upcoming primary. As an independent, she qualified without having to meet these requirements.

A large percentage of her funds came from members of New Alliance or related groups. The campaign raised a total of $2.2 million in almost 102,000 individual contributions, and received $1.9 million in federal matching funds.

Nearly all of the $4.1 million budget was spent on travel, room and board for campaign workers, and an expanded media campaign. Often, New Alliance-related businesses were hired for campaign needs. More than $450,000 was paid to supporting businesses tied to the party. Some $25,000 was spent for copies of the *National Alliance*, the party newspaper. Again, it is legal for a political campaign to purchase services from companies owned by the candidate's close associates but these services must be offered at no more than fair market value.

In mid-1994, the FEC undertook an investigation into the Fulani campaign, following published reports that several former members of the party made payments to themselves and that certain campaign workers never saw checks that were made out in their names. The diversion of taxpayer funds, of course, would be a violation of federal law.[80]

Hagelin

John Hagelin was the nominated candidate of the Natural Law Party. The party qualified as a "national committee" of a political party because it demonstrated sufficient activity at the national level. Its presidential candidate was on the ballot in twenty-nine states, and it had candidates for the Senate and House on the ballots in twenty-two states.

It was not until October 15, 1992, that the FEC found that Hagelin was eligible for federal matching funds for his prenomination campaign, enabling him to pay debts and winding-down expenses.[81] Hagelin's pre- and post-nomination funding totaled $1.3 million, as shown elsewhere.[82]

LaRouche

Lyndon H. LaRouche, who has run for the Democratic nomination in every election since 1980, was convicted of mail fraud, conspiracy, and tax evasion in 1988 in a fund-raising scheme that involved $30 million in defaulted loans. LaRouche first applied for matching funds in 1976 but was not found to be eligible. Then he violated federal campaign law in 1980, and post-campaign audits in 1984 and 1988 revealed suspicious activity. Matching funds in 1984 were not disbursed until his campaign organization paid a civil penalty and made other repayments. By 1992, LaRouche had received $1.8 million in matching funds for his previous campaigns. Two states, Massachusetts and Virginia, opened criminal investigations. The FBI raided LaRouche's headquarters and seized its records when he failed to provide financial information.

While LaRouche campaigned from prison for the nomination in 1992, his supporters raised $139,000 in twenty-two states, enough to qualify for matching funds from the U.S. Treasury. Federal law prohibits a felon from voting but not from running for office. The FEC denied the request for federal matching funds on December 19, 1991, citing LaRouche's conviction and imprisonment for fraud and fund-raising abuses. This was the first time the commission denied matching funds to a presidential candidate based on his past conduct. Commissioners said that LaRouche's violations of fund-raising rules led them to believe he would have done the same in 1992. LaRouche's attorney, Richard Mayberry, appealed the decision.

Supporters of LaRouche said the FEC did not have authority to deny funding based on a candidate's previous behavior. LaRouche claimed the FEC did not make its decision on the current application for funds, and the FEC failed in its bid to get Congress to enact legislation that would disqualify candidates who had violated campaign law from receiving matching funds.

On July 2, 1993, a federal appeals court ruled that the FEC could not deny an application for matching funds if the law's basic eligibility requirements were met. Circuit Judge Stephen F. Williams wrote, "The Commission is not authorized to appraise the candidate's good faith, honesty, probity or general reliability."[83] The Supreme Court refused to hear the case, letting the circuit court decision stand.

LaRouche was paroled on January 26, 1994, after serving five years of his fifteen-year sentence. In mid-February 1994, the FEC certified LaRouche's eligibility for a token amount, $100,000 in federal matching funds. LaRouche received an additional $468,435, for a total of $568,435 certified by the FEC. But an FEC spokesman maintained that LaRouche owed $146,000 to the U.S. Treasury following an audit of his 1988 campaign.

LaRouche also was on the ballot as an independent candidate in the general election in thirty states and the District of Columbia.[84] He spent $1.6 million on his prenomination campaign and $1.2 million on his general election campaign. In total, LaRouche spent $2.8 million seeking the presidency in 1992.

Reevaluating Reform

If the system of public funding of presidential campaigns described in this and previous chapters is to survive, it is necessary to think of making changes to keep up with the actual costs of campaigns in terms of contribution and expenditure limits, and the amounts of public funding.

While the federally imposed individual contribution limit of $1,000 per candidate per election may seem high to many Americans who could not make such a gift, the erosion of the dollar has been so severe that a $1,000 contribution in 1992 was worth a little more than one-third of the buying power in 1975 values, when the limit went into effect. Reflecting increases in the CPI, it cost $2,495 in August 1992 dollars to buy what $1,000 would have purchased in 1975.

Yet the costs of most items needed in campaigns have skyrocketed at a much higher rate. For example, from 1988 to 1992, the cost of a guaranteed thirty-second commercial during prime time on WAGA-TV in Atlanta rose about 20 percent, from $1,500 to $1,800. Broadcast costs in larger media markets were higher and escalating at an ever greater rate. From 1988 to 1992, one calculation showed a 17.6 percent increase in hotel rates; a bumper sticker, bought in lots of 1,000, rose from 11 cents to 20 cents each, representing an 81.8 percent increase; a campaign button, bought in lots of 1,000, rose 20 percent from 25 cents to 30 cents each; and a first-class postage stamp rose from 22 cents to 29 cents each, a 31.8 percent increase.[85]

The feasibility of public financing has depended on taxpayers' willingness to earmark a small portion of their tax liabilities for the PECF by using the federal income-tax checkoff. The $1 checkoff amount had not been increased since its inception in 1972, until 1993. From 1976 to 1992, the system provided enough money to cover the public funds certified to presidential prenomination and general election candidates, and to the major parties for their national nominating conventions; certifications by the FEC totaled $71.4 million in 1976, $101.6 million in 1980, $132.6 million in 1984, $176.9 million in 1988, and $175.4 million as of April 1993. The

1992 public financing payouts in the three phases of the presidential selection process were shown in Table 2.5.

While there was a small dip in 1992 amounts needed, the upward growth in spending over the course of five elections has resulted in a level of government payouts that now exceeds the amount of revenue generated by the system. Table 1.4 shows that, from 1976 through 1992, the approximate percentage of tax returns in which money was checked off for the PECF has ranged from a high of 28.7 percent in 1981 to a low of 17.7 percent in 1992. Prior to 1992, the FEC raised serious questions about the adequacy of the amounts of check-off funds. The 1993 increase in the rate of the tax checkoff to $3 was not only necessary but justified.

New ways of defining and dealing with soft money, and seeing that it is fully disclosed, are needed. New consideration of the role of political party committees, which spend most of the soft money, surely is necessary.

When monies spent on both major party conventions and the general election are twice as much as envisioned by spending limits, the time is at hand to reappraise the effectiveness of the law. The public funding could be conceptualized as "floors without ceilings," that is, an effort to give financial assistance that will permit candidates to have access to the electorate but without exacting the price of spending limits. But this is not a popular view. The notion of floors without ceilings has its supporters among some academics and others but has not gained popular acceptance (although most foreign nations that provide public funds do so without imposing expenditure limits). One might ask why in this formulation tax dollars should be added to unlimited private dollars. In the circumstances, then, most will interpret the spending as excessive, indicating a breakdown of the system envisioned by the Congress when it enacted public funding in the 1971 FECA and the 1974 amendments. But "floors without ceilings" well describes what was actually experienced in both 1992 and 1988. The development of a Campaign Cost Index, on which a revised system of public funding and expenditure limits could be pegged, would be an important first step.

Yet despite the high spending and the negative campaigns, any evaluation of the system should conclude that voluntarily donated campaign funds, as well as public funds earmarked by taxpayers to help finance campaigns, should be considered money well spent. The most costly campaigns are those in which voters choose poorly because they are ill-informed. For a candidate or party the most expensive election is a lost election. Accordingly, candidates and parties often spend as much as they can—and sometimes go into debt.

Conclusions

The FECA has achieved mixed results, if the experience of five presidential campaigns is any indication. In the prenomination period, the public funding provisions have improved access to the contest by supplementing the treasuries of candidates without the backing of wealthy contributors. Evidence may be found in the victorious campaign of the initially little-known Jimmy Carter in 1976, in the ability of George Bush and John Anderson to wage effective campaigns in 1980, or of Gary Hart and Jesse Jackson to make their marks in 1984, of Jackson again in 1988, and of Bill Clinton in 1992. In the 1992 prenomination period, several little-known Democrats needed the public money to gain attention.

Prior to 1988, contribution limits were thought to have reduced the possibilities that wealthy contributors could exert political influence. Disclosure provisions resulted in more campaign finance information than ever before being available to the public, and compliance requirements caused campaigns to place greater emphasis on money management and accountability. These effects suggest that in some ways the laws succeeded in altering the behavior or candidates, committees, and contributors to achieve some of the goals of campaign reform. But the incidence and amounts of soft money in 1988 and 1992 had implications for the effectiveness of both contribution and spending limits.

Another result of the law has been less favorable. The low individual contribution limit has caused wealthy contributors to be replaced by a variety of fund raisers upon whom candidates may become equally dependent for campaign funds. The large contributor, in effect, has been replaced by the large solicitor. Solicitors include direct mail consultants with access to mailing lists of proven donors to campaigns; PAC managers with their increasingly sophisticated means of fund raising; entertainment industry promoters who can persuade their clients to hold benefit concerts for favored candidates; and elite solicitors who can tap into networks of individuals capable of contributing up to the maximum allowed.

Even with public matching funds, the low contribution limit makes it difficult for candidates to raise sufficient money to conduct their campaigns. In 1984, for example, every eligible Democratic candidate ended his prenomination campaign with a substantial debt, and the combined indebtedness for all those candidates reached as much as $15 million. Debt repayment activities continued throughout the general election period—and well beyond—distracting attention and draining resources from the Democratic campaign. While few 1992 campaigns had lingering debts, the low contribution limits required candidates to spend considerable time raising money.

The low individual contribution limit and the expenditure limits have reduced campaign flexibility and rigidified the campaign process. The contribution limit tends to work to the advantage of well-known candidates capable of raising money quickly, forcing lesser-known candidates to begin their fund raising early, thereby lengthening the campaign season. The expenditure limit makes it difficult for candidates who have spent close to the maximum allowed to alter campaign strategy to fend off new challenges or to take other new developments such as Super Tuesday into account. The spending limit also tends to encourage candidates to favor mass media advertising, which may be more cost-effective than grass-roots campaigning but may not be as informative. It has caused candidates to centralize control of their campaign at the expense of local authority. Problems of cash flow and cash management abound.

The limits also have spurred the creation of several means of avoidance, including the presidential PACs, delegate committees, soft money, and independent expenditures. Restricting money at any given point in the campaign process often results in new channels being carved through which monied individuals and groups can seek to bring their influence to bear once more.

Despite the increase in campaign finance information available to the public because of the FECA disclosure provisions, there has been some significant erosion in the ability of these provisions to bring important data to light. For example, in December 1983, the FEC voted 4 to 2 to allow candidates who contract with outside consultants to conduct campaign-related activities on their behalf to meet their disclosure obligations merely by reporting payments made to those consultants.[86] The decision allowed the Mondale for President Committee to avoid public disclosure of its itemized media costs, permitting the committee instead merely to report the lump sums it paid to its media firm. The FEC failed to heed a warning from its own legal staff that under such a ruling campaigns could defeat the purpose of public disclosure of all campaign expenditures. Finally, the complexities of the compliance requirements have contributed to the professionalization of campaigns, possibly chilling enthusiasm for volunteer citizen participation in politics.

In the general election, public funding combined with a ban on private contributions to the major party nominees—except to defray compliance costs—was intended to equalize spending between major party candidates, to control or limit campaign spending, and to eliminate the possibility of large individual or interest group contributions influencing presidential election results. In 1976, with a few exceptions, those purposes appeared to have been achieved. But starting in 1980 and since, due in large part to increased familiarity with the law, as well as some changes in the law, political partisans discovered a variety of ways to upset the balance and reintroduce substantial amounts of private money into the campaigns: soft money contributions to state and local party committees to pay for activities beneficial to the presidential candidates; contributions to tax-exempt organizations conducting nominally nonpartisan voter drives that actually were intended to benefit candidates; independent expenditures; and spending by labor unions and other activities in parallel campaigns designed to help candidates. Thus, despite the spending limit of $65.5 million on the candidates and national party committees, general election costs for or on behalf of Bush and Clinton were well above the limit.

Notes

1. Stephen Bates, "The Future of Presidential Debates," The Annenberg Washington Program, 1993, pp. 12–14.
2. Dan Quayle, *Standing Firm: A Vice-Presidential Memoir* (New York: HarperCollins, 1994), p. 355.
3. Michael Wines, "Baker Returns, Bringing Tried-and-True Tactics," *New York Times,* August 24, 1992.
4. Michael Wines, "Baker's Double Role Is Raising Eyebrows," *New York Times,* August 14, 1992.
5. Doyle McManus, "Bush Appoints Mosbacher as Chief GOP Fund-Raiser," *Los Angeles Times,* August 28, 1992.
6. Howard Fineman, "Clinton's Team: The Inner Circles," *Newsweek,* October 26, 1992, pp. 28–31.
7. For an extended analysis of soft money, see Herbert E. Alexander, *Strategies for Election Reform* (Washington, DC: Project for Comprehensive Campaign Reform, 1989), pp. 44–57; also see Herbert E. Alexander, "Soft Money," *Vox Pop Newsletter of Political Organizations and Parties* 8, no. 1 (1989), pp. 1–3, 7.
8. Comparisons with 1988 are from Herbert E. Alexander and Monica Bauer, *Financing the 1988 Election* (Boulder, CO: Westview Press, 1991), pp. 37–38.
9. "Politics: Firm Grip on 'Soft' Money," *National Journal,* August 14, 1992, p. 2042.
10. Josh Goldstein, "Soft Money, Real Dollars: Soft Money in the 1992 Elections" (Washington, DC: Center for Responsive Politics, August 1992), p. 14.
11. This section is based on Herbert E. Alexander, "Outspending the Big Spender," *Baltimore Sun,* October 30, 1992.
12. To compare with 1988, see Alexander and Bauer, *Financing the 1988 Election,* pp. 40–43.
13. Sara Fritz, "Democrats Copy Fund-Raising Techniques of Experts: The GOP," *Los Angeles Times,* July 16, 1992.
14. "Clinton Seeks $1.79 Million in Federal Money," *New York Times,* August 5, 1992.
15. Ronald Brownstein, "Clinton Takes Big Lead as Perot Backers Shift," *Los Angeles Times,* July 19, 1992.

16. Michael Wines, "How Bush Lost: For Want of a Strategy, Chaos Ruled," *New York Times*, November 19, 1992.

17. Joe Klein, "On the Road Again," *Newsweek*, August 17, 1992, pp. 31, 33.

18. Brownstein, "Clinton Takes Big Lead as Perot Backers Shift."

19. Sam Fulwood III, "Jackson Will Help Recruit Black Voters for Democrats," *Los Angeles Times*, September 8, 1992.

20. Quoted in Calvin Sims, "Silicon Valley Takes a Partisan Leap of Faith," *New York Times*, October 29, 1992.

21. James Gerstenzang, "Clinton TV Ad 'Misleading,' GOP Charges," *Los Angeles Times*, September 1, 1992.

22. Gabe Martinez and Jeffrey A. Perlman, "8 Orange County Republicans Defect," *Los Angeles Times*, August 22, 1992.

23. Edwin Chen, "100 Business Leaders Join to Support Clinton," *Los Angeles Times*, September 22, 1992.

24. Susan Moffat, "Clinton Competes for the Votes of Business," *Los Angeles Times*, October 31, 1992.

25. Stephen Labaton, "Angry at Bush, Republican Contributors Are Helping Clinton," *New York Times*, September 22, 1992.

26. Fritz, "Democrats Copy Fund-Raising Techniques of Experts."

27. Terry Pristin, "Hollywood's Romance with Bill Clinton Heats Up," *Los Angeles Times*, August 10, 1992.

28. David Lauter, "Clinton Gala Raises Over $1 Million," *Los Angeles Times*, August 14, 1992.

29. Elaine Dutka, "See, This Is Like a Bonus Night: Bill Clinton and Barbra Streisand," *Los Angeles Times*, August 30, 1992.

30. Ronald Brownstein, "Democrats Eagerly Flaunt Hallowed Totems of GOP," *Los Angeles Times*, September 23, 1992.

31. "DNC Coffers Filled Briskly After Clinton Was Picked; RNC Fundraising Slowed After Bush's Nomination," *Political Finance & Lobby Reporter*, March 10, 1993, p. 4.

32. David Lauter, "In Homestretch, Clinton Topped Bush in Fund-Raising," *Los Angeles Times*, March 4, 1993.

33. Quoted in Douglas Jehl, "Clinton Campaign Seeks Loan as Funds Run Low," *Los Angeles Times*, October 30, 1992.

34. See chapter 8, pp. 235–37.

35. Quoted in Jehl, "Clinton Campaign Seeks Loan as Funds Run Low."

36. "Clinton-Gore Shift Monies From Legal Fund for Bills," *Election Administration Reports*, November 23, 1992, p. 3.

37. "Compliance Funds: The Use of Private Money in Presidential Campaigns," The Center for Responsive Politics, Washington, DC, June 1992, p. 8.

38. Ibid., p. 1.

39. Complaint letter from the CRP to the FEC, dated March 1, 1994, p. 4.

40. Sara Fritz, "Many Contributors' Jobs, Employers Not Told to FEC," *Los Angeles Times*, June 25, 1992.

41. "Candidates Get Reminder on Disclosure Obligations," *PACs & Lobbies*, Washington, DC, July 1, 1992, pp. 1, 5.

42. FEC, "Chapter Five: Legislation Recommendations," *Annual Report, 1993* (Washington, DC: FEC, 1994), pp. 37–38.

43. "FEC's 'Best Efforts' Rule Survives Legal Test," *Political Finance & Lobby Reporter*, August 10, 1994, pp. 1, 4.

44. Sara Fritz, "Perot Candidacy Stirs Up Issue of Wealth in Politics," *Los Angeles Times*, May 24, 1992.

45. FEC, *Federal Elections 92* (Washington, DC: FEC, 1993), p. 9.

46. Alexander, "Outspending the Big Spender."

47. R.W. Apple Jr., "Why Perot Could Be a Threat with $100 Million: It's His Own," *New York Times*, April 24, 1992.

48. Quoted in Steven A. Holmes, "Perot Running on His Money and Against Other People's," *New York Times*, June 18, 1992.

49. Quoted in ibid.

50. Douglas Schwarz, "Perot *Is* Buying the Election, and That's Bad," *Newsday*, July 8, 1992.

51. Holmes, "Perot Running on His Money."

52. Louise Overacker, *Money in Elections* (New York: Macmillan, 1932), p. 79.

53. Alexander Heard, *The Costs of Democracy* (Chapel Hill, NC: The University of North Carolina Press, 1960), Table 4, p. 54.

54. Herbert E. Alexander, *Financing the 1968 Election* (Lexington, MA: D.C. Heath, 1971), p. 92.

55. Herbert E. Alexander, with the assistance of Brian A. Haggerty, *Financing the 1980 Election* (Lexington, MA: D.C. Heath, 1983), p. 350.

56. "If Drafted, Perot Says He'd Run," *Los Angeles Times*, February 22, 1992.

57. Thomas C. Hayes, "Perot Is Showing Clear Signs of Joining Race for President," *New York Times*, April 17, 1993.

58. David Lauter, "Perot Spent Nearly $400,000 in March," *Los Angeles Times*, April 21, 1992.

59. David E. Rosenbaum, "Perot, Though Not in Race, Still Spends $400,000," *New York Times*, April 21, 1992.

60. Jack Cheevers, "Perot Chooses Ex-Admiral as Interim Running Mate," *Los Angeles Times*, March 31, 1992.

61. James Gerstenzang, "Perot Laughs Off White House 'Silliness,'" *Los Angeles Times*, May 23, 1992.

62. Steven A. Holmes, "Perot Hires Pair of Top Managers to Run Campaign," *New York Times*, June 4, 1992.

63. John Mintz and David von Drehle, "The Day Perot Pulled the Plug," *Washington Post National Weekly Edition*, July 27–August 2, 1992, p. 9.

64. Adam Clymer, "Perot Gave $12 Million to Aborted Campaigns," *New York Times*, August 25, 1992.

65. Bill Boyarsky, "A Change of Address for Perotists," *Los Angeles Times*, September 11, 1992; and Charles R. Babcock and Michael Isikoff, "The Off-and-On Candidate with His Personal War Chests," *Washington Post National Weekly Edition*, October 5–11, 1992.

66. Doyle McManus, "Perot Meets With Baker, Brown Amid Hints of Re-entering Race," *Los Angeles Times*, September 23, 1992.

67. See chapter 8, pp. 238–39.

68. Robin Toner, "Perot Re-Enters the Campaign, Saying Bush and Clinton Fail to Address Government 'Mess,'" *New York Times*, October 2, 1992.

69. Elizabeth Kolbert, "Perot to Launch a Big Ad Pitch, But Will It Sell?" *New York Times*, October 3, 1992.

70. Steven A. Holmes, "Perot Pouring Millions of Dollars into Major Onslaught of TV Ads," *New York Times*, October 14, 1992.

71. Richard L. Berke, "Perot Leads in $40 Million TV Ad Blitz," *New York Times*, October 27, 1992.

72. Steven A. Holmes, "Perot Wraps Up His Campaign Where He Mostly Ran It: On TV," *New York Times,* November 3, 1992.

73. Robert L. Jackson and Lianne Hart, "Perot Kicks Off Recruitment for Citizens' Lobby," *Los Angeles Times,* January 12, 1993.

74. James A. Barnes, "Still on the Trail," *National Journal,* April 10, 1993, p. 861.

75. Michael Wines, "Perot Continues His Campaign on Capitol Hill," *New York Times,* March 3, 1993.

76. Gwen Ifill, "Both Sides Assert Gain After Debate Over Trade Accord," *New York Times,* November 11, 1993.

77. Reference is to a study by Professor John Zaller, reported in *Public Affairs Report* 35, no. 2 (March 1994), pp. 1, 6–7.

78. Derived from Seymour Martin Lipset's ideas, in Barnes, "Still on the Trail," p. 863; also see John M. Broder, "Not Ready to Launch a Third Party, Perot Says," *Los Angeles Times,* November 7, 1992; and Theodore J. Lowi, "Mr. Perot, Form a Party," *New York Times,* April 6, 1992.

79. Quoted in Martin Gottlieb, "Minor Candidate's Fund-Raising Success Turns Spotlight on Party," *New York Times,* December 31, 1991.

80. "FEC Opens Inquiry into Fulani's Presidential Campaign," *Political Finance & Lobby Reporter,* September 14, 1994, p. 2.

81. FEC, *Annual Report 1992* (Washington, DC: FEC, 1993), pp. 5–6.

82. See Tables 2.4 and 2.5.

83. Quoted in "High Court Decision Lets LaRouche Apply for Presidential Campaign Funds," *Political Finance & Lobby Reporter,* December 8, 1993, p. 1; *LaRouche v. FEC,* 996 F. 2d 1263 (DC Cir. 1993), cert. denied.

84. FEC, *Federal Elections 92,* pp. 110–18.

85. "Campaign Costs Then & Now, 1988 and 1992," *New York Times,* March 3, 1992.

86. FEC, AO 1983–25, *FEC Record,* February 1984, pp. 4–5.

6

Soft Money:
The Last Hurrah?

The soft money finances of Democratic and Republican party organizations received considerable attention in 1992 due to the highly visible competition for dollars between the major parties on behalf of their presidential nominees. This attention was also a function of new FEC regulations that required detailed reporting of soft money contributions and expenditures for the first time since 1979, the year this form of funding was incorporated into the federal campaign finance system. As noted in chapter 5, soft money refers to funds that are raised from sources outside the restraints of federal law but spent on activities intended to affect federal election outcomes. By contrast, hard money is raised, spent, and publicly disclosed under terms mandated by federal laws and regulations.

In the 1991–92 election cycle, both parties spent substantial amounts of soft money in conjunction with federal elections. Most of these funds were spent to influence the outcome of the presidential general election, but sizable sums also were devoted to assisting candidates for nonfederal offices and improving the party organizations. The large amounts spent on the presidential race and the size of some of the soft money gifts accepted by the parties led many observers to call for further regulation of such funds, or even the complete prohibition of such donations. Others considered the use of soft money in federal elections to be a healthy development because it encouraged citizen participation in the electoral process and helped to restore a meaningful role for party organizations in federal elections. This chapter highlights some of the issues in the debate over soft money by providing a detailed analysis of the soft money funds raised and spent during the 1991–92 election cycle.

Background

While there are many kinds of soft money, in the context of national elections this term is used to describe the funds raised by party organizations under the provisions of the 1979 FECA Amendments.[1] These amendments exempt three types of party committee activity from the FECA's contribution and expenditure limits:[2]

- State and local party committees may prepare and distribute—including distribution by direct mail—slate cards, sample ballots, palm cards, or other printed listings of three or more candidates for any public office for which an election is held in a given state. None of the candidate listings mentioned, however, may be displayed by such means of general public political advertising as broadcast, newspaper, magazine, or billboard media.
- State and local party committees may pay for grass-roots campaign materials, such as pins, bumper stickers, handbills, brochures, posters, yard signs, and party tabloids or newspapers. These may be used only in connection with volunteer activities and may not be purchased by national party committees and delivered to the local committees or paid for by funds donated by the national committees to the local committees for that purpose. Nor may funds designated by donors for particular federal candidates be used to purchase such materials.
- State and local party committees may conduct voter registration and turnout drives on behalf of their parties' presidential and vice presidential nominees, including the use of telephone banks operated by volunteers, even if paid professionals develop the telephone bank system and phoning instructions and train supervisors. If party candidates for the U.S. House or Senate are mentioned in such drives in more than an incidental way, the costs of the drives allocable to those candidates must be counted as contributions to them. As in the case of volunteer-oriented campaign materials, state and local party committee voter drives may not involve the use of general public political advertising, nor may the drives be paid for by funds donated by the national party committees or designated by donors for particular candidates.

In all three types of exempted activity, only the portion of the costs allocable to federal candidates must be paid with hard money, that is, from contributions subject to the limitations and prohibitions of the FECA. The remainder may be paid from funds raised under applicable state laws, which often permit contributions from sources prohibited from giving in federal contests, such as corporations and labor unions, and tend to be less stringent with respect to the amounts that may be contributed by individuals and PACs.[3]

The exemption of these activities from the FECA limits was justified on the basis that such activities are designed to promote party-building and grass-roots political activity that benefit candidates at all levels of government, not just those seeking federal office. Consequently, the adoption of the 1979 law raised the question of whether the activities specified in the regulations were the only activities that qualified as party-building or grass-roots efforts. Party officials, for example, asserted that strengthening a party's infrastructure was a necessary condition for participating in both federal and nonfederal elections. Accordingly, they argued that parties should be allowed to finance a portion of overhead and administrative expenses with soft money.[4] The FEC accepted this position but required that party committees would have to maintain separate bank accounts for the hard and soft monies they received.[5] Similarly, although the 1979 amendments prohibited the direct use of soft money for public broadcast advertising, subsequent FEC decisions allowed for its use in cases in which the advertising clearly identified no candidates but promoted party themes or use of party symbols.[6]

The regulations also raised questions as to how to determine what portion of the costs of a particular activity could be financed with soft money funds. Until 1991, these decisions were largely left to the party organizations themselves. The FEC required only that parties use any reasonable method in allocating costs between federally regulated funds and soft money, which led to a variety of allocation schemes. In addition, parties were required to report only the portion of shared expenses or joint activities that were paid with federal funds. No disclosure of soft money expenditures or the sources of such receipts was required under federal law. These funds were subject to state disclosure laws, which are relatively ineffective and require widely varying types of information from party organizations and contributors.[7] As a result, information about the soft money finances of national, state, and local party committees was severely limited and fragmented, largely dependent on the reporting requirements of the states in which the monies were spent.[8] Starting in 1988, the DNC and then the RNC began to disclose voluntarily the sources of their state-related soft money, as well as some of the expenditures and transfers to state organizations made from soft money accounts. But most of this information related to the contributions received from donors of $100,000 or more; little information was released concerning the soft money activities conducted by state party committees on behalf of presidential candidates or other candidates for federal office.[9]

Regulatory Reform

As the amount of soft money spent in conjunction with federal elections has grown (see Table 5.1), there have been sporadic attempts to impose stricter regulations on this type of funding. As early as 1984, Common Cause advocated rulemaking by the FEC, but in 1986, the FEC denied the group's petition for rulemaking on the basis that it lacked hard evidence. Congress also was urged to take action, but it did not. Meanwhile, a consensus seemed to develop to require public disclosure of soft money.

Common Cause sought relief in federal court, filing a suit contesting the denial of its petition. The court rejected the group's request to prohibit the allocation of party expenses to soft money accounts, but directed the FEC to revise its allocation regulations to give party committees more guidance in complying with the soft money provisions of the FECA.[10] Thus, in September 1988, the FEC began a complicated rulemaking procedure that included the solicitation of written comments, public hearings, the mailing of a questionnaire to 110 Democratic and Republican state party chairs, and the input of chief party fund raisers. The commission then used this information to develop regulations pertaining to soft money, which were issued on June 21, 1990, and went into effect on January 1, 1991.[11]

The regulations changed the disclosure requirements for soft money funds and the methods by which party organizations could allocate their expenditures. Under these rules, all party committees raising and spending soft money funds in conjunction with federal elections must file regular disclosure reports of their contributions and disbursements with the FEC. These reports must identify any contributors who give $200 or more to soft money accounts or building fund accounts. Monies raised and spent by state and local committees that are unrelated to federal election activity, however, do not have to be reported to the FEC; these funds remain subject to the reporting requirements of applicable state disclosure laws.

The rules also replaced the FEC's "any reasonable method" approach to allocating hard and soft monies with a complicated system of formulas that accounted for different types of party committees and different types of soft money activities. In an effort to establish some consistency in the formulas, the regulations require that during a presidential election year, national party committees must allocate at least 65 percent of the costs of generic voter drives and administrative expenses to their hard money accounts; in nonpresidential election years, at least 60 percent of these costs must be paid with hard money. For state and local party organizations, these costs must be allocated on the basis of the composition of the particular state's general election ballot; that is, the percentage must reflect the proportion of federal offices to total offices on the general election ballot.[12] In the 1992 election cycle, this ballot composition ratio ranged from a low of 25 percent federal (hard) funds in Delaware, Mississippi, Montana, Rhode Island, and West Virginia, to a high of 75 percent federal in Maryland.[13]

Flexible allocation methods are retained for other types of activity. Fund-raising costs are allocated according to the relative amounts of federal and nonfederal monies raised. For example, if 20 percent of the funds received from a specific event meet FECA requirements, then 20 percent of the costs of the event must be paid from federal funds. Party committees must include in their disclosure reports the specific allocation percentages used for different fund-raising events or mail solicitations. Communication and phone bank costs are apportioned on the basis of the relative benefit that each candidate receives from space in a publication or time on the air, or from the telephoning conducted by the phone bank.

Soft Money in 1991–92: An Overview

The new soft money regulations require party committees to provide a detailed accounting of their nonfederal financial activity to the FEC. As a result, the 1991–92 FEC disclosure reports offered for the first time a fairly comprehensive summary of the soft money raised and spent on activities related to federal elections. These data show that Democratic and Republican party organizations at the national and state level raised and spent more than $150 million in soft money during the 1992 election cycle (see Table 6.1). Of this amount, slightly more than one-half, approximately $80 million, was the result of Republican Party efforts. Democratic Party committees raised about $71 million in soft money and spent about $73 million, or around 10 percent less than their Republican counterparts.

At the national level, the Republican Party committees raised and spent substantially more soft money than the Democratic committees. The RNC, National Republican Senatorial Committee (NRSC), and National Republican Congressional Committee (NRCC) spent a combined $49.8 million, as compared to about $35.1 million for the DNC, Democratic Senatorial Campaign Committee (DSCC), and Democratic Congressional Campaign Committee (DCCC). The RNC spent $5.5 million more than the DNC, and the Republican congressional committees spent about $9.2 million more than the Democratic congressional committees, most of which was due to a $7.3 million difference in spending between the NRSC and DSCC. The NRSC's expenditures exceeded those of the DSCC by a substantial margin, largely because the Republican committee spent $5 million more in soft money from a building fund to help pay for the cost of a new Washington headquarters.

Table 6.1

Summary of Soft Money Receipts and Expenditures, 1991–92

	Receipts	Expenditures
Democratic		
DNC	$31,616,094	$30,187,913
DSCC	617,052	520,201
DCCC	4,705,795	4,366,614
State parties[a]	34,273,618	38,113,972
Total	$71,212,559	$73,188,700
Republican		
RNC	$36,207,832	$35,627,908
NRSC	9,046,482[b]	8,156,160
NRCC	6,281,040	6,330,895
State parties[a]	27,976,081	31,109,295
Total	$79,511,435	$80,908,921

Source: Federal Election Commission.

Note: Figures include all soft money funds raised and spent in conjunction with federal election-related activities between January 1, 1991, and December 31, 1992.
[a]Includes only the nonfederal share of funds raised and spent on activities related to federal elections. Figures do not include funds raised and spent solely in conjunction with state and local election activity, which are not reported to the FEC.
[b]This figure has been reduced by $4.5 million to account for the amount borrowed by the NRSC building fund to repay earlier loans. It also reflects an adjustment of $200,000 to account for transfers between the NRSC nonfederal account and building fund account.

While this disparity in spending between the national Republican and Democratic Party organizations was widely reported by the FEC and noted by journalists, it is important to note that the Democrats made up much of this margin as a result of the soft money expenditures of state party committees. As noted in Table 6.1, at the state level the Democrats raised and spent significantly more than the Republicans, soliciting about $34.3 million in soft money funds versus $28 million for the Republicans, and disbursing $38.1 million, as opposed to $31.1 million for the Republicans. When these funds are taken into account and the amounts spent from building funds are excluded, the difference between Democrats and Republicans with respect to federal election–related soft money spending is reduced to about $2.9 million. Thus, the Republican Party enjoyed only a slight advantage with respect to the amount of soft money it spent on federal election–related activities in the 1992 election cycle. Moreover, as noted in chapter 5, when these totals are disaggregated, the results show that the Democrats spent significantly more soft money when it mattered most, during the 1992 presidential general election period, despite the Republicans' greater aggregate spending over the course of the election cycle.

Soft Money Contributions: The Return of the High Roller

Because the contribution limits established by state laws are less stringent than those set forth in federal regulations, individuals, PACs, corporations, and labor unions can donate sums to party soft money accounts that greatly exceed the amounts that can be given to federal accounts. Common Cause and other advocates of reform have, therefore, been highly critical of soft money funding, arguing that it violates the intent of the FECA by permitting large private contributions. They further contend that such gifts are often made by individuals and organized interests seeking access to government officials. This criticism became particularly acute after the 1988 election, when the national party committees revealed that some 267 Bush supporters had each contributed $100,000 or more in soft money to various Republican Party accounts, while some 130 Dukakis supporters each donated or raised $100,000 for Democratic Party accounts.[14] Others, however, argue that these soft money donors make a valuable contribution to the political system, because they provide party organizations with sorely needed revenues for voter registration and mobilization efforts, as well as other activities designed to promote citizen participation in the electoral process.[15]

The controversy over soft money donations was reignited by what started out as the largest single soft money contribution from any one individual to the Republican Party during the 1991–92 election cycle. Michael Kojima, a previously unknown businessman who was believed to be living in Los Angeles, gave $400,000 in connection with the 1992 President's Dinner, the Republican Party's largest annual fund-raising event, which generates both hard and soft money for the party's national campaign committees.[16] As the most generous individual contributor to the event, Kojima was seated next to Bush at the dinner, which attracted the attention of reporters and other observers, who became interested in knowing more about his background. Republican officials said that as far as they knew, Kojima was just a wealthy businessman with connections in both the United States and Asia.[17] When the press reported additional information on Kojima's background, his donation became an embarrassment to the president and his party.

Soon after the media began to circulate reports of this record gift, people who had dealings with Kojima became enraged. A New York attorney who had represented a North Carolina seafood company, which had sued Kojima for $280,000, was unpleasantly surprised when he learned of the donation.[18] Kojima's two ex-wives, each with two children from their marriages to Kojima, were furious. One of them already had secured a $100,000 court judgment for unpaid child support. Kojima also owed $600,000 to Lippo Bank, an Indonesian bank with offices in the United States, for another business deal. Once these claims surfaced, the Republicans quickly put the $400,000 contribution in escrow pending the resolution of the claims against him.[19]

Once Kojima's alleged history of dodging creditors and child support payments was made public, the Republicans claimed that they knew very little about the businessman, noting that they are not in a position to ask questions of potential donors. They said they knew only that Kojima was involved in setting up international business deals.[20] In criticizing the Republicans for accepting a gift from such a donor, the Democrats said they conducted thorough background checks on their soft money contributors using systems such as Lexis/Nexis, which stores court records electronically. Upon completing these checks, party officials then decide if it would be in their best interest to accept a gift from a particular donor. Contributions had reportedly been refused in the past based on the information obtained from such searches.[21]

Kojima was not the only contributor to donate a substantial sum to a party soft money account. Following the pattern established in the 1988 election cycle, both parties placed an emphasis on large donations in seeking out soft money funds. The Republicans sought to build on the success of the Team 100 approach. They maintained this program after the 1988 election and asked the more than 250 Team 100 members to donate $25,000 a year during each of the four years in the presidential election cycle, as well as an additional $100,000 in the election year.[22] The Democrats also sought to build on their 1988 efforts by developing their own version of a Team 100 approach, in which they sought to identify individuals who would donate or raise at least $100,000 for the party's soft money accounts.

Both parties solicited soft money donations throughout the 1992 presidential election cycle, with the RNC raising a total of $36.2 million and the DNC raising $31.6 million. As noted in chapter 5, the major portion of these funds was received during the general election period as a result of the fund-raising efforts of the former Bush and Clinton staff members, who raised the monies needed to finance their candidate's prenomination campaign, then shifted to the national party committee payrolls and began to solicit soft money. An analysis of the election-related soft money accounts disclosed by the RNC and DNC as part of their regular FEC filings shows that the Republicans received about $20.1 million in soft money gifts between January 1991 and June 1992, compared to about $10.4 million for the Democrats.[23] From July 1, 1992, to the end of the election year, however, this pattern was reversed; during this period, the DNC raised close to $20.9 million in soft money funds for its election-related activities, as compared to $13.4 million for the RNC. Thus, of the combined $64.8 million in soft money solicited in 1991 and 1992 by the two major party organizations for election-related purposes, about $34.3 million, or 53 percent, was raised in conjunction with the presidential general election.[24]

As in 1988, a significant portion of the soft money raised by the national party committees came from a relatively small group of donors who each contributed a total of $100,000 or more. A Common Cause study of the soft money contributions accepted by the DNC revealed that seventy-two contributors had each donated $100,000 or more, including twenty-three who each gave more than $150,000. The Democrats received gifts of more than $200,000 from seven individuals and five labor unions, including $398,876 from the United Steelworkers and $344,180 from the National Education Association. They also received seventeen corporate contributions of $100,000 or more, including $171,573 from the Atlantic Richfield Company and $152,000 from the Philip Morris Company.[25] The study did not examine soft money gifts to the RNC, but FEC reports show that more than sixty contributors gave at least $100,000 each in soft money.[26] These included a combined total of $977,000 from the Archer Daniels Midland Corporation and its chair, Dwayne Andreas, who was the leading Bush and Republican contributor in the 1991–92 cycle, giving a total of more than $1 million in soft and hard money combined to Bush's prenomination campaign committee and Republican Party coffers; $520,300 from the Atlantic Richfield Company; and $450,000 from Edgar Bronfman, whose company gave an additional $58,727.[27]

The Democrats also received sizable contributions from individuals or corporations that had donated funds to the RNC earlier in the election cycle. In most instances, these gifts were offered late in the race, as the likelihood of a Democratic victory increased. For example, on October 30, four days before the election, Archer Daniels Midland donated $90,000 in soft money to the DNC through seven separate contributions from seven subsidiary corporations, and Andreas made an individual gift of $50,000 to a DCCC soft money account. Bronfman gave $200,000 to the Democrats in early October. Revlon Inc. balanced $140,000 in Republican contributions with $120,000 in donations to Democrats. Another major soft money contributor, Pacific Telesis, gave $60,000 to the RNC during the two weeks prior to the election, then gave $50,000 to the DNC after the election.[28]

Moreover, these cases were not unique. A study conducted by the Center for Responsive Politics found that donors representing five traditionally Republican industries shifted their patterns of soft money giving in the period after the Democratic convention. In three industries (investment and securities; pharmaceuticals and health; and beer, wine, and liquor), soft money contributions shifted from an average of 3 to 1 or 4 to 1 in favor of the Republicans to an advantage in favor of the Democrats, while in two others (oil and gas, and insurance), the gap between Republicans and Democrats narrowed significantly.[29] These disclosures prompted further debate concerning soft money fund raising, with some observers contending that these shifting patterns of donations demonstrated that donors were more interested in gaining influence than in assisting the parties. Other observers noted that contribution patterns might simply reflect the diverse interests represented by these donors.

Finally, it is important to note that although the total number of $100,000 donors reported in 1992 is well below the number reported in 1988, this does not mean that the national party committees placed less reliance on large donors or were less successful in soliciting such gifts than they had been four years earlier. The Democrats actively sought large contributions, but they also encouraged supporters to raise $100,000 or more for the party, if they could not donate this amount themselves. One report that included those who gave $100,000 or more and those who were responsible for raising this amount estimated that the Democrats had about 250 of these large soft money donors.[30] Also, the FEC disclosure reports analyzed by Common Cause and others only include soft money contributions made in 1991 and 1992. Individuals who made a contribution relatively early in the presidential election, such as those who might have made a generous contribution in 1990 or those who might have given an aggregate $100,000 by donating $25,000 a year in soft money (as Republican Team 100 members were asked to do), would not be included among those identified as large donors on the basis of FEC disclosure lists.

National Party Committee Spending

In the 1992 election cycle, both national party committees mounted aggressive soft money financial operations. Overall, the Democrats and Republicans raised $67.8 million in soft money and spent $65.8 million (see Table 6.2), or approximately $22 million more than the estimated $45 million spent in the 1988 election cycle.[31] The RNC raised about $36.2 million

Table 6.2

National Party Committee Soft Money Activity, 1991–92

	Receipts	Disbursements
Democratic National Committee		
Nonfederal individual	$11,953,013	$11,340,293
Nonfederal corporate	15,143,206	14,865,896
Nonfederal general (labor)	3,847,775	3,467,492
Nonfederal Max PAC	426,050	360,486
Building fund	161,550	71,508
Democratic news service	84,550	82,238
Subtotal	$31,616,094	$30,187,913
Republican National Committee		
Republican National State Election Committee	$33,469,431	$33,017,693
Committee to Preserve Eisenhower Center	2,687,824	2,575,445
National Republican Legislators Association	50,577	34,770
Subtotal	$36,207,832	$35,627,908
Total	$67,823,926	$65,815,821

Source: Federal Election Commission.

through three nonfederal accounts: the Republican National State Election Committee (RNSEC) account, their primary soft money account for election-related activities, which received about $33.5 million; the Committee to Preserve the Eisenhower Center, their building fund, which took in $2.7 million; and the National Republican Legislators Association, which received slightly more than $50,000 for activities related to state legislative races.

The DNC maintained six major nonfederal accounts. Four of these accounts were designed to segregate soft money contributions on the basis of the source of a given donation: one for individual gifts, another for corporate gifts, a third for labor contributions, and a fourth for PAC monies. These four accounts, which took in about $31.4 million of the party's $31.6 million total, were the primary accounts for election-related activities. Of this $31.4 million, almost half, $15.1 million, came from corporate donors; approximately $11.9 million came from individual contributors; about $3.8 million came from labor organizations; and $426,000 came from PACs, most of which had already contributed the maximum amount allowed under federal law to the party's hard money accounts. In addition, the party had a building fund and an account for a Democratic Nonfederal News Service, but neither of these accounts received significant sums ($161,550 and $84,500, respectively).

The Democrats maintain separate nonfederal accounts for different types of donations, largely because this approach makes it easier to disburse these monies, given the complexity of state campaign finance laws. Some states allow unlimited individual gifts to state and local candidates or party committees; some permit contributions from corporations or labor union treasury funds; others place relatively few restrictions on PACs. Funds from different sources can thus be matched with particular states to facilitate an efficient distribution of funds. The Republicans, on the other hand, have essentially established only one nonfederal account as the vehicle for their election-related activity, which simplifies administration of these monies but raises questions about the party's ability to segregate monies and fulfill any restrictions mandated by state law.

Although a significant percentage of the soft money raised by the national party committees was expended during the 1992 general election period, FEC disclosure reports show that the presidential race is not the only focus of the parties' soft money financial activity. Instead, both parties appear to be increasingly incorporating soft money into their overall financial schemes. For example, about 25 percent of the soft money spending during the 1991–92 election cycle, approximately $15.8 million, occurred in 1991, long before the presidential nominees had been determined. Much of this sum was spent on administrative and overhead expenses, fund-raising costs, and other general party-building activities. In fact, the RNC spending pattern suggests that nonfederal funding may be becoming a relatively standardized component of the party's finances; the party spent $5.4 million from its soft money accounts during the first six months of 1991, $5.3 million in the next six months, and $6.6 million in the first six months of 1992, which included at least a few months of heightened activity associated with the beginning of the 1992 general election period. The RNC then spent about $15.6 million during the last six months of 1992.

The DNC had a more uneven spending pattern, disbursing about $22 million, or 74 percent of its total soft money expenditures, in the last six months of 1992. This pattern, however, was largely determined by the availability of funds. FEC reports show that the party generally spent the soft money as the funds were received; for example, in 1991 the DNC raised about $5.4 million and spent $5.2 million. The Democrats' problem was that the party had little success in soliciting substantial amounts of soft money until after the presidential nominee was selected. In the future, it is

Table 6.3

National Party Committee Nonfederal Disbursements, 1991–92

Type of Expenditure	Democrats	Republicans
Joint activity		
Administrative/voter drive	$15,334,343	$18,858,891
Fund raising	1,573,599	2,964,765
Unidentified	1,019,073	3,224
Subtotal	$17,927,015	$21,826,880
Transfers to state/local parties	9,495,328	5,338,595
Contributions to state/local candidates	212,091	1,249,000
Miscellaneous	2,553,479	7,213,433
Total	$30,187,913	$35,627,908

Source: Federal Election Commission.

likely that the DNC will try to develop a steadier flow of nonfederal funds and begin to invest these monies on an ongoing basis as the RNC has apparently done.

The FEC disclosure reports also indicate that the disbursement and use of soft money is much more complex than has been assumed. In general, the national party committees spent soft money on four broad types of political activity: (1) joint federal and nonfederal activities, which include such items as administrative costs shared with state parties, costs of fundraising efforts designed to raise federal and nonfederal funds, and voter registration and mobilization drives to benefit federal and nonfederal candidates; (2) direct financial transfers to state and local parties; (3) contributions to state and local candidates; and (4) miscellaneous expenditures, which include such items as building funds, redistricting efforts, and the costs associated with ancillary party organizations like the Association of State Democratic Chairs and the College Republicans.

As noted in Table 6.3, the RNC and DNC each spent the largest share of their soft money funds on joint activities. The RNC spent $21.8 million, or 61 percent of its soft money expenditures, on activities financed with a combination of federal and nonfederal funds, while the DNC spent close to $17.9 million, 59 percent of its total, on such activities. The parties differed significantly with respect to the proportion of funds they devoted to other activities. The Democrats distributed $9.5 million, about 31 percent of their total, in the form of direct transfers to state and local party committees, almost twice the amount the RNC gave to its state and local affiliates. One of the main reasons for the larger Democratic total is that the DNC transfers included monies transmitted to state parties that represented their share of the receipts from a series of joint Democratic Party Victory Fund events. These fund-raising events were conducted throughout the 1992 general election period to raise hard and soft money to finance general election voter identification and turnout programs, as well as other general election-related activities.

The Republicans placed greater emphasis on direct contributions to state and local candidates than did the Democrats, donating $1.2 million to their candidates as compared to the DNC's $212,000. The RNC also allocated more than $4 million more than the DNC to miscellaneous expenditures, in part because the RNC reported hundreds of thousands of dollars of in-kind media and consulting expenditures made on behalf of its 1991 gubernatorial candidates in this category. The committee's miscellaneous spending also included approximately $2.6 million in building fund expenditures for its party headquarters; the DNC reported less than $72,000 in building expenses. In addition, the RNC spent more than $2.2 million in soft money funds on redistricting activities in at least twelve states.[32] In some cases, the RNC sent soft money payments to data analysis and computer graphics firms to research and develop redistricting models; in others, the national party transferred funds directly to ad hoc groups organized to coordinate redistricting efforts in particular states, such as the Massachusetts Redistricting Task Force.

The DNC and RNC adopted strongly centralized approaches in administering these funds in an effort to maintain control over the ways soft money was spent. Even in the case of monies transferred to state and local party organizations, the national committees usually allowed little autonomy with respect to how these funds were to be spent. In most instances, transferred funds were to be used for purposes approved by the national organization. This centralized focus was undoubtedly due in part to each national committee's desire to expend these funds in as effective a manner as possible, as well as to ensure the proper implementation of planned programs. It also might have been in part a result of the new FEC disclosure regulations; parties may have demanded greater control over these monies to ensure proper disclosure and to comply with the complex allocation rules. Whatever the reason, both parties held a relatively tight rein over soft money disbursements while using these funds for a wide variety of purposes.

Joint Activity

Both parties spent the major share of their soft money on joint activities, which are activities related to both federal and nonfederal elections. Some insight into the types of activity financed by the national party committees can be obtained from FEC disclosure reports, since the disclosure rules adopted in 1990 require party committees to differentiate the amounts spent on fund raising from those associated with administrative costs and voter drive expenses. Parties are not required, however, to specify the exact amounts spent in conjunction with voter registration and mobilization drives or any of the other types of joint activity detailed in the exemptions established by the 1979 FECA Amendments. It is, therefore, impossible to determine precisely what percentage of the monies spent on joint activities was used to increase voter participation or finance other grass-roots volunteer efforts. But the general patterns of joint activity financing can be determined and these patterns are helpful in understanding the role of soft money in the political system.

Table 6.3 indicates the amounts spent by the national party committees on different types of joint activity. Overall, the Republicans disbursed $21.8 million on this type of activity, including approximately $18.9 million for administrative and voter drive expenses, and almost $3 million for fund raising. According to FEC figures, about 33 percent of this $21.8 million, or $7.1 million, was spent between July and December 1992, the period in which most of the RNC's efforts were directed toward the general election. During this period, the RNC spent $6.1 million on administrative and voter drive expenses, and $1 million on fund raising.

The DNC spent $17.9 million on joint activities. The party's financial summaries, as reported by the FEC, show that the DNC allocated $15.3 million to administrative and voter drive costs, and about $1.6 million to fund-raising costs, while the particular purpose of another $1 million in joint activity spending is not specified. A detailed analysis of monthly disclosure reports suggests that almost all of this $1 million was spent on fund raising, since the estimated total of the itemized fund-raising transfers identified in these reports is about $2.7 million. About 65 percent of the DNC's total expenditures, $11.9 million, were made during the 1992 general election period, including about $10 million for administrative costs and voter drives, and $1.9 million for fund raising. Thus, although the RNC spent more on such activities than the DNC over the course of the entire 1991–92 cycle, the Democrats outspent the Republicans by about $4.8 million between July 1992 and the end of the election year.

There is a certain logic behind the fact that a majority of each party's joint activity expenses are incurred during the general election period. Parties generally avoid involvement in primary races, preferring to concentrate their efforts on general election contests. Voter identification and mobilization drives are usually conducted in the three-month period before the election and are especially important in presidential election years, which involve not only the presidential contest but also Senate and House races, as well as a majority of state elections. Therefore, it makes sense that most of the monies spent on activities designed to influence federal and nonfederal elections are disbursed during this period.

Perhaps more noteworthy are the sizable amounts spent outside the period of the presidential general election. Because most party staff members are assumed to spend at least some of their time working with state party officials or assisting individuals involved in nonfederal political activities, both parties use soft money to finance part of their administrative and overhead expenses. Soft money is, therefore, used to defray some of the "institutional maintenance" costs of the national party organizations. Under FEC regulations, up to 40 percent of these expenses in a nonpresidential election year and 35 percent in a presidential election year may be paid with soft money funds. So, for example, during the 1991–92 election cycle, the Democrats spent about $2.9 million in soft money on payroll expenses, while the Republicans spent about $5.1 million for the same purpose. Both parties also used soft money to defray a variety of overhead expenses, such as postage and overnight delivery service, office supplies, and utilities. This use of soft money has allowed the party organizations to improve their staffs and provide more services to their constituents. It also has helped free up federally regulated dollars, to be used to make contributions or coordinated expenditures on behalf of party candidates, rather than to pay bills at the national headquarters.

Transfers to State and Local Parties

Both national party committees also rely on soft money as a vehicle for providing direct financial assistance to state and local party affiliates. According to FEC reports, about one-quarter of the soft money raised nationally by the DNC and RNC during the 1991–92 cycle was transferred to state and local party organizations. The Democrats transferred a total of $9.5 million, about $9 million of which was distributed between July and November 1992. The Republicans transferred a total of $5.3 million, with about $4.7 million of this amount distributed between July and November 1992. These funds were generally used to purchase, update, and computer-

Table 6.4

Soft Money Transfers to State and Local Parties, 1992

Top Ten Democratic States		Top Ten Republican States	
1 California	$1,204,814	1 Ohio	$968,891
2 Texas	1,035,383	2 California	492,150
3 Pennsylvania	637,935	3 North Carolina	325,452
4 Georgia	632,711	4 Georgia	292,860
5 New York	611,885	5 Michigan	289,825
6 North Carolina	582,633	6 Washington	256,725
7 Illinois	459,539	7 North Dakota	253,775
8 Louisiana	373,914	8 South Carolina	239,500
9 Michigan	339,694	9 Pennsylvania	227,381
10 Missouri	332,387	10 Florida	222,432
Total	$6,210,895		$3,568,991
Percentage of soft money transfers	65.4		66.8

Source: Federal Election Commission.

Note: Figures represent the dollar amounts of nonfederal funds transferred from the Democratic National Committee and Republican National Committee.

ize voter lists; to develop targeting programs; to pay fund-raising expenses; to conduct telephone voter identification programs; and to hire party workers and poll watchers on election day. While party organizations used the funds they received from their national organization to finance a variety of activities in 1992, the bulk of the funds went to generic phone bank operations designed to identify party supporters and turn out the vote.

According to FEC disclosure reports, most of the state party organizations received a share of the soft money funds raised by their national party committees. The Democrats transferred $9.5 million in soft money funds to forty-seven states.[33] Federal party funds were sent to all fifty states; when this hard money is added to the soft money transfers, the total amount sent to state committees by the DNC reached $14.3 million. The Republicans sent about $5.3 million in soft money to forty-two states and about $3.5 million in federal party funds to forty-three states, for a total of about $8.8 million.[34]

Most of the soft money sent to state committees was focused on a small group of targeted states that were considered essential to a presidential victory. The Democrats disbursed two-thirds of the nonfederal funds transferred to states to ten key electoral battlegrounds (see Table 6.4). These ten states, which contained 219 electoral college votes, or 81 percent of the total needed to win the presidency, included most of the large electoral states and three crucial southern states the Democrats thought they could win: Georgia, Louisiana, and North Carolina. All of these states, with the exception of Texas and Michigan, also held U.S. Senate elections in 1992 (with California holding elections for both seats). North Carolina and Missouri also were the sites of gubernatorial contests.

The Republicans also disbursed two-thirds of their transferred funds to ten states (see Table 6.4). These states, which contained 190 electoral votes, or 70 percent of the number needed to win the presidency, also included a number of large states and three key southern states. Again, with the exception of Michigan, all of these states were the sites of U.S. Senate races, and three states, Washington, North Carolina, and North Dakota, were holding gubernatorial elections. The one oddity on the list of top Republican states was North Dakota. But North Dakota was an important state for the Republicans in 1992, since it was viewed as a needed base state in the presidential election and was the site of a gubernatorial contest that the party ultimately won.

Direct Candidate Assistance

The RNC and the DNC used some of their soft money funds to assist party campaign organizations and candidates. There were, however, some major differences in the tactics employed by these competing organizations. For instance, the RNC devoted special attention to a selected group of state legislative races. One of the problems the Republican Party has faced in recent decades is its lack of success in gubernatorial and state legislative elections. Despite winning five of the six presidential races held between 1968 and 1988, the Republicans have consistently failed to win a majority of the nation's statehouses. As part of the effort to reverse this pattern, the Republicans transferred funds to state legislative campaign committees, as well as to state party committees, in at least fifteen states. These transfers were made to help elect Republicans to state legislative office and enhance Republican voting strength in state assemblies. The RNC also hoped that in the long term such spending might help the party to improve its pool of candidates for statewide office and congressional contests.

The Republicans also directly contributed a total of $1.2 million in non-federal funds to candidates seeking office at the state level. During the 1992 general election period, the party contributed about $804,000 to candidates in twenty-three states. Most of these funds were used to assist the Republican nominee in key gubernatorial contests. A total of about $550,000, representing about 68 percent of the soft monies donated to candidates, was given to gubernatorial candidates in five states: Missouri, New Hampshire,

North Dakota, Utah, and Washington. The leading recipient was William Webster of Missouri, who was given $225,000; Ken Eikenberry of Washington received $125,000; and Edward Schafer of North Dakota received $95,000. Other major gifts included $20,000 for the Pennsylvania attorney general's race and $21,000 for Georgia legislative candidates. In addition to these direct contributions, the RNC also provided more than $220,000 in media assistance to state and local candidates. The primary beneficiaries of this support were the Republican nominees in the Los Angeles mayoral race and the Mississippi and Louisiana gubernatorial contests.

The DNC spent no soft money during the 1992 general election period on direct contributions to candidates. Although the committee reported about $148,000 in contributions to candidates during the general election period, this sum actually represented the funds expended to provide survey research to state parties and candidates. The DNC hired six Washington-based polling firms, including Stanley Greenberg's firm, to conduct surveys in thirty-one states. In twenty-seven of these states, polls were conducted at least two or three times during the course of the campaign.[35] The results were shared with state party officials so they could target their appeals and voter canvassing efforts. The polls included questions related to particular state races and the results were provided to these campaigns. In addition to gubernatorial candidates, the polling gathered information for some of the candidates seeking the office of lieutenant governor, attorney general, secretary of state, state auditor, associate justice, and, in Texas, railroad commissioner. This research was financed through a combination of hard and soft money, with part of the expense included in the amounts reported as transfer payments and another part counted as contributions to candidates.

Soft money thus allowed the Democrats to provide state parties with a resource, statewide polling data, that most of these organizations could not otherwise afford. The Republicans also did some polling, but on a much more modest scale. In an operation like that of the Democrats, the RNC spent some $220,000 on polls and surveys in thirty-nine states that were shared with state parties and Republican candidates. This service offered a number of benefits. First, it provided high-quality survey research to many party organizations and candidates. Such information aids in the development of more effective communications with voters, and helps parties and candidates target their resources more efficiently. In particular, this polling benefited the Clinton and Bush campaigns, which relied on the party polling to gain access to information on the status of the race in targeted states without having to bear the full cost of these polls. This sharing of information thus reduced the aggregate amount the presidential campaign had to spend on polling. Second, by conducting coordinated, centralized polling operations, the national committees eliminated at least some of the need for duplicative efforts by different candidates. While some candidates still conducted their own polling, they could reduce the amount their campaigns had to spend on survey research by piggybacking onto a poll that was primarily being conducted to track the progress of the presidential race.

It should further be noted that polling services were not the only means by which the DNC and RNC used soft money to assist their candidates. In 1991, for example, the DNC used soft money in a number of ways to assist its candidates in Pennsylvania. According to FEC reports, the DNC transferred $50,000 from its nonfederal individual account to the Pennsylvania Democratic Party between August and October. The DNC also directly contributed $25,000 to Ed Rendell, the party candidate in the Philadelphia mayoral race. In the special election for U.S. senator, the party supplemented its coordinated spending made on behalf of Harris Wofford by spending $50,000 in soft money funds on media expenses and by paying a portion of the salaries, per diem expenses, and travel costs of a dozen party organizers who were sent to Pennsylvania to help coordinate an election day get-out-the-vote program.

The national party organizations thus used soft money in a variety of ways during the 1991–92 election cycle. These funds served as an important supplement to the public funds and coordinated spending made on behalf of the parties' respective presidential tickets. They also provided the resources needed to conduct extensive voter identification and mobilization programs. Finally, they were a means of financing a significant portion of the ongoing expenses of the national party organizations, which allowed them to use a greater share of their federally regulated receipts for election-related purposes.

Senatorial and Congressional Committee Spending

The national senatorial and congressional campaign committees also raised and spent soft money to influence the outcomes of federal elections. Like the DNC and RNC, the Democratic and Republican campaign committees worked with state and local affiliates to pay for voter identification and registration programs, as well as fund-raising events and other generic party programs. Generally, they spent soft money funds on the same types of activities as the national party committees, although most of their expenditures were devoted to transfers to state parties and their share of the costs of activities jointly conducted with state and local party organizations.

Table 6.5

Senatorial and Congressional Campaign Committees, Soft Money Activity, 1991–92

	Receipts	Disbursements
DSCC		
Building fund	$617,052	$520,201
DCCC		
Nonfederal #1	2,398,337	2,039,270
Nonfederal #2	221,029	200,485
Nonfederal #3	290,314	297,599
Nonfederal #4	122,500	56,700
Nonfederal #5	43,000	42,300
Nonfederal #6	5,000	4,002
Building fund #1	1,622,454	1,684,187
Building fund #2	3,161	42,071
Subtotal	$4,705,795	$4,366,614
NRSC[a]		
Building fund	992,091	943,920
Nonfederal account	8,054,555	6,896,903
Subtotal	$9,046,482	$7,840,823
NRCC		
Nonfederal account	$6,281,040	$6,330,895

Source: Federal Election Commission.

Note: Figures are based on available Federal Election Commission data as of August 1994.
[a]The NRSC building fund totals have been reduced by $4.5 million to account for a loan used to pay earlier loans. The nonfederal account totals reflect an adjustment of $200,000 to account for transfers between this account and the building fund.

The Republicans

The Republican campaign committees' soft money activity significantly exceeded that of their Democratic counterparts. Overall, the two Republican committees raised a combined total of $15.3 million and spent about $14.2 million, as compared to the Democrats' $5.3 million and $4.9 million (see Table 6.5). The NRSC spent $7.8 million in soft money, $4 million of which was spent on joint activities (see Table 6.6), which included $2.3 million in fund-raising expenses. The committee also used about $1 million to finance the costs of its new Washington office, not including a $4.5

Table 6.6

Senatorial and Congressional Committee Soft Money Disbursements, 1991–92

Committee	Transfers to State Parties	Contributions	Joint Activity	Other
DSCC	0	0	0	$520,201
DCCC	$34,550	$561,649	$1,896,303	$1,874,112
NRSC	1,479,603	0	4,077,646	2,283,574
NRCC	1,753,250[a]	N.A.[b]	673,776	3,903,869

Source: Federal Election Commission.

Note: Figures include all soft money funds spent in conjunction with federal election-related activities between January 1, 1991, and December 31, 1992.
[a]This figure does not include a transfer of $300,000 on October 19, 1992, to a committee established by Governor Pete Wilson of California.
[b]The NRCC did not provide a separate summary of contribution activity to the FEC.

million bank loan it negotiated to repay prior loans for building costs. The committee's other major disbursements were made in the form of transfers to state party organizations. In total, about $1.5 million was transferred to ten states. More than half of this amount was transferred to four states with open-seat Senate races: Idaho received $372,000; Colorado, $225,000; Washington, $115,000; and Utah, $100,000. The committee also transferred $211,000 to Indiana, where Republican Dan Coats was waging an ultimately successful reelection campaign, and $180,000 to Georgia, where Republican Paul Coverdell defeated incumbent Democrat Wyche Fowler in a runoff election.

The NRCC spent $6.3 million in soft money. But unlike the NRSC, the congressional committee devoted a relatively small percentage of its total spending, only about 10 percent, to joint activity. Moreover, almost all of the $674,000 in joint activity expenses reported by the committee were for the nonfederal share of fund-raising costs; the NRCC allocated no monies to voter identification or mobilization programs. The committee also did not report any aggregate figure for contributions to candidates, but its FEC disclosure filings did show about $2 million in transfers, including $1.7 million to seventeen state parties and a 1992 transfer of $300,000 to the campaign committee of Governor Pete Wilson of California. Most of the monies transferred to state parties were sent to states holding key Senate elections: Oregon received $236,250; Florida, $200,000; Illinois, $175,000; Indiana, $150,000;

Idaho, $112,000; and Georgia, $106,000. The only other state to receive more than $100,000 was New Jersey, which was sent $180,900.

The Democrats

Most of the soft money activity by the Democratic campaign committees was conducted by the DCCC. The DSCC maintained only one soft money account, a building fund, which raised about $617,000 and spent $520,000 (see Table 6.5). These building fund expenses were the only soft money expenditures reported by the committee. The DCCC, on the other hand, maintained eight nonfederal accounts, including two building fund accounts, which totaled $4.7 million in receipts and close to $4.4 million in expenditures.

As noted in Table 6.6, the DCCC disbursed soft money funds for four purposes: transfers to state parties, direct candidate contributions, their non-federal share of joint activity, and other costs, including building funds and administrative expenses. The Democratic organizations transferred relatively little money to state party organizations. The DCCC sent less than $35,000 in soft money to six states; $12,500 was sent to the top recipient, Montana, and $10,000 was sent to Maryland. But the committee did spend a relatively sizable sum, more than $561,000, in contributions to state and local candidates or legislative campaign committees. In contrast, the Republican committees showed a preference for transferring significant amounts to state parties instead of making contributions to candidates.

Most of the $4.4 million spent by the DCCC was devoted to its nonfederal share of joint fund-raising expenses and building expenses. The committee spent about $1.9 million on joint activity, $1.4 million of which was for fund-raising expenses. The committee spent $1.7 million on building expenses, which represented most of the amount reported in the category of "other expenses." The balance in this category, about $150,000, primarily consisted of administrative and other overhead expenses.

State-Level Activity

The FEC's revised soft money disclosure regulations require that state parties disclose any monies raised and spent in connection with federal elections. As a result, the FEC reports for the 1992 election cycle provide an accounting of the funds state parties raised and spent on their share of joint activity expenses. The regulations, however, do not require party committees to disclose at the federal level funds spent on activities that are solely designed to influence the outcome of state and local elections. These monies remain under the jurisdiction of applicable state and local regulations. The FEC rules also do not require state parties to provide a detailed listing of their soft money contributors; instead, state parties simply have to provide information about their aggregate receipts. The new FEC data thus provide some insight into the soft money activity of state parties, but the picture they present is far from complete. Given the limits of the regulations, it is impossible to identify the sources of contributions, the particular federal candidates state parties are trying to assist, or the specific purposes for which soft money funds are spent. Under the law, state parties may use soft money for a wide range of activities designed to influence federal elections, including the printing and distribution of slate cards and sample ballots, the production of campaign paraphernalia, and their share of joint fund-raising activities, voter mobilization programs, and other volunteer programs.

Table 6.7 provides a summary of the soft money receipts and expenditures reported to the FEC by Democratic and Republican state party organizations. All of the state parties reported soft money contributions and disbursements to the FEC during the 1991–92 cycle, with the exception of the South Carolina Republican Party, which reported that it did not raise or spend any soft money outside the amount it received through transfers from the national party committees (FEC reports show that the party received $239,500 in soft money from the RNC). The amounts raised and spent by state parties varied widely, ranging from $15,180 in spending by the Kansas Democratic Party to $4.2 million by the California Democratic Party. Among Republicans, the disparities were not so great, but the differences were still sizable; for example, the West Virginia state party spent only $16,443, while the New Jersey state party spent more than $3.2 million.

As Robert Biersack of the FEC has observed, the data suggest that "party organizations at the state level have for the most part developed substantial financial resources."[36] Thirteen Democratic state committees reported more than $1 million in soft money expenditures, and three others, Arkansas, Kentucky, and Wisconsin, spent more than $900,000. Ten Republican state committees spent at least $1 million, while two others, Colorado and Missouri, disbursed more than $900,000. Furthermore, the Democratic state committees in only 20 percent of the states raised less than $500,000 during the election cycle. For Republicans, only 26 percent of the states reported receipts under this amount. By contrast, about 96 percent of all PACs that reported raising funds in 1991–92 raised less than $500,000.[37]

The state party committees that spent $1 million or more were primarily from large states where the state parties tend to be well-financed. They also were the sites of crucial electoral contests. All of these states, with the possible exception of Indiana for the Democrats, were battlegrounds in the presidential race. Nine of these states were the sites of U.S. Senate races: California, Florida, Georgia, Illinois, Indiana, New York, Ohio, Pennsylvania, and Washington. Indiana, North Carolina, and Washington also were

Table 6.7

State Party Soft Money Receipts and Expenditures, 1991–92

	Democratic		Republican	
	Receipts	Expenditures	Receipts	Expenditures
Alabama	$483,980	$483,980	$185,154	$179,239
Alaska	113,853	115,054	88,207	88,207
Arizona	121,090	307,286	115,015	115,015
Arkansas	1,001,852	994,013	125,520	119,331
California	4,609,070	4,207,923	1,881,045	2,155,111
Colorado	509,207	575,023	979,741	980,750
Connecticut	323,319	369,835	146,765	154,149
Delaware	265,855	270,231	619,599	550,825
Florida	308,685	318,323	1,946,822	1,967,160
Georgia	2,596,958	2,621,214	1,101,313	1,095,819
Hawaii	708,092	638,631	60,000	61,734
Idaho	93,951	93,951	568,292	571,365
Illinois	911,622	1,020,891	530,516	497,579
Indiana	1,038,018	1,354,029	1,091,611	1,162,840
Iowa	630,363	630,362	284,976	290,307
Kansas	15,180	15,180	126,772	126,772
Kentucky	812,836	961,660	154,742	153,467
Louisiana	992,424	1,050,933	30,177	42,497
Maine	223,660	347,831	20,356	20,356
Maryland	275,341	337,225	44,725	43,600
Massachusetts	535,240	699,688	554,216	617,502
Michigan	1,775,564	2,110,972	2,524,396	2,552,195
Minnesota	1,480,178	1,474,271	1,068,995	1,194,382
Mississippi	215,350	227,896	0	16,679
Missouri	849,669	892,251	950,680	919,195
Montana	16,584	715,877	93,668	212,371
Nebraska	175,041	200,291	490,445	486,046
Nevada	228,687	496,181	101,564	104,350
New Hampshire	187,800	196,163	0	72,143
New Jersey	1,298,287	2,084,670	3,125,032	3,220,474
New Mexico	454,146	454,146	285,591	293,547
New York	938,182	1,400,286	617,332	770,830
North Carolina	1,238,918	1,077,486	245,599	245,598
North Dakota	270,193	409,877	127,141	279,050
Ohio	1,725,764	1,621,669	2,639,701	2,561,583
Oklahoma	43,392	147,830	80,903	286,467
Oregon	408,589	451,426	24,375	79,579
Pennsylvania	1,170,519	1,097,040	655,318	586,880
Rhode Island	39,901	36,663	147,943	143,581
South Carolina	206,861	217,352	0	0
South Dakota	255,987	250,553	179,195	179,195
Tennessee	219,608	231,438	45,898	391,305
Texas	2,284,825	2,358,341	1,334,929	2,487,955
Utah	318,656	381,714	432,541	457,681
Vermont	222,702	223,080	189,922	192,618

(continued)

Table 6.7 *(continued)*

	Democratic		Republican	
	Receipts	Expenditures	Receipts	Expenditures
Virginia	421,109	435,331	373,458	363,808
Washington	235,281	394,278	1,058,522	1,377,088
West Virginia	152,332	175,326	0	16,443
Wisconsin	837,345	906,641	470,464	567,789
Wyoming	31,552	31,660	56,905	56,838
Total	$34,273,618	$38,113,972	$27,976,081	$31,109,295

Source: Federal Election Commission.

Notes: Figures include only the nonfederal share of funds raised and spent on joint activities related to federal elections and reported to the FEC. Any funds related solely to state and local election activity are not included. Figures represent the dollar amounts raised and spent from January 1, 1991, to December 31, 1992.

holding gubernatorial elections during this election cycle.

A 1994 study of soft money contributions by the Center for Responsive Politics offers some additional understanding of the soft money activities of state committees. The center's study, which examined contributions to state party committees in nine states—Colorado, Florida, Illinois, Iowa, Missouri, Ohio, Oregon, Pennsylvania, and Texas—revealed that the Democratic and Republican party organizations received a total of $41.6 million during the 1991–92 election cycle in what the study describes as soft money.[38] This figure includes $12.7 million in transfers from national party committees, which have already been accounted for in discussing the soft money activity of these organizations. When these transfers are subtracted from the total, the aggregate amount received by these nine party committees is approximately $28.8 million, with the Democratic committees raising about $15.3 million and the Republicans around $13.5 million. It also is important to note that all of this amount might not be considered soft money under federal statutes. While none of these gifts were subject to federal contribution limits, the center's aggregate figure for receipts is not limited to monies raised by state parties for the purpose of influencing federal elections; therefore, it may also contain funds raised for purposes unrelated to federal contests. Even with these caveats, however, the center's study is useful for the light it sheds on the contribution patterns that characterize state party fund raising.

The center's analysis found that these nine state committees raised significant sums from a variety of sources. Of the $28.8 million total, $10.6

million came from business donors, $10.1 million from individuals, $4.2 million from candidate committees, $3.3 million from labor unions, and about $650,000 from other or unidentified sources. The Democratic committees raised the majority of their funds from businesses and labor unions, receiving $5.7 million from corporate sources and $3.2 million from labor unions, with another $3.4 million from individual donors. The Republican committees raised $6.7 million from individual donors and $4.9 million from business sources, and only $38,250 from labor. Most of these contributions came from in-state sources. Excluding party transfers, about 84 percent of the funds received by these state committees came from donors within each state.

As with the national party committees, state party organizations received a number of large contributions to help finance their political activities. The center study identified thirty contributors who donated $100,000 or more to the nine state parties they surveyed. Of these top thirty contributors, ten were business interests, eight were individuals, six were labor unions, four were candidate committees, and two were single-issue groups. Among the leading donors were the National Education Association, which gave $1.3 million to Democratic committees; Bruce Benson, owner of Benson Mineral Group, an oil, gas, and mining company, who gave $465,360 to the Colorado Republican Party; the Association of Trial Lawyers of America, which gave $419,000 (94 percent of which went to Democrats); the AFL-CIO, $409,855 to Democratic committees; Philip Morris, $394,650 (60 percent to Democrats); the Teamsters Union, $374,507 (99 percent to Democrats); and EMILY's List, which gave $265,000 to Democrats. The center further found that forty-four donors gave at least $10,000 each to Democratic and Republican party organizations.

The new FEC regulations and state disclosure reports have provided more information on soft money financing than was previously available. But a comprehensive accounting of soft money activities, especially those conducted by state and local party organizations, remains elusive, since federal regulators do not require state parties to report the sources of their contributions or specify the particular purposes of their expenditures. Further improvement of disclosure laws will be needed before a full accounting of soft money and its role in the political process is possible.

Notes

1. For a comprehensive discussion of the various types and role of soft money in the political system, see Herbert E. Alexander, *"Soft Money" and Campaign Financing* (Washington, DC: Public Affairs Council, 1986).
2. 11 C.F.R., Section 100.7(b).

3. See Anthony Corrado, *Paying for Presidents* (New York: Twentieth Century Fund Press, 1993), pp. 65–66.

4. See, for example, John F. Noble, "Soft Money," *Campaigns & Elections,* summer 1984, p. 44.

5. 11 C.F.R., Section 102.5 (a)(1).

6. For example, see FEC, Advisory Opinion 1984–15.

7. On the problems of state disclosure laws, see Herbert E. Alexander, *Reform and Reality: Financing State and Local Campaigns* (New York: Twentieth Century Fund Press, 1991), pp. 51–71.

8. For a discussion of soft money financing in the 1980 election, see Elizabeth Drew, *Politics and Money: The New Road to Corruption* (New York: Macmillan, 1983); and Herbert E. Alexander and Brian A. Haggerty, *Financing the 1980 Election* (Lexington, MA: Lexington Books, 1983), pp. 367–440. For the 1984 election, see Alexander, *"Soft Money" and Campaign Financing*; and Herbert E. Alexander and Brian A. Haggerty, *Financing the 1984 Election* (Lexington, MA: Lexington Books, 1987), pp. 329–42.

9. For a discussion of soft money financing in the 1988 election, see Herbert E. Alexander and Monica Bauer, *Financing the 1988 Election* (Boulder, CO: Westview Press, 1991), especially pp. 74–82.

10. *Common Cause v. Federal Election Commission,* 692 F. Supp. 1391, 1396 (D.D.C. 1987).

11. For background and a summary of the regulations, see *Federal Register* 55 (June 26, 1990): 2605ff; FEC, *Record,* August 1990, p. 1; and *Record,* September 1990, pp. 9–12.

12. In these cases, each type of race—president, U.S. Senate, U.S. House, governor, other statewide offices, state senate, state representative, and local offices—receives one point, and the allocation ratio is based on the federal to nonfederal point totals. In 1991, the FEC amended the 1990 rules to add an additional nonfederal point for each state.

13. Robert Biersack, "Hard Facts and Soft Money: Party Finance in the 1991–1992 Election Cycle" (paper presented at the State of the Parties Conference, Ray C. Bliss Institute of Applied Politics, Akron, OH, September 23–24, 1993), p. 9.

14. Alexander and Bauer, *Financing the 1988 Election,* pp. 75–77; and Jean Cobb, Jeff Denny, Vicki Kemper, and Viveca Novak, "All the President's Donors," *Common Cause Magazine* 16 (March/April 1990), pp. 21–27, 38–39.

15. See, for example, Gerald Pomper, "Soft Money is Good Money," *PartyLine: The Newsletter of the Committee for Party Renewal,* spring/summer 1993, pp. 4–5; and Beth Donovan, "Much-Maligned 'Soft Money' is Precious to Both Parties," *Congressional Quarterly Weekly Report,* May 15, 1993, pp. 1195–1200.

16. "Republican Donation Put in Escrow," *Los Angeles Times,* May 11, 1992. According to FEC reports, this event, which is also known as the annual Republican Senate–House Dinner since most of the funds raised are for the NRSC and NRCC, raised a total of about $4.9 million in 1992.

17. Neil A. Lewis, "Big G.O.P. Donor Becomes Large Embarrassment," *New York Times,* May 9, 1992.

18. Ibid.

19. "GOP Holds Controversial $400,000 Contribution in Escrow Account," *Los Angeles Times,* May 9, 1992.

20. Lewis, "Big G.O.P. Donor Becomes Large Embarrassment."

21. Sara Fritz, "Democrats Copy Fund-Raising Techniques of the Experts: The GOP," *Los Angeles Times,* July 16, 1992.

22. Cobb, Denny, Kemper, and Novak, "All the President's Donors," p. 23.

23. This analysis was conducted by one of the coauthors. The figures presented here are based on the soft money contributions deposited in the accounts used by the DNC and RNC to finance activities designed to influence federal election outcomes. These accounts represent more than 99 percent of the total unadjusted soft money receipts of the DNC and about 93 percent of the total unadjusted soft money receipts of the RNC. The figures do not include any building funds and the account maintained by the RNC for the National Republican Legislators Association, which had total receipts of only $50,577.

24. A similar analysis by Common Cause of all DNC and RNC soft money accounts found that the Democrats raised $19.8 million in soft money between July 1, 1992, and November 23, 1992. The Republicans received $12.5 million. These totals included nearly $5 million received by the Democrats and $2.2 million by the Republicans during the five-week period immediately before and after the election (October 15 through November 23, 1992). See Common Cause, "Clinton and Democrats Raise Nearly $20 Million in Soft Money During the Presidential General Election Period; Bush and Republicans Raise $12.4 Million, According to Reports Filed with FEC," press release, December 17, 1992, p. 1.

25. Common Cause, "Soft Money for President Clinton & Democratic National Committee Tops $29 Million During 1991–1992 Election Cycle," press release, March 3, 1993.

26. Jeffrey Denny, "Democrats Play the Soft Money Game," *Common Cause Magazine* 18 (winter 1992), p. 9.

27. Common Cause, "Clinton and Democrats Raise Nearly $20 Million in Soft Money," p. 2.

28. Ibid., pp. 2–3; and Charles R. Babcock, "GOP Donors Open Wallets for Democrats," *Washington Post,* October 24, 1992.

29. Cited in Jill Abramson, "Crowd of Usually Stalwart Pro-GOP Industries Stopped Feeding Elephant as Clinton Surged," *Wall Street Journal,* November 19, 1992.

30. Elizabeth Nueffer, "New Interest Groups Emerge as Big Donors," *Boston Globe,* September 17, 1992.

31. Alexander and Bauer, *Financing the 1988 Election,* p. 41.

32. These states included Illinois, Virginia, California, Massachusetts, New Mexico, Maryland, New Hampshire, Oregon, Ohio, Georgia, North Carolina, and Arkansas.

33. The three states that did not receive nonfederal funds were Massachusetts, Oklahoma, and West Virginia. These states received close to $350,000 in hard money.

34. The eight states that did not receive nonfederal funds were Connecticut, Hawaii, Maryland, Massachusetts, Nebraska, New York, Utah, and West Virginia. Of these, Utah received some hard money, but the amount was only $494.

35. The DNC conducted polls in Arizona, Nevada, and Virginia in early September but financed no subsequent surveys in these states. The committee also financed one poll in Florida in early October. This was probably due to the fact that the surveys indicated that the Democrats were unlikely to win these states. The only one of these states the Democrats carried in the presidential race was Nevada. In his remarks delivered at the National Press Club on January 19, 1993, James Carville, Clinton's campaign manager, cited Nevada as the one state the Democrats won but had not expected to win. Also see presidential polling set forth in chapter 5, pp. 121–26.

36. Biersack, "Hard Facts and Soft Money," p. 12.

37. Ibid.

38. CRP, *Soft Money in the States* (Washington, DC: Center for Responsive Politics, 1994).

7

Senate and House Financing and PAC Trends

In recent decades, congressional elections have rarely produced surprising results. In a typical election year, relatively few House incumbents are seriously challenged and a significant number face no opposition at all. Those who are challenged usually outspend their opponents by substantial amounts and are reelected by sizable margins. As a result, most House members win reelection. In the 1986 elections, for example, only eight lost their bids for reelection; in 1988, only seven lost; and in 1990, only sixteen of the 406 incumbents were voted out of office.[1] These results were not atypical. In the congressional elections between 1980 and 1990, an average of 95 percent of those seeking reelection won their primary and general election races. When turnover in membership did occur, it was usually due to retirement, redistricting, death, or a candidate seeking another office rather than as a result of an incumbent losing in a stable district.

Senate contests are generally more competitive than House elections because incumbents usually face more well known and better-financed opponents. From 1980 to 1990, an average of 83 percent of incumbent senators won their bids for reelection, although the rates varied widely, ranging from 53 percent in 1980 to 97 percent in 1990. But in recent elections, a number of incumbents have run without having to face a serious challenger or have outspent their opponents by significant margins, and from 1982 to 1990, no incumbent seeking reelection lost in the primaries. This experience has led some observers to conclude that recent Senate elections have been less competitive than those of previous decades.[2]

The 1992 elections dramatically departed from these historical patterns. The elections produced a turnover of 110 members in the House, the largest change since 1948, when 118 new members took office. This extraordinary level of turnover was due largely to an unusual number of retirements: fifty-four members, a postwar high, decided to leave public office, and thirteen others withdrew to seek another office.[3] The elections also produced an unusual number of incumbent defeats, particularly because only 371 members decided to seek reelection, the lowest number since World War II. Nineteen of these individuals were defeated in primaries, another postwar record, and twenty-four were defeated in general elections. In recent decades, only the Watergate elections of 1974 had produced as many incumbent losses.[4]

Turnover in the Senate was more modest, with twelve new members seated as a result of the elections.[5] This change was in part due to retirements, as seven senators decided to retire from office, the most since 1978, when a postwar record ten chose not to seek reelection. In addition, one senator, Illinois Democrat Alan Dixon, was defeated in a primary race, and four others (Democrats Terry Sanford and Wyche Fowler, and Republicans Bob Kasten and John Seymour) lost in general elections.

In other postwar election years, a high level of turnover has been accompanied by a large partisan swing in the composition of the Congress, but the 1992 election also proved to be unusual in this regard. The Senate races yielded no change in partisanship, with the Democrats maintaining the 57-to-43 advantage they held before the election. In the House, a change in more than one-quarter of the membership resulted in a net gain of only ten seats for the Republicans, making 1992 the first election since 1892—and only the second in American history—in which the party that lost the White House gained seats in the Congress.[6] If the election had followed the average historical pattern since 1942, it would have produced a net partisan swing of fifty-four seats.[7]

The election did, however, lead to major demographic changes in the composition of the national legislature. Many political observers declared 1992 the "Year of the Woman" due to the record number of women seeking federal office and the high level of political activity on the part of women and women's groups around the country. This activity was spurred by the controversy surrounding the hearings on Clarence Thomas's nomination for the Supreme Court, which was dominated by Anita Hill's testimony that she had been sexually harassed by Thomas. The 1992 elections produced a substantial increase in the number of women holding federal office, with the number of female representatives growing from twenty-eight to forty-seven, and the number of women senators from two to six. Minority representation in the House also rose significantly, with the number of African American members rising from twenty-five to thirty-eight, and Latinos from eleven to seventeen.[8] Carol Moseley-Braun of Illinois became the first African Amer-

Table 7.1

Congressional Campaign Expenditures, 1972–92 (in $ millions)

Election Cycle	Total	Senate	House
1971–72	$77.3	$30.7	$46.5
1973–74	88.2	34.7	53.5
1975–76	115.5	44.0	71.5
1977–78	194.8	85.2	109.7
1979–80	239.0	102.9	136.0
1981–82	342.4	138.4	204.0
1983–84	374.1	1,170.5	203.6
1985–86	450.9	211.6	239.3
1987–88	457.7	201.2	256.5
1989–90	446.3	180.4	265.8
1991–92	678.3	271.6	406.7

Source: Citizens' Research Foundation compilation, based on FEC and other data.

ican woman elected to the Senate. The 1992 elections thus produced much greater diversity on Capitol Hill.

The 1992 elections departed from historical patterns in one other crucial way: they were the most expensive congressional contests in American history. As shown in Table 7.1, from 1986 through 1990, congressional spending was relatively stable, averaging about $450 million in each of these election cycles. In 1990, spending declined slightly to $446.3 million, from $457.7 million in 1988. In 1992, the amounts jumped to more than $678 million, an increase of 52 percent over 1990 and the largest single-election surge since the FEC began reporting congressional finances. The most dramatic rise occurred in House campaign expenditures, which rose 53 percent to $406.7 million. Senate expenditures rose sharply, from about $180.4 million in 1990 to $271.6 million. Part of this increase was due to the amounts spent on special elections in Pennsylvania and North Dakota, as well as two Senate elections in California.[9] Another reason for the extraordinary growth in spending was the increased number of candidates; there were 2,956 House and Senate candidates in the 1992 cycle, or about 1,200 more than in 1990 or 1988.[10] Yet even when these considerations are taken into account, the total for 1992 represents a substantial increase over the amount spent in the previous two election cycles.

The Context of the 1992 Elections

The high turnover and extraordinary levels of spending were both results of the unique dynamics of the 1992 elections. The election year was marked by a rising tide of public discontent with the Congress. This deep disapproval of Congress's performance began in the 1990 election cycle, stimulated by the controversies associated with pay raises, the ethical lapses of some members, including House Speaker Jim Wright, and the 1990 budget accord that mandated a sizable tax increase. In 1990, voter dissatisfaction was not intense enough to result in a large number of incumbents being voted out of office. Yet it was strong enough to register at the polls, as the average share of the vote received by incumbents in both parties dropped sharply, reaching its lowest point since 1974.[11] In 1991 and 1992, the public perception of Congress grew worse, as gloomy economic predictions and continuing criticism of partisan bickering gave rise to an "anti-incumbent mood" in which a significant share of the public expressed disapproval not only of the Congress, but also of their own representative.[12] Accordingly, many analysts felt 1992 would prove to be a tough year for incumbents seeking reelection.

Many observers also believed that 1992 would be a difficult year for incumbents because of redistricting. The 1992 elections were the first to be held after the decennial reapportionment. Such elections tend to produce greater than average turnover in Congress since some members will choose to retire rather than run for a redistricted seat, while others will lose races in redrawn districts. The potential effects of redistricting on the electoral prospects of incumbents were especially pronounced in 1992, due to the extensive amount of remapping that was required. Nineteen seats were shifted, affecting twenty-one states. Most of the states that did not lose or gain seats had to redraw districts to meet the equal-population requirement.[13] Furthermore, the effects of the process were exaggerated by Voting Rights Act considerations. In 1986, the Supreme Court in *Thornburgh v. Gingles* construed the act to require that minorities receive a fair chance of obtaining representation through redistricting and that district lines not discriminate, even unintentionally, against minorities. This decision was widely interpreted as meaning that districts should be designed to assist racial and ethnic minorities where residency patterns made this possible. Accordingly, a number of districts were redrawn for the purpose of promoting minority representation, usually by creating districts in which a majority of the residents were minority voters.[14] This consideration led some states, particularly North Carolina and Louisiana, to undertake a more extensive revision of districts than otherwise might have been required. The creation of such "minority majority" districts was one of the key reasons for the increased number of minority candidates elected to the House in 1992, as the process resulted in fifteen new districts with black majorities and nine new districts that were majority-Hispanic.[15] But it also had the effect of stripping crucial blocs of minority voters from some districts, which weakened the electoral prospects of some House Democrats, especially in the South.[16]

The effects of redistricting were expanded by other procedural circumstances. In some states, districts were not devised, as is usually the case, by state legislatures, which are often willing to consider partisan interests or to protect incumbents when revising congressional seats. Some districts were determined by courts or other entities, paying little regard to the interests of incumbents or other political concerns. For example, in California, the district map was determined by a group of "special masters," retired judges appointed by the state supreme court. In Florida, a court-appointed expert determined the districts without considering where the incumbents lived.[17] Judges also determined the new district lines in New York and Michigan. In all, eleven states with a total of 170 House seats ended up with a redistricting plan devised by a court.[18] As a result, some incumbents were presented with districts in which the population differed by as much as 75 percent from their previous race. In California, six incumbents were paired against each other, even though the state gained seven seats as a result of the 1990 census.[19]

The electoral prospects of House incumbents were further undermined by the House Bank scandal. Since the early 1800s, House members have received their paychecks at the office of the House Sergeant at Arms, which maintains a depository called the House Bank, where members may deposit their checks and other monies in noninterest-bearing checking accounts. The bank routinely used the funds in its accounts to cover any overdrafts by a member, essentially providing members with interest-free loans, so long as the overdraft was less than a member's next paycheck, and sometimes even more.[20]

Overdrafts at the bank had been reported in yearly audit reports since 1947, but they became a focal point of media attention in 1991 as a result of a General Accounting Office report that revealed that the bank had covered 8,331 bad checks in the past year without imposing a penalty or interest.[21] The release of the report created a public uproar, and although House leaders initially sought to keep secret the names of those who had written bad checks, pressure from inside and outside Congress forced the issue and led the House to vote to disclose the identity and accounts of all members who had written overdrafts since 1988. This disclosure was released in April 1992, when the House Ethics Committee revealed the names of 325 current or former members who had been responsible for one or more overdrafts, including forty-six sitting representatives who had each written 100 such checks or more.[22]

Although the bank's practices involved no cost to taxpayers and the House quickly moved to adopt reforms in its procedures, the revelations

ignited a widespread public perception of congressional privilege and
abuse, and thus had a significant effect on the outcome of the 1992 congressional elections. The scandal was a major cause of the record number of
retirements and was a key factor in the defeat of a number of well-established incumbents.[23] Of the 269 sitting members on the Ethics Committee
list, seventy-seven, or more than one out of four, retired or were defeated in
primary or general election races.[24] Twenty-five of the forty-six members
with 100 or more overdrafts did not return to the Congress: twelve retired,
eight were defeated in primaries, and five lost in the general election.[25]
Eight of the thirty-two with more than fifty overdrafts each did not return:
four retired, two lost in primaries, and two lost the general election.[26] Many
of the worst abusers who lost their bids for reelection were well-entrenched
incumbents, including Democrats Joseph Early of Massachusetts, Mary
Rose Oakar of Ohio, Jerry Huckaby of Louisiana, Gerry Sikorski of Minnesota, Thomas Downey of New York, Peter Kostmayer of Pennsylvania, and
Albert Bustamante of Texas, as well as Republican Bob McEwen of
Ohio.[27] Those who survived the election despite many overdrafts, such as
Democrats Ronald Coleman of Texas with 673 overdrafts and Dan Glick-
man of Kansas with 105 overdrafts, found themselves in vulnerable positions for the first time since they had entered the House and often faced
strong challengers, who made the "bounced checks" the centerpiece of their
campaigns. This strategy generally benefited challengers; in fact, one post-
election analysis found that the scandal had a significant effect on the support
given to incumbents who were perceived as having abused their bank privileges, reducing their vote by an average of about five percentage points.[28]

Given these circumstances, it is not surprising that congressional candidates spent a substantially greater amount than they had in the previous
election cycle. Fewer House seats went uncontested than in any previous
postwar election, and many incumbents were running scared or at least
facing tougher contests than they had in the past. In 1990, more than one
out of five House members faced no major opposition in the general election, and five Senate candidates were unopposed. In 1992, less than 6
percent of those who sought reelection to the House faced no opposition,
and no senator lacked a major party opponent (excluding Democrat John
Breaux of Louisiana, who won a majority of the vote in the primary and
thus, in accordance with Louisiana law, had no opponent in the general
election).[29] Many of those who were opposed faced well-financed challengers, while others decided to protect themselves against any anti-incumbent feelings among the electorate by conducting more extensive, and
expensive, campaigns. There also was a noteworthy increase in the number
of open seats, which are generally more hotly contested and expensive than

races involving challengers against incumbents. In 1990, there were open seats in only twenty-eight districts and three Senate contests. In 1992, the number of open seats tripled, with eighty-six in the House and nine in the Senate.[30]

Therefore, although 88 percent of the House members and 85 percent of the senators who sought reelection were successful, the 1992 races were more competitive than others in recent decades. Even though many of the most vulnerable incumbents retired, the average share of the two-party vote won by sitting members was the lowest since 1966, with virtually no difference recorded between Republicans and Democrats.[31] Moreover, the proportion of House incumbents who won with less than 60 percent of the vote rose to 33.4 percent, the highest percentage since 1964.[32] In the Senate races, 56 percent of the incumbents won with less than 60 percent of the vote.[33] Many incumbents, therefore, found themselves in contested races in which they felt a need to spend more than in the past. Thus, as in previous elections, those seeking reelection significantly outspent their opponents, and most won another term in office. Yet despite this outcome, 1992 was not a typical election year.

Financial Activity in the 1992 Elections

During the 1991–92 election cycle, 2,956 House and Senate candidates raised $658.6 million and spent $678.3 million on their campaigns (see Table 7.2). Expenditures thus exceeded receipts by about $20 million, a marked contrast from 1990, when congressional candidates raised about $471 million and spent $446 million, or 1988, when $478 million was received and only $457 million spent.

House and Senate candidates spent more than they received, with House contenders spending about $11 million more than they raised and Senate hopefuls spending close to $9 million more than they collected. As noted in Table 7.2, almost all of the additional spending can be attributed to incumbents, who spent $22.5 million, or about 7.4 percent more than they raised during the election cycle. The balance was made up by dipping into funds left over from previous elections. Incumbents began the 1992 cycle with about $86 million in excess funds; after the election they had about $54.5 million left over, a drop of 42 percent from their holdings after 1990 and the smallest remaining balance for incumbents since 1984.[34]

Even if they had not dipped into their coffers, House incumbents would have had significantly more money available to spend than their opponents. The 400 incumbents who solicited funds during the 1992 cycle raised $300.4 million, as compared with $182.8 million for their 1,774 chal-

Table 7.2

Congressional Campaign Financial Activity, 1991–92 (in $ millions)

Campaign[a]	Receipts	Expenditures
Senate	$262.9	$271.6
Democrats	142.8	146.7
Incumbents	45.4	48.2
Challengers	62.8	62.8
Open Seats	34.6	35.7
Republicans	118.8	123.7
Incumbents	51.9	57.4
Challengers	27.6	27.4
Open Seats	39.3	38.9
Others	1.3	1.3
Challengers	1.1	1.1
Open Seats	0.2	0.2
House	395.7	406.7
Democrats	217.3	227.8
Incumbents	126.6	138.7
Challengers	34.7	34.0
Open Seats	56.0	55.1
Republicans	174.4	175.0
Incumbents	75.9	77.6
Challengers	53.9	53.2
Open Seats	44.6	44.1
Others[b]	4.0	3.9
Incumbents	0.6	0.6
Challengers	2.7	2.6
Open Seats	0.7	0.7
Total	$658.6	$678.3
Democrats	360.1	374.5
Republicans	293.2	298.6
Others	5.3	5.2
Incumbents	300.4	322.5
Challengers	182.8	181.2
Open Seats	175.4	174.6

Source: Federal Election Commission.

Note: Figures are rounded off.

[a]The FEC defines open seat races as those in which the incumbent did not seek reelection. Accordingly, general election candidates in the fourteen congressional districts where an incumbent decided to retire after receiving his party's nomination for reelection are listed as challengers.

[b]These totals reflect the campaigns of incumbent Bernard Sanders of Vermont, Lynn Taborsak of Connecticut, and Carlos Romero-Barcelo of Puerto Rico.

lengers. Most of this disparity was due to the fund-raising efforts of House incumbents, who outraised their opponents by more than 2 to 1, generating $203.1 million as compared with $91.3 million for their challengers. Senate incumbents enjoyed less of an advantage, raising $97.3 million as compared to $91.5 million for their challengers. Incumbents thus accounted for 45.6 percent of the total monies raised during the cycle, as compared to 27.7 percent for challengers. The 782 open seat candidates received $175.4 million, or about 26.6 percent of the total monies raised.

Sources of Funds

Congressional candidates were able to spend more money in 1992 than in any previous election because they raised more money than ever before. Major party House and Senate candidates raised $653.3 million during the 1992 election cycle, which was about $180 million more than they raised in either 1990 or 1988.[35] This substantial influx of funds came from no one particular source, as the amounts received from each major source increased significantly. Most of the $180 million increase, however, was due to a substantial rise in the amounts solicited from individual contributors, which yielded about $104 million more in net receipts than in 1990. The amount candidates contributed or loaned to their own campaigns, which rose from $37.8 million in 1990 to $87.8 million in 1992, accounted for slightly less than one-third of the increase in total 1992 receipts. In addition, PACs gave about $30 million more to these candidates than they did in 1990, providing $180.1 million in total receipts, as compared to $149.6 million in 1990.

Individual Contributions

Most of the funds raised by congressional candidates during the 1992 election cycle came from direct contributions from individuals. Democratic and Republican House and Senate candidates raised $352.8 million, or 54 percent, of their $653.3 million in total net receipts from individual contributors. As shown in Table 7.3, Senate candidates raised $162.5 million, or 62 percent of their funds, from individual donors. This percentage represented a slight decrease from 1990 and 1988, when Senate candidates relied on individuals for about 64 percent of their total funds. But the dollar amount rose significantly, reversing a 1986 to 1990 decline in which the amounts contributed by individuals fell from $140 million to $119.6 million. Overall, Democrats and challengers raised a slightly higher proportion of their funds from individuals, with challengers leading all categories with 65.7 percent.

When the cumulative figures in Table 7.3 are disaggregated, however, greater differences are revealed. The twelve Republican Senate incumbents raised $34.5 million, or 66.6 percent of their total funds, from individuals, while the seventeen Democratic incumbents received $24.4 million, 53.9 percent of their total, from individuals. There also was a significant difference between Democratic and Republican candidates running for open seats, with the twenty-nine Democrats raising 70 percent of their monies, $24.2 million, from individuals, and the thirty-one Republicans getting only 50.6 percent of their funds, $19.9 million, from this source. Challengers in both parties received about 65 percent of their revenues from individuals, with the seventy-six Democrats taking in $41.5 million and the eighty-two Republicans $17.9 million.

House candidates raised $190.3 million from individuals, which represented a substantial increase over the sums received from individual donors in previous elections. From 1986 to 1990, House contenders raised an average of about $128 million from individuals, with little growth from election to election. The primary reason for the dramatic increase in giving in 1992 was the larger number of candidates soliciting individual donations. There were 2,049 House contenders in 1992, as opposed to an average of just less than 1,400 candidates in each of the three previous election cycles. On average, each of these candidates raised about $92,800 from individuals, as compared to an average of $94,400 per candidate in 1990. As in the past, however, challengers failed to keep pace with incumbents; the average amounts solicited by incumbents rose from about $190,500 in 1990 to $249,400 in 1992, while challengers' average receipts rose from about $35,600 in 1990 to about $42,000 in 1992. The substantial rise in the amounts contributed from individuals was, therefore, also influenced by the fund-raising efforts of incumbents, who raised significantly more from their supporters than they had in the previous election cycle.

In general, House candidates are less dependent on individual gifts than their Senate counterparts because the former receive a greater proportion of their revenues from PACs. In 1988 and 1990, House candidates raised about 46 percent of their total funds from individual contributors; in 1992, despite the surge in revenues from individual donors, this percentage increased only slightly, to 48.6 percent. Overall, incumbents raised about 46 percent of their funds from individuals, as compared to about 52 percent for challengers and open seat candidates. The 143 Republicans who sought reelection, however, relied on individual gifts to a greater extent than their Democratic colleagues. Republican incumbents raised $39.7 million, 52.4 percent of their total, from individuals, while the 227 Democrats raised $52.6 million, 41.5 percent of their total, from this source. That Democratic

Table 7.3

Sources of Congressional Campaign Receipts, Major Party Candidates, 1991–92 (in $ millions)

	Net Receipts	Individual Contributions	Political Committee Contributions[a]	Candidate Contributions	Candidate Loans	Other Loans
Senate	$261.6	$162.5 (62.1)	$51.8 (19.8)	$6.6 (2.5)	$28.2 (10.8)	$0.4 (0.2)
Democrats	142.8	90.1 (63.1)	30.1 (21.1)	1.7 (1.2)	14.2 (9.9)	0.4 (0.2)
Republicans	118.8	72.3 (60.9)	21.7 (18.2)	4.9 (4.1)	14.0 (11.8)	0.0 (0.0)
Incumbents	97.3	59.0 (60.6)	31.9 (32.8)	0.7 (0.1)	0.1 (0.0)	0.1 (0.0)
Challengers	90.4	59.4 (65.7)	8.9 (9.8)	1.7 (0.2)	16.8 (18.6)	.03 (0.0)
Open Seats	73.9	44.1 (59.7)	11.0 (14.9)	4.2 (5.7)	11.3 (15.3)	0.0 (0.0)
House	391.7	190.3 (48.6)	128.3 (32.8)	11.2 (2.8)	41.8 (10.7)	1.8 (0.5)
Democrats	217.3	98.5 (45.4)	85.8 (39.5)	3.4 (1.6)	18.5 (8.5)	1.0 (0.5)
Republicans	174.1	91.8 (52.6)	42.5 (24.4)	7.8 (4.4)	23.3 (13.4)	0.8 (0.5)
Incumbents	202.5	92.3 (45.6)	94.7 (46.8)	0.4 (0.2)	2.7 (1.3)	0.6 (0.3)
Challengers	88.6	45.9 (51.8)	12.3 (13.9)	8.3 (9.4)	17.8 (20.1)	0.6 (0.7)
Open Seats	100.6	52.1 (51.8)	21.3 (21.2)	2.5 (2.5)	21.3 (21.2)	0.6 (0.6)

Source: Federal Election Commission.

Note: Figures in parentheses represent the percentage of total receipts from each source.
[a]Figures in this column represent mostly PAC contributions but also include monies from other nonparty political committees.

incumbents raised a smaller share of their funds from individuals than other candidates is not unusual, especially given the substantial amounts Democrats tend to receive from PACs. There was little difference between Republican and Democratic challengers with respect to the proportion of funds they received from individuals, although the average Republican took in more from this source, since the 578 Republican challengers received $28.2 million, while the 513 Democrats deposited $17.8 million. The more important disparity with respect to individual giving was between incumbents and challengers. Incumbents netted $92.3 million from individual gifts, which was more than twice the amount solicited by their challengers. This disparity gave incumbents a sizable financial advantage over their opponents, which was increased by the donations they received from PACs.

PAC Contributions

As in previous elections, PACs were the second largest source of funding in congressional elections, donating $51.8 million to major party Senate candidates and $128.3 million to major party contenders for House seats, for a total of $180.7 million, or 27.4 percent of the major party candidates' total receipts. Despite the anti-Washington rhetoric and widespread condemnation of "special interests" that characterized the election year, almost all of those who sought federal office solicited PAC money. All of the Senate incumbents accepted PAC gifts, while only seven major party general election candidates accepted no PAC money, none of whom won. Five of those who received no PAC funding were Republicans and two were Democrats: Republicans Richard Sellers of Alabama, Brook Johnson of Connecticut, Richard Reed of Hawaii, Demar Dahl of Nevada, and James Douglas of Vermont, and Democrats Jean Lloyd-Jones of Iowa and John Rauh of New Hampshire.[36] Only eleven of the 371 House incumbents who sought reelection did not take PAC money. Moreover, only eleven of the 110 new members elected in 1992 refused these funds: Republicans Jay Dickey of Arkansas, Terry Everett of Alabama, Peter Hoekstra of Michigan, Martin Hoke of Ohio, Steve Horn of California, Michael Huffington of California, Bob Inglis of South Carolina, Nick Smith of Michigan, and Peter Torkildsen of Massachusetts, and Democrats Scotty Baesler of Kentucky and Martin Meehan of Massachusetts.[37] Six of the eleven who rejected PAC money defeated incumbents, and another won in a district that rejected the incumbent in the primary.[38]

Most of the money donated by PACs went to incumbents. Senate incumbents received $31.9 million in PAC money, which represented about one-third of their total funds and was more than three times the $8.9 million given to their opponents. The seventeen Democratic incumbents raised about $17.8 million in PAC money for 39.2 percent of their total receipts, while the twelve Republicans were given $14.1 million, which represented 27.2 percent of their total. The average Democratic incumbent received about $1 million in PAC money; the typical Republican veteran received about $1.2 million.

In the House, the margin was greater, with incumbents receiving $94.7 million from PACs, which represented about 47 percent of their total funds and was more than seven times the $12.3 million received by their challengers. The Democratic members who ran raised $64.4 million from PACs, as compared to $4.7 million for their Republican challengers, while Republican members raised $30.3 million, as opposed to $7.6 million for their Democratic challengers. In open seat races, the 318 Democratic candidates raised $13.7 million in PAC gifts, or 24.5 percent of their total monies, while the 270 Republican candidates received $7.6 million, or 17 percent of their total.

Candidates' Personal Loans and Contributions

With many incumbents aggressively soliciting funds from individuals and PACs, and such a large number of competitive races, many challengers and open seat candidates had to look to sources other than individuals and PACs to ensure that they had the revenues needed to conduct a viable campaign. Many of those who could afford to dipped into their own pockets. Indeed, one of the most noteworthy aspects of the financing of congressional elections during the 1992 cycle was the significant increase in the extent to which candidates relied on their own resources. Overall, candidates directly gave their campaigns $17.8 million and made loans of $70 million for a total of $87.8 million, or about 13.4 percent of the total monies raised during the cycle.[39] This amount was more than double the comparable sum for 1990, when candidates contributed $7 million and loaned $30.8 million, for a total of $37.8 million, which represented 8 percent of total receipts.

As noted in Table 7.3, both Senate and House candidates raised similar proportions of their campaign monies from personal contributions and loans. Senate candidates donated $6.6 million and loaned $28.2 million to their campaigns. Almost all of this money came from challengers and open seat candidates. Incumbents provided an estimated total of only $800,000 in support to their own campaigns, and most of this sum came from Democrat John Glenn of Ohio, who gave or loaned his reelection campaign $706,800. The only other incumbent to commit as much as $10,000 in campaign funding was Democrat Wendell Ford of Kentucky, who provided his campaign with $19,000.[40] Similar patterns characterized House races. House candidates gave $11.2 million and loaned $41.8 million to their campaigns, but only $400,000 of the total amount contributed and $2.7 million in loans came from incumbents.

In contrast, a number of challengers invested significant amounts of their own money in their bids. Overall, Senate challengers put $18.5 million into their campaigns, which constituted 18.8 percent of their total receipts. Six general election challengers each provided more than $100,000 in self-financing: Connecticut Republican Brook Johnson, $1,935,000; North Carolina Republican Lauch Faircloth, $760,530; Pennsylvania Democrat Lynn Yeakel, $305,700; Ohio Republican Michael DeWine, $200,000; Iowa Democrat Jean Lloyd-Jones, $175,057; and Missouri Democrat Geri Rothman-Serot, $143,000. Of these, only Faircloth won election, defeating Sanford, who fell ill during the election and was briefly hospitalized, in a close contest. While the others lost, they were all facing vulnerable incumbents (with the possible exception of Lloyd-Jones, who ran against Charles Grassley) and were thus willing to expend some of their own monies in an effort to provide their campaigns with the resources they felt were needed to win. In addition, a number of primary challengers relied heavily on self-financing, including Illinois Democrat Albert Hofeld, who was responsible for $4.6 million of his $4.9 million in receipts; Wisconsin Democrat Joseph Checota, who provided $3.6 million of his campaign's $4 million; and New York Republican Laurance Rockefeller, who directly contributed $305,700 in addition to a loan of $130,000.

Similarly, in races without an incumbent, a number of candidates decided to use some of their own resources in an effort to win. Overall, $1 out of every $5 raised by these candidates came from their own pockets. Of the $15.5 million total, more than 25 percent was the result of the activity of three general election candidates: Utah Republican Robert Bennett, the major Senate candidate-donor, raised about $4.2 million, $3.5 million of which he provided himself; Colorado Republican Terry Considine provided $371,000; and New Hampshire Democrat John Rauh provided $338,066. Bennett won and the others lost in close races. It also should be noted that a significant portion of Bennett's contribution was made during the primary election. Bennett, a former chairman of Franklin International, spent $1.4 million of his own in his primary campaign against Joe Cannon, chairman of the board of the Utah-based Geneva Steel Company. Cannon invested close to $6 million of his own money in that race, contributing $1.4 million and loaning a net $4.4 million, and was considered the heavy favorite until the final weeks of the campaign, when Bennett overtook him with an aggressive advertising campaign that highlighted Bennett's "Washington

outsider" image and Geneva Steel's poor environmental record.[41] In Utah's
Democratic primary, Douglas Anderson, who lost to Wayne Owens, loaned
his campaign more than $1 million. The Utah race alone thus accounted for
about two-thirds of the total amount raised through self-financing by candidates in races lacking an incumbent.

In House elections, close to 30 percent of the money raised by challengers was self-financed. These candidates directly gave $8.3 million to
their campaigns and provided another $17.8 million in loans. In races for
open seats, about 23 percent of total revenues came from the candidates,
who directly contributed $2.5 million and loaned $21.3 million. In most
instances, these candidates were not injecting large sums into their campaigns; they were providing what they could afford in hopes of winning
their races, especially in hotly contested contests.

There were, however, some notable exceptions, the most prominent
being Republican Michael Huffington, who won a primary election against
incumbent Robert Lagomarsino in the newly drawn 22nd District in California and went on to defeat Democrat Gloria Ochoa, a Santa Barbara
County supervisor, in the general election. Huffington, the son of Houston
oil man and longtime Republican contributor Roy Huffington, made a fortune in oil, natural gas, and banking ventures before deciding to run for
Congress. He raised a total of $5.4 million for his primary and general
election campaigns, more money than any other House candidate in the
1992 election cycle. But he took in only $254,000 from individual do-
nors and received no money from PACs. Instead, he contributed $5.2
million of his own money to his campaign, and told supporters he did not
need theirs.[42]

The only other House candidate to contribute an extraordinarily large
sum was California Democrat Jane Harman, who donated $673,000 in win-
ning the 36th District. Other major self-donors gave substantially less. After
Harman, some of the leading donors were Virginia Democrat Stephen
Musselwhite, who gave $69,158; Wisconsin Republican Mark Neumann,
$34,552; Texas Republican Dolly McKenna, $33,401; and Alabama Republican Robert Everett, $26,586. A significant number of House candidates,
however, loaned money to their campaigns. In all, at least forty-two general
election candidates each loaned more than $100,000 in net receipts to their
campaign committee, with ten of these individuals loaning more than
$250,000.[43] Only four of these candidates were incumbents: Ohio Demo-
crat Mary Rose Oakar and Georgia Democrat Richard Ray, who lost their
seats, and Connecticut Democrat Sam Gejdenson and Nevada Democrat
James Bilbray, who both won with less than 60 percent of the general
election vote.[44] Among the leading lenders were Michigan Republican

Richard Chrysler, $1.6 million; Maine Republican Linda Bean, $1.2 million; Alabama Republican Robert Everett, $904,700; New York Democrat Stephen Orlins, $775,000; Wisconsin Republican Mark Neumann, $752,400; and New Jersey Democrat Herbert Klein, $639,000.[45]

The increase in the amount of candidate self-financing and the media attention paid to the handful of wealthy individuals who deposited large sums into their campaigns generated a substantial amount of debate about the role of wealth in congressional elections.[46] Some analysts noted that the 1992 experience, as symbolized by such candidates as Perot or Huffington, may be the latest step in a trend toward wealthy individuals running for national office. In their view, the rising costs of campaigns and the inability of challengers to raise large sums from individuals and PACs have created a situation in which the most viable candidates for federal office, especially in Senate races, are increasingly those who are capable of donating or loaning significant sums of money to their campaigns.[47] To support this claim, proponents often cite a number of recent examples in addition to Perot and Huffington, such as Democrat Jay Rockefeller, who spent $12.1 million— most of it his own money—in winning a Senate seat in West Virginia in 1984; and Democrat Herbert Kohl, who provided $6.9 million to his campaign in winning a Senate race in Wisconsin in 1988.

The rise of wealthy challengers willing to spend millions of dollars out of their own pockets certainly raises serious questions about the role of personal wealth in federal elections and the ability of the campaign finance system to ensure equitable opportunities for candidates of lesser means to compete for federal offices. But the Supreme Court's ruling in Buckley declared that such contributions represent a form of personal political speech and cannot be controlled unless public funding is provided by the government and accepted by the candidate. Accordingly, some advocates of campaign finance reform have cited the finances of wealthy candidates as yet another reason for extending public funding to congressional campaigns. It is important to note, however, that relatively few candidates in each election are able or willing to donate large sums in support of their own cause. Many of those who do rely on self-financing, including most of those who did so in 1992, do not win office. Moreover, it may be that the sizable increase in the amount candidates were willing to spend was a function of the dynamics of the 1992 races; because a relatively large number of contests were close and it was perceived to be a "bad year" for incumbents, more challengers might have been willing to assist their campaigns than in the past. It remains to be seen whether the proportion of congressional campaign receipts will continue to rise in the future. If an upward trend is established, then it is likely that candidate self-financing will join PAC funding and soft money as a major issue in debates over campaign finance reform.

Spending Patterns

Overall, $678.3 million was spent in the 1992 congressional elections, with $526.7 million disbursed by general election candidates in the primaries and general elections combined, and $151.6 million by candidates who lost in the primaries. The 112 general election candidates in Senate races spent $196.6 million, while 1,137 House competitors spent $330.1 million. The forty-three minor party Senate challengers and 294 minor party House challengers were responsible for a relatively insignificant share of these expenditures, with Senate candidates totaling $1.3 million, an average of less than $30,000 each, and House candidates totaling $3.3 million, an average of less than $11,000.[48]

Senate Contests

The Democratic and Republican candidates who competed for the thirty-five Senate seats at stake in the general election spent $195.3 million (see Table 7.4). In both parties, the average amount spent by general election contenders was about $2.8 million, with the thirty-five Democrats disbursing a total of $98.6 million and the thirty-four Republicans a total of $96.7 million. Incumbents outspent their challengers by $100.1 million to $56.5 million in the primary and general election campaigns combined. The average expenditure for incumbents was $3.7 million versus about $2 million for challengers. The majority of incumbent spending, $57.4 million, was done by the twelve Republicans seeking reelection. Their Democratic challengers spent $37.3 million. The fifteen Democratic incumbents spent $42.7 million, as opposed to $19.2 million for their Republican challengers. The seven open seat races attracted almost $38.7 million in spending by general election contenders in their primary and general election campaigns, with Democrats disbursing about $18.6 million and Republicans $20.1 million.[49]

Much of the money spent by Senate general election candidates can be attributed to the exceptionally heavy spending in a handful of races. The most expensive races occurred in California, where elections were held for both of the state's Senate seats due to the retirement of Democrat Alan Cranston, which created an open seat, and the 1990 election of Wilson to the governor's office, which led to the need for a special election. In the open seat race, Barbara Boxer, who had to defend herself against attacks for having bounced 143 checks at the House Bank, spent $10.4 million in the

Table 7.4

Senate and House Campaigns, General Election Spending, 1991–92

Campaign	Number of Candidates	Net Disbursements (in $ millions)[a]
Senate	69	$195.3
Democrats	35	98.6
Republicans	34	96.7
Incumbents	27	100.1
Challengers	28	56.5
Open Seats	14	38.7
House	843	326.8
Democrats	426	186.5
Republicans	417	140.3
Incumbents	350	203.0
Challengers	349	62.9
Open Seats	144	60.9

Source: Federal Election Commission, "1992 Congressional Election Spending Jumps 52% to $678 Million," press release, March 4, 1993.

Note: Figures include only Democratic and Republican Party candidates; minor party candidates are excluded, which excludes one House incumbent, Independent Bernard Sanders of Vermont, who spent $575,791.

[a]Total disbursements (minus transfers), including primary campaign costs, for candidates in the general election; the FEC does not issue separate primary spending figures.

primary and general election campaigns combined to defeat conservative former television commentator and Nixon White House official Bruce Herschensohn, who spent a total of $7.9 million. In the special election, incumbent John Seymour, who was appointed in January 1991 to fill Wilson's seat, was considered vulnerable because he was not as well known as most incumbents. Seymour faced Democrat Dianne Feinstein, who had lost the 1990 governor's race to Wilson. Feinstein spent a total of $8.1 million to defeat Seymour, who spent $6.8 million. In all, the campaigns of these four general election candidates in California cost about $33.2 million.

Moreover, both Senate races in California featured competitive primary contests in both parties. Boxer defeated Representative Mel Levine, who spent $7.2 million in the primary, and veteran lieutenant governor Leo McCarthy, who spent $3 million. Herschensohn defeated Thomas Campbell, who spent $5.1 million. In the other race, Gray Davis spent $2.6 million against Feinstein, while Representative William Dannemeyer spent about $3.5 million against Seymour. When the amounts disbursed by these primary challengers are added to the monies spent by the four general election candidates, the total cost of the two California races comes to $54.6 million, or about 20 percent of the total amount disbursed by all major party Senate candidates in the 1992 election cycle.

The Senate campaigns in New York and Pennsylvania also were expensive. In New York, Republican Alfonse D'Amato spent $9.2 million in his successful reelection effort against Democrat Robert Abrams, who spent $6.6 million. In Pennsylvania, Arlen Specter faced a strong challenge from Yeakel. Specter won, spending $8.9 million in the process, while Yeakel, who received substantial support from women's groups, spent $5.2 million. When the amounts disbursed by these four candidates are added to that of the general election candidates in California, total spending reaches $63.1 million. Thus, eight candidates in four races were responsible for 32 percent of the total amount spent by the sixty-nine major party Senate general election candidates. Other expensive contests included the Illinois race, where Moseley-Braun spent $6.7 million and her opponent, Richard Williamson, spent $2.3 million, and Oregon, where Republican Robert Packwood won reelection at a cost of $6.1 million, while his opponent, Representative Les AuCoin, spent $2.6 million.

House Contests

In House elections, Democratic and Republican general election candidates spent a combined $326.8 million in their primary and general election campaigns (see Table 7.4). The 426 Democrats disbursed $186.5 million, an average of $437,800 per candidate, while the 417 Republicans disbursed $140.3 million, an average of $336,400 per candidate. In 1990, Democrats spent an average of $316,500 and Republicans $250,500.

This growth in average costs was driven by the large amounts spent by fifty-four candidates. In 1990, fourteen House general election candidates reached the $1 million amount in spending; in 1992, forty-nine general election competitors and five primary losers reached this level. One 1992 challenger, Huffington, conducted the most expensive House campaign to date, spending $5.4 million, or more than triple the sum disbursed two years earlier by Democrat Marguerite Chandler of New Jersey, who led all 1990 congressional candidates with $1.7 million in total expenditures. Three other candidates expended more than $2 million in their primary and general election campaigns combined: Gephardt spent $3.3 million in his successful bid for reelection; Representative Stephen Solarz of New York spent $3.2 million but lost in the primary election to challenger Nydia Velazquez in a newly drawn minority-majority district; and Democrat Jane

Harman spent about $2.3 million. The expenditures of the forty-five general election candidates who reached $1 million totaled $69.4 million. Six percent of the candidates were, therefore, responsible for 21 percent of the aggregate amount spent by House general election contenders. Thirteen of the forty-nine candidates lost in the general election, including two whose opponents also spent $1 million or more.[50]

House incumbents outspent their challengers by a margin of $203 million to $62.9 million in the primary and general election campaigns combined. The average expenditure for incumbents was $580,000, more than three times the average $180,300 spent by challengers. The 213 Democratic incumbents outspent their Republican challengers by a margin of 3 to 1, disbursing $128.4 million versus $40.5 million for their opponents. The 137 Republican incumbents enjoyed a similar advantage, outspending their Democratic challengers by $74.6 million to $22.4 million. The unusually large number of open seat races generated a combined $60.9 million in primary and general election spending by those who contested the general election, with seventy-four Democrats disbursing about $35.7 million and seventy Republicans about $25.2 million. The average cost of an open seat campaign was about $422,600, or more than double the average spent by candidates opposing incumbents.

Challenger Spending

With a significant percentage of House members facing tough campaigns due to the anti-incumbent mood of the electorate and the effects of redistricting, more challengers than usual were considered to be competitive candidates with a chance of winning. These challengers enjoyed greater fund-raising success than their counterparts in previous elections and were, therefore, able to spend more than many past challengers. According to FEC data, the median amount spent by general election challengers more than doubled from two years earlier, with median spending by Democrats rising from $33,800 to $68,234, and for Republicans from $26,230 to $83,201.[51] The number of challengers who had received $200,000 or more by mid-October also rose, increasing from forty-eight to seventy-nine. This group included thirty-six Democrats, as compared with nineteen in 1990, and forty-three Republicans, as compared with twenty-nine in 1990.[52]

Despite this rise in the number of well-financed challengers, most incumbents outspent their opponents by significant sums. Of the 252 congressional candidates able to spend $500,000, 184 were incumbents, 53 were candidates for open seats, and only 15 were challengers. Of the 548 candidates who spent $200,000 or more, 324 were incumbents, 135 were open seat candidates, and 89 were challengers. Thus, even in a supposedly anti-incumbent year, almost three-quarters of the incumbents (250 of 349) did not have to face a challenger who could afford to spend as much as $200,000.[53] As a result, many incumbents were involved in races that were not financially competitive. A study by Common Cause, for example, found that 290 of the 349 incumbents in the general election were either unopposed or paired against a challenger who had less than one-half as much money to spend. In forty-eight close races in which incumbents won with less than 55 percent of the vote, the incumbents had more than three times the campaign resources of their challengers—$34 million to $10 million.[54]

While some analysts explained electoral outcomes by focusing on the sizable financial advantage realized by incumbents, others emphasized another pattern in spending. Political scientist Michael Malbin, for example, concluded that challenger spending was a more important factor in determining the competitiveness of the 1992 elections than the amount expended by incumbents. His analysis of expenditures in the 1992 congressional elections revealed that challengers have to be good fund raisers to win, but they do not have to match the resources of their opponents. Those who beat incumbents, for example, spent an average of $451,201. This amount was less than one-half the average sum spent by their opponents; the incumbents who lost in these races spent an average of $965,537. Malbin further notes that challenger spending is directly related to electoral outcomes; the more challengers spend, the better they tend to do in the election. In 1992, challengers who lost but received 40 percent to 49 percent of the vote spent an average of $281,261 versus $89,931 for those who received less than 40 percent of the vote. On the other hand, Malbin found little evidence to suggest that the amount spent by incumbents influenced their level of support. While the campaigns of defeated incumbents cost an average of almost $1 million, members who won with 50 percent to 59 percent of the vote averaged $784,303 and those who received 60 percent or more averaged $486,681.[55]

The reason why money means more for challengers than incumbents, according to Malbin, is that challengers need to boost their name recognition and the electorate's familiarity with their candidacies if they are to mount competitive campaigns. Challengers who can raise $250,000 or more will have the resources needed to improve their name recognition significantly, but such spending does relatively little to enhance incumbents' prospects since these individuals are fairly well known. Malbin estimates that expenditures up to the $500,000 level increase the percentage of the electorate who recognizes the name of a challenger, on average, from 22 percent to

75 percent, as opposed to an average increase of from 88 percent to 92 percent for an incumbent.[56] Adequate funding thus provides a challenger with an opportunity to become better known and shifts the dynamics of a congressional race to one in which the electorate gives greater consideration to issues and the relative strengths of the candidates. "An incumbent with effective opposition naturally will spend more money than an incumbent whose opposition is unknown," wrote Malbin. "That explains why higher spending incumbents do worse than incumbents who spend less. They do worse because the challengers have managed to shift the debate to more meaningful grounds."[57]

Malbin's findings were supported by the results of a study by political scientists Jonathan Krasno and Donald Green that examined 1,540 House races from 1976 to 1990 in which an incumbent faced a major party challenger in consecutive elections. This analysis also concluded that although money is essential for challengers, they do not necessarily have to spend as much as incumbents to win.[58] Both studies suggest that if congressional elections are to be made more competitive, the direction of reform should be toward finding ways to increase the resources available to challengers, rather than limiting the receipts and expenditures of incumbents.[59]

Party Spending in Congressional Elections

In addition to the funds detailed in Table 7.3, many congressional candidates receive substantial assistance from national, state, and local party organizations. National party organizations, especially the Democratic and Republican senatorial and congressional campaign committees, are important sources of money and support in congressional elections. These committees provide contributions and campaign services directly to candidates and otherwise assist them in obtaining access to resources. Most of the assistance distributed by the four committees is targeted to candidates in close elections, especially challengers running against incumbents. This practice reflects the principal goal of these committees, which is to increase the number of seats their party controls in each house of Congress.[60]

The monies spent by party organizations in conjunction with congressional elections are limited by the FECA. National party committees and party senatorial committees combined may contribute a maximum of $17,500 to each of their senatorial candidates during the calendar year in which the election takes place. Any contributions these committees make in any other year count toward the election-year limit. State party organizations can contribute a maximum of $5,000 per election to a Senate candidate. National and state party organizations also are allowed to make coordinated expenditures on behalf of their candidates in general election contests. These expenditures are made in cooperation with each candidate's campaign committee, giving the party and the candidate some control over how these resources are spent. Such coordinated expenditures are limited under the 1974 FECA to the greater amount of $20,000 plus an adjustment for inflation since 1974, or two cents times the voting-age population of the candidates' states plus the adjustment for inflation. In 1992, these limits ranged from $55,240 in the smallest states to $1,227,322 in the most populous state, California. Under federal regulations, a state political party also may make coordinated expenditures in connection with the campaign of a Senate candidate in the state. The state committee–coordinated expenditure limit is the same as for the national committees. Under the law, a state committee may make the national committee its agent for spending within the state's limit; that is, it may cede its statutorily permitted spending to a national committee. Such agency agreements, in most cases, effectively double the amount a national party committee may spend in coordinated expenditures.

In House races, national and state party organizations are each allowed to contribute up to $5,000 per election to a candidate. As in Senate races, national and state party committees also may make coordinated expenditures on behalf of candidates. The limit set for these expenditures is lower than in Senate contests; under the 1974 law each committee may spend up to $10,000, plus an adjustment for inflation. In 1992, the most a national or state party could expend on behalf of a House candidate reached $27,620.

In the 1992 election cycle, Republican Party organizations disbursed close to $30 million in contributions and coordinated expenditures for House and Senate candidates, as compared to $19.6 million for Democratic Party organizations. As detailed in Table 7.5, party committees at all levels spent more in coordinated expenditures than in contributions, which reflects the higher limits for coordinated spending under the FECA. Republican committees contributed a total of about $2.2 million to their House contenders and almost $800,000 to Senate contenders, while making $6.9 million in coordinated expenditures on behalf of House candidates and $20.1 million in coordinated expenditures on behalf of Senate candidates. Democratic organizations contributed a total of about $1.2 million to House contenders and $675,000 to Senate contenders, while spending $5.8 million on coordinated expenditures in House races and $11.9 million in Senate races.

Republican Party Contributions and Expenditures

NRSC was the leading contributor to federal candidates among party organizations. According to FEC reports, the NRSC raised $72.3 million and spent $71.8 million during the 1991–92 election cycle.[61] The committee disbursed $17.2 million, about 24 percent of its spending, in the form of direct candidate assistance, including $691,195 in contributions to fifty federal candidates and almost $16.5 million in coordinated expenditures on behalf of thirty-five candidates. The NRSC reported contributions to thirty-eight Senate candidates. The committee donated the maximum $17,500 to each of the thirty-five Republicans competing in general election races and made contributions to three others.[62] It made coordinated expenditures on behalf of thirty-five candidates, but more than one-half of the amount spent in this manner, approximately $8.4 million, was directed toward elections in three states: the committee spent $4.9 million on behalf of Seymour and Herschensohn, close to $2 million on behalf of Thornburgh in the 1991 Pennsylvania special election and Arlen Specter in the 1992 race, and $1.5 million on behalf of D'Amato. The NRSC spent no money on behalf of five of the party's general election candidates, one of whom, Senate Minority Leader Robert Dole of Kansas, won easily in his bid for reelection. The other four were challengers, each of whom received less than 35 percent of the vote.[63]

The NRSC also gave the maximum $5,000 each to twelve House candidates, all of whom were involved in close elections. Such contributions, which are known as "crossover spending," are a relatively new phenomenon among national party organizations and occur when a senatorial campaign committee spends money in House elections or a congressional campaign committee spends money in Senate races.[64] As evident from Table 7.5, all of the four party congressional campaign committees had some crossover expenditures. These disbursements, which are usually reported as contributions rather than coordinated expenditures, may consist of direct donations to a candidate's campaign committee, but usually they are in-kind contributions, resulting from shared polling or some other coordinated campaign activity that is conducted by one of the campaign committees in cooperation with another campaign committee, a Senate candidate, or one or more House candidates who typically reside in the same state as a Senate candidate.[65]

The NRCC raised $34.4 million and spent $33.5 million, including approximately $5.9 million in direct candidate assistance, about 18 percent of its total spending. The NRCC contributed $760,276 to 360 candidates. It gave the maximum $5,000 each to seven Senate candidates and a total of about $725,000 to 351 House candidates, including a $1,000 gift to independent Stephen Grote, who ran in Ohio's 1st District where there was no Republican challenger. The committee disbursed close to $5.2 million in coordinated expenditures on behalf of 197 House candidates, with sixty-two of these candidates receiving $40,000 or more in this type of assistance.

Republican candidates also benefited from financial support offered by

Table 7.5

Party Contributions to Congressional Candidates, 1991–92

	House		Senate	
	Direct Contributions	Coordinated Expenditures	Direct Contributions	Coordinated Expenditures
Democratic				
DNC	0	$913,935	0	$195,351
DSCC	$10,000	2,600	$583,500	11,233,112
DCCC	819,146	4,135,861	18,682	0
State and local	366,477	750,451	72,699	487,415
Total	$1,195,623	$5,802,847	$674,881	$11,915,878
Republicans				
RNC	780,003	823,347	5,000	0
RSCC	60,000	0	631,195	16,477,387
RCCC	725,276	5,186,095	35,000	0
State and local	626,057	868,908	127,960	3,617,303
Total	$2,191,336	$6,887,350	$799,155	$20,094,690

Sources: Figures for the national party committees are based on Federal Election Commission data as of August 11, 1994. Figures for state and local party committees are based on the data reported in Paul S. Herrnson, "The Revitalization of National Party Organizations," in L. Sandy Maisel, ed., *The Parties Respond,* 2d ed. (Boulder, CO: Westview Press, 1994). Used by permission of Westview Press.

the RNC and state and local party committees. In addition to the generic support these party organizations provided to their candidates through their election-related spending and soft money activities, the RNC and numerous Republican state and local party committees directly contributed money to congressional candidates and made coordinated expenditures on their behalf. The RNC devoted most of its resources in congressional elections to House races, reporting only a single contribution of $5,000 in Senate elections, which was given to Clark Durant, who ran against incumbent Democrat Carl Levin in Michigan. The national party contributed $780,000 to 181 House candidates, an average of more than $4,000 per candidate, and spent funds on behalf of fifty-four House contenders, totaling more than $832,000. The Republican state and local party committees that registered with the FEC reported total contributions of $754,000, including $626,000 to House candidates and $128,000 to Senate candidates, and coordinated spending of $4.5 million, including $867,000 on behalf of House contenders and $3.6 million in support of Senate contenders.

Democratic Party Contributions and Expenditures

For the Democrats, the DSCC reported the largest sums spent on congressional elections. The DSCC reported receipts of $24.4 million and expenditures of $25.5 million during the 1991–92 election cycle. It disbursed $11.8 million in the form of direct candidate assistance, which represented about 46 percent of its total spending, a percentage about twice that of its wealthier Republican counterpart. The DSCC contributed $593,500 to thirty-nine federal candidates, including two House candidates who each received the maximum gift of $5,000: John Olver of Massachusetts, who won a close contest in his bid for reelection, and Tony Center of Georgia, who was challenging Republican House Minority Whip Newt Gingrich. Of the thirty-seven Senate candidates, thirty-one were Senate general election candidates who each received the maximum gift of $17,500. Three other general election candidates, Christopher Dodd of Connecticut, Wendell Ford of Kentucky, and Barbara Mikulski of Maryland, received only token gifts since they were involved in safe races, and Breaux received no money (and only $656 in coordinated spending) since he was running in the general election without opposition, having won his primary with more than 50 percent of the vote. Three other candidates received the maximum $17,500: Wofford; Brock Adams of Washington, who retired before the primary election; and Alan Dixon.

The DSCC made $11.2 million in coordinated expenditures on behalf of fifty candidates, including a reported $2,600 in such spending for two House candidates.[66] As in the case of the NRSC, a significant portion of this sum, $6.1 million or about 54 percent of the committee's total coordinated spending, was directed toward the Senate races in California, Pennsylvania, and New York. The DSCC spent $2.9 million in support of Dianne Feinstein and Boxer in California (about $2 million less than the amount spent by the NRSC on behalf of their Republican opponents), $1.7 million in support of Wofford in the 1991 special election and Yeakel in the 1992 race, and $1.5 million in support of Abrams in New York. The DSCC also spent more than $500,000 each in support of vulnerable incumbents Glenn (who was reelected with 55 percent of the vote), Sanford, and Fowler.

The DCCC raised $12.8 million and spent $12.6 million during the election cycle, including almost $5 million in direct candidate assistance, which represented 39 percent of its total spending, more than twice the percentage of the NRCC. The committee's contributions totaled $837,800, including more than $18,000 in donations to ten Senate candidates, three of whom received the maximum of $5,000: Byron Dorgan of North Dakota and Sanford in 1992, and Wofford in 1991. The DCCC gave about $819,000 to

437 House candidates for an average of about $1,900, or about the same amount as the average contribution of the NRCC.[67] The committee also spent $4.1 million in coordinated expenditures on behalf of 395 House contenders but spent $40,000 or more in only nineteen of these races.

Like the Republican committees, the Democrats' national committee and state and local party organizations spent substantial amounts to assist their congressional candidates. The DNC, however, did not follow the RNC in providing both contributions and coordinated expenditures to its candidates. Instead, the DNC disbursed all of the monies it devoted to congressional contests in the form of coordinated expenditures, spending about $914,000 in support of 116 House candidates and $195,000 on behalf of fifteen Senate candidates. The state and local Democratic organizations registered with the FEC reported total contributions of $439,000, including $366,000 in gifts to House candidates and $73,000 to Senate candidates, and about $1.2 million in coordinated spending, including $750,000 in support of House contenders and $487,000 in support of Senate contenders.

Parties as a Source of Candidate Funding

The sums expended by political party organizations in the 1992 elections indicate that these committees were a major source of funding for many congressional candidates. These party contributions play an important role in the financing of congressional campaigns because they are usually made early in the general election period and often function as seed money that candidates use to generate more funds.[68] The contributions and coordinated expenditures made by party committees often take the form of in-kind campaign services that are worth much more than their reported value or that provide candidates with professional services that they might not otherwise be able to obtain.

While Republican committees generally provide more assistance to their candidates than Democratic committees, candidates in both parties rely on these monies and consider them an essential component in the financing of their campaigns. This is especially true for those candidates who are challenging incumbents. In general, Republican and Democratic party organizations tend to give substantially more support to candidates seeking open seats and to challengers than to incumbents. Moreover, most of these funds are targeted to candidates in close races; challengers with little prospect of being elected and incumbents running in safe seats are usually given only token sums from party coffers.

According to Paul Herrnson, a specialist in political party finance, party money was a particularly important source of challenger funding in the 1992 election cycle. Herrnson analyzed the contributions and coordinated expenditures made by national and state party organizations to congressional general election candidates on the basis of each candidate's status (incumbent, challenger, or open seat), and combined the amounts reported with the amount spent by each candidate's campaign committee to determine the total amount spent by or on behalf of different types of candidates. This analysis revealed that party money (including coordinated expenditures) accounted for more than 11 percent of the general election funds spent by or on behalf of 1992 House challengers and in excess of 14 percent of the money spent by Senate challengers. In House races, Democratic challengers received about 12.5 percent of the total amounts spent on their campaigns from party committees; the figure for Republican challengers was 11.3 percent. In Senate races, Republican challengers relied more heavily on party donations, which represented 17.2 percent of the totals spent on their campaigns; party funds represented about 14.5 percent of the amounts spent on Democratic challengers. In contrast, party monies represented less than 3 percent of the total amounts spent by Democratic and Republican House incumbents, and less than 10 percent for Senate incumbents, with parties providing only 5.4 percent of the Democrats' total spending and 9.7 percent of the Republicans' total. In open seats, the percentages of total funds provided by party committees were 3.5 percent for House Democrats, 7.1 percent for House Republicans, 5.6 percent for Senate Republicans, and 11.2 percent for Senate Democrats.[69]

This financial assistance is not the only way national party committees spend money to assist their candidates. The national party organizations also offer many candidates a wide range of services and benefits. For example, in 1992, the NRCC's media center produced 188 television commercials for twenty-three incumbents and twenty-two challenger and open seat candidates. The DCCC's Harriman Communications Center produced television advertisements for 171 incumbents and seventy challenger and open seat candidates. Both committees also provided candidates with strategic advice and employed field workers who visited campaign headquarters to help candidates develop campaign plans, improve their messages, and build their organizations.[70] The Hill committees also provide an array of other services for candidates, including such activities as conducting public opinion polls, undertaking political research, assisting with fund raising, and helping candidates solicit PAC contributions.

The Financial Activity of PACs

In the 1991–92 election cycle, the 4,729 PACs registered with the FEC reported adjusted receipts of $379 million, adjusted expenditures of $385.7 million, and contributions of $188.7 million to federal candidates, including $178.4 million in contributions to congressional candidates seeking election

Table 7.6

Financial Activity of PACs, 1972–92

Election Cycle[a]	Adjusted Receipts[b]	Adjusted Expenditures[b]	Contributions to Congressional Candidates[c]
1972	N.A.	$19,168,000	$8,500,000[d]
1974	N.A.	25,000,000[e]	12,526,586
1976	$54,045,588	52,894,630	22,571,912
1978	79,956,291	77,412,860	35,187,215
1980	137,728,528	131,153,384	55,217,291
1982	199,452,356	190,173,539	83,620,190
1984	288,690,535	266,822,476	105,330,090
1986	353,429,266	339,954,146	132,671,437
1988	384,617,093	364,201,275	147,846,057
1990	372,091,977	357,648,557	149,891,723
1992	378,954,279	385,745,089	178,387,905

Sources: For 1972–80 data, Joseph E. Cantor, *Political Action Committees: Their Evolution and Growth and Their Implications for the Political System* (Washington, DC: Congressional Research Service, 1982), p. 67. For 1982–92 data, various FEC compilations.

[a]The periods covered by the election cycles vary. Data for 1972 are relatively limited for the period prior to April 7, 1972, the effective data for disclosure under the FECA of 1971. Until then, campaign finance disclosure was governed by the Federal Corrupt Practices Act of 1925, under which much activity went unreported. The 1974 data cover September 1, 1973, to December 31, 1976. The 1978 data cover January 1, 1977, to February 22, 1980. Data for the 1980 election cycle and those thereafter cover the periods beginning on January 1 of the preelection year and ending on December 31 of the election year.
[b]Adjusted receipts and expenditures exclude funds transferred among affiliated committees.
[c]For 1974–78, figures represent the total amount contributed to congressional candidates during the election cycle, regardless of whether a candidate was seeking election in that cycle. For 1980–92, figures represent the total amount contributed to congressional candidates seeking election in the particular cycle noted.
[d]Figure excludes contributions to candidates defeated in primary elections.
[e]Figure is estimated.

in the cycle. In each of these categories, the amounts realized in the 1992 cycle surpassed those of previous elections (see Table 7.6). The net receipts reported by PACs were about 2 percent higher than the receipts of the 4,681 committees active in 1990, while net expenditures were about 8 percent higher. The amounts contributed to federal candidates rose by about 19 percent, the largest percentage increase since 1986.

For the first time since 1977, PACs drew on surplus funds from previous years to spend about $6.7 million more than they raised.[71] This escalated level of spending reflected the larger number of competitive races in 1992 and might have been a result of greater demand for funds from many House incumbents who were concerned about getting reelected, especially after the early and unexpected defeats of a number of well-entrenched members in primary contests.[72] Yet even after spending more than $6 million from their reserves, PACs maintained an aggregate balance of about $95 million in surplus funds after the election.[73]

PACs vary widely in their levels of financial activity, depending on the type of committee and their success in soliciting funds. The FEC classifies PACs into six categories based on their sponsoring organizations, which determines whom the PAC may solicit for contributions. Connected PACs, which are committees sponsored by organizations with separate identities, may solicit funds only from their restricted classes. Corporate PACs may solicit their stockholders, executive or administrative personnel, and their families at any time. They may solicit employees who are not stockholders or administrative personnel twice a year, but only through mail addressed to their residences. Labor PACs may solicit their members and their families at any time. Twice a year they may solicit through written communications employees who are not members of the labor organization sponsor and other individuals associated with corporations (e.g., executive and adminis-trative personnel and stockholders) in which the labor organization repre-sents members working for the corporations. PACs sponsored by membership organizations, cooperatives, and corporations without stock may solicit without restriction members and executive or administrative personnel and their families. Trade association PACs may seek donations from stockholders and executive or administrative personnel of the association's member corporations so long as these corporations approve the solicitation. Member corporations, however, may not approve any such solicitation by more than one trade association in a calendar year. All of these types of connected PACs may have their administrative and fund-rais-ing costs paid for by their sponsoring organizations. Nonconnected PACs, which are usually committees formed by ideological organizations or other political groups, have no sponsoring organizations to pay for their adminis-trative and fund-raising costs. But because they are not tied to a specific organization with a separate identity, they are not restricted to a circum-scribed group when raising funds and may solicit contributions from mem-bers of the general public.

As noted in Table 7.7, corporate PACs were the only group of commit-tees to receive more than they spent in 1992, raising $111.6 million and spending $111.3 million. In every other category, the committees' aggre-

206

Table 7.7

PAC Financial Activity by PAC Categories, 1991–92

Type of PAC	No. of Committees	Adjusted Receipts[a]	Adjusted Disbursements[a]	Contributions to Federal Candidates[b]	Independent Expenditures[c]
Corporate	1,930	$111,593,793	$111,272,548	$68,442,883	$47,883
Labor	372	86,884,100	89,005,839	41,339,090	298,497
Nonconnected	1,377	72,627,400	75,119,091	18,183,052	6,276,696
Trade/member/health association	836	94,416,089	96,346,778	53,746,146	3,422,300
Cooperative	61	4,705,663	4,795,331	2,981,390	0
Corporation without stock	153	8,727,234	9,205,502	3,983,542	385,300
Total	4,729	$378,954,279	$385,745,089	$188,676,013	$10,430,676

Source: Federal Election Commission.

[a]Adjusted receipts and expenditures exclude funds transferred among affiliated committees.
[b]Figures for all contributions made to federal candidates, including $9,511,659 in contributions to candidates not seeking election in 1991–92 and $810,211 in contributions to presidential candidates.
[c]Figures for all independent expenditures made during the 1991–92 cycle, including $393,278 in expenditures not associated with candidates seeking election in 1991–92.

gate spending in this election cycle exceeded their revenues. Trade association PACs spent $96.3 million, or about $1.9 million more than they received. Labor PACs spent $89 million, which was about $2.1 million more than they received, and nonconnected PACs spent $75.1 million, $2.5 million more than they received. PACs organized by cooperatives or corporations without stock spent a combined $14 million, about $600,000 more than they received. Although corporate and trade associations spent larger aggregate sums than labor PACs, labor committees spent much larger amounts than committees in these other categories, averaging $239,200 in expenditures, as compared with $115,200 for trade association groups and $57,600 for corporate committees. PACs in the other three categories each had less than $80,000 in average spending.

As in previous elections, most PAC financial activity was the result of the sizable sums raised and expended by a small group of well-financed committees. Of the more than 4,700 committees filed with the FEC in 1992, 910 reported no expenditures at all and 962 others spent $5,000 or less. About 67 percent of the total amount spent by PACs was a result of the activity of 304 committees—6 percent of all PACs—that each disbursed more than $250,000 during the election cycle. These committees accounted for an unadjusted total of $264.9 million in expenditures. More than one-half of this amount, $160.9 million, was disbursed by seventy-four committees, each of which spent more than $1 million. Twenty-eight of these committees were labor PACs that spent a total of $67.5 million; nineteen were trade, membership, or health association PACs that spent $44.3 million; the top eighteen nonconnected PACs, $35.9 million; seven corporate PACs, $10.1 million; and two others, $3.1 million.

Of the top ten PACs ranked according to expenditures, four were labor committees, four were trade association, membership, or health committees, and two were nonconnected committees. These ten committees spent a combined $55.2 million:

1. Democratic-Republican-Independent Voter Education Committee (Teamsters-labor)	$11,825,340
2. American Medical Association Political Action Committee (trade/member/health association)	6,263,921
3. National Education Association Political Action Committee (labor)	5,817,975
4. NRA Political Victory Fund (National Rifle Association) (trade/member/health association)	5,700,114
5. Realtors Political Action Committee (National Realtors' Association) (trade/member/health association)	4,939,014
6. Association of Trial Lawyers of America Political Action Committee (trade/member/health association)	4,392,462

7. American Federation of State, County and Municipal
   Employees—People, Qualified (labor)   4,281,395
8. UAW Voluntary Community Action Program
   (United Auto Workers-labor)   4,257,165
9. National Congressional Club (nonconnected)   3,864,389
10. National Abortion Rights Action League Political
    Action Committee (nonconnected)   3,831,321

Other committees that spent at least $2.5 million were: EMILY's List, a nonconnected PAC organized to assist women running for federal office, which reported $3,389,276 in expenditures; the International Association of Machinists' Non-Partisan Political League (labor), $3,357,403; Voice of Teachers for Education/Committee on Political Education of New York State United Teachers (labor), $2,559,787; and the American Telephone and Telegraph Company PAC, the top corporate PAC with $2,553,485.

PAC Contributions

PACs disbursed about 51 percent of their adjusted expenditures in the form of direct or indirect assistance to federal candidates, donating $188.7 million directly to candidates through an estimated 214,000 separate contributions and making $10.4 million in independent expenditures for or against candidates.[74] Of the $188.7 million contributed to candidates, about $178.4 million was donated to congressional candidates seeking election in the 1992 cycle, $9.5 million was donated to candidates not seeking office in this cycle (most of which consisted of contributions to Senate incumbents up for reelection in 1994 or contributions to defeated candidates, especially defeated incumbents, to help retire debts incurred in their 1990 campaigns), and $921,000 in gifts to presidential candidates, the lowest amount given to presidential contenders since 1976, which was the first presidential contest conducted under the FECA.

Nonconnected PACs contributed a far smaller percentage of their funds to federal candidates than did PACs in any other category. These committees donated a total of $18.2 million to federal candidates, or 24.2 percent of their total expenditures. In contrast, corporate PACs contributed $68.4 million, 61.5 percent of their total expenditures; cooperative PACs, $3 million, 62.2 percent of their total expenditures; trade, membership, and health association PACs, $53.7 million, 55.8 percent; labor committees, $41.3 million, 46.4 percent; and corporations without stock, $4 million, 43.3 percent. Nonconnected PACs, however, lack sponsoring organizations that can pay a share of their administrative and fund-raising costs. Consequently, these committees have to devote a substantial share of their resources to operational expenses, which is the primary reason why they have a smaller percentage of their funds available to donate to candidates.

According to FEC reports, almost a quarter of the total amounts donated by PACs, $45.6 million, came from twenty-seven PACs that each donated more than $1 million to federal candidates. Another $28.4 million came from forty-two PACs that each gave more than $500,000. The top 100 PACs contributed a total of $86.5 million, accounting for 46.1 percent of all PAC contributions. This represented practically no change from the 1990 election cycle, when the top 100 PACs contributed $74.5 million, or 46.7 percent of the total sum donated by these committees.[75] Five labor committees and five trade, membership, and health committees were among the ten top contributors in the 1992 cycle. These were:

1. Realtors Political Action Committee (National Realtors' Association) (trade/member/health association) $2,950,138
2. American Medical Association Political Action Committee (trade/member/health association)   2,936,086
3. Democratic-Republican-Independent Voter Education Committee (Teamsters-labor)   2,442,552
4. Association of Trial Lawyers of America Political Action Committee (trade/member/health association)   2,366,135
5. National Education Association Political Action Committee (labor)   2,323,122
6. UAW Voluntary Community Action Program (United Auto Workers-labor)   2,231,917
7. American Federation of State, County and Municipal Employees—People, Qualified (labor)   1,950,365
8. Dealers Election Action Committee of the National Automobile Dealers Association (trade/member/health association)   1,784,375
9. NRA Political Victory Fund (National Rifle Association) (trade/member/health association)   1,738,446
10. Committee on Letter Carriers Political Education (labor)   1,714,777

In contrast to these committees, many PACs gave little or no money to federal candidates. About 44 percent of all PACs contributed a total of $1,000 or less to federal candidates, with 1,685 committees making no contributions and 414 others giving less than $1,000. Another 644 PACs donated a total of more than $1,000 but less than $5,000. Many of these committees were nonconnected PACs that were not required to register with the FEC until they raised or spent $1,000 on federal election–related activities during a single calendar year.[76]

A number of PACs exhibited significant increases in their level of giving during the 1992 election cycle. A study by the Center for Responsive Politics found that PACs representing lawyers and lobbyists gave $6.3 million to candidates in 1992, increasing their level of giving by 38 percent over 1990. Much of this growth was due to a 55 percent increase in the amount donated by the Association of Trial Lawyers of America PAC, which gave $2.3 million to candidates. Analysts argued that this heightened activity reflected the organization's concern over tort-reform legislation pending before Congress.[77] PACs associated with the health care industry gave 32 percent more than in 1990, donating about $14.4 million. Among the most active health care committees were the American Medical Association PAC, whose contributions grew by 23 percent to $2.9 million; the American Dental Association, up 70 percent to $1.4 million; and the American Chiropractic Association, whose $628,000 in donations represented a 234 percent increase.[78] The National Rifle Association's PAC also raised its level of giving significantly, donating more than $1.7 million to federal candidates, an increase of 132 percent.

Ideological and single-issue groups also gave more than in previous elections, led by a dramatic surge in contributions by PACs representing women's groups, which increased their level of giving by more than 300 percent from that of 1990, donating more than $1.5 million to federal candidates.[79] This enhanced activity was facilitated by a noteworthy improvement in their ability to raise funds, which was largely a response to the 1991 Senate Judiciary Committee confirmation hearings on Clarence Thomas's nomination to the Supreme Court, during which Anita Hill, one of Thomas's former co-workers, went before the committee in a nationally televised appearance and charged that Thomas had sexually harassed her. Hill and others thus argued that Thomas was an unsuitable nominee. Hill's testimony generated substantial public controversy, which was heightened by the Senate's decision to confirm Thomas despite the charges. This decision led many organized interests and political observers, especially women's groups, to attack the Senate for being insensitive to such an important concern, with many of these critics claiming that more women legislators were needed in Congress before the body could be considered to be truly representative of the public.

Women's groups seized on the Anita Hill episode as a vehicle for encouraging women to get involved in politics. In the months following the hearings, many women decided to pursue elective office at all levels, especially for Congress. As a result, a record number of women sought positions in the House and Senate. In 1990, seventy women ran for the House, more than in any prior election; in 1992, 150 women entered races for House seats, thirty-five in California alone. In 1990, eight women ran for the Senate; in 1992, twenty women entered Senate races.[80] Of these, 108 House candidates—seventy-one Democrats and thirty-seven Republicans—made it to the general election, as did eleven of those running for Senate, including ten Democrats and one Republican.

The hearings also provided women's groups with an issue they could use as a vehicle for raising funds. For example, the Women's Campaign Fund, a federal PAC that helps candidates from both parties who support abortion rights, issued fund-raising appeals urging women to contribute with the slogan, "This one's for Anita"; and in the first three months of 1992 the committee raised twice the amount it had raised for the comparable period in 1990.[81] By October 1992, the fund had doubled its membership and raised close to $2 million, almost double the $1.2 million it had received during the 1990 cycle.[82] The National Organization for Women, which usually attracts about 2,000 new members a month, signed up 13,000 new members in the two months immediately after the Thomas hearings.[83] The organization's PAC, NOW/PAC, more than doubled the amount it raised in 1990 and donated more than $322,000 to federal candidates. The National Women's Political Caucus Victory Fund, a nonconnected PAC, had donated less than $90,000 to federal candidates during the 1990 election cycle, but it gave more than $136,000 to House and Senate candidates in 1992 and more than $500,000 to candidates in federal, state, and local races combined.[84]

EMILY's List

The most successful, and controversial, women's PAC in 1992 was EMILY's List. This PAC, whose name is an acronym for "Early Money Is Like Yeast," was formed in 1985 to provide early seed money to Democratic women running for office who support abortion rights and are regarded as potentially viable candidates.[85] Like most nonconnected PACs, EMILY's List solicits funds from the public and directly contributes funds to the candidates it endorses. But unlike most PACs, EMILY's List primarily helps candidates by administering a "donor network," that is, by encouraging its members to make direct contributions of their own.[86] Individuals join EMILY's List by contributing $100 to the PAC and by pledging to give $100 to at least two candidates of their choice from a list of recommended candidates the PAC provides.[87] These checks, which are made out to each candidate's campaign committee rather than to EMILY's list, are then collected by the PAC, sorted by candidate, bundled together and sent to the appropriate candidates without ever being deposited in the PAC's bank account. Since these checks are not made from the PAC's funds, they do not count against the PAC's contribution limit of $5,000 per election per candidate. Instead, they are treated as contributions from the specific donors, subject to the $1,000 per election limit on individual donations.

During the 1990 election cycle, EMILY's List raised approximately $973,000, spent $800,000, and made direct contributions of less than $90,000 to candidates for federal office. In addition, the PAC raised $1.5 million for fourteen candidates from the contributions it solicited from its 3,000 members.[88] The PAC thus generated an average of more than $100,000 for the candidates it endorsed, or an amount ten times greater than the combined maximum ($10,000) the PAC itself could give in a primary and general election under the FECA's $5,000 per election limit.

In the five months after the Thomas hearings, EMILY's List's membership more than tripled, rising to more than 11,000 members by April 1992.[89] According to Deborah Hicks, the PAC's communications director, this rapid growth was due in part to the hearings and in part to a late March 1992 profile of the organization on "60 Minutes."[90] Membership continued to grow throughout 1992, and by early 1993 the PAC was reported to have an estimated 24,000 members.[91]

With this broader membership base, EMILY's List was able to increase its financial activity substantially. It raised $4.1 million and spent $3.4 million during 1991–92, a fourfold increase over the previous cycle, making it the top fund raiser among nonconnected PACs and third in terms of spending in the 1992 cycle. The committee directly contributed $365,318 to sixty-five federal candidates, including sixty-four Democrats and one Independent House contender, Lynn Taborsak of Connecticut. More important, it generated $6.2 million for fifty-five candidates from 63,000 individual donations solicited from its members.[92] It thus raised an average of close to $113,000 in members' gifts for each of its endorsed candidates. This, in effect, made EMILY's List the biggest PAC donor to House and Senate candidates in the 1992 cycle, easily outdistancing the National Association of Realtors, which ranked first among all PACs with $2.9 million in direct contributions to federal candidates. EMILY's List also solicited soft money gifts from its members to provide additional assistance to candidates involved in key contests. These funds were raised solely through small individual donations (no corporate, union, or large individual gifts were accepted) and were spent on programs that sought to persuade women registered as Republicans or Independents to vote Democrat.[93] In total, the PAC donated more than $620,000 to the soft money accounts of selected state party committees, with the largest sums given to California ($245,000), Illinois and Pennsylvania ($95,000 each), and Washington ($70,000), where women the PAC had endorsed were involved in tight Senate races.[94]

The success of EMILY's List encouraged the formation of similar PAC operations. In December 1991, a group of Republican women formed WISH List (Women in the Senate and House), a PAC designed to provide financial support to Republican women candidates who support abortion rights. This committee, which raised $150,000 in its first two months of existence, had 1,500 members and more than $300,000 in receipts by the end of 1992. It donated about $250,000 to candidates in direct contributions and bundled checks from members during the 1992 election cycle.[95] After the election, another Republican committee modeled on EMILY's List, the Republican Network to Elect Women, was formed to solicit the support of working women and others, and to persuade them to support the party's economic goals.[96] America's Fund, whose title is an acronym for "Achieving More Equitable Representation in the Congress and the States," was created by a group of Democratic Washington-based professionals, including Michael Brown, an attorney and the son of Ron Brown; former New Mexico governor Jerry Apodaca; and Lynn Cutler, a former DNC vice chair. The PAC's mission is to raise money and channel bundled contributions to minority candidates, regardless of their party affiliation.[97] The success of EMILY's List was even felt overseas, as a group of British women formed EMILY's List UK, a group completely independent of the American organization, which will raise money to help elect more women to Parliament.[98]

The financial practices of EMILY's List and similar PACs have been a focal point of extensive debate and commentary. Many observers believe that the committee's actions, although legal, are little more than a device for circumventing the limits on PAC donations. Accordingly, they argue that "bundling" should be prohibited and advocate reform of federal campaign finance laws to stop this tactic. Otherwise, the bundling of checks, which is practiced by a number of PACs (although less overtly than in the case of EMILY's List), and is suspected to be widespread among many others, will become increasingly common.[99] Others contend that PACs such as EMILY's List should be allowed to continue to solicit contributions in their current manner, since such funding is an important source of revenues for challengers or other candidates who may not have access to the resources needed to launch a competitive campaign. They further note that the contributions solicited for federal candidates by such PACs are subject to the $1,000 individual contribution limit and are disclosed by the candidates who receive them. In 1993, Congress responded to the success of EMILY's List and the accompanying debate by reconsidering the need for more detailed bundling provisions in future campaign finance legislation. Such provisions were incorporated into the main campaign finance reform proposals submitted to the 103d Congress, as noted in chapter 9.

Patterns of PAC Donations

With respect to their patterns of giving, all types of PACs heavily favored incumbents and gave more to open seat candidates than to challengers. PACs contributed $126.4 million to incumbents, which was 71 percent of the $178.4 million contributed to all candidates seeking election in 1991–92. They gave $31.4 million, 17 percent of their total contributions, to candidates pursuing open seats, while challengers received $20.6 million, 12 percent of the total. Incumbents, however, received a smaller percentage of the money contributed by PACs than they did in either of the previous two election cycles; incumbents received 79 percent of all PAC donations in 1990 and 74 percent of such gifts in 1988. This decline was largely a function of the greater share of donations given to open seat candidates, who had received less than 11 percent of all contributions made by PACs in 1990. This shift in funding patterns, however, does not represent a major change in PAC contribution strategies; rather, it is primarily due to the fact that there were seventy-five open seats in 1992 as opposed to forty in 1990.[100] The most incumbent-oriented PACs were those formed by cooperatives and corporations, which respectively gave 82 percent and 77 percent of their total contributions to incumbents. Those least likely to give to incumbents were labor committees and nonconnected groups, but these PACs still gave the majority of their gifts to incumbents; committees in both of these categories gave about 59 percent of their donations to senators and representatives seeking reelection.

Since the Democrats controlled Congress, the preference for incumbents displayed by PACs worked to the Democrats' advantage. Democrats seeking election in the 1992 cycle raised $114.3 million from these committees, 64 percent of all PAC contributions, as compared with $63.8 million for Republicans and $316,000 to independents and minor party candidates. Labor committees were the mostly heavily Democratic PACs, giving almost 95 percent of their gifts, $37.5 million, to Democrats versus only $1.9 million to Republicans. Even corporate PACs, which have tended to favor Republicans, gave slightly more to the Democrats, splitting their gifts almost evenly between candidates of the two major parties, with $32.3 million going to Democrats and $32.0 million to Republicans. Among other types of PACs, the average share of contributions received by Democrats ranged from 58 percent to 68 percent.

While PACs generally favored incumbents, they were relatively generous to those challengers who won their elections. The twelve new members of the Senate all accepted PAC money. PACs gave an aggregate $7.2 million to these candidates, an average of $600,000 each. The leading recipients were all Democrats: Feinstein, who received $941,000; Boxer, $898,500; Dorgan, $786,000; Ben Nighthorse Campbell of Colorado, $741,600; and Moseley-Braun, $646,700.[101] Their success in soliciting PAC funds, however, might have been due to factors other than their partisan affiliation. Feinstein and Boxer were both running in California, the most populous and expensive state in which to seek office. Boxer was a former House member with the experience and access needed to solicit PAC donations, as were Dorgan and Campbell. The new senator who received the lowest amount from PACs, Robert Bennett, was relatively unknown among the Washington PAC community but solicited more than $343,000 in PAC contributions.[102]

Of the 110 candidates who won election to the House for the first time in 1992, ninety-nine accepted PAC money. These ninety-nine collected nearly $15 million in PAC contributions, an average of about $149,000 each, which represented about 26 percent of their total campaign funds. Twenty received $200,000 or more each from PAC donors, while fifty-five received more than $100,000 each. The top PAC recipient among entering House members was Democrat Gene Green of Texas, who solicited $409,700 from PACs, 58 percent of his total campaign funds. But Green's case was unusual, since he faced the voters four times during the 1992 election cycle: in a primary, in a runoff election that was invalidated by the courts, in a second runoff, and finally in the general election. He also made a tactical decision to emphasize PAC contributions in his fund-raising strategy, which he could do as a twenty-year veteran of the Texas legislature.[103] The other leading recipients of PAC money among new House members were also Democrats, including Leslie Byrne of Virginia ($309,300), Lynn Schenk of California ($300,100), Anna Eshoo of California ($296,300), and Earl Pomeroy of North Dakota ($296,300).

After the election, PACs gave significant sums in additional contributions to these candidates, who were now considered incumbents in the eyes of most PAC managers. In the fifty-eight-day period between the election and December 31, 1992, the twelve newly elected senators received almost $456,000 from PACs, an average of $38,000 each. Only one, Dorgan, received no PAC money during this period. PACs gave $82,000 to Bennett, $74,200 to Feinstein, and more than $42,000 to Faircloth. Between his runoff election on November 24 and December 31, Coverdell accepted $105,845 from PACs.[104]

PACs concentrated most of their post-election giving on House newcomers, many of whom were readily willing to accept these funds to help pay off sizable campaign debts. Collectively, the campaign committees of the 110 new House members held a debt of $7.2 million after election day.

Between election day and December 31, ninety-four of the ninety-nine new members who accepted PAC money in 1992 received additional PAC contributions, totaling $1.2 million. Eighteen members of this group—ten Democrats and eight Republicans—each collected more than $20,000.[105] Furthermore, the PACs that donated these funds showed little partisan bias in post-election giving. Before the election, the newly elected Republicans who accepted PAC money received an average of 74 percent of the amount given to newly elected Democrats. After the election, the average Republican collected 95 percent of the amount given a Democratic counterpart.[106]

PAC donations to new members took on an even more familiar pattern during the early months of 1993. According to a Common Cause analysis, after their first six months in office the fund-raising patterns of freshman members generally followed the typical pattern for incumbents. By mid-1993, first-term members had raised nearly one-half of their reelection funds from PACs, more than double the 26 percent average share they had received in 1992.[107] A survey of mid-year FEC reports conducted by the Gannett News Service came to a similar conclusion. This study revealed that first-term members had solicited 50 percent of their reelection funds from PACs, and that 55 percent of these representatives had raised more than one-half of their total funds from PACs, as compared with 51 percent for the comparable group in the 1991–92 election cycle. In addition, the study found that the new senators also had fallen into typical fund-raising patterns, raising about 34 percent of their reelection funds from PACs, compared with 31 percent for incumbents in the 1991–92 election cycle.[108] Most observers interpreted these early patterns as indicating that there would be little change in the general pattern and flow of funds in congressional races during the 1994 election cycle.

Independent expenditures made by PACs are noted in chapter 8.[109]

Grandfathered Funds

Under federal law, most members of Congress may not convert their leftover or excess campaign funds to personal use; they must return the funds to campaign donors, contribute these funds to other political committees or charitable organizations, or dispense of them in some other manner approved by the FEC. Rules adopted by the House Ethics Committee that were incorporated into the 1979 FECA,[110] however, allow House members who were in office on January 8, 1980, to convert any excess campaign funds to monies for their personal use upon leaving office. This provision, which is known as the "grandfather clause" because it maintains the old rules for the more senior representatives, originally allowed eligible representatives to convert unlimited sums to personal use. But as part of the Ethics Reform Act of 1989, Congress amended this clause in two ways. First, the law limited the time period within which grandfathered members could exercise this option, declaring that members who served in the 103d Congress or a later Congress would be unable to convert funds to personal use after January 3, 1993. Second, it limited the amount that could be converted, guarding against the possibility of members engaging in fund-raising practices designed to pad their retirement funds rather than finance their next campaign. The act mandated that eligible members could convert only an amount equal to their campaign's unobligated balance as of November 30, 1989. In 1991, the FEC revised its regulations to conform to the Ethics Reform Act's modifications.[111]

The Ethics Reform Act thus forced grandfathered members to make a decision to retire before the 1992 election if they wished to keep their leftover funds. While there was some speculation that this provision might encourage some members to retire early and thus take advantage of this windfall, none of the representatives who chose not to run cited this benefit as a reason for retiring, which is not surprising given the public criticism that would undoubtedly accompany such a decision. In fact, only a few of the retiring members announced before the election that they would be converting their leftover campaign monies to personal use. Representative Don Pease, an Ohio Democrat, announced that he would dispose of the last $130,000 in his campaign accounts through a trust established by the Community Foundation of Greater Lorain County, which would make contributions for political and charitable purposes. By November 1992, this foundation had already given away more than $62,000 to various national and local Democratic committees, as well as $25,000 to Oberlin College, where Pease would be teaching part time after completing his term in office.[112] Similarly, New Jersey Republican Matthew Rinaldo, who had the largest excess of any departing member, $994,348, announced that he had set up a committee to dispense this sum to political and charitable causes.[113] The only members to admit that they were converting their funds to personal use were North Carolina Democrat Walter Jones, who died before the election, leaving $295,601 to his estate; and Arizona Democrat Morris Udall, who resigned because of failing health and turned over more than $56,000 in campaign funds to his family after leaving office.[114]

While few members were willing to declare publicly their intention to convert grandfathered funds to personal use, many of those who are eligible to do so have exercised this option. In 1994, the Center for Public Integrity, a Washington-based, nonprofit organization devoted to the study of public service and ethics-related issues, released a comprehensive study of grandfathered funds, which revealed that 112 former members of Congress had used an estimated $10.5 million in unspent campaign funds since 1979 for essentially nonelection-related purposes.[115] The largest part of this total, approximately $6 million, was transferred by former members or, in the case of their deaths, by their campaign committees to personal accounts or to the members' beneficiaries. The remaining portion, an estimated $4.5 million, was used to cover post-retirement office, travel, entertainment, or other political expenses, or, in a few cases, to pay personal legal fees in criminal trials or congressional ethics probes.[116]

Few of the former members with grandfathered funds returned significant portions of their monies to campaign contributors. Among those who did were Robert Mrazek of New York, who gave back more than $218,000 to PACs and individual donors; William Brodhead of Michigan, $72,000; Dan Mica of Florida, $69,000; and Harley Staggers of West Virginia, $59,000. Many others contributed all of their funds to state and local party organizations and candidates, charitable organizations, or educational entities. Longtime Representative Charles Bennett of Florida, for example, gave $270,835 to the U.S. Treasury for use by the National Park Service. His Florida colleague Don Fuqua gave more than $100,000 to Florida State University, while Robert Whittaker of Kansas contributed in excess of $509,000 to Kansas State University. Representative Charles Luken of Ohio gave $110,000 to the state treasury to help pay the costs of a special primary to select his replacement.[117] A number of other former members have established personal foundations or charitable trusts that are responsible for administering contributions to various organizations and causes. These entities have received a total of $2.7 million in leftover funds.[118]

The Center for Public Integrity study reported that twenty-six former members since 1979 have relied on the grandfather clause to transfer more than $100,000 or more apiece for personal use or to pay for post-retirement expenses. In these cases, a former member may use the funds for any purpose so long as they are reported as income to the IRS and the appropriate amount in taxes are paid. The former member who received the largest sum in this manner was Larry Hopkins of Kentucky, who converted $665,000 despite having pledged not to use his leftover campaign funds "for personal benefit" in his failed 1991 gubernatorial campaign. Others who converted significant amounts to personal use included John Duncan of Tennessee, whose campaign committee transferred $605,000 to his heirs after his death in 1988; Gene Taylor of Missouri, who converted $345,000 to personal use; Bob Traxler of Michigan, who converted in excess of $295,000; and Carroll Hubbard of Kentucky, who converted $216,000.[119]

Among those who left office in 1992, fifty-one were eligible to convert leftover funds, including thirty-two who retired, eleven who were defeated in primaries, and eight who lost in the general election.[120] Those who retired reported an average of approximately $303,000 in remaining campaign funds, as opposed to an average of $82,000 for those who lost elections.[121] According to the Center for Public Integrity study, twenty-three of these members had converted approximately $2.4 million to personal use or used leftover monies for various post-retirement expenditures by the end of 1993.[122] A number of others established personal charitable trusts that allowed them to contribute funds to other organizations without having to disclose the beneficiaries publicly. Those who pursued this option included Larry Coughlin of Pennsylvania, who transferred his remaining $208,000 to a Coughlin Family Charitable Trust; William Broomfield of Michigan, who placed more than $517,000 into his Broomfield Charitable Foundation; Norman Lent of New York, who put $570,000 in the Lent Family Charitable Trust; and John Paul Hammerschmidt of Arkansas, who put almost $400,000 into his JPH Education Fund.[123]

The analysis particularly highlighted the ethical concerns associated with the practice, adopted by a number of former members, of transferring leftover campaign funds to personal PACs that former members could use to make political donations. Nine of the members who retired in 1993 pursued this option, transferring a total of $1.5 million.[124] This approach was cited because it provides former members with an ability to distribute funds to lawmakers whom they may be attempting to influence in post-retirement lobbying careers. The study identified twenty-one "grandfathered" members who were working as post-retirement lobbyists. Lent, for example, who was the ranking Republican on the House Energy and Commerce Committee when he left office and now has his own Washington lobbying firm, donated about $15,000 in leftover campaign monies to twenty-one representatives, including seven Democrats, in his first year out of office. Another former member working as a lobbyist, Ronnie Flippo of Alabama, who left Congress to run unsuccessfully for governor in 1990, had nearly $500,000 in his campaign fund when he left the House, more than $47,000 of which he donated to members of Congress from both parties.[125]

Although members who leave Congress in the future may no longer convert leftover campaign funds to personal use, as of the end of 1993 there were still twenty-three grandfathered former members of Congress who had not yet disposed of their excess campaign funds and were still eligible to transfer an estimated $3.2 million to personal use.[126]

Notes

1. Norman J. Ornstein, Thomas E. Mann, and Michael J. Malbin, *Vital Statistics on Congress 1991–1992* (Washington, DC: Congressional Quarterly, 1992), p. 58.
2. Donald Gross and David Breaux, "Historical Trends in U.S. Senate Elections, 1912–1988," *American Politics Quarterly* 19 (July 1991), pp. 284–309.
3. Richard E. Cohen, "No Honeymoon Cruise," *National Journal*, November 7, 1992, p. 2544.
4. Ornstein, Mann, and Malbin, *Vital Statistics on Congress*, p. 58.
5. This figure does not include Harlan Mathews of Tennessee, who was appointed to fill the vacancy created by Al Gore's election to the vice presidency.
6. Dave Kaplan and Charles Mahtesian, "Election's Wave of Diversity Spares Many Incumbents," *Congressional Quarterly Weekly Report*, November 7, 1992, p. 3570.
7. Gary C. Jacobson, "Congress: Unusual Year, Unusual Election," in Michael Nelson, ed., *The Elections of 1992* (Washington, DC: Congressional Quarterly, 1993), p. 154.
8. Ibid., pp. 154–55.
9. FEC, "1992 Congressional Election Spending Jumps 52% to $678 Million," press release, March 4, 1993, p. 1.
10. According to FEC reports, there were 1,792 House and Senate candidates in the 1988 cycle and 1,764 in the 1990 cycle.
11. Marjorie Randon Hershey, "The Congressional Elections," in Gerald M. Pomper, ed., *The Election of 1992: Reports and Interpretations* (Chatham, NJ: Chatham House, 1993), pp. 173–74.
12. "Congress, My Congressman," *Public Perspective* 3 (May/June 1992), p. 102.
13. Jacobson, "Congress: Unusual Year, Unusual Election," p. 164.
14. Ibid., p. 165; and Hershey, "The Congressional Elections," p. 165.
15. Paul R. Abramson, John H. Aldrich, and David W. Rohde, *Change and Continuity in the 1992 Elections* (Washington, DC: Congressional Quarterly, 1994), p. 264.
16. Ibid.
17. Jacobson, "Congress: Unusual Year, Unusual Election," p. 165.
18. Abramson, Aldrich, and Rohde, *Change and Continuity in the 1992 Elections*, p. 263.
19. Jacobson, "Congress: Unusual Year, Unusual Election," p.165.
20. Hershey, "The Congressional Elections," p. 163.
21. Ibid.
22. Abramson, Aldrich, and Rohde, *Change and Continuity in the 1992 Elections*, p. 267. For a list of those included on the Ethics Committee list, see *Congressional Quarterly Weekly Report*, April 18, 1992, pp. 1006–7.
23. For an analysis of the factors that influenced the number of retirements in the 1992 cycle, see L. Sandy Maisel, "Opting Out and Opting In: The Impact of Voluntary Retirements on the 1992 Congressional Election" (Washington, DC: The Progressive Foundation, 1993); and Timothy Groseclose and Keith Krehbiel, "Golden Parachutes, Rubber Checks, and Strategic Retirements from the 102nd House," *American Journal of Political Science* 38 (1994), pp. 75–99.
24. Phil Kuntz, "Bank Issue Yields 25% Return for Hill Challengers," *Washington Times*, November 9, 1992.
25. Hershey, "The Congressional Elections," p. 175. These figures do not include Barbara Boxer.
26. Hershey, "The Congressional Elections," p. 175.
27. Kaplan and Mahtesian, "Election's Wave of Diversity," p. 3571.

28. Michael A. Dimock and Gary C. Jacobson, "Checks and Choices: The Impact of the House Bank Scandal on Voting Behavior in the 1992 Elections" (paper presented at the annual meeting of the Midwest Political Science Association, Chicago, IL, April 14–16, 1994).

29. Hershey, "The Congressional Elections," p. 171.

30. Ibid.

31. Ibid., p. 174, and Jacobson, "Congress: Unusual Year, Unusual Election," p. 168.

32. Jacobson, "Congress: Unusual Year, Unusual Election," p. 168.

33. Ibid., p. 174.

34. Cassandra Burrell, "Congressional Campaign Spending Jumps 52 Percent," Associated Press news release, March 5, 1993; and Tim Curran, "Incumbents' War Chests Fall Off 42%," Roll Call, March 8, 1993.

35. The figures for previous elections noted in this section are drawn from the tables in FEC, "1992 Congressional Election Spending Jumps 52% to $678 Million."

36. Based on an analysis of PAC receipts reported by the FEC.

37. Beth Donovan with Ilyse J. Veron, "Freshmen Got to Washington With Help of PAC Funds," Congressional Quarterly Weekly Report, March 27, 1993, pp. 723, 726.

38. Hoekstra, Huffington, and Meehan defeated incumbent members in primary elections. Hoke, Inglis, and Torkildsen defeated incumbents in general election contests. Jay Dickey of Arkansas won in the district in which incumbent Democrat Beryl Anthony lost in the primary to Bill McCuen.

39. The figures for candidate contributions and candidate loans are based on the data reported by the FEC. It is important to note, however, that specific figures for funding in these categories are difficult to estimate due to the complicated accounting that often accompanies such transactions. For example, candidates sometimes loan their campaigns large sums and then take back a portion of the loan for one reason or another, thus essentially giving their campaigns additional funds that are never used in the campaign. Candidates also have loaned their campaigns money and repaid the loans in another election cycle or converted a loan to a direct contribution; or they may have paid off an initial loan with a second loan that may be for a different sum and from another source. Reported figures for candidate contributions and loans, therefore, may vary. The data reported here are based on the data reported in FEC, "1992 Congressional Election Spending Jumps 52% to $678 Million," unless otherwise specified.

40. In the 1989–90 election cycle, Senator Robert Kasten of Wisconsin provided $246,231 to his campaign.

41. Ines Pinto Alicea, "Big Spenders End Up Losers in Primaries for Senate," Congressional Quarterly Weekly Report, September 12, 1992, p. 2739.

42. See Ronald D. Elving, "Huffington's Wealth Becomes the Issue," Congressional Quarterly Weekly Report, May 23, 1992, p. 1473; and "The Waning Aversion to Wealth in Politics," Congressional Quarterly Weekly Report, April 3, 1993, p. 874. For background, see Michael Barone and Grant Ujifusa, The Almanac of American Politics 1994 (Washington, DC: National Journal, Inc., 1993), pp. 141–42.

43. This figure is based on FEC records as of August 8, 1994, and is based on the amount of the net outstanding balance on loans made to the campaign after any repayments. If repayments are not included, at least fifty candidates loaned their campaigns $100,000 or more during the course of the 1992 election cycle.

44. One other incumbent, Republican Charles Taylor of North Carolina, loaned his campaign $438,278, all but about $10,000 of which was repaid, so he does not appear in this list being discussed here. Taylor won reelection with 54 percent of the general election vote.

45. Harman loaned $823,000 to her campaign, $673,000 of which had been repaid by August 8, 1994. Therefore, her net loan balance was $150,000.

46. For a discussion of personal spending in the 1988 congressional elections, see Herbert E. Alexander and Monica Bauer, *Financing the 1988 Election* (Boulder, CO: Westview Press, 1991), pp. 65–68.

47. See, for example, Elving, "The Waning Aversion to Wealth in Politics," p. 874.

48. The House total for minor party candidates includes one incumbent, independent Bernard Sanders of Vermont, who spent $575,791.

49. The FEC compilation of candidate expenditures does not include Illinois as an open seat race, even though there was no incumbent in the general election, since Senator Alan Dixon was defeated in the Democratic primary. Instead, the FEC lists both general election contenders as challengers.

50. In the race in Michigan's Eighth District, incumbent Democrat Bob Carr spent $1.4 million to defeat Republican Richard Chrysler, who spent $1.8 million. In Montana, redistricting forced two incumbents, Democrat Pat Williams and Republican Ron Marlenee, to face each other and each spent about $1.3 million. Williams was reelected.

51. FEC, "1992 Congressional Election Spending Jumps 52% to $678 Million," p. 12.

52. Tim Curran, "Up Against the Wall," *Roll Call,* November 2, 1992.

52. Michael J. Malbin, "Campaign Finance Reform: Some Lessons from the Data," *Rockefeller Institute Bulletin,* 1993, p. 49.

54. Reported in "Political Reform," *Washington Post,* November 10, 1992.

55. Malbin, "Campaign Finance Reform," p. 49.

56. Ibid., p. 51.

57. Ibid.

58. Jonathan S. Krasno and Donald Philip Green, "Stopping the Buck Here: The Case for Campaign Spending Limits," *The Brookings Review,* spring 1993, pp. 17–21.

59. See ibid., pp. 20–21; and Malbin, "Campaign Finance Reform," pp. 52–53. Also see Gary C. Jacobson, *Money in Congressional Elections* (New Haven, CT: Yale University Press, 1980), and *The Politics of Congressional Elections,* 2d ed. (Boston, MA: Little, Brown, 1987).

60. Paul S. Herrnson, "National Party Decision-Making, Strategies, and Resource Distribution in Congressional Elections," *Western Political Quarterly* 42 (1989).

61. Figures reported in FEC, "Democrats Narrow Financial Gap in 1991–92," press release, March 11, 1993. All figures on national party committee receipts and expenditures discussed in the following section of this chapter are based on the data reported in this press release.

62. The NRSC gave $17,000 to Thornburgh and reported small gifts to Jane Brady of Delaware and Milt Erhart of Idaho. The committee also spent $951,183 on Thornburgh's behalf. This amount is included in the figure reported for total coordinated spending in the 1991–92 election cycle.

63. These candidates were Richard Sellers of Alabama, Richard Reed of Hawaii, Alan Keyes of Maryland, and Bill Grant of Florida.

64. Paul S. Herrnson, "The Revitalization of National Party Organizations," in L. Sandy Maisel, ed., *The Parties Respond,* 2d ed. (Boulder, CO: Westview Press, 1994), p. 61; and Michelle Mittelstadt, "Republican Senatorial Committee Lends Helping Hand to House Candidates," Associated Press news release, October 23, 1992.

65. Herrnson, "The Revitalization of National Party Organizations," p. 61.

66. The DSCC spent $1,300 each in support of Dan Glickman of Kansas and Jim Moody of Wisconsin. The aggregate figure includes $881,429 in coordinated expenditures made in 1991 in support of Wofford.

67. This total includes contributions to two minor party candidates. Independent

Lynn Taborsak of Connecticut received $200 and Ruben Franco of New York, who ran on the Liberal ticket, received $150.

68. Herrnson, "The Revitalization of National Party Organizations," p. 63.

69. Ibid., Table 3.3.

70. Ibid., p. 64.

71. FEC, "PAC Activity Rebounds in 1991–92 Election Cycle," press release, April 29, 1993, p. 1. In this release, the FEC reported unadjusted figures on PAC receipts and expenditures that showed that PACs spent about $9 million more than they received in the 1991–92 election cycle.

72. Keith White, "Incumbents Got Most Money from PACs, FEC Study Shows," Gannett News Service release, April 29, 1993.

73. FEC, "PAC Activity Rebounds in 1991–92 Election Cycle," p. 1.

74. Glenn R. Simpson, "Study: PAC Spending Jumps 18% in 1992," Roll Call, June 3, 1993. The figure is based on a study of PAC contributions conducted by the Center for Responsive Politics.

75. "Realtors, Doctors Had Most Generous PACs in 1991–92 Election Cycle," Political Finance & Lobby Reporter, April 28, 1993, p. 2.

76. Ibid., p. 102; and FEC, "PAC Activity Rebounds in 1991–92 Election Cycle," p. 7.

77. Simpson, "Study: PAC Spending Jumps 18% in 1992."

78. Richard Benedetto, "Health PACs' Giving Rises," USA Today, March 12, 1993.

79. Simpson, "Study: PAC Spending Jumps 18% in 1992."

80. R. W. Apple Jr., "Steady Local Gains by Women Fuel More Runs for High Office," New York Times, May 24, 1992.

81. Steven V. Roberts and Gary Cohen, "Will 1992 Be the Year of the Woman?" U.S. News & World Report, April 27, 1992, pp. 38–39.

82. Charles R. Babcock, "Women are Filling Coffers of Female Candidates," Washington Post, October 22, 1992. Figures for receipts are based on FEC reports on PAC activity for the 1990 and 1992 election cycles.

83. Apple, "Steady Local Gains by Women Fuel More Runs for High Office."

84. Figures for contributions to federal candidates based on FEC reports on PAC activity for the 1990 and 1992 election cycles. Figure for total contributions reported in Babcock, "Women are Filling Coffers of Female Candidates."

85. Helen Dewar, "EMILY's List Falls Prey to PAC Hunt," Washington Post, March 7, 1993.

86. "Look Who's Bigger Than the Teamsters," Political Finance & Lobby Reporter, October 27, 1993, p. 1.

87. Maralee Schwartz, "Female Candidates Break Record, Mold," Washington Post, May 25, 1992.

88. Ibid.

89. Roberts and Cohen, "Will 1992 Be the Year of the Woman?" p. 39.

90. Schwartz, "Female Candidates Break Record, Mold."

91. " 'Soft Money' Role of EMILY's List," Washington Post, May 30, 1993.

92. Dewar, "EMILY's List Falls Prey to PAC Hunt."

93. " 'Soft Money' Role of EMILY's List."

94. Ibid.

95. Apple, "Steady Local Gains by Women Fuel More Runs for High Office"; and Babcock, "Women are Filling Coffers of Female Candidates."

96. "A GOP EMILY's," Washington Times, November 29, 1993.

97. "From the K Street Corridor," National Journal, August 7, 1993, p. 1986.

98. "EMILY's List Cloned by British Women," Political Finance & Lobby Reporter, March 10, 1993, p. 4.

99. Dewar, "EMILY's List Falls Prey to PAC Hunt."

100. FEC, "PAC Activity Rebounds in 1991–92 Election Cycle," p. 1.

101. Donovan with Veron, "Freshmen Got to Washington With Help of PAC Funds," p. 727.

102. Ibid.

103. Ibid.

104. Ibid.

105. Beth Donovan with Jennifer S. Thomas and Ilyse J. Veron, "PAC Faith in First-Time Candidates Takes Big Jump After Election Day," *Congressional Quarterly Weekly Report,* March 27, 1993, p. 724.

106. Ibid.

107. Peter Montgomery, "In Common," *Common Cause Magazine,* winter 1993, p. 40.

108. Keith White, "Congress' Freshmen Rake in PAC Dollars," *USA Today,* August 24, 1993.

109. See chapter 8 in this volume, pp. 242–48.

110. See *Federal Election Campaign Act, U.S Code,* vol. 2, sec. 439a.

111. For background, see FEC, *Record,* September 1991, pp. 5–6, and December 1991, p. 2. The new regulations concerning grandfathered funds can be found in *Federal Register* 56 (July 25, 1991): 34124.

112. Lee Bowman, "Hill Retirees Pledge Good Intentions," *Washington Times,* November 16, 1992.

113. Ibid.

114. Ibid.

115. Kevin Chaffee, "Saving for a Rainy Day II: How Congress Uses Leftover Campaign Cash" (Washington, DC: Center for Public Integrity, 1994). See also Kevin Chaffee, "Saving for a Rainy Day: How Congress Turns Leftover Campaign Cash into Golden Parachutes" (Washington, DC: Center for Public Integrity, 1991); and "Money Under the Mattress: What Congressmen Don't Spend," *Washington Monthly,* September 1984.

116. "Saving for a Rainy Day II," p. 1. For example, former representative Mario Biaggi of New York used $386,000 in leftover campaign funds for legal fees in his 1987 criminal trial; former Speaker of the House Jim Wright used $354,000 in excess campaign funds for the legal fees incurred as a result of a House Ethics Committee probe into his financial improprieties; William Bonner of Tennessee used $197,000 to pay legal fees in connection with House Ethics Committee and Justice Department probes of alleged kickbacks from defense contractors; Robert Garcia of New York spent about $147,000 on legal fees in his 1989 trial on racketeering charges in the Wedtech case; and Larry Smith of Florida used $76,000 to pay legal fees related to his indictment on tax and campaign finance violations.

117. Ibid., p. 9.

118. Ibid., p. 2.

119. Ibid.

120. Bowman, "Hill Retirees Pledge Good Intentions"; Peter H. Spiegel, "Five Grandfathered Ex-Members Keep Cash, Including Hopkins Who Pockets Record Sum," *Roll Call,* August 5, 1993.

121. Bowman, "Hill Retirees Pledge Good Intentions."

122. "Saving for a Rainy Day II," p. 1.

123. Spiegel, "Five Grandfathered Ex-Members Keep Cash."

124. "Saving for a Rainy Day II," p. 2.

125. Ibid., p. 3.

126. Ibid.

8

Communicating with the Voters

This chapter sets forth the laws and regulations governing political broadcasting. It also covers media expenditures in the presidential campaigns and national political broadcast costs, as well as developments relating to the presidential debates and forums.

Broadcast Media Regulations

Basic federal law governing candidates' use of broadcast media to appeal to the electorate is embodied in the Communications Act of 1934, which is administered by the Federal Communications Commission (FCC). Section 315 of the act regulates political broadcasting. "If any licensee shall permit any person who is a legally qualified candidate for any public office to use a broadcasting station," states Section 315, "he shall afford equal opportunities to all other such candidates for that office in the use of such broadcasting station."[1]

The equal opportunities requirement is triggered when the identity of a candidate who appears on a broadcast can reasonably be presumed to be known by the audience, and when the appearance is of sufficient magnitude to be considered an integral part of the broadcast. The appearance does not necessarily have to be related to, or make mention of, an individual's candidacy to be considered a "use" entitling a political opponent to an equal opportunity to appear.

The equal opportunities requirement is not absolute. In 1959, Congress amended the law, exempting candidate appearances in four news situations from the requirement: newscasts; news interviews; news documentaries, provided the candidate's appearance is incidental to the subject matter of the documentary; and on-the-spot coverage of news events. In 1960, Section 315 was suspended as it applied to presidential and vice presidential nominees. This one-time suspension permitted John Kennedy and Richard Nixon to appear in a series of broadcast debates without requiring broadcasters to provide equal opportunities for minor party candidates. Similar attempts to suspend Section 315 to allow presidential debates in 1964, 1968, and 1972 failed. In 1975, however, the FCC, in response to a petition filed by the Aspen Institute Program on Communication and Society, ruled that broadcast political debates qualify as exempt, on-the-spot coverage of news events provided they are sponsored by outside parties and are covered contemporaneously.[2] This administrative ruling permitted presidential debates sponsored by the League of Women Voters (LWV) to be broadcast in 1976, 1980, and 1984.

In November 1983, the FCC relaxed its 1975 ruling regarding broadcast debate sponsorship. In response to a petition filed by Henry Geller, a former Carter administration Commerce Department official, the National Association of Broadcasters (NAB), and the Radio and Television News Directors Association (RTNDA), the commission ruled that broadcasters may stage their own debates, inviting candidates of their choice to participate, without violating Section 315, provided the broadcasters do not favor or disfavor any particular candidate.[3] The commission also lifted its 1975 restriction limiting rebroadcast of political debates to within twenty-four hours of the original event. Then-FCC chairman Mark S. Fowler maintained the ruling would "encourage increased political debate, especially at the smaller and local levels."[4] Broadcasters, predictably, hailed the decision. Edward O. Fritts, then-NAB president, said it would allow the broadcast industry to serve the public interest better. He called "the public and our form of government the obvious winners."[5] Gene Mater, then-senior vice president of CBS News, said he thought broadcasters would do a far better job of staging political debates than "people not in the business, who [are] not journalists."[6]

The 1983 FCC ruling was not universally acclaimed. Andrew Schwartzman, director of the Media Access Project, agreed with Fowler that the ruling would have its greatest effect at the state and local levels. He warned, however, that local broadcasters' judgments about which candidates to include in a debate might be influenced by the broadcasters' business or family relationships. The LWV, which sponsored presidential forums and debates during the prenomination and general election campaigns in 1976 and 1980 and had already launched similar plans for 1984, strongly objected to the decision. League president Dorothy S. Ridings observed that the ruling permitted broadcasters to make as well as cover the news and made voters "even more vulnerable to the influence of the TV networks on campaigns and elections."[7] She upheld the league's position that debates should be sponsored by independent outside organizations that are nonpartisan and nonprofit. "Our purpose is not to entertain, it is to inform," she said.[8]

The league appealed the FCC decision, but in March 1984, the U.S. Court of Appeals in Washington issued a brief, unsigned, unanimous judgment affirming the commission's ruling. The court held that the commission's decision was a "legitimate exercise of its discretion."[9]

Although the FEC has no jurisdiction over the broadcasting of candidate debates, it has been required to reconcile FECA provisions that prohibit contributions and expenditures by corporations in connection with federal elections with the FCC decisions to permit news media corporations first to broadcast debates staged by others and, more recently, to broadcast debates they themselves stage.[10] In 1979, the FEC prescribed regulations to create a narrow exception to the ban on corporate expenditures in connection with federal elections to permit news media organizations and certain nonprofit corporations to sponsor nonpartisan candidate debates.[11] Under the exception, debate structure is left to the discretion of the staging organization, provided the debate includes at least two candidates and is nonpartisan, that is, it does not promote or advance one candidate over another.[12] The FEC promulgated these regulations because it considered the staging of candidate debates to be outside an existing exemption from the law's definition of "expenditure," which encompassed money spent by news media corporations on news stories, commentaries, or editorials.[13] The 1983 FCC decision, however, clearly included broadcaster sponsorship of candidate debates within a broadcast media organization's news function. The FEC, accordingly, was faced with the decision whether to revise its regulations to follow the FCC's 1983 interpretation or to retain the approach the FEC formulated in 1979. In large part because it wanted to avoid suggesting that all activities of broadcasters were to be exempted from the FECA requirement, the election commission chose to retain its 1979 regulations.

Debates and Forums

The 1992 election was the fifth consecutive presidential election to feature nationally televised debates between the major presidential candidates. But the 1992 presidential debates were unique in many ways. For the first time they provided the electorate with an opportunity to see an independent candidate, Ross Perot, share the stage with the Republican and Democratic party nominees on live national television. An independent candidate had not participated in the general election debates since 1980, when John Anderson faced Ronald Reagan in a forum that Carter chose not to attend. The debates also included a number of innovative formats, including the use of a single moderator instead of a panel of journalists asking questions of the candidates, and a "town hall meeting" format that gave undecided voters a chance to question the candidates directly. These innovations prompted extraordinary public interest in the debates, making them one of the most widely viewed political events in modern broadcast history. As one analysis noted: "By nearly all measures, the 1992 debates were an enormous success. They employed more formats, featured more candidates, reached more voters, and influenced more voting decisions than ever before."[14]

In 1988, developments had led to political party sponsorship of the general election debates. The debates in 1976, 1980, and 1984 were sponsored by the LWV. The Commission on National Elections, sponsored by the Center for Strategic and International Studies, issued a report in April 1986, calling for the institutionalization of joint appearances by major party nominees for the presidency.[15] It was proposed that to improve voter education, the two major political parties should assume direct responsibility for sponsoring the debates, subject to candidate acceptance. One reason was that in all prior presidential campaigns in which there were debates, protracted negotiations among candidates and sponsor took place, often threatening to undermine the debates themselves.

Accordingly, a Memorandum of Agreement on Presidential Candidate Joint Appearances, signed by DNC chairman Paul G. Kirk Jr. and RNC chairman Frank J. Fahrenkopf Jr., was included in the report.[16] Subsequently, in early 1987, a bipartisan, nonprofit organization was established, called the Commission on Presidential Debates. This commission sponsored the 1988 and 1992 debates. After the 1988 election, the commission conducted surveys of voter attitudes and held a conference in an effort to identify ways to improve the debate planning process and sponsor future forums more effectively. One of the decisions made as a result was to present a debate plan early in the election year, before the major party nominating conventions, in order to start negotiations with the candidates soon after they were selected in hopes that final arrangements could be made shortly after the conventions had concluded.[17] Accordingly, on June 11, 1992, the commission issued a proposal that called for four ninety-minute debates—three presidential and one vice presidential—to be held on a schedule of roughly one debate per week between September 22 and October 15. The plan also called for all debates to use a single moderator instead of the press panel used in previous elections. About the same time, in anticipation of the likelihood of Perot's major independent candidacy, the commission also announced its selection criteria under which third party or independent candidates would be invited to participate. These standards, which were used to determine whether a candidate had a "realistic chance" of winning the election and were similar to those used by the commission in 1988, included evidence of national organization, signs of national news-worthiness and competitiveness, and indicators of national enthusiasm or concern.[18]

Historically, the individual challenging an incumbent president is eager to debate, while the incumbent or a candidate enjoying a large lead in the polls has been more reticent about engaging his opponent on national televi-sion. It was, therefore, not surprising that Clinton readily accepted the commission's debate proposal after he received the Democratic nomination in July. The Bush campaign, however, was not so eager to place the presi-dent on the same stage with his challenger. Although the president and his strategists acknowledged there would be debates, the Bush campaign wanted to determine the debate schedule and logistics in candidate-to-can-didate negotiations, as had been the case in 1988. As a result, an agreement to debate was delayed for more than a month as the candidates engaged in political posturing and negotiations over where and under what conditions to debate.[19]

The Bush campaign would not agree with the format proposed by the nonpartisan Commission on Presidential Debates, which suggested just one moderator. Bush wanted a panel of reporters, and he indicated a preference for the 1988 schedule of two presidential debates and one vice presidential meeting.[20] The commission and the Clinton campaign were still suggesting three presidential debates. Clinton accused Bush of being afraid to debate "man to man."[21] The uncertainty surrounding Bush's willingness to debate hindered Clinton's campaign schedule and the first two dates suggested by the commission passed without an agreement on the part of the candidates to debate. Schedules had to be rearranged and preparation time allocated in the event the debate would take place. Days kept open for the debates had to be filled at the last moment, and Clinton had to slow down his sched-ule.[22] By mid-September, polls began to show that close to a majority of the public felt that Bush was avoiding debates. With Clinton maintaining a lead in the polls, Bush shifted his position in late September, calling for a series of four debates between the major contenders. This signaled an end to the stalemate, and within a few days an agreement was reached.[23]

Finally, on behalf of the parties, the commission conducted four general election debates in 1992: three between the presidential candidates, George Bush, Bill Clinton, and Ross Perot; and one between the vice presidential candidates, Vice President Dan Quayle, Albert Gore, and James B.

Stockdale. The Perot and Stockdale appearances were unique additions to the debates. The debates were held in St. Louis, Missouri; Richmond, Virginia; East Lansing, Michigan; and Atlanta, Georgia. One reached an audience of approximately 99 million, garnering a larger audience than the 1992 Super Bowl, traditionally television's highest-rated event of the year. The January 1992 game "earned a 40.3 rating on CBS—meaning 40.3 percent of the nation's television households were tuned in. But Thursday's presidential debate from Richmond, Virginia, got a 43.4 combined rating on the ABC, CBS, NBC, and Fox networks, according to the A.C. Nielsen Co."[24]

The debates not only spurred viewer interest, but there is also some evidence to suggest that they proved helpful to the electorate in making decisions as to which candidate to support. According to a Times Mirror survey conducted after the election, 70 percent of the public said the debates were helpful in making their decision as to which candidate to support. In contrast, a comparable survey conducted on the weekend before the election four years earlier found that 48 percent of the electorate rated the debates as very helpful in deciding who to support.[25] Another survey by Markle/Princeton Survey Research Associates showed that one-half of those interviewed in late October rated the debates as highly influential to their voting choice.[26]

The funding for the commission and the debates was derived mainly from corporations and foundations. An example of corporate donors sponsoring a debate was the first one held at Michigan State University in East Lansing. While it was an honor for the university to be chosen, it had to find donors to underwrite the $500,000 cost of the event. "A dozen corporations and labor unions, which are ordinarily prohibited from making contributions or expenditures in connection with federal elections, made contributions of $20,000 or more to underwrite the event's cost," the *Detroit Free Press* reported.[27]

A talk show format was introduced into the debates, after a consensus emerged that more creative formats were needed.[28] In a 1993 conference on the presidential debates sponsored by the Annenberg Washington Program of Northwestern University and the Joan Shorenstein Barone Center at Harvard University, the 1992 debates were thought to have played a more decisive role than any in the three previous decades. The institutionalization of the debates was a hot topic of discussion at the conference, with the Markey bill being one of the issues on the agenda. Congressman Edward J. Markey (D-MA) proposed that candidates receive the "$55 million in federal funds for the general election only by agreeing to take part in five debates (four presidential and one vice presidential)."[29] While opponents of Markey's bill said that such a requirement would raise questions about First

Amendment rights, others pointed out that debates were inbred into the system to meet voter expectations. In addition, it was suggested that "the statute might prove unenforceable as a practical matter, given the Federal Election Commission's slow pace."[30]

Under varying sponsorship, a series of debates—better called forums—were scheduled in the prenomination period among the Democratic presidential candidates and received varying public response. The forums were an opportunity for the candidates to discuss the issues. Starting in December 1991 and running through March 1992, they were held in various locations, ranging from Atlanta, Georgia, to Denver, Colorado, and to other locations northward and eastward. The appearances, some featuring as many as six candidates, were carried on cable, network, and local television. But a study showed that, "in fact, the many debates which began on NBC and continued on other networks represented a revenue loss for television, which rendered what should have been a public service."[31] Despite efforts by broadcasters to stop him, former governor Edmund G. Brown Jr. of California used a number of the forums to blurt out his 800 number, to seek funding for his campaign.

Reasonable Access

Although Section 315 of the Communications Act requires broadcast stations to afford political candidates equal opportunities to appear on stations or to respond to other candidates in the circumstances described, it does not require stations to allow candidates to appear in the first place. Another section of the act, Section 312(a)(7), however, warns licensees that among grounds for revocation of license is the "willful or repeated failure to allow reasonable access to or to permit purchase of reasonable amounts of time for the use of a broadcasting station by a legally qualified candidate for federal elective office on behalf of his candidacy." State and local candidates are not mentioned in this section, but the FCC interprets Section 307, which grants licenses only "if the public convenience, interest or necessity will be served thereby," to mean, among other things, that stations cannot choose to avoid equal opportunities requirements simply by refusing to provide political candidates with any access to station facilities. Even state and local candidates must be provided with access, although there is no fixed formula by which to measure reasonableness in that case.

Section 312(a)(7) does not require broadcast licensees to sell broadcast time to candidates at any level. Rather, licensees may fulfill the requirement this provision imposes by inviting candidates for specific offices to participate in forums and debates.[32] The requirement is that some broadcast time, whether purchased or free, must be made available. This provision became a matter of litigation during the 1980 presidential campaigns. The three major commercial television networks refused to sell candidates Ronald Reagan, Jimmy Carter, and John Connally broadcast time late in 1979 to announce and promote their presidential candidacies. The networks maintained it was much too early for such advertisements. When the FCC sided with the Carter campaign committee, which had filed a complaint based on the reasonable access provision of the law, the networks brought suit against the FCC. The matter was carried to the Supreme Court, which ruled in July 1981 that the First Amendment rights of candidates to present their views and of voters to obtain information outweigh the constitutional rights of broadcasters.[33]

Lowest Unit Rate

If a broadcast licensee does sell time to a candidate, the licensee must do so in accordance with Section 315(b) of the Communications Act, as amended. Under this provision, the broadcast media cannot charge political candidates more than the lowest unit rate charged to any other advertiser for the same class and amount of time for a period extending forty-five days before a primary election and sixty days before a general or special election. At other times, rates cannot exceed the charges made for comparable use for other purposes. Thus, during the designated campaign period, political candidates are to be given the same discounts as a broadcast station's most favored advertiser.

Some broadcasters, however, have succeeded in frustrating the provision by making the rate available only on an immediately preempt basis. "If a candidate does not like the idea that his announcement may be preempted," explained political consultant and media time buyer Jack Fiman at a 1983 congressional hearing, "he can elect to pay a fixed rate—usually the highest rate ever offered, but almost never used by regular clients of the stations. Television stations have interpreted the lowest unit rate to mean that they offer the lowest rate with no guarantee of airing and a choice of paying a higher rate in order to secure the desired time."[34] Thus, despite the lowest unit-rate provision, candidates who feel strongly that their advertising must air at specific times in the weeks before an election often have no choice but to pay the high rates for fixed time charged by the stations.

An FCC audit of thirty television and radio stations in five selected cities during part of the 1990 election year produced preliminary findings that they had been charging political candidates more money than other customers to broadcast advertisements. In one city in one week, all candidates paid in excess of the highest rate paid by any commercial advertiser. In one case, candidates paid an average of $6,000 for a thirty-second spot announcement, while the average cost for commercial advertisers was $2,713. The FCC also found that some stations created new classes of time for candidates, called "news adjacencies," for which there were no comparable commercial rates and hence higher charges were made.[35] As noted, most candidates seek to buy fixed air time, at a specific time aimed to reach certain audiences; this traditionally has drawn higher rates than preempt air time, meaning there is no guarantee the spot will be broadcast if other advertisers are willing to pay higher rates for the time. Since an election may be imminent, candidates are willing to pay higher rates for the time the consultants and time-buyers tell them they need. The audit findings moved the FCC to rule that broadcasters must stop charging premium rates for political advertising on television and radio.

Thus, since 1972, federal law has required broadcasters to sell political time at the lowest unit charge, giving candidates a price comparable to the lowest rate sold to a most favored advertiser for a spot in a comparable time period. Since some broadcasters auction off given time periods to the highest bidder, political or commercial, one can conclude that some broadcasters have not been fair to political candidates, and that some political consultants and time-buyers have not bargained for the better rates required by law. Moreover, some observers maintain that high television costs are a cause of negative advertising, because candidates cannot afford softer positive spots but resort to hard-hitting negative spots to get their messages across.[36]

The Costs of Television, Radio, and Cable

Among the few functional expenditures that have been estimated across the country at all levels of candidacy, the most prominent is political broadcasting on television, radio, and cable. A report issued by the Television Bureau of Advertising indicated that the political expenditure volume on the broadcast networks and local television stations hit an all-time high of $300 million in 1992. Included in this figure are advertising for presidential, state, and local elections, with 75 percent of the spending concentrated on local television stations. Los Angeles was the leading political spending market in the country, with $19.2 million, followed by New York with $13.9 million, and Philadelphia with $10.6 million.[37] Most candidates for political office at the state and local levels never buy any television advertising time or even get near a television camera. Usually, only serious candidates for major offices—presidential, senatorial, and gubernatorial— make substantial use of television advertisements. Probably only about one-half of the House candidates purchase television time, and its cost often represents just a small portion of their campaign spending.

The costs of television in a given election year are difficult to pinpoint due to the design of the FEC disclosure forms. For example, the costs of writing, producing, and running the spot may be hidden in other categories on the disclosure form—such as the unspecified "consultant" category—making it difficult to ascertain the exact broadcast-related costs. The Television Bureau of Advertising figures show the growing costs of airing advertisements for political campaigns in aggregate terms, combining federal, state, and local candidates and committees, but do not estimate production costs—which can be as much as 25 percent to 33 percent of air time costs.

As noted, not every candidate uses television advertising. For some, it is simply too expensive. Most House challengers, for example, did not raise enough money in 1992 to produce and run a single professionally written television spot. Then there are the cases of incumbents running without opposition who would appear foolish to voters if they spent a great deal of money on television advertisements. And House candidates whose districts are covered by the costliest media markets—such as New York City, which includes forty congressional districts in a tristate area—are more likely to spend their money on direct mail and radio rather than buy television time that blankets not only their district but sections of huge metropolitan areas whose viewers are unable to vote for the candidate. And there are many local campaigns for which television is simply not cost-efficient. And many candidates simply cannot afford television.

Estimates also are available for radio expenditures across the country. According to an official at the Radio Bureau of Advertising, who conducted a survey, expenditures for political campaigns in mainly large and medium radio stations totaled some $22.4 million; with small markets included, perhaps the total would be $30 million, or 10 percent of television costs. Of the $22.4 million recorded, which includes spending by candidates and parties, and on issues, the heaviest months of expenditure were October, with $7.5 million, and November, with $7 million.[38]

Political broadcasting is a growth industry on cable. According to a Cable Network executive, "both national and statewide races are making spot cable an integral part of their television advertising mix."[39] The estimated amount spent on national spot cable political advertising is $4.5 million. This figure does not include locally placed cable spots, time costs for infomercials, or any program-length usage. The typical cable buy is only a few networks, not across the spectrum—the largest buys being on CNN, Headline News, USA, TNT, Lifetime, and ESPN channels.

Table 8.1

Television Expenditures: Presidential Prenomination, 1992

	Clinton	Bush
National network	0	$145,128
Local spots	$4,222,000	4,733,197
Cable	257,000	0
	$4,479,000	$4,878,325

Source: Citizens' Research Foundation.

Note: Clinton also reported radio, $681,000; print media, $50,000.

Media Expenditures: Presidential Prenomination

Media costs in the presidential campaigns, calculated internally by campaign operatives, were made available to the authors for this study, separately for the pre- and post-nomination campaigns.

Table 8.1 shows the media placement, or on-air, expenditures for the Clinton and Bush prenomination campaigns. It is surprising that Bush—an incumbent, challenged only by Pat Buchanan, and certain to be renominated—spent more than Clinton, who was heavily challenged early on in the Iowa caucuses and the New Hampshire primary, the two earliest state events. In all, Clinton spent $4,479,000 on television, while Bush media expenditures on television were $4,878,325. Clinton used significant amounts of cable advertising, costing $257,000. None of Clinton's opponents for the Democratic nomination were heavy media spenders because none had large amounts of money available. Nevertheless, Kerrey spent $1,530,000 on media production and time expenses, and Tsongas spent in excess of $1.1 million. Brown's media spending was close to $300,000.

A case study by L. Patrick Devlin estimates that in the New Hampshire primary, Democratic candidates spent about $2.5 million on television advertising, and Republican candidates spent about $1.5 million. There is only one television station in New Hampshire, WMUR, but candidates also advertise in adjacent cities, mainly Boston, Massachusetts, Portland, Maine, and Burlington, Vermont, each with viewing ranges into New Hampshire. Devlin studied the WMUR logs and calculated amounts spent on that channel, and in some campaigns total amounts spent on television advertising related to the 1992 New Hampshire primary, as shown in Table 8.2.[40]

Table 8.2

Television Advertising in New Hampshire, 1992

Candidate	WMUR	Total in New Hampshire
Democrats		
Kerrey	$155,000	$700,000[a]
Clinton	133,000	
Harkin	72,000	650,000
Tsongas	54,000	430,000
Brown	25,000	60,000
Cuomo (write-in)	20,000	
Republicans		
Buchanan	135,000	
Bush	104,000	
Lennane	42,000	

Source: L. Patrick Devlin, "Television Advertising in the 1992 New Hampshire Presidential Primary Election," *Political Communication* 11 (1994), pp. 81–99. Reproduced with permission of Taylor & Francis, Inc. All rights reserved.

[a]Other information, including spending on cable, radio, and production costs, indicates that Kerrey media expenditures relating to New Hampshire were close to $1.2 million. See chapter 3, p. 59.

Media Expenditures: Presidential General Election

The authors received exclusive internal compilations of media expenditures from each of the three major general election campaigns—Clinton–Gore, Bush–Quayle, and Perot–Stockdale—totaling $92.3 million, as shown in Table 8.3. The Clinton and Bush compilations include coordinated expenditures made on media advertising by the Democratic and Republican national committees on behalf of their presidential tickets. If production costs, undeclared in two of the three campaigns, are added in, there is no doubt that a combined total of more than $100 million was spent on broadcasting from the time of the conventions for Clinton and Bush, until election day, and for the entire Perot campaign.

Additionally, as shown in the previous section, for the Clinton and Bush prenomination campaigns, advertising expenditures totaling $5,210,000 (including television, radio, and print media) and $4,878,325, respectively, were divulged and should be added into the overall total of presidential broadcast costs—$102.4 million. Thus the presidential amounts account for about one-third of all political broadcast costs, estimated at $300 million in 1992 by the Bureau of Television Advertising.

The Clinton campaign specified additional radio costs at $1,949,000,

Table 8.3

Television Expenditures: Presidential General Election, 1992

Candidates	Clinton	Bush	Perot
National network	$7,247,000	$5,521,662	$19,870,387
Local spots	24,246,000	21,683,011	11,297,816
Cable	1,195,000	448,017	716,133
Totals	$32,688,000	$27,652,690	$31,884,336

Source: Citizens' Research Foundation.

related print or "tune-in" advertising at $34,000, and production and creative charges separated out at $2,943,000; additional Clinton production and creative costs may have been included within certain of the television or radio categories.

Table 8.3 shows that Bush spent $27.7 million, almost $5 million less than Clinton, who spent $32.7 million, although that figure includes radio and production cost extras. In all, Clinton showed thirty television ads while Bush aired twenty-four; both actually produced more.[41] Clinton spent the most on local spot announcements—$24.2 million—indicating a targeting strategy pointing to specific states, presumably those thought to have winnable electoral votes. Clinton also spent the most on cable, $1.2 million, as much as Bush and Perot combined, indicating a strategy using inexpensive means to reach certain special audiences. Perot spent by far the most on national networks, $19.9 million, suggesting a national strategy seemingly not dictated by electoral vote considerations but by an approach designed to maximize scattered individual votes, to get as high a national vote percentage as possible. Perot also spent $761,133 on cable, seeking to reach special audiences, such as CNN's.

Position Papers and Books

Position papers and candidates' books were highly touted. In the prenomination period, Tsongas published the first and the longest paper, "A Call to Economic Arms." Clinton's paper, "A Plan for America's Future," was part of a commercial early in the campaign, in which he suggested people visit a local library to see a copy. He also put out a position paper on his economic plan. Harkin's paper, "A Blueprint to Build a New America," was the shortest at twenty-five pages and was apparently published to keep up with the competition. Although position papers themselves are by no means new to campaigns, they had never been quite so visible in the past.[42]

In the general election, Clinton and Gore published a book, *Putting People First*. And Perot had published *United We Stand*, a book whose title became the name of his post-election organization. While both books ranged over a great number of public policy issues, what the candidates said about election reform is most pertinent to this book.

The book Clinton and Gore wrote set forth their ideas about campaign finance reform, which was covered in a page and one-half. The ideas were more explicit than those in the Democratic platform but were laid out in only the most sketchy way. Starting strongly by saying that "American politics is being held hostage by big money interests," and blaming Bush for vetoing the 1992 campaign reform bill, the authors called for spending limits; reducing PAC contribution limits to $1,000; reducing the cost of television air time; eliminating soft money contributions; and eliminating tax deductions for special interest lobbying expenses.[43] All the ideas were conventional reformist positions and failed to offer any new or elaborated arguments. They were precursors to positions taken by the Clinton administration once it took office. Curiously, in the book, Clinton and Gore did not tie spending limits to public funding, as is necessary under *Buckley;* there was no mention of public funding in the book, only expenditure limits.

As for Perot, he suggested that contributions be limited to $1,000, even for PACs and parties, although at times he spoke of eliminating PACs entirely. He wanted to reduce the influence of the "special interests" but was not very specific on how. He recommended restrictions on lobbyists and on political and administrative government employees quitting and then working as lobbyists (the revolving door). Clinton's proposal regarding lobbyists was very much along the same lines. Perot suggested strengthening the FEC, making it a nonpartisan rather than a bipartisan agency. He proposed that the commission consist of five members, appointed at staggered times, to avoid tie votes. The reconfigured FEC would need a new approach to enforcement and would be given increased powers to prosecute violations.[44]

Perot was quick to attack the use of government jets for cabinet members and White House staffers. Perot suggested, "They should go out to the airport, get in line, lose their baggage, eat a bad meal, and stay in touch with how normal people live."[45] This was in contrast to Clinton, who was eager to point out that the use of government aircraft gives the incumbent president an advantage over the challenger.[46]

Some of Perot's most strident remarks about the political system were those concerning foreign lobbyists. Perot also wanted to eliminate the "lawyers' loophole," which allows lawyer-lobbyists to disguise lobbying activities on behalf of corporations and foreign governments, and Clinton followed suit on this idea. While Perot was eager to attack foreign lobbyists, several of his suggestions for reform, such as prohibiting foreigners from making campaign contributions, already exist in the law. He urged the tightening of disclosure laws as well as government employee ethics codes but was no more specific than other candidates as to how this would be done. Perot would prohibit anyone lobbying for a "foreign interest" to serve on a congressional or presidential campaign, even as a volunteer.[47]

Perot put some of his ideas to work. He had input with certain members of Congress on the pending campaign finance and lobbying legislation, he engaged constitutional scholars to develop ideas on campaign finance and ethics, he reiterated his ideas in a spring 1993 television program, and he commissioned a poll to measure public support on the issues.

The New Age of High-Tech Campaigning

The 1992 campaign became the locus for a struggle between the new and old media. One columnist wrote: "There's Old Media: the nets, big newspapers and news magazines, Washington-based op-ed chin-pullers, public TV and influential journals of political opinion. Then there's New Media: CNN, C-SPAN, 'infotainment' talk shows like 'Larry King Live' and 'Donahue,' computer bulletin boards and satellite hookups."[48] The mainstream press competed with a more populist, democratic style of televised presidential coverage that emphasized viewer participation.

Election year 1992 was a milestone in the introduction of new technology into campaigning. Clinton as well as Harkin used videos of five to fifteen minutes in length to raise money and recruit volunteers. The announcements of their candidacies were designed to serve as key components of both Clinton's and Harkin's tapes. Early on, in December 1991, all of the 2,000 delegates to a Florida convention, who were holding a straw poll, received a videotape from Clinton sent directly to their homes. Harkin's tape was shown at more than 1,100 events. Bob Kerrey used videos in focus groups, testing what voters thought about him. Since the tapes cost about $1 each to produce, they are a rather inexpensive and potentially a very useful medium.[49]

While videos are not meant to be a widespread replacement for conventional campaign methods, many believe they complement these. They seem to be especially useful in getting the support of the undecided. For example, in New Hampshire, Clinton distributed 20,000 copies of a twelve-minute video to undecided voters in a door-to-door canvass; Clinton operatives phoned a sample of the voters and claimed 70 percent said they had watched. Also in New Hampshire, Clinton aired a one-half-hour question-and-answer program with undecided voters and also did a one-half-hour live call-in show. These were innovations as well.[50]

Fax broadcast services also were a new high-tech campaigning mechanism. The Clinton–Gore campaign was said to have faxed at least 10,000 messages of one type or another every day. Before Bush had finished his acceptance speech at the convention, the Clinton campaign already had sent out more than 100 faxes to the news media disputing Bush's claims. Fax broadcast services can handle more than 500 transmissions per hour with the use of multiple transmissions simultaneously on different lines. Due to the bulk quantities, these services can negotiate lower rates, thus reducing telephone expenditures.[51]

Brown and Perot used 800 numbers to facilitate the raising of campaign contributions from the general public. Brown mentioned his toll-free number every chance he got during radio and television interviews, debates, and forums. This was not very well received by the media. Sometimes Brown's hand-held sign was blacked out or he was silenced by a beep to prevent the audience from getting what could be considered free advertising or solicitation of money. Perot's 800 number had the capability of identifying the callers' numbers, making for easy compilation of statistics.[52]

Brown also tried in New Hampshire a "documercial," a form of an "infomercial" in which fund raising was part of the format. Some $10,000 was spent to test it in four cities, and with widespread use of Brown's 800 number, it was said to have brought in $21,000. Brown's campaign produced 10,000 copies of the "documercial" edited down to twenty-one minutes and distributed it to anyone who volunteered to hold a party for him or come out to see him.[53]

In mid-September, Clinton ran a thirty-second commercial in twenty states touting his plan to create jobs, which was directed at Democrats who had voted for Reagan and Bush. At the end of the ad, an 800 number appeared for people who wanted a copy of the plan. Clinton used 800 numbers before this ad to advance his proposals, but Bush did it for the first time in an advertisement on the economy in mid-September.[54]

Television also was used in an alternative way. Talk shows such as comedian Arsenio Hall's, on which Clinton appeared playing the saxophone, are not traditionally programs where presidential candidates used to appear. The candidates appeared on talk shows on radio and television. Town hall meetings connected by satellite also experienced a boom. In the 1992 general election period, all three major candidates—Clinton, Bush, and Perot—used a Perot innovation, "infomercials." Brown spent hours on CompuServe talking to computer users throughout the country. The Perot campaign used computers intensively to help distribute campaign literature, for scheduling, and to send messages around the country. Computers also were used in identifying potential contributors. The Clinton–Gore campaign used electronic mail to distribute press releases.[55]

Other applications of high-tech computer technology were mapped out in a 1988 Annenberg Washington Program special colloquium, "New Technologies in Political Communications." Developments included the ability of campaign managers to "trace out a proposed district on a computer screen and receive a complete breakdown of the area's demography and voting behavior, [the ability to] produce an audio/visual message aimed at a specific group of voters and see it delivered to thousands of them at a cost of often less per/contact than broadcast advertising."[56]

The three major television networks and CNN shared videotape coverage in the New Hampshire primary to cut down on costs. In 1988, the networks had been criticized for focusing "too much effort on staged events, and for televising some less-than-newsworthy events simply to justify the money spent covering them."[57] Network executives also discussed a proposal to have an outside organization, such as the Election Satellite Network, provide videotape of all the candidates' daily activities.[58]

Marvin Kalb, director of the Shorenstein Barone Center at Harvard, commented on the extraordinary changes in the televised coverage of the presidential election, pointing out that the ground rules for television campaigning have changed: "It's a turf war between the new media and the old—between the talk shows and traditional evening news, between electronic populism and an elite corps of political reporters, between 'the people' (of all people!) asking questions of substance in the White House Rose Garden and inside-the-beltway pros asking about what interests them—process, polls and 'character.' "[59]

Prenomination television formats ranged from call-in shows to talk shows to town halls. Referring to Tsongas, who won the Democratic primary in New Hampshire, one reporter stated: "The Democratic primary was won by a homely candidate with a small advertising budget who was initially written off by the press and did not run any negative or even very interesting commercials."[60] Clinton addressed negative publicity with "several novel media strategies, including answering questions from voters on two live thirty-minute television programs bought by his campaign."[61] One reporter observed that Perot made his own contribution to broadcasting to "short-circuit government gridlock with nationwide electronic town halls."[62] In a study by the Freedom Forum Media Studies Center at Columbia University, it was suggested that town hall meetings "allow candidates to direct the discourse on their own terms. But the high costs involved in creating their own programs make talk shows an attractive alternative."[63]

Other dimensions of the 1992 campaigns and their coverage by the electronic media were discussed in a report of a Task Force on Television and the Campaign of 1992, sponsored by the Twentieth Century Fund. While much of the subject matter of this report is beyond the purview of this book, several items are well worth the reader's time.[64]

Independent Expenditures

In *Buckley,* the Supreme Court ruled that individuals and groups may spend unlimited amounts on communications advocating the election or defeat of clearly identified candidates, provided the expenditures are made without consultation or collaboration with the candidates or their campaigns.[65] Following the ruling, the 1976 FECA Amendments imposed no limitations on independent expenditures on behalf of, or in opposition to, federal candidates. Individual donations to independent expenditure committees, however, are restricted to a maximum of $5,000 to each multicandidate committee and $1,000 to each single-candidate committee. Moreover, any contributions to committees making independent expenditures are counted against the contributors' $25,000 overall limit to all federal campaigns annually. But there can be no limit on direct or out-of-pocket independent expenditures by an individual or a PAC.

By 1980, groups and individuals inclined to make independent expenditures had developed sufficient familiarity with the election law to spend about $2.7 million in the presidential prenomination campaigns, about $1.6 million of it reported as expenditures on Reagan's behalf. Subsequently, independent expenditures became the object of considerable litigation.

In July 1980, Common Cause and the FEC filed suit against a number of groups that had announced plans to spend money independently on behalf of Reagan in the general election. Among other things, the complainants argued that the proposed independent spending would violate a provision of the Presidential Election Campaign Fund Act that prohibited organized political committees from spending more than $1,000 on behalf of a candidate who has become eligible to receive public funds. The specific provision, Section 9012(f)(1) of the Internal Revenue Code, never was directly considered in *Buckley* and was left untouched when Congress rewrote the election law in 1976 to conform with the court's ruling. A three-judge federal district court panel rejected the suits, striking down Section 9012(f)(1) as an unconstitutional restriction of the First Amendment rights of individuals. The complainants appealed the decision, but it was too late to affect independent spending in the 1980 general election. Groups and individuals reported spending substantial sums independently, with the bulk of it, $10.6 million, reported on Reagan's behalf. In January 1982 the Supreme Court upheld the decision by reaching a 4-to-4 deadlock in the case, but issued no opinion. Since the vote was equally divided, the Court's decision had no value as a precedent and applied only in the District of Columbia circuit.

Faced with the possibility that groups and individuals might spend large amounts independently on behalf of Reagan in the 1984 campaign, in 1983 the FEC and the DNC brought suit in the U.S. District Court for the Eastern District of Pennsylvania against the National Conservative Political Action Committee (NCPAC) and the Fund for a Conservative Majority (FCM), two groups that had announced plans to conduct pro-Reagan independent expenditure campaigns in 1984. The court refused to allow the FEC to implement Section 9012(f)(1), and the commission filed an appeal with the Supreme Court. The high court declined to expedite the appeal and did not hear oral arguments in the case until late November 1984, after the general election. In March 1985, the court, in a 7-to-2 vote, struck down Section 9012(f)(1) as unconstitutional.[66] Justice William Rehnquist, writing for the majority, declared that the provision failed to serve a compelling government interest, such as avoiding corruption or its appearance, and that, accordingly, the provision's restrictions of First Amendment rights could not be upheld. In dissent, Justice Byron White took issue with the identification of money and speech, arguing, as he had in *Buckley,* that the First Amendment protects the right to speak, not the right to spend.

Some observers argue that in many cases in which the commission appears to be at odds with the First Amendment, the fault lies with the campaign law and not with the agency mandated to administer and defend it. That argument was made regarding the NCPAC case. Commission defenders maintain the FEC had no choice but to seek an injunction of NCPAC's proposed independent spending because Section 9012(f)(1) prohibited such spending beyond $1,000. In light of a number of court decisions castigating the commission for its insensitivity to First Amendment rights, however, critics question whether involvement in such cases represents a wise use of FEC resources or an appreciation by the agency of the importance of freedom of speech in the political arena.

1992 Overview

During the 1991–92 election cycle, 217 entities—182 political groups (mainly PACs) and thirty-five individuals—reported independent expenditures of about $11 million for or against presidential and congressional candidates, as shown in Tables 8.4 and 8.5. In comparison with the 1984

Table 8.4

Independent Expenditures: Presidential and Congressional Campaigns, 1980–92 (in $ millions)

	Presidential	Congressional
1980	$13.7	$2.3
1984	17.4	6.0
1988	14.3	7.1
1992	4.4	6.6

Source: Citizens' Research Foundation, based on Federal Election Commission data.

Table 8.5

Independent Expenditures: Presidential and Vice Presidential, Prenomination and General Elections, 1992

	For	Against
General Election		
Bush	$2,027,531	$34,648
Clinton	533,116	506,758
Duke	0	16,306
Gore	0	0
Perot	59,715	12,254
Quayle	333	684
Subtotal	2,620,695	570,650
General election total	$3,191,345	
Prenomination[a]		
Brown	$627	0
Buchanan	296	0
Bush	1,021,586	24,000
Clinton	32,224	45,603
Duke	0	43,135
Jackson	0	4,727
Quayle	0	44,352
Tsongas	22,983	4,242
Subtotal	1,077,716	166,059
Prenomination total	1,243,775	
Total presidential	$4,435,120	

Source: Federal Election Commission, 1991–92, Candidate Index of Independent Expenditures, as of November 9, 1993.

[a]Presidential prenomination period includes all expenditures made through July 15 for the Democratic candidates and all expenditures made through August 15 for the Republicans. The difference is based on the timing of the nominating conventions.

and 1988 election cycles, independent spending in 1991–92 represented a decrease of about 50 percent.[67]

In 1992, the major part of the total amount of independent expenditures—nearly $8.8 million—was spent on behalf of candidates. The lesser part—$2.2 million—was spent against certain candidates.

While there was a sharp decrease in independent expenditures, there was no significant change in the number of individuals and PACs making these kinds of expenditures. PACs made the most independent expenditures, spending almost 98 percent of the total. Of the $10.8 million, $8.6 million was spent on behalf and $2.2 million against federal candidates. The following list, compiled by the FEC, shows the top ten independent spending PACs:

1. Presidential Victory Committee (nonconnected)	$2,057,757
2. National Right to Life PAC (National Right to Life Inc.)	1,609,884
3. American Medical Association PAC (American Medical Association)	1,024,210
4. Realtors PAC (National Association of Realtors)	999,016
5. NRA Political Victory Fund (National Rifle Association)	957,666
6. National Abortion Rights Action League PAC (National Abortion Rights Action League)	718,756
7. Freedom Leadership PAC (nonconnected)	189,950
8. Clean Up Congress FKA Accountability Project (Willamette Citizens)	169,433
9. American Citizens for Political Action (nonconnected)	169,250
10. Public Citizen Inc. Fund for a Clean Congress (Public Citizen Inc.)	150,193

The amounts spent by individuals on independent expenditures were approximately $240,000 on behalf of, and nearly $93,000 against, specific candidates.

Independent Expenditures and Congressional Elections

Independent expenditure campaigns in congressional races tend to mirror a growing tendency of PACs supporting incumbents to get their attention and appreciation. One reason PACs may lean toward independent expenditures is to influence the behavior of congressional candidates, and to circumvent the restrictions on direct contributions by an alternative way of participation.[68] This is especially true for trade and industry PACs, as opposed to ideological PACs.

To compare one, the Realtors PAC was number one in independent expenditures in 1988—with an amount of $3,045,769—and it was only number four in 1992, spending $999,016.

Table 8.6

Independent Expenditures: Congressional Elections, 1992

	For	Against
House	$3,110,104	$889,686
Senate	1,919,924	693,351
Total		$6,613,065

Source: Federal Election Commission, 1991–92, Candidate Index of Independent Expenditures, as of November 9, 1993.

About the same amount of independent money was spent in favor of candidates of both major parties: $2.5 million for Republicans, with about $2.4 million for Democratic congressional candidates. In contrast, spending against candidates was in an imbalance. While $1 million in negative spending was targeted against Democrats, only $600,000 was spent against Republicans. The development of independent expenditures in congressional campaigns shows that although the overall amount remained quite stable—$5.8 million in 1984, $7 million in 1988, and, as shown in Table 8.6, $6.6 million in 1992—negative spending decreased from $2.5 million in 1984 to $1.6 million in 1992, and did not play the excessive role it had earlier.[69]

Independent spending, while an important factor in political finance, should not be overrated. The trend since 1980 shows that it is not a widespread alternative used by wealthy contributors or PACs, because massive amounts of money from these sources are more likely to be contributed as "soft money." Nor have independent expenditures become an important source of negative campaigning. It remains to be seen whether independent expenditures will increase and become a significant political finance instrument if reform legislation outlaws or reduces PAC giving in its present form.

Independent Expenditures and Presidential Elections

In 1984, the amounts of independent expenditures during the presidential campaigns were nearly three times higher than in the congressional races. In 1988, the sum was two times higher. The 1991–92 cycle shows a reversal: presidential independent expenditures were about 30 percent less than in the congressional campaigns (see Table 8.7).

Table 8.7

Independent Expenditures in the Presidential General Election, 1992

	For	Against
George Bush (total)	$2,027,531	$34,648
Groups	1,972,712	34,648
Individuals	54,819	0
Bill Clinton (total)	533,116	506,758
Groups	529,214	472,030
Individuals	3,902	34,728
Ross Perot (total)	59,715	12,254
Groups	45,502	12,254
Individuals	14,213	0

Source: Citizens' Research Foundation compilation, based on Federal Election Commission data.

More than 75 percent of independent expenditures on behalf of a presidential candidate in the general election period was spent in favor of Bush. About 70 percent of independent expenditures made against a candidate advocated the defeat of Bill Clinton (see Table 8.5).

Floyd G. Brown, a conservative political strategist who operated the National Security PAC in 1988 in its direct-mail operation and production of the controversial Willie Horton television commercial, set up the Presidential Victory Committee in 1992.[70] This group created an independent expenditure campaign for Bush under the banner "Citizens for Bush." As with the National Security PAC in 1988, the effort was financed mainly by direct-mail receipts.

But the 1992 committee raised less than its 1988 counterpart, which put Brown under financial pressure. Therefore, Brown, who believes in aggressive messages, combined new technology with his innovative skills. He aired as sixty-second spots Flowers' allegations about a twelve-year love affair with Clinton.[71] In addition to the ads, which addressed the issue of Clinton's suitability and character, Brown offered a phone service on a Nevada long-distance line and a 900 telephone number. On this "Bill Clinton Fact Line," which cost $4.99 per call and contributed to the Presidential Victory Committee's fund raising—about 38,000 calls during the first thirty-six hours of operation—people could listen to "12 minutes of stale talk about sex, draft evasion and marijuana use."[72]

In contrast to the National Security PAC's financial success and effectiveness in the Horton commercial in 1988, Floyd G. Brown had somewhat less success in 1992. First, his attempt failed to convert a modest television buy into millions of dollars' worth of free publicity. Second, while the committee's independent expenditures exceeded $2 million, Brown clearly missed the self-set goal to raise $8 million to $10 million. And although his PAC's independent expenditures were the highest in 1992, administrative costs and fund-raising expenses swallowed up the largest portion of the amount.[73]

Nevertheless, the Horton and Flowers commercials show one serious concern about independent expenditures: the lack of accountability.[74] Although this type of expenditure mostly benefits a certain candidate, it may jeopardize a campaign strategy. Bush's campaign management, aware that Brown's activities were out of their control, filed a complaint with the FEC against Brown. The complaint asked the FEC to find Brown in violation of statutes that require a political group to state clearly who pays for its solicitations. Bush's campaign took further measures, including letters informing Brown's contributors that "Citizens for Bush" was not affiliated with Bush–Quayle '92.[75] Although the Presidential Victory Committee PAC's efforts neither helped nor hurt the Bush campaign very much, the independent expenditures "lack of accountability" remains a major problem.

Communication Costs in the 1992 Campaigns

In addition to the independent expenditure campaigns, there is another form of participation by groups not affiliated with the candidate that falls outside the FEC guidelines on PACs. This is the so-called "communication costs" category. The FECA prohibits corporations and labor unions from using their treasury funds to make contributions or expenditures in connection with federal elections. But corporations and labor organizations may participate in the federal election process by using their treasury funds to make partisan and nonpartisan communications. Partisan communications may be made only to the organization's restricted class—meaning by a corporation to its stockholders and executive and administrative staff and their families, or, in the case of a labor union or membership organization, to its members. Nonpartisan communications may be made to all employees and, in some cases, to the general public.

Corporations, labor unions, and trade, membership, and health organizations may conduct four types of unlimited partisan communications: (1) meetings between candidates or political party representatives and the organizations' restricted classes; (2) publications written and produced by the organizations; (3) telephone banks; and (4) voter registration and turnout drives. The costs of partisan communications that aggregate more than

Table 8.8

Communication Costs in Presidential and Congressional Campaigns, 1980–92 (in $ millions)

	1980	1984	1988	1992
For presidential candidates	$2.0	$4.7	$2.0	$4.2
Against presidential candidates	0.6	0.05	0.1	0.05
For House candidates	0.8	1.0	1.1	2.3
Against House candidates	0.1	0.06	0.0	0.01
For Senate candidates	0.3	0.6	1.2	1.9
Against Senate candidates	0.05	0.0	0.02	0.07
Total	$3.9	$6.4	$4.4	$8.5

Source: Citizens' Research Foundation, based on Federal Election Commission data.

Table 8.9

Communication Costs: Presidential Campaigns, 1992

	Prenomination		General	
	For	Against	For	Against
Brown	$45,451	0	N.A.	N.A.
Bush	0	5,727	760,081	51,099
Clinton	646,494	0	2,730,989	0
Harkin	4,615	0	N.A.	N.A.
Perot	N.A.	N.A.	0	1,727
Subtotal	$696,560	$5,727	$3,491,070	$52,826
Total	$702,287		$3,543,896	

Source: Federal Election Commission, 1991–1992, Communication Cost Index by Communication Filers, as of July 10, 1993.

$2,000 per election must be reported to the FEC by the organizations that conduct them, unless those communications are primarily devoted to subjects other than candidate advocacy.[76] In that case, no reporting is required.

Communication costs in the 1992 presidential campaigns, which accounted for $4.2 million (see Table 8.8 and 8.9), increased about 50 percent from 1988, when only $2 million was spent. But the amount did not reach the 1984 high, when some $4.8 million in communication costs was spent.

Table 8.10

Communication Costs: House and Senate Campaigns, 1992

	For	Against
House	$2,263,781	$12,673
Senate	1,945,695	76,162
Subtotal	$4,209,476	$88,835
Total	$4,298,311	

Source: Federal Election Commission, 1991–92, Communication Cost Index by Communication Filers, as of July 10, 1993.

Communication costs in House campaigns have risen continuously since 1980: from $800,000 in 1980 to $1 million in 1984, $1.1 million in 1988, and a record of $2.3 million in 1992. The Senate campaigns show a similar picture. Spending in these cases increased from $300,000 in 1980 to $600,000 in 1984, $1.2 million in 1988, and $1.9 million in 1992 (see Table 8.10). In the 1991–92 election campaigns, about $88,835 was spent on negative attacks.

Although the total amounts in the 1991–92 election cycle show a new high with $8.5 million in communication costs spending (see Table 8.8), there is no continuous upward trend since 1980, particularly in the presidential campaigns. There are several reasons for this. It is a question of interpretation by the filers as to the numbers and data which will be made available or which must be reported to the FEC. For example, no data are available regarding the amounts of money spent on partisan communications that did not reach the $2,000 reporting threshold or on communications advocating the election or defeat of candidates that were part of larger communications (such as regularly published newsletters) devoted primarily to subjects other than candidate advocacy. Nor is it possible to determine with precision the value of ostensibly nonpartisan communications, which in fact were targeted to reap maximum benefit for specific candidates or parties. Such communications include the publication of incumbents' voting records, voting guides describing candidates' positions, and joint sponsorship of nonpartisan voter drives with nonpartisan, tax-exempt organizations or state and local administration agencies. Costs for these types of communications may be paid for out of treasury funds, but the payments need not be reported to the FEC.[77] If there were more uniformity in reporting, the real amount of communication costs would probably be much higher.

The membership groups most likely to incur communication costs are labor unions, which explains why so much was spent in support of Clinton. Most of the largest labor unions give the maximum allowable contributions to their endorsed federal candidates through their PACs. Then they are free to spend whatever they feel is needed to communicate with their members about their endorsement of a particular candidate. This is the equivalent of a direct-mail campaign on behalf of a candidate, but it is considered as a communication cost, apart from other political spending.

In comparison with the 1988 prenomination period—when the AFL-CIO decided not to endorse any candidate and most unions waited until the general election to weigh in with their communications on behalf of a candidate—the communication cost spending in the 1992 prenomination period can be seen as a sign of early endorsement of Clinton's candidacy. The AFL-CIO/COPE Political Contributions Committee sent a clear signal to its affiliates and members by spending about $350,000 in communication costs during the pre-convention period on behalf of Clinton. This effort was supported by the American Federation of State, County, and Municipal Employees and certain other state and local unions, which together spent about the same amount as the AFL-CIO/COPE. In the general election, the endorsement of Clinton was echoed by other unions such as the American Federation of Teachers, the Communication Workers of America (CWA), the Amalgamated Clothing and Textile Workers Union (ACTWU), and the National Education Association (NEA). In all, they spent an aggregate amount of $2.7 million on behalf of Clinton. Communication costs on behalf of Bush accounted for only $760,000, and were spent without exception by the National Rifle Association.

Notes

1. *United States Communications Act (U.S.C.A.), U.S. Code,* vol. 4, sec. 315. Only circumstances in which the candidate himself or herself appears on a broadcast are covered by section 315.

2. Aspen Institute, 55 FCC 2d 697 (1975), *aff'd sub nom, Chisolm v. F.C.C.,* 538 F. 2d 349 (DC Cir. 1976).

3. Regarding Petitions of Henry Geller and the National Association of Broadcasters and the Radio-Television News Directors Association to Change Commission Interpretation of Certain Subsections of the Communications Act, BC Docket 82–564, FCC 83–529 (released November 16, 1983), *Federal Register* 48 (November 25, 1983): 53166.

4. Penny Pagano, "FCC Broadens Rule on Equal Time for Debates," *Los Angeles Times,* November 9, 1983.

5. Phil Gailey, "F.C.C. Lets Broadcasters Hold Political Debates," *New York Times,* November 9, 1983.

6. Michael Isikoff, "Networks Win in '84 Debates," *Washington Post National Weekly Edition*, November 21, 1983.

7. Gailey, "FCC Lets Broadcasters Hold Political Debates."

8. Isikoff, "'Networks Win in 84 Debates."

9. Robert B. Abeshouse, "FCC Watch: On the Impact of Televised Debates and Advertising," *Campaigns & Elections*, Spring 1984, p. 41.

10. *Federal Election Campaign Act (FECA), U.S. Code*, vol. 2, sec. 441B.

11. See 11 CFR 110.13; also 110.7(b)(21), 100.8(b)(23), and 114.4(e).

12. For a discussion of the circumstances surrounding the 1979 candidate debate regulations, see Herbert E. Alexander and Brian A. Haggerty, *Financing the 1980 Election* (Lexington, MA: Lexington Books, 1983), pp. 155–158.

13. *FECA, U.S. Code*, vol. 2, sec. 431(9)(B)(i).

14. Stephen Bates, *The Future of Presidential Debates* (Washington, DC: The Annenberg Washington Program in Communications Policy Studies of Northwestern University, 1993), p. 5.

15. Robert E. Hunter, ed., "Electing the President: A Program for Reform," *Final Report* of the Commission on National Elections (Washington, DC: The Center for Strategic and International Studies, 1986), pp. 41–44.

16. Ibid., back cover.

17. See the statement of Frank Fahrenkopf, co-chair, Commission on Presidential Debates, in U.S. Congress, Committee on House Administration, *Presidential Debates*, Hearings before the Subcommittee on Elections, 103d Cong., 1st sess., June 17, 1993, pp. 45–46.

18. Commission on Presidential Debates, "Commission on Presidential Debates Announces 1992 Plans, Releases Candidate Selection Criteria," press release, June 11, 1992.

19. "Bush Accepts Debates, Subject to Negotiations," *New York Times*, August 19, 1992; and Thomas Oliphant, "Baker Moves to Make the Debates More Comfy for Bush," *Boston Globe*, August 30, 1992, p. 67.

20. B. Drummond Ayres Jr., "Bush Rejects Panel's Plan for 3 Debates," *New York Times*, September 4, 1992.

21. Michael Kelly, "Clinton Says Bush is Afraid of Debating 'Man to Man,'" *New York Times*, September 19, 1992.

22. Edwin Chen, "Debate Uncertainty Hindering Clinton Schedule," *Los Angeles Times*, September 24, 1992.

23. Richard L. Berke, "Bush Shifts Stand, Saying He's Ready to Hold 4 Debates," *New York Times*, September 30, 1992.

24. Steven Herbert, "Debate Draws a Bigger TV Audience Than Super Bowl," *Los Angeles Times*, October 17, 1992.

25. Times Mirror Center for the People & the Press, "The People, The Press, and Politics: Campaign '92: Voters Say 'Thumbs Up' to Campaign, Process, & Coverage," Survey 13, November 15, 1992.

26. See the statement of Andrew Kohut, in Committee on House Administration, *Presidential Debates*, p. 70.

27. "Beltway," *PACs & Lobbies*, November 18, 1992, p. 8.

28. "Infofile," *National Journal*, May 22, 1993, p. 1257.

29. Bates, *The Future of Presidential Debates*, p. 8.

30. Ibid., p. 9.

31. The Freedom Forum Media Studies Center, "Covering the Presidential Primaries," *The Media and Campaign '92*, June 1992, p. 85.

32. *U.S.C.A., U.S. Code*, vol. 47, sec. 312(a)(7).

33. For the full story and citations, see Alexander and Haggerty, *Financing the 1980 Election*, pp. 220–22.

34. U.S. Congress, House Committee on House Administration, Task Force on Elections, *Campaign Finance Reform*, 1984 Hearings, 98th Cong., 1st sess. (Washington, DC: U.S. Government Printing Office, 1984), p. 684.

35. FCC, "Mass Media Bureau Report on Political Programming Audit," September 7, 1990, pp. 1–8.

36. Thomas B. Rosenthiel, "Candidates' Ad Rates Too High, FEC Says," *Los Angeles Times*, September 8, 1990.

37. Television Bureau of Advertising Inc., "Broadcast Television Political Ad Volume Hit Record High of $300 Million in 1992," press release, February 11, 1993.

38. Interview with Ken Costa, vice president for marketing information, Radio Bureau of Advertising, November 3, 1993.

39. Cable Networks Inc., "Political Advertising Outlays on Spot Cable Reach $100,000 Per Day," press release, July 10, 1992, pp. 1–2.

40. L. Patrick Devlin, "Television Advertising in the 1992 New Hampshire Presidential Primary Election," *Political Communication* 11, pp. 81–99.

41. L. Patrick Devlin, "Contrasts in Presidential Campaign Commercials of 1992," *American Behavioral Scientist* 32, no. 2, p. 286.

42. Elizabeth Kolbert, "Campaigns' New Prop: A Prescription in Print," *New York Times*, January 25, 1992.

43. Governor Bill Clinton and Senator Al Gore, *Putting People First: How We Can All Change America* (New York: Times Books, 1992), pp. 45–46.

44. Ross Perot, *United We Stand: How We Can Take Back Our Country* (New York: Hyperion, 1992), pp. 24–27.

45. Ibid., p. 28.

46. Associated Press, "Review Finds Bush Campaign Is Slow to Repay Taxpayers," *New York Times*, October 18, 1992.

47. Perot, *United We Stand*, pp. 24–27.

48. Jonathan Alter, "Why the Old Media's Losing Control," *Newsweek*, June 8, 1992, p. 28.

49. Thomas B. Rosenthiel, "Candidates Hope to Turn on Voters Via Campaign Videos," *Los Angeles Times*, January 8, 1992.

50. Devlin, "Television Advertising," p. 95.

51. Frank Tobe, "High Tech Campaigning Helped Produce Big Wins for Clinton/Gore in '92," *Politea*, April/May 1993, p. 4.

52. Ibid.

53. Devlin, "Television Advertising," p. 95.

54. Richard L. Berke, "Clinton Addresses Unemployment," *New York Times*, September 17, 1992.

55. Tobe, "High Tech Campaigning."

56. Newton N. Minow, correspondence to Herbert E. Alexander, January 5, 1988.

57. John Tierney, "Networks to Save in New Hampshire," *New York Times*, January 10, 1992.

58. Ibid.

59. Marvin Kalb, "From Sound Bite to a Meal," *New York Times*, July 3, 1992.

60. John Tierney, "Setback for the Media Manipulators," *New York Times*, February 20, 1992.

61. Ibid.

62. Robert Wright, "Washington Diarist," *The New Republic*, June 15, 1992, p.46.

63. Referred to in a study by the Research Group of the Freedom Forum Media

Studies Center, "An Uncertain Season Reporting in the Postprimary Period," *The Media and Campaign '92,* Columbia University, September 1992, p. 21.

64. Report of the Twentieth Century Fund Task Force on Television and the Campaign of 1992, *1–800-PRESIDENT,* with background papers by Kathleen Hall Jamieson, Ken Auletta, and Thomas E. Patterson (New York, NY: Twentieth Century Fund Press, 1993).

65. *FECA,U.S. Code,* vol. 424, sec. 51.

66. *Federal Election Commission v. National Conservative Political Action Committee, et al.,* 105 Sup. Ct. 1459 (1985).

67. In 1983–84, $23.4 million; in 1987–88, $22.1 million. See Herbert E. Alexander and Brian A. Haggerty, *Financing the 1984 Election* (Lexington, MA: Lexington Books, 1987), p. 116; and Herbert E. Alexander and Monica Bauer, *Financing the 1988 Election* (Boulder, CO: Westview Press, 1991), p. 84.

68. Candice J. Nelson, "Loose Cannons: Independent Expenditures," in Margaret Latus Nugent and John R. Johannes, *Money, Elections, and Democracy: Reforming Congressional Campaign Finance* (Boulder, CO: Westview Press, 1990), pp. 56–69.

69. See Nelson, "Loose Cannons"; and Alexander and Bauer, *Financing the 1988 Election,* pp. 84–86.

70. Carol Matlack, "The Thunderbolt from the Right," *National Journal,* May 30, 1992, p. 1309.

71. Ibid.

72. Ruth Marcus, "Bush Camp Files Complaint Against Horton Ad Maker," *Washington Post,* July 15, 1992; Laurence I. Barrett, "Baby Huey on Attack," *Time,* July 20, 1992, p. 31; and "Group Will Air TV Spots About Clinton," *Los Angeles Times,* July 9, 1992.

73. Howard Kurtz, "Hitting Clinton with Flowers by Wire," *Washington Post,* July 9, 1992.

74. Nelson, "Loose Cannons," p. 60.

75. Marcus, "Bush Camp Files Complaint."

76. CFR Sec. 114.2 and CFR Sec. 100.8.

77. For nonpartisan communications, see CFR Sec. 114.4.

9

Shaping Campaign Reform

Election reform was a charm issue in the 1970s. The FECA was enacted in 1971, strengthened in the wake of Watergate in 1974, and fine-tuned in response to the *Buckley* decision in 1976. Amendments in 1979 provided for what has come to be called soft money, in an attempt to recoup the faltering fortunes of political party organizations.

Since that time, all attempts to revise federal law have failed. The Republican ascension to the White House and control of the Senate in 1980 put reform into abeyance. It finally reemerged in 1986, when Senators David Boren (D-OK) and Barry Goldwater (R-AZ) offered a bill that would have capped the total amount of PAC money a member could accept. This effort to set aggregate limits elicited much positive response on and off Capitol Hill but failed to draw conclusive action before the 99th Congress adjourned.

After the Democrats regained control of the Senate in the 1986 elections, the Boren bill returned, this time co-sponsored by Majority Leader Robert Byrd (D-WV). By the time it had cleared the Rules and Administration Committee on a partisan vote, the bill was considerably broadened in scope and strengthened in character. Provisions in the new version of the bill included partial public financing for the general election campaigns of Senate candidates who agreed to limit their spending and raised an eligibility amount for individual contributions—the precise levels depending upon the voting-age population of the state. Aggregate PAC receipts were capped for all candidates (whether they had agreed to spending limits or not) and national party committees. Other prescribed restrictions included a bundling ban on PACs and their affiliated organizations, and broadened disclosure of soft money expenditures.[1]

While the goal of the bill was to reduce candidate dependence on PACs, the likely upshot would have been a shuffling of fund-raising tactics that would have diminished the influence of only the smaller committees. The aggregate limits were a new wrinkle that probably would have raised constitutional questions in the courts. And the provisions for public financing and spending limits guaranteed nearly unified Republican opposition, while providing the public relations cover needed by Democrats to withstand the pressures to enact reform. Cognizant that their own challenging and open-seat candidates tended to raise funds more easily than their Democratic counterparts, and determined to reverse their minority status, Republican leaders decried spending limits as a form of incumbent protection. They succeeded in taking advantage of popular distrust of government by casting the bill's public finance provisions as an attempted raid on the Treasury by greedy politicians.

Efforts to salvage the bill raised some innovative alternatives to public financing, such as lower rates on broadcast advertising and reduced postal rates for candidates accepting spending limits. But after a Republican caucus in June 1987 voted not to accept any public financing or spending limits, it gradually became evident that the bill was doomed.[2] Byrd was reduced at one point to ordering the arrest of Republican members to maintain a quorum; a leading opponent of the legislation was even forcibly carried into the chamber.[3] Partisanship immediately hardened beyond recall, and all eight cloture votes taken to shut off the filibuster against the bill came up at least five votes short.

In desperation, Sen. Ernest Hollings (D-SC) tried to float a constitutional amendment that would have short-circuited part of *Buckley* by allowing mandatory spending limits without the public funding trigger. Although a few Republicans were on record as favoring limits but opposing public financing, support for his resolution was far short of the necessary two-thirds majority. It ultimately failed to clear the sixty-vote cloture bar.[4]

While the 100th Congress had heard little public outcry for campaign finance reform, the climate would soon change for the 101st Congress. Presidential campaign fund raisers revealed their rosters of $100,000 donors during the 1988 general election race, awakening the media to the realities of soft money. When the new Congress tried to boost its pay by 25 percent in its first session, the subsequent public furor forced the Senate to abandon the raise and the House to forsake the taking of honoraria. Despite these displays of contrition, many voters took the episode as confirmation their representatives were becoming more venal and less responsive.[5]

That perception became rampant when the 1989 collapse of the savings and loan industry promised to leave the taxpayers a tab of several hundred billion dollars, and the search for scapegoats quickly came to the door of federal campaign finance. It was revealed that five senators, appearing together as a group in 1987, had pressured federal regulators into easing up on lender/developer Charles Keating, whose empire eventually collapsed, leaving the government a $2 billion liability. The Keating Five had received contributions totaling $1.3 million from the fallen financier for their various electoral projects.[6]

Disturbing evidence emanated from the 1988 elections as well: of the six House incumbents defeated in November, only one had not been tainted by scandal. Overall, the reelection rate was the highest in 198 years.[7] Incumbents took in six times more PAC money than their challengers, up from a 2.4-to-1 ratio only eight years before.[8] A new conventional wisdom was forming, one that ascribed an alleged congressional invulnerability to challengers, and devotion to special interests, to a political finance system increasingly dominated by lobbyists.

Republicans moved to take advantage of the new climate in the fall of 1989, expanding Bush's radical proposals into a twenty-five-point program for reform that surfaced in the House. The plan moved to emasculate PACs, by then predominantly sources of Democratic funds, and lifted all restraints on contributions from party committees, where the GOP had a 3-to-1 fund-raising advantage. Obviously, such a proposal had no assistance from Democrats.

In February 1990, Senate leaders George Mitchell (D-ME) and Bob Dole (R-KS) assembled a panel of experts on campaign finance, including the senior author, and charged it with charting a way through the partisan logjam. Its recommendations were presented one month later, and both Mitchell and Dole expressed optimism that reform could be achieved.[9]

The critical provisions dealt with a scheme for reasonably high and flexible voluntary spending limits that avoided the stumbling block of direct public financing. Postal and broadcast advertising discounts and 100 percent tax credits for in-state individual contributors, up to a certain level, were employed. Such in-state contributions from individuals would be exempt from spending limits. PAC money was only lightly discouraged, but its influence would have been reduced by the effect of the various incentives for sources of less interested campaign cash.[10] The common thread of the plan was its determination to expand selectively rather than restrict the resources available to campaigns. The day after the panel report was released, the latest incarnation of the Boren bill, labeled S 137, and by now popularly known as "Boren Again," was reported out of the Senate Rules Committee in seven minutes on a party-line vote. Whereas the new bill was basically a return to where the Democrats had left off on the issue in the previous Congress, the committee's quick action was instead a handoff to the Senate leaders, who were now charged with negotiating a compromise.[11]

Boren and Mitchell appear to have made a legitimate effort in that direction; within six weeks they had gotten the Democratic Caucus to sign onto the concept of exempting small, in-state individual contributions from spending limits, retaining flexibility up to 25 percent beyond the spending limit. By that time, however, Republican leaders had discarded their enthusiasm for the panel report and had set a plan in motion to use the campaign finance issue as a public relations tool for the 1990 elections.[12]

The Democratic leaders also faced a mutiny within their own ranks. DNC chairman Ronald Brown blasted the bill's tightening of soft money procedures, and the eleven Senate Democrats facing their first reelection in 1992 agitated against the spending limits, which an independent study suggested were low enough to crimp campaign communications seriously.[13] Most of the Class of 1986 had been narrowly elected from conservative states and had already raised and spent large sums. Potential challengers were likely to push the modest limits, allowing them to outspend the incumbents in the campaign's crucial stretch drive. Small-state senators were particularly livid; heavily dependent on PACs and out-of-state cash (which S 137 sought to curtail), they were especially vulnerable to last-minute infusions of national party cash, a GOP strong point whose influence would now be enhanced.

Partisan pressures and public clamor soon turned campaign finance reform into a political football game. Each party began loading popular reform ideas into legislative packages it knew the other could never accept. As soon as the Republicans offered an alternative bill that would have eliminated PACs, the Democratic Caucus proposed banning PAC contributions, after resurrecting the scheme for nearly full public financing. Each side concerned itself primarily with casting the other as the defender of PACs or high spending, and the enemy of reform. Senate negotiators found common ground on such provisions as broadcast ad discounts, a ban on bundling, mitigating the excessive use of personal funds, curbing independent expenditure campaigns, and toughening FECA penalties.[14] But the parties squabbled over exemptions and means of implementation, and ultimately broke off negotiations altogether over the issue of spending limits.[15]

Because members of the House were more dependent on PAC money than their colleagues in the Senate, action in the lower chamber was characterized by even less ambitious reform and even more determined pursuit of partisan interests. Democratic leaders, for example, pushed a sliding scale contribution limit on PACs that would have had the effect of severely constraining corporate committees while leaving those of labor unions untouched, an unmistakably partisan tack.

Egged on by mounting savings and loan cleanup bills and an advertising campaign against PAC supporters staged by Common Cause, constituents gave members an earful about campaign finance practices over the July 4, 1990, recess.[16] On returning, Dole sent Mitchell a letter endorsing the concept of spending limits, provided an exemption was made of in-state contributions of $250 or less.[17] But the Democratic Caucus rejected the Dole proposal and began retooling its bill into material for the fall election campaign; popular reforms (such as a blatantly unconstitutional PAC ban) were added, while unpopular ones (such as public financing) were dropped or severely curtailed.[18] Anticipating a veto from Bush over the spending limit provision, the Democrats were plainly loading their legislation with public relations features designed to satisfy reform groups and editorial writers, but which few of them actually wished to see enacted.

To allow each side to go on record as supporting campaign reform, Mitchell and Dole cut a deal: Republicans were permitted to move their amendments in exchange for eschewing a filibuster. After the GOP's alternative was defeated, S 137 passed on August 1 with but five Republican votes. Two days later, the House passed its much less restrictive Democratic bill (HR 5400), which had been further relaxed at the last minute by the Democratic Caucus: criminal penalties against excess spenders were dropped, soft money usage loosened, and a ban on bundling by lobbyists stricken.[19]

Public interest lobbies praised S 137 as an important step but derided HR 5400 as a sham.[20] In the end, the whole exercise proved much ado about nothing. When Congress reconvened after its August/Labor Day recess, it was immediately consumed by two crises: the Gulf War and the budget deficit. The unwieldy, forty-member conference committee charged with reconciling the bills never met, as achieving a quorum promised to be too daunting a task.[21]

Calculations and Miscalculations, 1991–94

Observers could be forgiven if they had by now concluded that members of Congress had not been serious about reforming the means of their own election. Each party seemed purposefully to craft its proposals for rejection by the other side of the aisle while avoiding practical compromise. While members assured themselves that the issue was arcane to the folks back home, in fact, an atmosphere for reform had been slowly building in the electorate. Over the years 1991–94, that would begin to change, as the infrastructure for change began to take shape.

The first seminal event unfolded on the nation's television sets in the late summer and fall of 1990, as the Senate probed the wreckage of the savings and loan debacle in general, and the Keating Five scandal in particular. Premonitions of doom became evident: a CBS News/*New York Times* poll found 71 percent of those surveyed believing that "most members of Congress are more interested in serving special interests than the people they represent," and the percentage of constituents who said their member deserved reelection routinely dropped ten points.[22]

Incumbents breathed more easily after the November 1990 elections brought little turnover, but it was a false sense of security. Only fifteen congressmen and one senator had gone down to defeat, but that was six more members than had lost in 1988. Moreover, the competition had been the thinnest in memory: only 10 percent of the House faced challengers who had held public office, while one-fifth faced no opposition whatever. Almost one-half, 47 percent, who had major party opposition in both 1988 and 1990 saw their winning percentages drop five points or more.[23]

Disturbing trends had continued relentlessly through each cycle since 1982: overall spending was up, the share of candidate contributions received from PACs was up, candidacies were down, contested races were down, successful challengers were down. In 1982, House incumbents spent $2.02 for every challenger dollar; eight years later that figure had risen to $3.65. Any viable potential challenger could not possibly miss the message: Running for Congress meant almost certain defeat. Voters had little reasonable alternative to voting for incumbents.[24]

Members were soon thrown on the defensive. "Unless these trends are recognized and dealt with," warned Senate Ethics Committee counsel Robert Bennett, ". . . the reputation of this body and its members will be utterly ruined."[25] It was a prophecy that Common Cause, Public Citizen, and Citizen Action mobilized to fulfill at the grass roots. For the first time, they were joined in this endeavor by the 33-million-member American Association of Retired Persons.[26]

In 1991, both Senate camps moved quickly to capitalize on campaign reform's newfound popularity. Boren, Mitchell, and Rules Committee chairman Wendell Ford (D-KY) trotted out S 137, stripped it of most of the concessions that had been made to Republicans, boosted its public financing provisions, and relabeled it S 3. Under this latest scheme, a candidate who complied with spending limits would receive a 75 percent discount on first-class mail, and a two-cent reduction for third-class mail. Such candidates also would be eligible for federal vouchers worth 50 percent of the spending limit for their states, to be redeemed for television ad time in blocks of one to five minutes. Restricting voucher use to long-form television spots was part of a conscious effort to make campaign communications more substantive. These provisions echoed the final, passed version of S 137, although the voucher's value had been increased 150 percent. In addition, the new bill would have required broadcasters to slash their rates for these candidates by half, making the total boost in voucher value fivefold.[27] This dramatic sweetening was addressed to both the spiraling cost of TV advertising and the deficient incentives of S 137.

Practical solutions were, in fact, much in evidence in S 3, but it appeared to be financially irresponsible. Only the postal discounts were accounted for by congressional appropriations. Public subsidies that would kick in for candidates who faced a noncomplying opponent could climb to double the spending limit and keep the complier better-financed than the offender up to that point. And TV vouchers, the main incentive, were still expected to be drawn on government funds, even though they need not have cost the taxpayers a cent: broadcasters could have been required to absorb their lost revenues as part of the public obligation carried by their federally granted licenses. The mood for such an imposition ripened in Congress, after a July 1990 FCC audit of twenty TV stations found sixteen of them charging candidates higher rates than any other client.[28] But the power of the TV news media apparently proved too intimidating for the Democratic leadership.

But the bill remained an easy one for Republicans to oppose. In addition to S 3's drains on the treasury and attempts to compromise the First Amendment (e.g., requiring candidates to appear in their ads, claiming sponsorship), nonpartisan research suggested its basic spending limits, $950,000 to $5.5 million, depending on the size of the state, were so low as to be unfairly constrictive to challengers.

Alternative Senate bills were floated, though none was expected to pass. Perhaps getting out ahead of his troops, Dole displayed innovative flexibility in two bills, S 6 and S 7, that embraced the concept of aggregate limits on large out-of-state donations and required broadcasters to provide five hours of free broadcast time for division among Senate candidates in lots as small as sixty seconds. And perhaps in an effort to make the Democratic leadership's bill look moderate, Senators John Kerry (D-MA), Bill Bradley (D-NJ), and Joe Biden (D-DE) floated a measure, S 128, that would have provided general election candidates with 90 percent public financing.

At a May 14 meeting of the Senate Democratic Caucus, six conservatives voiced opposition to the expense and lack of appropriation specifics in S 3, jeopardizing the fragile Democratic majority. The voucher values were scaled back to 20 percent of the spending limit, and two days later the leadership succeeded in passing a sense of the Senate resolution that called for the reforms to be funded by the elimination of tax deductibility for lobbying expenses. Boren assessed the revamped bill as costing $25 million per year, and the deduction elimination as yielding $1 million annually.[29]

Floor action on S 3 reprised that for S 137 the previous year in almost every respect. In both instances, an amendment calling for almost total government subsidization of campaigns was rejected, as was another that would have stricken spending limits. A proposal prohibiting senators from accepting speaking fees won approval both times, and the particulars of the final bills passed were a close match. The 1991 version, the Senate Election Ethics Act, passed the Senate on May 23, virtually untouched since it left the Democratic Caucus.[30]

Those who thought the reputation of Congress had nowhere to go but up in the spring of 1991 were quickly proved wrong by events that unfolded over the rest of the year. Following the example the House had set in the previous Congress, the Senate voted on July 17 to raise its pay to $125,100, a 24 percent boost. No matter that senators banned the keeping of honoraria at the same time; the message received outside the Beltway declared that greedy Washington politicians had lined their pockets again.[31]

A pair of embarrassing scandals were revealed in the fall. On September 18, the General Accounting Office reported that 8,331 bad checks had been drawn against members' accounts at the House Bank over a twelve-month period ending June 30, 1990. The checks had been paid out by the bank without penalty or interest charged to the offending congressmen.

The uproar sent reporters looking about for more egregious perquisites, leading them to the House restaurant, where members had run up tabs totaling hundreds of thousands of dollars. The news hit the front pages on the morning of October 3, sending Speaker Tom Foley into conference with House leaders. That afternoon, he announced that the House Bank would close, and that its operations would be the subject of an ethics panel investigation.[32]

The Democratic House bill had been in careful preparation for months, though the leadership had repeatedly delayed attempts to move it toward the floor. Staff members from the House task force on campaign finance had individually briefed Democrats on how the bill would affect their own campaigns, and the chamber's leading reformer, Mike Synar (D-OK), had agreed to be a co-sponsor rather than push his own more ambitious proposals.[33]

Drafted by task force chief Sam Gejdenson (D-CT), the bill differed markedly from the Senate version. House campaigns would be limited to $600,000 in spending, with no more than $200,000 coming from PACs. Candidates who won their primaries by less than ten percentage points could spend an additional $150,000, while those subjected to a runoff could tack on another $100,000. Legal and accounting expenses would not count toward the limit. Candidates accepting these restrictions could have their contributions of $200 or less matched by federal funds, up to an aggregate of $200,000. As in the Senate version of the bill, there was no formal provision for appropriating the money, only a suggestion that it come from the repeal of tax deductibility for lobbying expenses.[34]

With the various scandals raining down on their heads, members of the Democratic Caucus approved the Gejdenson bill on October 9, and the leadership formally proposed it on November 12 as HR 3750. The Conservative Democratic Forum (CDF), a group of forty-six Democratic congressmen led by Glen Browder (D-AL), asked the House Administration Committee to replace the direct public financing features in the bill with a 100 percent tax credit for contributions of $50 or less. Browder contended that credits were a more politically palatable form of public financing, but Gejdenson countered with evidence indicating such a plan would be much more expensive than the $75 million price tag on his direct approach. The committee approved an intact HR 3750, but it was becoming evident that the bill's provisions for direct public financing would have to be jettisoned in order for it to pass.[35]

Ten days later, Administration Committee chairman Charlie Rose (D-NC), Gejdenson, and three CDF leaders worked out a compromise that dropped the tax squeeze on lobbyists as a suggested means of funding the bill. The question of appropriations was left largely open, though language was added that called for incentives for individual contributions, and the Make Democracy Work Fund, created by voluntary donations to assist eligible candidates with funding, was included. The modified bill passed the House on November 25, 1991, in a 273-to-156 party-line vote.[36]

After four months of seeming inactivity on the subject, the conference committee on election reform finally met on March 31, 1992, with Mitchell and House Majority Leader Dick Gephardt presiding. As most of the details had been prearranged beyond the view of the Republican conferees, the proceedings advanced smoothly, and the Congressional Campaign Spending Limit and Election Reform Act was reported out on April 2, just eight days before the spring recess. The only serious conflict had been over soft money, with the House finally accepting most of the Senate's tougher restrictions and lower spending ceilings.

Committee Republicans denounced the agreement as a partisan sham hours before it was announced. Mitchell had conceded as much, saying, "It's important that the American people know we're trying to change the system," even though the bill faced a certain veto.[37] There could be no mistaking Bush's intentions. He had vowed to veto any package that included one of three features: an artificial ceiling on spending, the providing of public funds to candidates, and differing rules for House and Senate campaigns. The conference bill contained all three. Among other features were further restrictions on PACs; reductions of party spending, including prohibitions on soft money; curbs on bundling and independent expenditures; and a provision that the bill would not take effect until funds were appropriated for it.[38]

The conference bill passed the House on April 9, one day before the recess adjournment, by a vote of 259 to 165, far short of the 290 votes needed to override the anticipated veto. Only nineteen Republicans voted for the bill, only twenty Democrats against.

The Senate added its approval on April 30, shortly after returning from the recess. The 58-to-42 vote fell more starkly along party lines than the tally on S 3, with only three Republicans joining the majority. Two of those, David Durenberger (R-MN) and John McCain (R-AZ), had recently been under investigation for alleged breaches of ethics.

Reaction to the bill among opinion makers was not entirely positive. "The campaign finance reform drama has been played according to script," sneered syndicated columnist David Broder,"with winks and leers signaling the hypocrisy of all sides."[39] Most editorial writers for prominent dailies, however, continued to follow the lead of the good government lobbies, whose long knives began to hang over Bush. Common Cause wheeled its publicity machine into line behind the bill; group president Fred Wertheimer declared that a Bush veto would make "the corrupt campaign system in Washington . . . his personal responsibility."[40] Public Citizen joined in with a report that showed the president had taken more taxpayer money for his campaigns than any candidate in history, headed for a total of nearly $200 million by the end of the year.[41]

Bush was indeed vulnerable on the issue. Just two weeks before the election reform bill cleared the Congress, his reelection campaign listed five corporations as sponsors (major donors) on the program for a Bush-Quayle fund-raising dinner in Michigan, a blatantly illegal practice.[42] Speculation began to rise that the president might pull a fast one on the Democrats by signing the bill and forcing them to appropriate funds for it, in effect making them put the taxpayers' money where their mouths were.[43] In the end, however, the administration seemed satisfied with the marketability of its long-stated stance, and Bush vetoed the bill on May 9. Despite the negative editorial reaction, the Senate sustained the veto on May 13.

Change at the Ballot Box

When judgment day arrived on November 3, 1992, some thought it anticlimactic. Only twenty-seven congressional incumbents had lost, notably fewer than most pundits had anticipated. But closer examination of the returns and FEC reports revealed a sea change in public sentiment and campaign characteristics.

Widely seen as out of touch with common Americans, Bush had been turned out of office after garnering little more than a third of the vote. After mercilessly deriding the political establishment for months, Ross Perot had polled the highest third-line percentage of the presidential vote since ex-president Theodore Roosevelt in 1912. Costs of congressional candidacies climbed 52 percent.[44] And while incumbent losses were less than catastrophic, twenty had gone down in the primaries while another seventy-four, including many of the most vulnerable, had retired or sought another office, creating a larger-than-usual number of open seats.

Some members of the reform lobby pointed to the sharp rise in spending with alarm, yet the boost in campaign dollars was actually an encouraging sign for those who worried that the vitality of democracy had been flagging. It was the result of redistricting and increased competition, with more candidates out raising and spending funds and some worried incumbents spending from large war chests they had been stockpiling through several cycles of light opposition. With more than a quarter of the House and more than a third of the Senate now composed of freshmen (elected within the past four years), an argument could convincingly be made that the system was rectifying itself, without the aid of term limits or campaign reform.

Despite such indications, the prospects for campaign finance reform were brighter than they had been in nearly two decades. Both houses of Congress and the presidency were now held by Democrats, the party usually more prone toward reshuffling the campaign rules. The last time there had been so many freshmen on Capitol Hill (1975), a raft of procedural reforms had been enacted. With this latest batch of new arrivals coasting in on a wave of revulsion against the status quo, it appeared big changes would soon be in the making.

The Clinton administration's efforts to enact significant election reform made a good deal of progress in the early months of the 103d Congress. In May 1993, both houses passed and the president signed conference bill HR 2, Motor Voter, which, among other provisions, requires states to allow citizens to register to vote at the same time they apply for a driver's license. The conference had dropped one House provision allowing voter registration at unemployment offices and modified another that called for enrolling voters at welfare offices. Both moves were made to avoid a filibuster by Senate Republicans, who claimed the House proposals were motivated by partisan advantage.[45] Bush had vetoed a similar measure in 1992 for the same reasons, and an earlier version of the same bill had been derailed by a Senate filibuster in February 1992.

Also in May, the Senate passed a dramatic tightening of the lax lobbyist registration laws, adding a last-minute amendment from Paul Wellstone

(D-MN) that required lobbyists to report any gifts valued at more than $20 that they made to members of Congress or their staffs.[46] A considerable loosening of the Hatch Act, which had severely restricted the political activities of public employees, easily passed the House and seemed certain to become law after two decades of frustrated efforts. And the White House had finally brought forth its proposals for campaign reform.

In his State of the Union address on February 17, President Clinton had called for the enactment of campaign finance reform legislation that year. His sense of urgency reflected a conscious effort by his advisers to continue the momentum of the presidential campaign. Quickly, the new administration would have to establish in the public mind a sense that it was breaking up business as usual in Washington. If it failed to do so, it would soon be identified as part of the establishment within the nation's capital and all prospects of majority popular support would vanish. Campaign finance practices also seemed an inviting initial target since they had been a complaint of Ross Perot, whose nearly 20 million voters would be vital to the Clinton reelection strategy.[47] And Clinton's campaign promises on the subject had been outlined in his 1992 book with Gore, *Putting People First.*[48]

Painfully aware that any legislation they now approved would become law, House Democrats balked at the ambitious Clinton program. Many returning members had survived close calls in 1992, and history suggested that as members of the "in" party in an off year, they would face severe obstacles to reelection in 1994. Significant amounts of their campaign funds had come from PACs, and they suspected they might need every penny to withstand the tide of anti-incumbency.[49] Such fears were considerably less pronounced in the Senate, where PAC money made up a lesser amount of reelection kitties.

PACs were not the only stumbling block to majority party unity. Beneficiary of a particularly strong state party organization, the powerful twenty-one member Democratic House delegation from Texas was easily alarmed by proposals to abolish or tightly constrain soft money, as was the DNC, which had raised more soft money than ever before.[50] Further complicating the pressures on the House majority, a large contingent of conservative, mostly southern, Democrats led by Rep. Glen Browder, was adamantly opposed to direct public subsidies to campaigns.

In the week leading up to February 3, the administration held an increasingly important series of closed-door meetings with key Democratic congressional players on the campaign reform issue. Initially, political consultant Paul Begala huddled with House members, followed by meetings between congressional leaders and the president himself, first in the Capitol, and the next day at the White House.

Quickly, the new reform-minded president was given a crash course in Washington realities. Speaker Foley had just been reelected by an unimpressive ten points after outspending his hitherto-unknown opponent 2 to 1; some 72 percent of his funds had been drawn from PACs. The Speaker told both the president and reporters before the conferences even began, there was no chance that any reform affecting the 1994 elections would be considered. Robert Torricelli (D-NJ), leader of the stand-pat faction in the House, told Begala the Democrats might "lose control of the House" if the Clinton promises were enacted.[51] Speaking before a roomful of majority whips, Romano Mazzoli (D-KY), who had already foresworn PAC money and would soon announce his retirement, urged Clinton to press for the immediate imposition of his proposed rules. "All the other stuff you want to do is going to be harder to do or impossible to do," Mazzoli warned, "unless you reform the way campaigns are financed." The silence in the room was deafening.[52]

Foley was ultimately more persuasive, telling Clinton that he would desperately need votes in the upcoming battle over the administration's budget package, and that running through campaign reform at the same time would give waverers too much leverage, allowing them to play one vote against the other. Clinton meekly agreed not to posture on the issue. It was assigned to Michael Waldman, a junior thirty-two-year-old White House aide with a Nader-related reform background, and pushed to the back burner. Clearly, the president had to consider what would best help Democrats while formulating his proposals.

The public interest lobby was alarmed; some warned that Clinton was repeating a mistake made by President Jimmy Carter, who had been swept into office on a wave of anti-establishment fervor, only to see his designs for reform scuttled after assenting to a delay.[53]

Republicans watched the Democrats' dissolution of resolve with barely concealed glee. On January 21, Senate Minority Leader Dole had suggested publicly that partisan point men David Boren and Mitch McConnell (R-KY) work out a compromise on their own over a thirty-day period, an idea that Mitchell endorsed. Boren sent McConnell a letter on February 1, suggesting logistics for such a cooperative effort, but the Kentuckian was soon gloating over the disarray apparent on the other side of the aisle.

Boren and McConnell finally met on February 25, but it was soon evident they would be unable to fashion a compromise bill.[54] The Democratic majority proceeded to push S 3 with little regard for Republican sentiment. Only senators supporting the bill, or variations of it, were invited to testify at hearings held by the Committee on Rules and Administration.[55] The panel approved S 3 on March 18 by a party-line tally of 8 to 5, leaving it essentially the same legislation Bush had vetoed, the only difference being the addition of an aggregate ceiling on PAC contributions that brought it more in line with the House version.[56]

Senator Dianne Feinstein, a new member of the committee, had come ready to offer an amendment excepting ideological PACs from the bill's virtual ban on bundling but was told to save it for another day. Her proposal was on behalf of EMILY's List, a network of bundled contributors who had given $6.2 million to pro-choice Democratic women in the previous cycle, including $375,000 to Feinstein. The campaign for EMILY's exemption was an effort to ensure funding for compatible women candidates, but it was reproved by reform-minded editorialists, Clinton, and even political allies of EMILY'S List. "We must support strict campaign finance reform, without exception," wrote the Hollywood Women's Political Committee's Margery Tabankin in the *New York Times*. "Campaign reform success will be undermined if we allow bundling by some and not by others. . . ."[57] Some women called her a traitor to the feminine cause.

Another key Democratic power base at odds with the legislation taking shape was the DNC, which feared the financial base of the party's organizations would be severely undercut by the proposed ban on soft money for federal elections. DNC chairman Wilhelm proposed that individuals be allowed to give a total of $150,000 per year to state grass-roots organizing committees, plus an aggregate limit of $25,000 each to national party committees and federal candidates. As the current aggregate annual limit for an individual's contributions to federal campaigns was only $25,000 total, the Wilhelm scenario was soon shot down by both the White House and the public interest lobby.[58]

But the most formidable Democratic obstacle faced by the Clinton campaign reform agenda was the House Caucus, with its heavy reliance on PAC money and resistance to public financing. It had moved into the reform camp the year before, but only after repeated assurances that Bush would veto the legislation. After Foley admitted on March 9 that he did not think he could muster the votes for significant public funding,[59] the president ordered the House Democratic leadership to poll members on a proposal that would fund incentives through a raise in the election checkoff on tax forms from $1 to $5; if those funds proved insufficient, the needed money would be raised by ending the tax exemption for lobbying expenses. On March 30, Democratic whips reported that with half the caucus surveyed, sentiment was running 2 to 1 in favor of the proposal.[60]

Clinton had told reporters on March 23 that his proposals for campaign finance reform would be out in a few days, but four release dates were subsequently set and missed. White House staffers were huddled with

Wilhelm and aides of Mitchell and Gephardt, and consensus was proving difficult. House Democrats refused to lower PAC contribution limits, demanded higher spending ceilings, and held out for a bundling exemption for EMILY's List. But the Senate contingent realized such conditions would make it all but impossible to hold onto enough Republican moderates to avoid a filibuster.[61] Wilhelm pointed out that the DNC stood to lose 40 percent of its budget under the proposal to ban soft money from federal elections, and he insisted something be done to make up the shortfall.[62] But after having been gathered in amounts as large as $100,000 or more from single individuals, such money was perceived as tainted in the public mind and Clinton seemed determined to wash his hands of it.[63]

Wilhelm again proposed a substitute: give the major party national committees, and perhaps their congressional campaign committees, $6 million a year each in public subsidies for grass-roots activities, ostensibly awarded as matching funds for individual contributions of $200 or less, though both parties were already raising several times that volume in small donations.[64] As was Wilhelm's earlier proposal, the idea was floated to the outside and quickly dropped in the face of sour reactions from Congress and editorialists.[65]

The House negotiators could not be so easily turned aside. From a partisan standpoint, their reluctance to lower PAC contribution limits was understandable: Democrats had taken in $50.3 million in such donations of $5,000 or more during the 1991–92 cycle, compared with only $20.3 million for Republicans.[66] Similarly, an analysis circulated on Capitol Hill by Fraoli/Jost, Democratic consultants who specialized in raising PAC money, indicated Democrats had much more to lose with the imposition of a $600,000 spending limit on House races.[67] The unquestioned dominance of EMILY's List in the field of ideological bundling lent a partisan urgency to that point as well.

When the Clinton package was finally unveiled on May 7, amid considerable fanfare, it was readily apparent the House had prevailed: the current PAC contribution limit of $5,000 per election would remain for lower chamber elections, and the old S 3 spending limits would be indexed for inflation as of 1992. The document punted on the issue of bundling, preferring it be hashed out in the legislative process.

Unlike the Bush-vetoed 1992 bill, the Clinton proposal employed the combination of tax checkoffs and lobbying deduction repeal that had polled well among House Democrats. Realistic projections already had decreed that the checkoff be raised to $3, just to make the existing presidential campaign fund solvent for 1996. The proposed boost to $5 would raise less than $120 million per cycle for congressional races, while most independent analysts figured about $200 million would be required by the S 3/Clinton incentives. The tax squeeze on lobbying would easily make up for the $80 million–plus shortfall, raising $340 million per cycle according to treasury estimates.[68]

Other Clinton proposals that marked departures from the 1992 bill included:

- Prohibiting soft money from campaign activities that affect federal races, though political parties would still be allowed to use it for nonadministrative building and office costs.
- Raising the amount individuals could contribute to federal races from $50,000 to $60,000 per election cycle. Within that limit, they could not exceed $25,000 to candidates, $20,000 to national party committees, and $20,000 to grass-roots organizations in the states. This plan would funnel at least $15,000 to party building in the states for each giver who wished to max-out, and served as a modest substitute for soft money.
- Lowering the amount PACs could contribute to a presidential campaign from $5,000 to $1,000. To make up for lost soft money assistance, the major party presidential nominees would be given another $11 million each in public money to fund grass-roots efforts.
- Prohibiting registered lobbyists from contributing or raising campaign money for any federal officeholder they had lobbied in the previous year. In the case of the president, a lobbying contact with any member of the executive branch would qualify.[69]

None of these Clinton innovations were thought to add significantly to the bill's vulnerability before Congress, though the lobbyist restrictions appeared to be fraught with loopholes and on shaky constitutional ground.[70] Republicans zeroed in on the public financing portion of the package, though even that appeared to be politically tenable, at least at the ballot box. An NBC News/*Wall Street Journal* survey in late April found respondents favoring public financing of congressional elections by a 52 to 38 percent margin, provided the funding came from eliminating tax deductions for lobbying.[71]

By and large, the reform lobby was satisfied with the Clinton plan. Common Cause reported it would take $130 million of special interest money out of federal politics, which satisfied that group. The Republican leadership was not particularly inclined toward bipartisanship. Dole announced his opposition to the Clinton package several weeks before it was completed, leading the *New York Times* to accuse him of "shilling for a corrupt status quo."[72] Republicans had introduced their own reform package, with restrictions on soft money and full prohibitions on PACs and bundling, and Dole continued to deride public financing as an entitlement program for politicians. When the Clinton plan was finally unveiled, he claimed it was "designed to protect the Democrat Congressional majority forever." A few days later, Dole admitted to reporters: "If [House Republicans] were smart, they would accept the public financing provision and sunset it after four years."[73] The statement seemed to suggest the minority leader actually felt the package might help Republicans and challengers.

At least five GOP senators, Dave Durenberger (MN), John Chafee (RI), William S. Cohen (ME), John McCain, and Jim Jeffords (VT), seemed ready to approve the Democratic designs, with modifications. They sent Mitchell a letter on May 6, outlining the points they would need to see in the bill to support it. All five had voted for one Democratic campaign finance bill or another in recent years, and their votes would be needed again if a filibuster was to be broken.[74]

These moderates were grudgingly willing to accept public financing, as long as it did not contribute to the deficit. But they demanded restrictions on the personal use of campaign funds, full disclosure of independent expenditures, limits on out-of-state fund raising, tougher restrictions on PACs, the dropping of language designed to strengthen the FEC, and a single set of contribution standards for House and Senate races. The letter came too late to have a direct impact on the Clinton plan, and the five rebuked the package in a new letter, presented by McConnell to the Senate Rules Committee two weeks later.[75]

Special interest lobbying on the bill was remarkably slight, considering it was a direct assault on that very culture. Active opposition was offered by the National Association of Broadcasters, aroused by the requirement of one-half-off ad discounts for candidates; the National Association of Business PACs, arrayed against new PAC restrictions; and the right-wing National Taxpayers Union, livid over public financing. But the provisions aimed specifically at lobbyists provoked little comment, even from lobbyists, despite their questionable constitutionality.

The new version of S 3, incorporating the Clinton proposals, made it to the Senate floor on May 25. Almost immediately, an amendment offered by Wellstone to limit individual contributions to $100 was soundly rejected. Another, calling for a ban on the personal use of campaign funds, was presented by repentant McCain, a member of the Keating Five, and passed on a voice vote. The bill already banned PAC contributions for Senate campaigns and incorporated Clinton's $1,000 limit only as a backup, anticipating the total ban would be rejected by the courts. On the second day of debate, an amendment by Larry Pressler (R-SD) to extend these provisions to House races passed 85 to 12. In this and other ways, the Senate was preparing to enter the conference not with the bill Bush had vetoed, but with their original version of S 3, plus Clinton additions.

Further accommodation by the Republican moderates was evident when the Senate approved an amendment from Chafee to ban out-of-state fund raising during the first four years of a senator's term. But the bill was nearly eviscerated on May 26, when Senator Judd Gregg (R-NH) proposed an amendment that would have earmarked the lobbying deduction elimination for deficit reduction. Quick maneuvering by Boren short-circuited the move on a procedural tally, but only by a two-vote margin, as five Democrats jumped ship. A subsequent stream of amendments, many of them from Democrats, led Mitchell to abandon his policy of scheduling votes and debates for the convenience of senators, and he was unable to bring the bill to a vote before the Memorial Day recess.[76]

After the Senate reconvened, debate dragged on for another week before Mitchell made his first attempt at cloture, failing on a 53-to-41 tally along party lines. Republicans denied they were filibustering the bill, but they refused to agree to a date for a final vote.

McCain offered another amendment, this one to apply the bill to the 1994 cycle, an apparent anathema to Foley. Democrats tried to approve it by voice vote, a method that would make the provision easier to discard in the conference process, but Dole demanded a recorded vote, and the amendment passed 85 to 7. An amendment by Cohen, stripping the language that toughened the FEC, also was approved. Despite the growing list of concessions to GOP moderates, a second attempt at cloture was thoroughly beaten on June 15, drawing not a single Republican vote.

But the threat to the bill was becoming bipartisan. Senator James Exon (D-NE) had opposed cloture and was a de facto member of the moderate bloc; moreover, there were cloakroom rumors that senators Robert Kerrey, Jay Rockefeller (D-WV), and Joseph Lieberman (D-CT) might join Exon and perennial deserter Richard Shelby (D-AL) in backing the filibuster if public financing were not scaled back. The beset Mitchell finally gave in, as much to keep his own ranks intact as to mollify the GOP moderates. After lining up crucial backing from Common Cause, he agreed to back an amendment by Durenberger and Exon that provided public funding only to candidates whose opponents had exceeded the prescribed spending limit. The funding mechanism also was changed: rather than a tax checkoff or elimination of tax breaks for lobbying, the bill now called for subjecting campaigns to the highest corporate income tax rate (35 percent) unless they assented to the spending limit. Republican leaders decried this latest move as confiscatory as well as an unconstitutional tax on the First Amendment, and McConnell declared the bill would be DOA in the courts.

Some liberals were appalled as well, and they balked at this considerable concession. It appeared at first that the amendment had failed, but the leadership managed to persuade four Democrats to change their votes, pointedly arguing the bill was dead otherwise.[77] Cloture soon followed, backed by sixty-two senators, two more than necessary. Of the seven Republicans bucking the party line, all but Nancy Kassebaum (R-KS) had been afforded the opportunity to amend the bill personally to address a pet concern.

Now stripped of most of its public financing features, "S 3 Lite" quickly cleared the Senate by a 60-to-38 vote. Although Clinton had not been apprised of the key compromise until it had already passed, he immediately backed the measure as "a vast advance over the present law in breaking the back of special interest domination of politics and elections." Many reformers, however, agreed with the grumbling assessment of Wellstone: "It's a great leap sideways."[78]

The Senate had acted out of turn in calling for a new tax on campaigns, as the Constitution requires all such bills to originate in the House. But the lower chamber was dragging its feet in addressing campaign reform and seemed unlikely to revisit the subject until the fall. Meanwhile, the president managed to steer his budget through both houses, succeeding by the barest of margins and expending an enormous amount of political capital. The poor public reception of the controversial package, which raised taxes on a large segment of Americans, left many House Democrats in no mood to ask for public financing of their campaigns.

Moreover, the budget reconciliation bill, passed in August, co-opted both means of taxpayer funding that had been targeted by the Clinton campaign finance proposals, still the working blueprint for the House. First, the bill latched onto the repeal of lobbying deductions for the purpose of deficit reduction, taking the most politically attractive means of raising public money for campaigns; second, it raised the income tax checkoff for public financing of presidential campaigns from $1 to $3, discouraging another trip to that well in the same session. The latter measure was politically defensible in that it was merely adjusting the 1974 amendments for inflation and the fund would be unable to meet its anticipated 1996 obligations without it.[79]

The same could not be said for the diminishing options open to the public funding of congressional campaigns. Democratic House leaders seemed to agree that the punitive campaign tax in the Senate-passed bill was unconstitutional, and that it was now up to them to come up with an alternative for the conference. But forty-seven Democratic congressmen had declared, in a letter to Foley in May, that they could not vote for public financing; influential reformers Mike Synar and Tony Beilenson (D-CA) also had given up on the idea, and each was offering bipartisan-backed alternative bills without spending limits or public funding.[80] Most significantly of all, Ways and Means Committee chairman Dan Rostenkowski (D-IL), whose support would be critical to any new finance mechanism, was known to look upon the whole concept of taxpayer-funded campaigns with a jaundiced eye.

Despite these sobering realities, Common Cause president Fred Wertheimer warned Foley and Gephardt his group would oppose their package if it avoided public financing. The pressure was maintained by editorial allies of the public interest lobby, such as the *New York Times,* which responded to a compromise solution floated in late September as a disgraceful retreat, and labeled Foley a grand artificer. The threats were particularly irksome to House Democrats in that Wertheimer had praised the Senate bill, even though its provisions of public funds were virtually gutted.[81]

No such pressures were forthcoming from the White House, however. After strongly backing the dual concept of spending limits and public funding in the spring, Clinton seemed to lose all enthusiasm for campaign reform after the Senate's retreat from those measures. Waldman had been reassigned to lobbying duty for the North American Free Trade Agreement (NAFTA), and the administration's campaign reform outpost seemed deserted.[82]

The next step was unveiled at a sparsely attended Democratic Caucus meeting on November 3, 1993. The mood was subdued, perhaps inspired by a GOP sweep of all the major off-year elections, held the day before. Once highly contentious over aggregate limits on PAC funds, the caucus now seemed resigned to them, in part because the members had been preparing for such an outcome: the DCCC had tripled its number of active individual donors to 145,000 during the previous two years.[83]

The leadership's bill, HR 3, was basically the same legislation that had initially passed the chamber in 1992, calling for a basic $600,000 spending limit for House races and a $200,000 aggregate PAC contribution limit. Those in compliance with the limits would receive federal matching funds for the first $200 of all contributions, up to an aggregate total of $200,000. But with the limit indexed for inflation and subject to exemptions for overhead (up to 10 percent of the total), competitive primaries, fund-raising expenses, legal and accounting fees and taxes, the true ceilings could easily exceed $1 million in marginal constituencies.

There were a few other notable changes:

• Public funding would come from PAC registration fees of up to $30,000 and a voluntary tax return add-on of $10. If these sources failed to generate the needed money, public funding would be doled out on a pro-rated basis. If the fund fell short of its 1996 cycle obligations by more than fifty cents on the dollar, a 5 percent tax on all federal campaigns would be instituted.

- All candidates would be made subject to the aggregate limit on PAC contributions, whether or not they complied with the spending limits.
- The ban on leadership PACs was dropped, as was the $600,000 ceiling on funds an incumbent could roll over from one campaign to the next.

The retreats from reform were directly attributable to the fact that House Democrats knew the bill they passed in 1993 could well become law, while the one they passed in 1992 obviously had been doomed to be vetoed. Leadership PACs were an obvious means of allowing powerful members of Congress to double-dip among their contributors to cover various campaign expenses and increase influence among their colleagues. Rollover war chests, particularly those in excess of $600,000, were maintained as much to scare off opposition as to free the member from repeated fund-raising chores. Both practices were often used, and excuses for their maintenance were weak. Foley later insisted he had been amenable to the leadership PAC ban, but others had objections. Asked why the rollover limit had been lifted, Gejdenson explained: "Some of our members are worried million-aires might run against them."[84]

Such examples of backsliding were essentially ignored by public interest groups and the news media but dutifully pointed out by Republicans as the legislation moved through the House Administration Committee and onto the floor. By that time, the leadership had already stripped out the funding provisions in the face of a hostile Ways and Means Committee; that issue would have to be revisited in the next session if the remaining parts of the bill were ever to take effect. Forcefully backed by the reform lobby, Foley and Gephardt also took the precaution of bringing HR 3 to the floor under a closed rule that would prohibit the consideration of all amendments or alternatives, except for the package offered by the Republican leadership.[85]

That design faced a formidable obstacle in Synar, who was determined to force consideration of his no public funding/no spending limits plan to cut contribution limits in half. Backed by discontented Democrats and a virtually unanimous Republican Conference, Synar announced on November 18 that he had the votes to block consideration of the bill under the closed rule. He was not bluffing.

Fifteen votes down, and with the House about to adjourn for a two-month recess, the Democratic leadership spared no effort. The vote was scheduled for a highly unusual Sunday session on November 21, and a series of innocuous bills were inserted onto the agenda in front of it to buy time. Foley buttonholed members on the floor, worked the phones, and even made a last-second speech from the well of the House on behalf of the rule, the first time his staff could recall his doing so.[86] In the end, it was enough; the rule passed 220 to 207, with thirty-nine Democrats, ominously including Rostenkowski, crossing the line. The bill was approved by a deceptively decisive 255 to 175 margin the next day, following a raucous debate in which GOP point man Bob Livingston donned a clown's hat and nose to deride the bill as goofy.

Ark of the Lost Covenant

> *The work of change, frankly, will never get any easier until we limit the influence of well-financed interests who profit from this current system. So I must now call on you to finish the job both houses began last year by passing tough and meaningful campaign finance reform legislation this year.*
> —President Clinton's State of the Union Address, January 25, 1994

His high-profile exhortation to the contrary, Clinton had disappeared from the campaign finance debate after unveiling his proposal package the previous May, and rarely materialized again. The seriousness of his commitment became progressively more questionable as the Democratic Party apparatus continued to take advantage of his White House occupancy, squeezing huge quantities of soft money from wealthy individuals and large corporations. Beginning in July 1992, when Clinton had become the nominee and shot to the front of the presidential polls, the DNC had collected more than $44 million in soft money in less than two years, culminating in a $1,500-a-plate presidential dinner in June 1994 that raised $3.5 million.[87]

Co-chair of that event was Dwayne O. Andreas, chairman of Archer Daniels Midland (ADM), a huge agribusiness conglomerate. Andreas had funneled more than $1.1 million to the RNC during Bush's presidency.[88] But in the two years since the rise of Clinton as the favorite in the presidential race, Andreas, his wife, and his company had together bestowed more than $400,000 on the DNC. About two weeks after Andreas gave the Democrats a $100,000 check and co-chaired the presidential dinner, the Environmental Protection Agency issued a ruling that would give ethanol an estimated 10 percent of the automotive fuel market by 1996, a big boost. As the producer of 70 percent of America's ethanol, ADM seemed poised to gain.[89]

Other good things had been happening to the Democratic Party's biggest contributors: Commerce Secretary Ronald Brown embarked for China in August with several major givers in tow, including Lodwrick Cook of ARCO ($171,500) and Edwin Lupberger of Entergy Corp. ($60,000). Lupberger alone returned with $800 million in contracts. And while the Clinton administration denied that contributions had influenced the choice of CEOs for such trips, Brown lieutenant Melissa Moss, until 1993 the finance director for the DNC, figured prominently in their selection.[90]

Such activities had long been standard practice in the Washington culture, but many had expected a different course from Clinton. "American politics is being held hostage by big-money interests," he had written during the campaign, ". . . political action committees, industry lobbies, and $100,000 donors buy access to Congress and the White House. . . . We believe it's long past time to clean up Washington."[91] Common Cause now labeled the president the "king of the corrupt soft-money system."[92]

Clinton's sincerity fell further into question when his fiscal year 1995 budget proposal called for trimming the FEC's funding by 12 percent, even though the commission was already overwhelmed by its caseload and would be required to expand greatly its regulatory role if the Clinton reform plan passed. FEC staff director John Surina estimated the agency would have to increase its budget by two-thirds to fulfill the new duties, and several commission observers suggested Clinton was "low-balling" it.[93]

In spring 1994, Clinton reappointed two-term commissioners Lee Ann Elliott (R) and Danny McDonald (D) to third terms, based on the recommendations of Mitchell and Dole. Many reform advocates had called for new commissioners dedicated to an activist agenda. They read their rejection as confirmation that reform was not a top agenda item.

Perhaps to prove his agency was worthy of the budget increase he was asking, or at least undeserving of the cut sought by Clinton, new FEC Chair Trevor Potter directed a new approach to the caseload: scores of older, minor cases were dropped, while more serious ones were pushed to resolution and subjected to much higher fines than in the past. New regulations were in the works that would restrict the personal use of campaign funds, similar to measures the Republicans had managed to add to S 3. As a reward for this diligence, on June 16, the House voted to slash the FEC's budget by 25 percent, double the cut sought by Clinton. "Many regulated entities would rather their regulators went easy on them," observed Potter. "But not many regulated entities actually get to vote to do that."[94]

As its attitude toward the FEC seemed to indicate, the House was even less interested in reforming the campaign finance system than Clinton. Its negotiators in the process of unifying the House and Senate bills quickly became intransigent, refusing to allow any diminution of the $10,000 ceiling on PAC contributions to a single campaign. Preliminary discussions were conducted between representatives of Democratic leaders Mitchell, Foley, and Gephardt, issue point men Boren and Gejdenson, and occasionally emissaries from the White House. These meetings were ostensibly necessitated because a formal conference might be subject to complicating instructions from the full House if no report were forthcoming within twenty days. More to the point, any conference committee had to be worked out beforehand, enabling the Democrats to keep the Republicans out of the loop while a conference bill was being crafted.

These negotiations dragged on for nearly a year, but it was clear that PAC limits were the most daunting obstacle to a deal. The Republican moderate bloc in the Senate, crucial to the bill's chances of clearing a filibuster, had demanded that any bill operate under the same rules for the Senate and House, where practicable. They would not countenance the stapling of the two bills together, as had been done with the legislation that passed in 1992.

Reconciliation was acceptable on most issues. The Senate seemed ready to accept the extension of public funding to all complying House candidates, not just those faced with noncomplying opponents, and agreed to loosen the probably illegal punitive tax their bill levied on noncomplying candidates. In its place, senators were ready to accept a package of funding devices: a $5 federal income tax add-on to be included on personal income tax returns; a 5 percent tax on PAC receipts; a $500 annual registration fee on professional lobbyists; higher registration fees for foreign agents; higher taxes on the investment income of campaigns. House negotiators accepted the Senate ban on leadership PACs, provided it was delayed for one cycle, and communication vouchers in lieu of cash matching funds as incentives to comply with spending limits. Although labor unions had howled about the Jeffords amendment, its provisions for greater disclosure of nonparty soft money were accepted by the House. The Senate team also agreed to the House's demand to exempt ideologically based PACs, such as EMILY's List, from the prohibition on bundling.

The seeming veto power that seven Republican moderates held over the legislation was beginning to anger members; by the time the differing PAC contribution limits came up for consideration, House sensitivity toward the fragile Senate coalition had all but vanished. Heavily dependent on PAC money, House Democrats refused to allow a reduction in the $5,000-per-election limit on PAC contributions to House candidates. An offer by Mitchell to meet them halfway with a $2,500 limit was rejected, despite an analysis by Common Cause that showed it would cost House incumbents very little, far less than the aggregate PAC contribution limit already in their bill.[95]

Deadlines were set to complete passage of the legislation before the Memorial Day recess, then the Fourth of July recess, and finally the August summer recess. But target dates came and went with little sign of progress. Boren complained to reporters that the bill was swirling down the drain due to House intransigence on PAC limits. Long the leading Democratic critic of PACs in the Senate, Boren refused to take their money for his own campaigns. But all through the late winter and early spring, he had squeezed money out of PACs on behalf of his former press secretary, who was then running in a special election for a House seat.[96]

Despite occasional lapses, Senate negotiators were lionized by the reform lobby, just as Foley was vilified. "Many Democrats in the House, including some in the leadership, seem eager to find a way to kill campaign finance reform in a way that would let them heap blame for its defeat on Republicans in the Senate," wrote the *Washington Post*. "[B]ut to their credit, Mr. Mitchell and Mr. Boren are refusing to play their assigned roles in this charade."[97] Desperately in need of high ground from which to defend their pro-PAC position, Foley and his troops fell back into an unexpected quarter.

The congressional Black Caucus had been complaining for more than a year that the aggregate limit on PAC contributions would discriminate against minority candidates, who generally run in low-income districts and are outsiders to networks of high finance. Such campaigns would find it virtually impossible to raise adequate funds were it not for PAC contributions. The argument was taken up by opponents of PAC reform, who echoed Foley's pious declaration, "I don't think it's a reform . . . to cut off the opportunity of women and African Americans and Hispanics and other minorities to seek office and be elected."[98]

One analysis showed that returning black House members had received 51 percent of their funds from PACs in the 1991–92, below the average proportion for all returning Democrats. The corresponding figures for Hispanics (43 percent) and women (45 percent) were even lower.[99]

Negotiations between the House and Senate "preconferees" did not resume immediately after the July 4 break, and S 3 and HR 3 appeared to be buried beneath the long-brewing, heated debate over health care policy. Events soon began to drift in the direction of campaign finance reform, however.

Eighteen freshman House Democrats wrote to Foley in late July, urging him to accept Mitchell's offer of a $2,500-per-election PAC limit. The Speaker responded by reopening the talks, and as the prospects for health care legislation slowly faded, the White House briefly became engaged. Very little had been accomplished in the second session of Congress, and the Democrats began to look to the reform of campaign finance and lobbying as their potential saving grace with an increasingly critical electorate.

Even so, progress was tortuous. With less than a dozen days left on the schedule, there was still no agreement. A disgusted *New York Times* fingered Foley as "the principal culprit."[100] That very day, the Speaker polled only 35 percent in his home district primary, while the high-profile Synar lost in a runoff, beaten by a seventy-one-year-old retired teacher who spent less than $20,000 and hand-painted his signs. The fear of voters descended upon the Democrats of Capitol Hill.

Two days after the primary, Foley agreed to lower the PAC limit to $3,000 per election if the aggregate limit on PAC money was raised. Anticipating an imminent agreement, Mitchell already had tried to get a conference call rolling in the Senate, only to run headlong into a Republican filibuster. Such a call requires a three-part motion: a declaration of disagreement with the House, a request for conference, and authorization for the appointment of conferees. Each has to be acted on separately, and is traditionally granted by unanimous consent. But each is subject to a filibuster, which kills at least thirty hours of floor time, debating the motion for cloture; and two more filibusters could result after the arrival of the conference bill. With only a handful of days left on the calendar, Republicans could delay the bill a minimum of 130 hours, if held in all-night sessions. They had plainly embarked on such a course, and neither the Senate historian nor parliamentarian could recall a precedent for it.[101]

The first cloture motion passed 96 to 2 on September 22, and the Senate voted unanimously the next day to disagree with the House. But on Wednesday, September 27, Mitchell found himself three votes short of the sixty needed for another cloture motion. Only one of the seven Republicans who had voted for S 3 had strayed, but four Democrats had joined Shelby on the other side of the fence: Robert Kerrey, Ben Nighthorse Campbell (CO), Bennett Johnston (LA), and lame duck Senator Harlan Mathews (TN). Was the bill dead? "It's on life support," a grave Boren said. "It's gasping."[102]

Faced with near-certain defeat, pre-conference negotiators announced an agreement the following day. PAC donation limits would be set at $6,000 per election cycle, $5,000 of which could be donated for the primary. But it was a futile act; the new provision actually lost votes. A new cloture motion fell eight votes short on September 30, drawing campaign finance efforts to a close for the 102d Congress. Lobbying reform suffered a similar fate.

Conclusions

For campaign reform to succeed, there must be a bipartisan bill reflecting compromise among Democrats and Republicans, Senate and House, Congress and the White House. In the 1970s, corporations and labor unions worked together to set the rules for PACs. Whatever one's views on PACs, the point is that Democrats and Republicans, business and labor, worked together—a climate mostly lacking in recent years.

What is needed is a reduction of polarization through compromise. Campaign reform is not neutral; it affects both parties and should be formulated jointly in a compromise bill that contains elements favorable to each. In the past four years, there has been little effort to include the Republicans in the deliberations. The strategy was to find a consensus among Democrats in each chamber, then to buy off enough Republican votes by way of amendments to beat the Senate filibuster. When that price proved too high for the Democratic leaderships, Republicans had the opportunity to kill the legislation. As for Clinton, he talked a good game before the cameras but was not willing or able to spend the needed political capital, given other legislative concerns such as health policy. Besides, the hard and soft money rolling into the DNC was too good to pass up.

Another failure can be laid at the feet of the public interest lobby and editorial writers across the country, who echoed the reformers and helped to misdirect the cause of campaign finance reform by fostering the perception that mixing private funds with the electoral process results in moral corruption. Their "all or nothing" stance, it can be argued, prevented any incremental improvements through the fifteen years since the 1979 amendments, on grounds that minor change would ensure that public financing and spending limits would not be enacted.

Under these circumstances, the sullied reputation of Congress can best be rehabilitated by reforming the electoral process in such a way that balances partisan concerns, keeps concentrations of power and influence in check, and raises public confidence in the fairness of the system. That means enhancing competitiveness, encouraging citizen participation, promoting voter education on the candidates and the issues, and increasing communication between the candidates and the voters.

That does not mean imposing draconian spending limits or severely restricting sources of funds—the approaches the parties have attempted to follow in recent years. Rather, it means assuring a platform for challengers to be heard by easing fund raising and providing modest government assistance. Such a system must diminish dependencies on PACs, not by tightening up on contribution limits but by cultivating alternative, less interested generators of campaign resources.

The convoluted dance of political finance reform, which has consumed so much attention on Capitol Hill, might all be considered a waste of time were it not for the public relations value and political mileage that Congress seems ultimately able to wring from the issue. Rather than make the public interest the guiding light behind the reform legislation—trading off partisan concerns about various particulars as the package was constructed—legislative strategists chose to immunize their proposals from adoption by potential allies across the aisle. Once safely insulated from the possibility of actually enacting a bipartisan law, Democratic and Republican parliamentary maneuvers stuffed bills with popular reform ideas, regardless of their legitimate merit or constitutional appropriateness.

The alternative view sees money in politics not as inherently evil but as a requirement if democracy is to function properly. If overly restricted, special interest and PAC money will find new channels to filter into the system one way or another; accordingly, the least offensive approach, constitutionally and practically, is to permit it via PACs in ways that are open and disclosed. More money properly spent on campaigns equates to more voters informed of their choices, more interest generated in public disclosure, and more motivation arousing citizens to vote. If the money is raised in a widely dispersed fashion—modest donations from great numbers of people—political interest and involvement on a large scale is further enhanced, and the system becomes more of a reflection of the popular will, the function of democracy. For example, tax credits for political contributions can be structured to act as incentives to wider contributions, perhaps through benefits only to in-state contributions of limited amounts, as the Senate Campaign Finance Reform Panel suggested.[103]

What Congress has never seriously considered is a system of "floors without ceilings." Some supporters of public funding advocate public funding floors without spending-limit ceilings. This concept is favored by many of the mature democracies in Western Europe; the idea is that partial public funding, or a floor, gives candidates (or parties, in Western Europe) at least minimal access to the electorate and provides alternative funds so that candidates (or parties) can reject undesirable private contributions. If this approach were accepted by the Congress, the absence of spending limits would avoid the constitutional issues raised in *Buckley*. Although this system appears to favor incumbents who have an advantage in raising funds, the floors assist challengers by providing them with money, thereby giving them some degree of access to the voting public.

Floors without ceilings were actually experienced in the presidential general elections of 1992, when public funds provided the floors but the ceilings or expenditure limits were not effective because of substantial soft money spending. It took from 1976 to 1988 for soft money to break out significantly, but the lesson again in 1992, as in 1988, was that as the system evolves, ceilings eventually collapse. Ensuring that all serious contenders have a reasonable minimum is more important than limiting how much candidates can spend. The bigger problem is how to provide money to candidates, not how to restrict it unduly. Some such formula would serve both parties well: Democrats would get public funding, and Republicans would not be burdened with expenditure limits.

A truly effective and well-directed public interest lobby would concentrate its efforts on legislation that would encourage a broader donor base (perhaps through tax credits for small contributions from constituents), maximize candidate competition, lower the cost of campaign communications, strengthen political parties, and broaden public disclosure of campaign activities. Its strategy would recognize partisan interests and balance them in winning concessions for the democratic process, exposing legislative theatrics and retreats from reform rather than excusing them.

For editorial writers to espouse "freedom of the press" while seeking to limit political spending—the voicing of political ideas—is ironic. Electronic and print media would prefer to frame the campaigns to the electorate in their own words rather than allow candidates to speak for themselves and amplify their views, even if through the unpopular spot announcements that candidates find effective. But no one seems to point out that elections are improved by well-financed candidates able to wage competitive campaigns, not by stifling political dialogue.

Despite Democratic control of the White House and, through 1994, both houses of Congress, and sporadic commitment to change, no change has come, despite a favorable atmosphere that opinion leaders formulated and developed but could not get enacted.

Notes

1. "Dole's Presidential Hopes Provide Target for S 2 Supporters," *Campaign Practices Reports,* June 29, 1987, p. 3.

2. "Senate Stymied Over Campaign Finance Bill," *Campaign Practices Reports,* June 15, 1987, p. 2.

3. Janet Hook, "Packwood Arrested, Carried into Chamber," *Congressional Quarterly,* February 27, 1988, p. 487.

4. David S. Cloud, "Senate Declines New Approach to Limiting Campaign Finances," *Congressional Quarterly,* April 23, 1988, p. 1108.

5. Alan Secrest, "A Year of Living Dangerously," *Polling Report,* July 23, 1990, p. 8.

6. James J. Kilpatrick, "The 5 Senators and Charlie Keating," *Washington Post,* November 2, 1989.

7. Hendrik Hertzberg, "Twelve is Enough," *The New Republic,* May 14, 1992, p. 22.

8. Robin Toner, "House Edgy as Elections Loom and Voters Glower," *New York Times,* August 5, 1990; and Larry J. Sabato, *PAC Power: Inside the World of Political Action Committees* (New York: W.W. Norton & Co., 1985), p. 75.

9. Peter Osterlund, "Panel Unveils Campaign Finance Plan," *Baltimore Sun,* March 8, 1990.

10. Campaign Finance Reform Panel, "Campaign Finance Reform: A Report to the Majority Leader and Minority Leader, United States Senate," March 6, 1990.

11. Richard E. Cohen, "Back Room Bargaining," *National Journal,* March 17, 1990, pp. 672–73.

12. Herbert E. Alexander and Monica Bauer, *Financing the 1988 Election* (Boulder, CO: Westview Press, 1991), pp. 121–22.

13. David Beiler, "DNC Plans Hit the Summer Doldrums," *Campaigns & Elections,* June/July 1990, pp. 9–10; Committee for the Study of the American Electorate, "A Study of Campaign Expenses of Winning Challengers for Senate and House 1987–88," released by the committee on May 17, 1990; and interview with Curtis Gans, July 1990.

14. Chuck Alston, "Negotiators Tread Carefully to Find Common Ground," *Congressional Quarterly,* May 26, 1990, p. 1621.

15. Richard L. Berke, "Senate Campaign Finance Talks Break Down," *New York Times,* May 11, 1990.

16. Tom Kenworthy, "Democrats Rip Common Cause," *Washington Post,* July 13, 1990.

17. Steven A. Holmes, "Weaker Limit on PACs Is Proposed," *New York Times,* July 31, 1990.

18. Helen Dewar, "Senate Democrats Accept Republican Proposal to Outlaw PACs," *Washington Post,* July 28, 1990.

19. Kim Mattingly, "House Disposes of Campaign Reform Bill," *Roll Call,* August 6, 1990.

20. Richard L. Berke, "Senate Votes to Curb Donations From Outside Groups," *New York Times,* August 2, 1990; and Berke, "Campaign Surgery," *New York Times,* August 5, 1990.

21. "House-Senate Conferees: All Dressed Up but Nowhere to Go," *PACs & Lobbies,* October 3, 1990, p. 5.

22. Chuck Alston, "Image Problems Propel Congress Back to Campaign Finance Bills," *Congressional Quarterly,* February 2, 1991, p. 277; and Alan Secrest, "A Year of Living Dangerously," *Polling Report,* July 23, 1990, p. 8.

23. W. D. McInturff, "A Republican Perspective: Is the 'Anti-Incumbency Revolt' Serious? How Will It Affect '92 Races?" *Campaign,* November 1991, p. 34.

24. Maura Keefe, "Political Business Cut in Half by Incumbent Security," *Campaign,* August 1991, p. 18.

25. Alston, "Image Problems Propel Congress Back."

26. Chuck Alston, "Fertilizing the Grassroots," *Congressional Quarterly,* February 2, 1991, p. 280.

27. Chuck Alston, "Senate Is Expected to Act First to Renew Debate on Hill Money," *Congressional Quarterly,* February 2, 1991, pp. 278–79.

28. FCC, "Mass Media Bureau Report on Political Programming Audit," September 7, 1990, pp. 1–8; see also chapter 8, pp. 232–33.

29. Chuck Alston, "Outlook for Law This Year Dim: Partisan Split Remains Wide," *Congressional Quarterly,* May 18, 1991, pp. 1255–56.

30. Richard L. Berke, "A Revival: The Campaign Finance Show," *New York Times,* May 26, 1991.

31. Janet Hook, "Senate's Ban on Honoraria Marks End of an Era," *Congressional Quarterly,* July 20, 1991, p. 1955.

32. Phil Kuntz, "Uproar Over Bank Scandal Goads House to Cut Perks," *Congressional Quarterly,* October 5, 1991, pp. 2841–45.

33. Chuck Alston, "Democrats Set to Offer Plan Based on Public Funding," *Congressional Quarterly,* October 12, 1991, pp. 2933–34.

34. Chuck Alston, "Bill's Approach: $600,000 Limit or Else.... In Effort to Tame Campaign Funding," *Congressional Quarterly,* November 16, 1991, pp. 3360–61.

35. Chuck Alston, "Public Payments May Prove Achilles Heel on Floor," *Congressional Quarterly,* November 16, 1990, pp. 3359–60.

36. Chuck Alston, "Democrats Strip Out Financing to Pass Spending Limits," *Congressional Quarterly*, pp. 3509–10.

37. Adam Clymer, "Showdown of Bush and Congress Shapes Up on Campaign Spending," *New York Times*, March 31, 1992. Also see Clymer, "Campaign Finance Measure Advances (Toward a Veto)," *New York Times*, April 3, 1992.

38. Senate/House Conference Committee, "Major Provisions of the Congressional Campaign Spending Limit and Election Reform Act of 1992, Compared with S.3 and H.R. 3750," dated April 3, 1992.

39. David Broder, "Campaign Finance Farce," *Washington Post*, May 3, 1992.

40. Clymer, "Campaign Finance Measure Advances (Toward Veto)."

41. Michael Ross, "Democrats Approve Campaign Reforms," *Los Angeles Times*, April 4, 1992.

42. "Bundles from Heaven," *Washington Post Weekly Edition*, May 4–10, 1992.

43. Richard E. Cohen, "The Campaign Finance Reform Charade," *National Journal*, May 2, 1992, p. 1072.

44. FEC, "1992 Congressional Election Spending Jumps 52% to $678 Million," press release, March 4, 1993, p. 1.

45. Michael Wines, "Accord Is Reached on Voter Measure," *New York Times*, April 29, 1993.

46. Karen Tumulty, "Senate Votes to Strengthen Lobby Laws," *Los Angeles Times*, May 7, 1993.

47. David Lauter and Karen Tumulty, "Campaign Reform Huddle Yields Few Signals for Action," *Los Angeles Times*, February 4, 1993.

48. Bill Clinton and Al Gore, *Putting People First: How We Can All Change America* (New York: Random House, 1992), pp. 45–46; also see chapter 8, pp. 237–39.

49. Bob Dole and Mitch McConnell, "Re: Campaign Finance Reform" (letter to Republican U.S. senators), February 4, 1993.

50. Editorial, "No Delays for Public Trust," *New York Times*, January 24, 1993.

51. Jeffrey H. Birnbaum, "Clinton's Plan for Campaign, Lobbying Reform Encounters Resistance From House Democrats," *Wall Street Journal*, February 3, 1993.

52. Helen Dewar, "Reform Clutters the Picture," *Washington Post Weekly Edition*, February 22–28, 1993, p. 14.

53. "No Delays for Public Trust."

54. James A. Barnes, "Capitol Hill Watch," *National Journal*, March 6, 1993, p. 576.

55. Edward Zuckerman, "Frontier-Style Lawmaking: First, a Pro Forma Hearing," *Political Finance & Lobby Reporter*, March 10, 1993, p. 1.

56. Helen Dewar, "Panel Votes to Revamp Campaign Finance Laws," *Washington Post*, March 19, 1994.

57. Margery Tabankin, "No Fund-Raising Favor for Women," *New York Times*, April 10, 1993.

58. Charles R. Babcock and Kenneth J. Cooper, "Clinton Campaign Finance Plan Would Eliminate Soft Money," *Washington Post*, March 26, 1993.

59. "Public Funding Fading Fast," *Congressional Quarterly*, March 13, 1993, p. 573.

60. Beth Donovan, "Democrats' Count Shows Hope for Tax Checkoff Idea," *Congressional Quarterly*, April 3, 1993, p. 814.

61. Beth Donovan, "Clinton Offers Details of Plan; Big Test Is GOP Senate Unity," *Congressional Quarterly*, May 8, 1993, p. 1121.

62. Ruth Marcus, "Changing the Way Washington Works," *Washington Post Weekly Edition*, May 17–23, 1993.

63. Beth Donovan, "Much-Maligned 'Soft Money' Is Precious to Both Parties," *Congressional Quarterly*, May 15, 1993, pp. 1196–97.

64. Charles R. Babcock, "Clinton Plan Envisions Millions for Two Parties in U.S. Matching Funds," *Washington Post,* April 29, 1993.

65. Associated Press, "Proposed Tax Funds to Parties Dropped," *Washington Times,* May 5, 1993.

66. James A. Barnes, "Sticky Wicket," *National Journal,* May 8, 1993, p. 1109.

67. Charles Cook, "House Dems Are Hooked on PACs, Heavy Spending," *Roll Call,* June 1, 1993.

68. David Lauter, "Clinton Offers Reform Plan for Campaigns," *Los Angeles Times,* May 8, 1993. Also see Beth Donovan, "Delay, Controversy Certain As Senate Takes Up Plan," *Congressional Quarterly,* May 22, 1993, p. 1274.

69. Richard L. Berke, "Clinton Unveils Financing Plan for Campaigns," *New York Times,* May 8, 1993.

70. James A. Barnes, "Lobbyists' Loopholes?" *National Journal,* May 22, 1993, p. 1238.

71. Barnes, "Sticky Wicket."

72. "Bob Dole Versus Political Reform," *New York Times,* April 25, 1993.

73. Quoted in "Campaign Reform With Smarts," *Los Angeles Times,* May 19, 1993.

74. David Lauter and Karen Tumulty, "Plan Seeks to Give Congress Hopefuls Vouchers for Ads," *Los Angeles Times,* May 7, 1993.

75. "Republicans Prepare Filibuster to Wreck Democrats' Campaign Reform Legislation," *Political Finance & Lobby Reporter,* May 26, 1993, p. 1.

76. Donovan, "Debate Slows to a Halt With Votes Uncertain," *Congressional Quarterly,* May 22, 1993, pp. 1338–39.

77. Adam Clymer, "Senate Democrats Reach Compromise on Campaign Bill," *New York Times,* June 17, 1993.

78. Beth Donovan, "Senate Passes Campaign Finance by Gutting Public Funding." *Congressional Quarterly,* June 19, 1993, p. 1533.

79. FEC, "Congress Increases Tax Checkoff: FEC Says '96 Presidential Elections Will Be Fully Funded," press release, August 20, 1993.

80. Michael Ross, "47 House Democrats Fault Clinton's Campaign Reform," *Los Angeles Times,* May 21, 1993. Also see "Reps. Beilenson, Leach Introduce Reform to Abolish PAC Contributions, Set Spending Limits in House Elections," *Political Finance & Lobby Reporter,* April 14, 1993, p. 5; and Richard E. Cohen, "Downsizing Goals for Campaign Reform," *National Journal,* June 26, 1993, p. 1659.

81. "Capital Hill Watch," *National Journal,* July 3, 1993, p. 1712. Also see Janet Hook, "Reforms Are Hard to Come By as 'Reform Month' Looms," *Congressional Quarterly,* October 2, 1993, p. 2614.

82. Ibid., p. 2615.

83. Richard E. Cohen, "Capitol Hill Watch," *National Journal,* July 31, 1993, p. 1928.

84. Quoted in David Broder, "Reform the PACs? They Were Just Kidding, Folks, " *Richmond Times-Dispatch,* December 5, 1993.

85. Beth Donovan, "House Takes First Big Step in Overhauling System," *Congressional Quarterly,* November 27, 1993, p. 3247.

86. Ibid., p. 3248.

87. Charles R. Babcock, "Soft Money Is Like the Man Who Came to Dinner," *Washington Post,* June 24, 1994.

88. Ibid.

89. Peter H. Stone, "Money Still Talks," *National Journal,* October 1, 1994, p. 2309.

90. Ibid.

91. Clinton and Gore, *Putting People First,* p. 45.

92. "New Democrats, Old Cynicism," *New York Times,* June 23, 1994.

93. James A. Barnes, "Wobbly Watchdog," *National Journal,* April 2, 1994, p. 775.

94. Charles R. Babcock, "Master Gets Hot, Leaves Watchdog in Fiscal Freeze," *Washington Post,* June 17, 1994.

95. Charles R. Babcock, "Effect on Halving PAC Donation Cap Would Be Slight, Analysis Finds," *Washington Post,* June 13, 1994.

96. David Beiler, "Return of the Plainsman," *Campaigns & Elections,* June 1994, p. 48.

97. "Standing Firm on Campaign Reform," *Washington Post,* June 30, 1994.

98. Quoted in Beth Donovan, "Black Caucus: PAC Funds a Must for Minorities," *Congressional Quarterly,* September 25, 1993, p. 2525.

99. Ibid.

100. "Before Congress Quits," *New York Times,* September 20, 1994.

101. Beth Donovan, "Republicans Plan Filibusters, Imperiling Senate Schedule," *Congressional Quarterly,* September 24, 1994, p. 2655.

102. Helen Dewar, "Campaign Finance Bill Suffers Setback," *Washington Post,* September 28, 1994.

103. Campaign Finance Reform Panel report.

10

Post-Election Trends

Clinton–Gore Transition

Prior to 1964, the transition from one presidential administration to another was largely dependent on funds from the president-elect's party and on the work of unpaid volunteer staff. For most of the nation's history, presidents took office with relatively little specific preparation or substantive communication with the outgoing administration. As the nation grew in size and presidential responsibilities became more complex, however, the need to maintain effective continuity in the executive branch of government increased accordingly. In 1962, the bipartisan Commission on Campaign Costs, which had been appointed by President John F. Kennedy, recommended that federal funds be made available to pay costs incurred in promoting an orderly change of presidential administrations. Congress responded by enacting the Presidential Transition Act of 1964, which directed government officials to promote orderly transitions in administrations and authorized Congress to appropriate funds to cover some of the costs involved in doing so.[1]

President-elect Clinton and Vice President–elect Gore jointly received $3.5 million from the U.S. Treasury to cover expenses between the November election and the January 20, 1993, inauguration, an amount increased through the years since the first payout in 1964. The General Services Administration, which administers the funds, has provided the data shown in Table 10.1. While the bulk of the money went for salaries of the 452 staff members, the table demonstrates the range of activities paid for by the government grant, mainly communications and rent.

But the government funding was only the base of transition spending. Clinton also established a tax-exempt foundation, the Presidential Transi-

Table 10.1

Clinton–Gore Presidential Transition, 1992–93

Personnel compensation		$2,259,118
Personnel benefits		169,861
Rents and utilities		188,755
Communications		319,679
Postage	$45,253	
Local telephone service	112,331	
Long distance telephone service	62,384	
Intercity service	99,711	
Printing		11,961
Other services		466,678
Supplies		56,482
Program travel (motor pool)		6,702
Total obligations		$3,479,236
Total available		3,500,000
Unobligated balance		$20,764

Source: General Services Administration, data as of June 30, 1994.

tion Planning Foundation, as a supplement to government funds. With a goal of raising $2.7 million, it turned into a larger fund than the available public funds.[2] The combination of the two led to the highest cost of a presidential transition in history, as follows:[3]

	Receipts	Disbursements
Public funds	$3.5 million	$3,479,236
Presidential Transition Planning Foundation	5.2 million	4,800,000
Total	$8.7 million	$8,279,236

According to one account, the foundation spending included $1.8 million for consultants and $1.1 million for travel, in addition to categories and amounts shown in Table 10.1. The foundation limited contributions to $5,000, with a further restriction that money be accepted only from individuals.[4]

During the transition period, President-elect Clinton presided over the Little Rock Economic Conference on December 14–15, 1992. While some twenty-four of the participants at the Little Rock conference were contributors to the foundation, the costs of holding the conference were paid for by the DNC and not by the foundation. While many staff persons from the Clinton–Gore campaign went on the transition payroll, and then into government jobs, other staffers were moved to the DNC payroll the day after the election.

The law also provides funding for the outgoing president and vice president. According to the General Services Administration, as of August 8, 1994, former President Bush and former Vice President Quayle had spent as follows:

	Total Available	Total Spent	Balance
Bush	$1,248,000	$874,770	$373,230
Quayle	252,000	243,846	8,154

Ethics

Clinton issued ethical guidelines for his transition team, barring officials for six months from lobbying federal agencies they dealt with, and banning officials' involvement in decisions that could affect their financial or business interests. The guidelines went beyond those of earlier transition teams.[5]

Clinton also set extensive standards for his administration, designed to curb influence peddling by former government officials. Applying to about one-third of the 3,500 appointments he could make, the rules prohibited officials from lobbying their former agencies for five years and from ever representing foreign governments or foreign political parties before the federal government. The purpose was to diminish, if not eliminate, the "revolving door," according to which many officials leave government to make large amounts of money by using their former government contacts.[6] While the guidelines were elevating standards, some observers raised questions as to whether they would prevent some qualified persons from accepting government jobs, would favor the independently wealthy who would be minimally affected by post-employment restrictions, and would attract persons without experience.[7]

Financing the Inauguration

The inauguration of Bill Clinton and Al Gore cost at least $25 million.[8] Adding in government costs and in-kind contributions, however, the total could have been more than $36 million. The major source of revenue was corporate, labor, and individual loans—totaling some $17 million—which was mainly repaid from ticket and souvenir sales.[9] Government costs were a substantial element: some $5.5 million appropriated by Congress for District of Columbia police and public safety expenses, and an additional $906,000 to cover the ceremony and stage at the Capitol, including $290,000 for construction of the stands.[10] An overview of costs (in $ millions) estimated by the Citizens' Research Foundation follows:

Inaugural Committee and foundation spending	$25.0
Washington, DC, police and safety	5.5
Ceremony and stage	0.9
In-kind contributions and services	5.0
Total	$36.4

To balance the costs, revenue (in $ millions) estimated by the Citizens' Research Foundation, not counting government appropriations or in-kind contributions and services, was:

Tickets and souvenirs to repay loans	$17.0
HBO broadcast rights to "Call for Reunion" concert	1.5
Inaugural Eve Gala broadcast (net profit)	5.6
Total	$24.1

Sales of tickets and souvenirs raised the $17 million necessary to repay the interest-free loans that corporations had made. Inaugural Commemoratives, Inc., which operated a store in Little Rock for the Clinton–Gore campaign, opened one in Washington, DC, in late December to sell inaugural memorabilia. During its first eleven days of operation, it sold about $350,000 worth of inaugural items. Ordinarily when officially licensed merchandise is distributed, the royalty fees to the trademark holder are 10 percent, but the Clinton inauguration received more than that.[11]

The Entertainment Profits

The entertainment industry had been very supportive of the Clinton candidacy during the campaign. This support was no less visible during the inauguration, with the exception of a few celebrities who did not show up out of pride when they did not receive official invitations.[12]

The interest-free loans and in-kind contributions received from the entertainment industry were worth less in value compared with the deals the inaugural committee struck with broadcasters. HBO paid $1.5 million for the exclusive broadcast rights to the "Call for Reunion" concert at the Lincoln Memorial. The committee justified selling the rights based on its assertion that HBO was the only company willing to make a commitment to televise the concert. CNN and C-SPAN carried the event, but some of the entertainment was cut off.[13]

The inaugural committee paid CBS $875,000 for the two-hour Inaugural Eve Gala. Since the time was "bought," the committee was free to sell advertising slots. In fact, about $6.5 million in commercial spots were sold, with TriStar Pictures as one of the major advertisers. According to others in the broadcasting business, CBS could have charged up to $2 million for the two-hour time block under ordinary circumstances. After deducting the $875,000 cost for the time, an estimate of the profits was $5.6 million.[14]

This analysis has used a $5 million estimate for in-kind contributions. Probably one-half that amount was accounted for by the costs of corporate parties. AT&T provided telephones and service, and the automobile makers donated use of some 470 cars for two days.[15] The Bakery, Confectionery and Tobacco Workers baked a 600-pound cake. Nestle-Carnation served 100,000 hot cocoa drinks. Clairol serviced "freshen-up lounges" for VIPs and featured Miss America.[16] Time-Life Video and Warner Books put together a commemorative book and video and produced them at cost, with profits going to the inaugural committee.[17]

The inauguration festivities included an array of receptions, brunches, lunches, dinners, balls, and star-studded entertainment. At least 192 corporations were counted as providing loans of up to $100,000, to be repaid from receipts.[18] Some made tax-deductible donations totaling $2.4 million to the Presidential Inaugural Foundation to pay for the many public and free events. Among the free events were a festival on the Mall and the concert at the Lincoln Memorial.[19] Other corporations and unions provided in-kind goods or services, sponsored parties, and paid $15,000 to $25,000 for eight-seat boxes at the Capitol Centre Gala, as well as $15,000 for tables at several inaugural dinners. While the Clinton–Gore inaugural was expensive, it cost about $5 million less than the Bush–Quayle inaugural in 1989.[20]

Controversial Inaugural Party Solicitations

The two brothers of the First Lady-to-be, Hillary Rodham Clinton, were engaged in solicitations for several inaugural parties. A Pennsylvania attorney made requests to various large corporations for $10,000 donations. Among those that declined to contribute were the Ford Motor Company,

Mobil Corporation, and Chevron Corporation, at least two of which were already contributors to the main events. Hillary Clinton's brothers wanted these parties to be held in recognition of those who were helpful during the campaign. The lack of a promise that the Clintons would attend, and the resultant publicity, had some impact on the lack of response from the corporations that were contacted.[21]

Three parties that were to have honored Ron Brown were canceled when criticism surfaced over the financing of the parties. Officially, the parties were canceled to avoid "distractions" from the main events.[22] The most spectacular of these parties was to be held in the Terrace Theater at the Kennedy Center. The rent for this facility was part of the major share of the contributions that had already been spent before cancellation. Other nonrefundable items apparently included catering and the production of a video honoring Brown. Once all expenses were paid, the remaining funds were returned to the contributors.[23] The Kennedy Center Gala was to be held Sunday night prior to the inauguration and was to be financed entirely with $10,000 donations.[24]

Ambassadorial Appointments

Among the 3,500 or so appointments a newly elected president can make, perhaps the most controversial are ambassadorial, especially when political contributors and supporters are chosen instead of Foreign Service professionals. The *Los Angeles Times* framed the debate in adjoining op-ed articles, and the headlines told all: "Diplomacy is No Job for Amateurs," versus "Hypocritical Posturing by Snobs of State."[25]

During the first fourteen months of the Clinton administration, 41 percent of ambassadorial appointments were political; of ninety-eight ambassadors named, thirty-eight were not from the career Foreign Service. The administration has stated that its goal was to appoint 70 percent of its ambassadors from the ranks of the Foreign Service.[26]

As of January 1994, the Associated Press compiled a list of the ten most generous Democratic donors nominated to ambassadorships during Clinton's first year in office, as follows:[27]

Country	Ambassador	Amount
Austria	Swanee Grace Hunt	$328,700
Netherlands	K. Terry Dornbush	253,750
Switzerland	M. Larry Lawrence	196,304
Denmark	Edward Elson	182,714
France	Pamela Harriman	130,902

Belgium	Alan Blinken	46,933
United Nations–Europe	Daniel L. Speigel	40,796
Germany	Richard Holbrooke	30,050
United Nations–New York	Madeleine K. Albright	29,350
Sweden	Thomas L. Siebert	28,935

The list was drawn from records of the Senate Foreign Relations Committee and the FEC, and represents hard and soft money contributed by the nominees, their immediate families, and corporations they controlled.[28] Some of the appointees not only gave money but served as fund raisers; for example, Harriman hosted a strategy-plotting event at her Middleburg, Virginia, estate in June 1991, inviting most of the presidential hopefuls and twenty-one of the party's most reliable contributors; some of those attending were reported to have made promises of contributions for the 1992 campaigns.[29]

One appointee, Larry Lawrence, was selected to be ambassador to Switzerland after having paid a $7,179 fine to the FEC; the amount represented the excess by which he exceeded the $25,000-per-year ceiling for hard money contributions.[30]

Democratic Aftermath

After Clinton was elected, David C. Wilhelm, the new chairman of the DNC, announced that the national party organization would become a central component of the administration's political operation. The DNC would act to restore the party's base and reach out to new activists, especially young voters, to transform the national party organization into a grass-roots network responsible for mobilizing support for the president's public policy agenda. This revival would begin by placing a new emphasis on expanding the party's small donor base.[31]

Throughout 1993, the DNC committed significant resources to programs designed to attract small donors. By the end of the year, Democrats claimed to have added more than 120,000 contributors to their rolls, and they had received $8.9 million in contributions of less than $200, a record for a nonelection year, representing about one-half of the party's total hard money receipts.[32] But these revenues came at a high cost; the party spent approximately $8 million on direct mail and telemarketing programs, and according to one report, only a relatively small share of those who did respond to an initial solicitation became sustained givers.[33]

Before long, DNC staff members came to realize how expensive it can be for the party controlling the White House to pay for presidential politics and for political consultants, among other costs, that cannot properly be paid for by government. In addition, the national committee had to finance the costs not only of its small donor programs, but also of a burgeoning staff, which had grown to include more than 200 persons, many of whom were former Clinton campaign staffers brought on to assist with the task of overseeing the party's grass-roots outreach efforts.[34] Soon fund raisers discovered it was easier to raise money from wealthy individuals and special interests, some of whom were very willing to give to a new administration, including some donors who were willing to contribute large sums in the form of soft money.

Accordingly, DNC fund raisers, led by new finance chairman Terence McAuliffe, a veteran of the 1980 Carter and 1988 Gephardt presidential campaigns and former finance director for the DCCC, actively solicited large donations to replenish the party's depleted coffers. McAuliffe reinvigorated the DNC's Business Leadership Forum, a special program for $10,000-a-year donors, increasing its membership from about 130 before Clinton's election to more than 600. The party also received substantial sums from a number of corporations and executives, including $265,000 from American Financial chief executive officer Carl Lindner, $71,000 from Anheuser-Busch, and $95,000 from Archer Daniels Midland.[35] In the first three months of 1994, the DNC brought in a total of $10.3 million, its largest quarterly total ever reported, but only $1.5 million of this amount came from small donors.[36]

Overall, during the first fifteen months of Clinton's presidency, the Democrats' national political committees, including the DNC, DSCC, and DCCC, raised a total of $45 million and spent $43.4 million, which represented a 50 percent increase in revenues and a 52 percent rise in expenditures over the comparable period in 1991 and 1992. More than one-half of this amount, $27 million, was received in the form of soft money, most of it to the accounts maintained by the DNC. In fact, during this period, the DNC took in more soft money than hard money, depositing $23.5 million in soft donations, or more than three times the amount raised in the comparable period two years earlier.[37]

A significant portion of the DNC's newfound resources was spent on activities designed to mobilize support for the president's legislative agenda. In the spring of 1993, the DNC mounted a public relations blitz to sell the Clinton budget plan to the public and counteract Republican charges that the president's proposal would increase government spending and raise taxes. The national party distributed daily "talking points" by fax to supporters throughout the country, and targeted one-half million pieces of direct mail and more than 1 million telephone calls to Democrats in selected congressional districts in an effort to generate grass-roots support for the plan.[38] The DNC also broadcast radio ads in about fifty media markets and television spots in six states at an estimated cost of $1.5 million to $1.7 million.[39]

The DNC also played a role in the debate over the president's health care initiative. Initially, efforts to educate the public on the health care issue were to be conducted by a bipartisan, nonprofit foundation external to the party apparatus. But this bipartisan National Health Care Campaign, which was to be established with $100,000 in seed money from the DNC, was soon criticized and its bipartisanship questioned, especially after a former Clinton campaign staffer was named to head the group. Consequently, this structure was scrapped, and on September 20, 1993, Wilhelm announced the formation of the National Health Care Campaign, a DNC project aimed at promoting the Clinton proposal at the grass roots and responding to critics, especially those in the insurance industry. A former Democratic governor of Ohio, Richard Celeste, was chosen to head the project and the DNC committed about $3 million to the issue in 1993 alone, which was much less than earlier plans called for but still a sizable drain on party funds.[40]

These efforts to assist the president came under increasing attack as time proceeded and the 1994 elections loomed. Although supporting the president's legislative agenda is one of the roles of a political party, Democratic candidates expected the DNC to focus on elections, even at the price of support for the Clinton agenda. This conflict became particularly pronounced after the 1993 elections, in which the Democrats lost gubernatorial races in Virginia and New Jersey, and major mayoral contests in New York and Los Angeles.[41] Political money is a scarce resource and there never seems to be enough to go around, so priorities had to be chosen. Although the DNC spent more than $2.5 million on elections in 1993, assisting Democratic campaigns in nineteen states, elected officials concerned about the rising tide of anti-incumbent sentiment felt the party was not doing enough to prepare for the approaching mid-term elections.[42] Some insiders also were alarmed because the DNC, despite a record fund-raising pace for a nonelection year, had only $1.4 million in the bank by March 1994.

A deeper conflict also emerged. During the 1992 campaign, Clinton had promised to promote election reform to reduce dependence on PACs, special interests, and soft money. But as noted in chapter 9, the move to advance campaign reform, undertaken in the early months of the new administration and reflected in the White House's May 7 proposals, threatened certain money sources. As time passed, it became increasingly clear that reform would cost the party money.

As discussed in chapter 9, White House efforts toward reform waxed and waned. The Senate and House Democratic leaderships offered support, but each was left to develop its own version of Senate and House reform, with some provisions—such as PAC contribution limits and soft money—affecting the White House, the Congress, and the national party as well. Further controversy developed when the Senate passed a bill quite different from one that later passed the House. Despite the activity on Capitol Hill, however, for long periods of time there seemed to be little interest on the part of the White House in participating in the negotiations or taking action to help resolve differences.

To spur action on reform, Common Cause produced a study in June 1994, indicating that the DNC had raised $40.5 million in soft money in a twenty-one-month period from the time Clinton received the presidential nomination in July 1992 through March 1994. This was almost twice as much as the $21.5 million in soft money the RNC raised during the same period. The report further noted that during the first fifteen months of the Clinton administration, Democrats had raised 50 percent more in soft money gifts than the Republicans had raised in the first fifteen months of the Bush administration in 1989–90.[43]

The Common Cause study was timed to appear just as Democrats were holding a major fund-raising event, and as the Senate and House campaign finance bills were awaiting appointment of a conference committee. That particular fund-raising event, which raised about $3.5 million for the national party committees, followed a pattern established in other events held during 1993: those who donated $1,500 were invited to attend a dinner at which the president spoke; those who donated $10,000 or more also received an invitation to attend a reception at the White House; and those who gave $50,000 or more were invited to a pre-dinner cocktail party, where they could have their pictures taken with President and Mrs. Clinton. Such three-tiered events had been held earlier in Miami and Los Angeles, and similar events with variations had been held in New York, Chicago, Boston, Cleveland, and Houston.[44] Questioned about the apparent differences between Clinton's call for reform and actual fund-raising practices, aides said the president remained dedicated to election reform but would continue to play by the old rules until a new law was enacted.[45]

And play he did. Like Reagan and Bush, Clinton actively participated in party fund-raising activities. According to one report, in his first twenty months in office, Clinton personally participated in events or activities that produced $40 million in party donations.[46] The First Lady, Vice President and Mrs. Gore, and a host of Cabinet officers and other administration officials also helped raise funds. In 1994 alone, President and Mrs. Clinton, the Gore family, and top White House and Cabinet officials were scheduled to appear at nearly 300 fund-raising events.[47] The president also allowed the DNC and other party organizations to make use of the perquisites available to the party in control of the White House as part of their fund-raising activities. Party donors were invited to attend White House parties or state dinners, or be present at important events, such as bill signings or visits by foreign leaders. Administration officials regularly conducted special briefings on issues or policy initiatives for major party donors and selected donors. Large corporate soft money contributors were especially invited to join Commerce Department trade missions or other foreign trips. These types of activities led advocates of campaign finance reform to question the president's commitment to reform, and led to renewed calls for major changes in the current system.

Republican Aftermath

Meanwhile, Republicans, under new chairman Haley Barbour, faced a long climb after the 1992 election. In addition to being the minority party in the Congress, they also lacked control of the White House for the first time in twelve years. Bush's defeat, which had seemed so unlikely given his approval ratings in 1991, deeply disappointed many party supporters and had a dramatic effect on the party's fund raising. By the beginning of 1993, Team 100 membership was down by more than 50 percent, and membership in the $15,000-per-year Eagles was down by 60 percent. A number of corporate donors who had favored the Republicans in the past began to shift their pattern of giving in favor of the Democrats. For example, the Atlantic Richfield Company, which had given more than $141,000 to Republican Party committees in 1991 as compared with only $54,000 to Democratic committees, contributed $115,000 to the Democrats in 1993 and only about $67,000 to Republican committees. An effort to refill party coffers by holding a series of dinners honoring living Republican presidents Nixon, Ford, Reagan, and Bush fell through for a failure of the principals to participate.[48]

Barbour sought to shore up RNC finances in part by improving the committee's financial management. The staff was cut from 340 persons in 1992 to 170 in 1993.[49] The committee ended the use of open-ended consulting contracts and put all work contracted out on a competitive bid basis.[50] It also began a number of projects to enhance the party's organizational strength, including expanded training programs for party leaders and campaign managers, a comprehensive voter list development program to standardize voter records, and renovation of the RNC's in-house television facilities to enable the national committee to transmit weekly programming by satellite to state party organizations and others.

To finance these and other activities, the RNC, like the DNC, sought to expand its small donor base. Following the 1992 election, the RNC had a small donor base of about 400,000 contributors. The party initiated direct mail and telemarketing programs that criticized the anticipated tax and spending increases in Clinton's budget plan, then focused similar efforts on the Clinton health care package. These solicitations proved to be highly successful. By the end of 1993, the RNC had added about 180,000 contributors to its small donor list and returned nearly that many to active giving status, for a total of 600,000 such contributors. These donors made more than 1 million contributions in 1993 alone, producing $38.2 million, including a tripling of the amount raised through telemarketing, and accounting for 78 percent of the RNC's total hard money receipts.[51] About 20 percent of the new donors were self-described independents, as compared with about 5 percent in previous years.[52]

The party also sought to build its grass-roots support and improve its responsiveness to party members by conducting a variety of outreach programs. The most important of these efforts was the National Policy Forum, which was designed to serve as an issues forum for discussing health care, crime, and other issues, as well as a vehicle for soliciting the opinions and ideas of the party faithful. But this project, which is clearly affiliated with the Republican Party, was not established as part of the party's formal apparatus; it was organized in June 1993 as a tax-exempt, nonprofit organization, which claimed as its primary purpose to promote social welfare and educational goals, not to elect particular candidates to public office. As such, it was not considered a political committee subject to FECA regulations; therefore, it did not have to disclose names of donors and the size of their contributions, nor itemize expenditures.

The National Policy Forum was criticized in editorials published in the *New York Times* and *Washington Post* as a "new loophole," whose purpose is "very much to elect Republican candidates to office."[53] (As has been noted, the Democrats had planned a similar organization to promote discussion of health care issues, then backed away from the idea, especially after the publication of a *Washington Post* report that questioned the plan.) Barbour responded to such criticisms by noting that the forum was modeled on the DLC, the centrist organization once led by Clinton.

In its first year of operation, the National Policy Forum spent about $4 million. Although it did not disclose its donors, internal documents reported in news accounts revealed that the organization primarily focused on soliciting large gifts from corporations and organized interests, including the Philip Morris Companies, American Telephone & Telegraph, United Parcel Service, the National Rifle Association, and the National Cattlemen's Association.[54] The funds collected were used to sponsor a series of sixty issues forums around the country, which allowed party supporters to share their ideas and discuss such topics as the economy, welfare, families, and crime as part of a broader effort to develop ideas and policy proposals that could serve as the basis for a new Republican Party policy agenda. By encouraging this type of grass-roots participation, the party hoped to attract not only rank-and-file members but others, especially Perot supporters.[55]

Although the Republican Party's fund raising slowed and the Democrats' fund raising rose significantly in the early months of 1993, the Republicans retained the financial advantage they had traditionally enjoyed over Democrats and led Clinton's party by a significant margin in the early months of 1994. The Democratic national party organizations raised about $27 million in soft money, or almost $8 million more than the combined soft money receipts of the RNC, NRSC, and NRCC during the first fifteen months of the Clinton administration, but the Republicans significantly outpaced the Democrats with respect to hard money. Overall, by March 1994, the Republican national party organizations held a 2-to-1 advantage over the Democrats in hard money funds and had raised $98.1 million in combined hard and soft money funds, which was slightly less than the $101.6 million raised in the comparable period in 1991–92 but more than twice the $45 million taken in by the Democrats. More important, the RNC reported $9 million in cash on hand as of March 1994, with no outstanding debts, which was more than $7.5 million greater than the DNC total.[56] The Republican Party was thus well-positioned to contest the 1994 mid-term elections, despite its sluggish fund raising in the months immediately following the 1992 presidential election.

Notes

1. See President's Commission on Campaign Costs, *Financing Presidential Campaigns* (Washington, DC: Government Printing Office, April 1962), pp. 23–24.
2. "Bill Clinton's Money Machine: Like 'Energizer Bunny' It Keeps Going . . . And Going . . . And Going," *Political Finance and Lobby Reporter,* January 13, 1993, p. 6.
3. Edward T. Pound, "Clinton–Gore Transition Fund-Raisers Tapped into Some Traditional Sources," *Wall Street Journal,* April 2, 1993.
4. Ibid.
5. Thomas L. Friedman, "Clinton Issues Ethics Policies for Transition Team," *New York Times,* November 14, 1992.
6. Pamela Fessler, "Ethics Standards Announced," *Congressional Quarterly Weekly Report,* December 12, 1992, p. 3792.
7. Richard A. Hauser, "Some Thoughts on Clintonian Ethics," *Los Angeles Times,* November 22, 1992.
8. Charles R. Babcock and Michele L. Norris, "Clinton's Big Donors: Interest Groups Helping Fund Inauguration," *Washington Post,* January 14, 1993.

9. Martin Tolchin, "The Corporate Sponsors: Groups Give $17 Million in Loans to Inauguration," *New York Times,* January 17, 1993.

10. *District of Columbia Self-Government and Governmental Reorganization Act* (PL 93–198), *U.S. Statutes at Large* 87 (1973): 774, as amended. Also see Robert L. Jackson, "Inauguration Crowd of 250,000 Foreseen," *Los Angeles Times,* November 13, 1992.

11. Jeanne Saddler, "Small Firms Await Clinton with Both Worry, Optimism," *Wall Street Journal,* January 12, 1993.

12. Bernard Weintraub, "This Inaugural Thing Just Irks Hollywood," *New York Times,* January 19, 1993.

13. Irvin Molotsky, "Viewers Upset by HBO's Deal for Inaugural Concert Rights," *New York Times,* January 19, 1993.

14. Michael Weisskopf and Charles R. Babcock, "The Glitziest Gala Money Could Buy: Regulated Industries Had a Special Interest in Picking Up the Inaugural Tab," *Washington Post National Weekly Edition,* February 1–7, 1993, p. 12.

15. Bruce Horovitz, "Corporations Capitalize on Inauguration," *Los Angeles Times,* December 29, 1992.

16. Kevin Goldman, "Firms Campaign for Inauguration Day Action," *Wall Street Journal,* January 12, 1993.

17. Weisskopf and Babcock, "The Glitziest Gala Money Could Buy."

18. Ibid.

19. Jill Abramson, "A Small Army Toils to Ensure Clinton Makes the Right Impression on His First Day at Work," *Wall Street Journal,* January 4, 1993.

20. Tolchin, "The Corporate Sponsors."

21. Jeffrey H. Birnbaum and Rick Wartzman, "Representative From Hillary Clinton's Brothers Asks Firms to Finance Parties," *Wall Street Journal,* January 14, 1993.

22. Ibid.

23. Sara Fritz and Karen Tumulty, "Replying to Critics, Brown Cancels Gala," *Los Angeles Times,* January 14, 1993.

24. Ibid.

25. "Diplomacy is No Job for Amateurs" is by F. Allen Harris, president of the American Foreign Service Association, and "Hypocritical Posturing by Snobs of State" is by George S. Mitrovich, a civic leader in San Diego, where M. Larry Lawrence comes from; both in *Los Angeles Times,* December 8, 1993.

26. Steven Greenhouse, "Clinton Envoy Choices are Faulted as Political," *New York Times,* April 13, 1994; also see Thomas Omestad, "Green with Envoy," *The New Republic,* August 8, 1994, pp. 20–22.

27. "Clinton Plays Politics in Picking Top Envoys," *Washington Times,* January 7, 1994.

28. Ibid.

29. Gwen Ifill, "Hopeful Democrats Meet on How to Unseat Bush," *New York Times,* June 15, 1991.

30. Barbara Slavin, "Capital Gains," *Los Angeles Times,* April 14, 1994; and "Ambassador Admits Breaking Federal Campaign Finance Law," *COGEL Guardian,* April 1994, p. 9.

31. Quoted in Barnes, "Greener Acres," *National Journal,* April 23, 1994, p. 950.

32. DNC, *1993 Annual Report* (Washington, DC: DNC, 1994), p. 2; and Barnes, "Greener Acres," p. 950.

33. Barnes, "Greener Acres," p. 950; and Susan B. Garland and Richard S. Dunham, "Empty War Chest: How the Dems Blew $30 Million," *Business Week,* March 14, 1994, p. 37.

302   CHAPTER 10

34. James A. Barnes, "Double Identity," *National Journal,* November 27, 1993, p. 2835.

35. Garland and Dunham, "Empty War Chest"; and "DNC War Chest Has Record Quarter," *Washington Times,* April 19, 1994.

36. Weston Kosova, "The Party's Over," *The New Republic,* June 20, 1994, p. 25.

37. FEC, "FEC Reports on National Political Party Finances," press release, June 15, 1994.

38. Steve Lilienthal, "Campaigning and Governing," *PartyLine,* spring/summer 1993, p. 3; and John Aloysius Farrell, "Clinton, Party Plan Media Blitz on Budget Plan," *Boston Globe,* July 17, 1993.

39. Barnes, "Double Identity," p. 2834.

40. Ibid., and Ceci Connolly, "DNC Aides to Approach Hill From Ground Up," *Congressional Quarterly Weekly Report,* October 16, 1993, pp. 2809–12.

41. Kosova, "The Party's Over," p. 21.

42. DNC, *1993 Annual Report,* p. 2.

43. Common Cause, "President Clinton Becomes King of Corrupt Soft Money System," press release, June 1994.

44. Laurence I. Barrett, "Million-Dollar Bill," *Time,* July 4, 1994, p. 31.

45. Rick Waltzman, "Clinton, Having Assailed Unlimited Donations to Party Groups, Benefits Greatly from Them," *Wall Street Journal,* June 22, 1994.

46. Michael Wines, "President Grows a Money Tree," *New York Times,* October 1, 1994.

47. Ibid.

48. Barnes, "Greener Acres," p. 951.

49. James A. Barnes, "Creating a Lean, Mean RNC?" *National Journal,* November 27, 1993, p. 2835.

50. RNC, *1993 Chairman's Report to the Republican National Committee,* January 1994, p. 3.

51. Ibid., p. 6.

52. Barnes, "Creating a Lean, Mean RNC?" p. 2835.

53. "The G.O.P. Pioneers a New Loophole," *New York Times,* July 10, 1993; and "Who Paid for Those Ideas?" *Washington Post,* October 1, 1993.

54. Richard L. Berke, "Grass-Roots G.O.P. Group With Big-Company Backing," *New York Times,* April 1, 1994.

55. Ibid.; and Peter A. Brown, "GOP Forum Series Airs Local Opinions," *Washington Times,* June 18, 1994.

56. FEC, "FEC Reports on National Political Party Finances," p. 1.

Index

About the Authors

Herbert E. Alexander is Director of the Citizens' Research Foundation and Professor of Political Science at the University of Southern California. The nation's foremost authority on political finance, he has also taught at Princeton University, Yale University, and the University of Pennsylvania.

Anthony Corrado is a Principal Research Associate at the Citizens' Research Foundation and Assistant Professor of Government at Colby College.